FROMMER'S
NEW ZEALAND
ON $20 & $25 A DAY

by Susan Poole

1984-85 Edition

Published by Frommer/Pasmantier Publishers
A Division of Simon & Schuster, Inc.
1230 Avenue of the Americas
New York, New York 10020

ISBN 0–671–46797–2

Manufactured in the United States of America

CONTENTS

MAPS

INFLATION ALERT: We don't have to tell you that inflation has hit New Zealand as it has everywhere else. In researching this book we have made every effort to obtain up-to-the-minute prices, but even the most conscientious researcher cannot keep up with the current pace of inflation. As we go to press, we believe we have obtained the most reliable data possible. Nonetheless, in the lifetime of this edition—particularly its second year (1985)—the wise traveler will add 15% to 20% to the prices quoted throughout these pages.

A DISCLAIMER: Although every effort was made to ensure the accuracy of the prices and travel information appearing in this book, it should be kept in mind that prices do fluctuate in the course of time, and that information does change under the impact of the varied and volatile factors that affect the travel industry.

Readers should also note that the establishments described under Readers' Selections or Suggestions have not in many cases been inspected by the author and that the opinions expressed there are those of the individual reader(s) only. They do not in any way represent the opinions of the publisher or author of this guide.

READ THIS FIRST

In a world of fast-disappearing budget travel destinations, New Zealand not only continues to be one of those rare places, but actually offers bigger travel bargains than in the recent past. Still, the scoffers will say that *New Zealand on $20 & $25 a Day* is fantasy. Not so! Consider the following.

First of all, as with all Frommer budget guides, the cover prices quoted are meant to take care of only your *basic* daily travel expenses, i.e., a roof over your head and three square meals a day. Transportation, entertainment, sightseeing, shopping, and any other expenses are in addition to that $20 or $25 a day. Of these, your transportation to New Zealand will be the single largest expense item, and I have included some money-saving tips to help you trim that as much as possible. This book will, however, point out best buys in each of these categories to help you hold down *all* costs.

Even in the days when New Zealand dollars and U.S. dollars were at or near parity, those basics were available within the price range quoted. As this book is written, however (late 1983), there is a second factor which makes budget travel not only possible, but actually more flexible than ever. Those US $20 & $25 translate into NZ *$29.80* and *$37.25* at the current exchange rate of NZ$1.49 for each U.S. $1! Thus in many cases what would be "moderate" in New Zealand currency becomes "budget" in U.S. dollars. Throughout this guide, I'll give you both New Zealand prices and their U.S. dollar equivalents so you can make your own comparisons.

A third factor, which may prove to be unique for this edition, is the price freeze now in effect in New Zealand, which may or may not be lifted in March 1984. For as long as the freeze lasts, no prices may be increased without a special appeal for government approval (see "A Word About Prices"). With political and economic conditions so uncertain, it is impossible to predict when the freeze will end or what will happen to prices when it does. In the meantime, it's a bonanza for the traveler.

Let's look at those basic expenses in detail. You'll find good accommodations listed that average about NZ$20 ($14) single, NZ$38 ($25.50) double. On a per-person basis, it's as true in New Zealand as it is in other parts of the globe that two people traveling together will travel more cheaply than those alone. With breakfasts averaging NZ$4 ($2.68), lunch at NZ$5 ($3.36), and dinner at NZ$8 ($5.37), you come in just at the US$25 limit. But one of the joys (in terms of the pocketbook) of traveling in New Zealand is that almost all of the "best buy" accommodations come in the form of bed-and-breakfast (B&B) or motel flats with complete kitchens, which means you can save as much or as little as you choose on the cost of meals.

Other bonuses for your budget are the absence of sales taxes and service charges, and a tipping policy of "when and if you want to" (no obligation!). And no matter how you budget your sightseeing, you'll be treated to some of the most magnificent scenery in the world at absolutely no cost.

One last word: I have researched all prices in this book as close to press time as possible, and I feel secure in assuring you of their accuracy *as long as the currency exchange rate and price freeze remain intact*. If there is a drastic change in either, you may look for upward changes in the prices quoted here, *especially in the second year of the book's life, 1985*. It's a virtual certainty, however, that even if that occurs, price *categories* will remain the same and what is budget today will be budget tomorrow, even if "budget" takes on a slightly different definition.

You have undoubtedly bought *New Zealand on $20 & $25 a Day* with finances uppermost in your mind. Well, they have been my foremost consideration too, but far more than currency has played a part in the preparation of this book. What you'll find in its pages is a guide to the *total* New Zealand travel experience—a sort of love letter to that country's inordinate sense of decency and order, its gorgeous landscape and its endearing people. Having made the decision to visit Kiwiland, you're in for one of the travel treats of your life, dear reader—enjoy every minute!

Susan Poole
November 1983

Introduction

NEW ZEALAND

THERE ARE PROBABLY as many misconceptions about New Zealand as there are people who have never been there, and one that is particularly popular with Americans is the notion that it is virtually a suburb of Australia. Don't you believe it! True, they *are* both in the southern hemisphere, and on any map they appear to be close South Pacific neighbors. But that's *1300 miles* of Tasman Sea separating them, and their separations are by no means limited to those of a watery nature.

One of the most basic differences between the two countries is also one of the most visible—the land itself. For while Australia presents a dramatic, hot landscape of brilliant reds and oranges ringed by splendid, white-surfed beaches shading out to the deep blue of its oceans, New Zealand offers the striking contrast of lush, semitropical rain-forest greenery, cascading waterfalls, playful geysers, wondrous thermal grounds sporting halos of live steam, and more than 5700 miles of glorious coastline winding in and out of island-studded bays and harbors. In fact there is such a wealth of nature's blessing that even the most hidebound urbanite cannot escape inner stirrings of those deep ties with which all mankind is bound to the universe in which we live—New Zealand is, above all else, the perfect setting for getting back in touch with the harmony that should (and so seldom does) exist between the human race and its environment.

Surely one of the world's most beautiful countries, New Zealand is composed of two major islands plus little Stewart Island pointing off toward Antarctica. It is bounded on the north and east by the South Pacific, on the west by the Tasman Sea, and on the south by the Southern Ocean. And it's a mere speck on the map—a small country, right? Well, not all *that* small. From tip to tip, it measures a long 1000 miles, although at its widest it's no more than 280 miles across.

Within those perimeters is such an astounding array of natural beauty, sporting activities, and sightseeing "musts" that you can banish any thought of "doing" it in a few days or just one week—you couldn't even scratch the surface in that short a time! On the North Island, you surely won't want to miss the very special Bay of Islands, rich in history and a haven of tranquility rare in this modern-day world of ours. Or a day or so along the eastern "Sunrise Coast," where New Zealand's first light of day illuminates breathtakingly beautiful headlands. Or Rotorua's steamy thermal hotpot. Or Auckland's surprisingly sophisticated urban scene. Or Waitomo's glowworms. All that takes time—and that's just a *taste* of the North Island!

Then there's that marvelous ferry ride across the Cook Strait to the South Island, where golden sunsets and exotic coastal drives lure you the length of the West Coast, where the Southern Alps cover more territory than the entire country of Switzerland, where glaciers beckon you to their mountaintop source, where Stewart Island dares you to come as close as possible to the South Pole without shipping out for Cape Horn, where every day's drive is an education in the definition of "sheep station," where Dunedin unfolds its Scottish charms, and where Christchurch is waiting to show you its mirror image of Mother England. More time.

Allow *at least ten days* just to sample the highlights—and I should issue the warning that once there, you'll want to spend months to see it all. Since most of us don't really have that kind of time, you'll find some suggested itineraries in Chapter I (see "How Long to Stay") to help you use whatever time you have to get around to the highlights that most interest you. My best advice is to study this book and any others you can lay your hands on to determine just what those highlights are—you're going to have to make some hard choices! And the chances are good that you'll go home busily planning your next trip back to see those things you missed.

No matter what your itinerary, one promise I can make unconditionally: you're going to fall head-over-heels in love with New Zealand's scenery. To that promise I can add another, just as unconditionally: even more, you're going to love her people!

New Zealanders are so . . . well, civilized! They have good manners (i.e., they don't push or utter rude remarks on the street, or mark public buildings with graffiti). They have an innate sense of decency that sends them rushing to the aid of strangers and keeps them on cordial terms with the brown-skinned original New Zealanders. Above all, a strong respect for order pervades their daily lives. Things work as they're supposed to work—and if they don't, somebody fixes them. In short, all the human virtues we remember (or remember hearing about) are in abundant supply in New Zealand. Now I'll wager you'll hear at least once the remark from another American that the country is so charming because "it's 20 years behind the times." Well, for my money, all the "progress" in all the rest of the world is miles behind the sort of human progress New Zealand has managed to achieve!

And all those nice people have come up with a cornucopia of travel goodies to make your stay so easy and so comfortable you won't believe you're traveling on a budget. For example, if a rental car is beyond your means (but *do* plan for it if you can), there's one of the best public transportation systems I've run across anywhere—rail, bus, ferry, or plane, you'll travel in comfort. Stopovers can be spent in accommodations, which will change forever your image of motels—they're motel *"flats,"* complete with lounge, separate bedroom in most cases, and a kitchen equipped right down to coffee, tea, and milk in the fridge! In fact, you may forget you're traveling on a budget.

Just one more thing. You're going to bring back many things from your New Zealand visit—memories, souvenirs, friendships—and unless I miss my guess, among them will be some irresistible expressions, which will have beguiled their way into your vocabulary. Just try not to adopt the lovable "Spot on!" Or the complimentary "Good as gold." And when tempers flare back home, what better way to cool them than with a smiling, "Just don't get your knickers in a knot, mate."

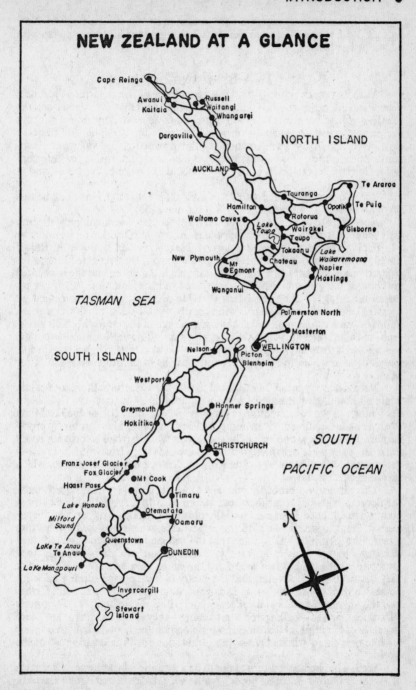

NEW ZEALAND AT A GLANCE

All the above is, of course, a very general overview of New Zealand. Now let's get down to specifics, and where better to begin than at the beginning, with a look at her history.

1. A Brief History

As to its very beginning, you have your choice of two theories on just how New Zealand came about. Geologists will tell you that its islands are the relatively young remnants of a continental mass, separated by violent shifts in the earth's crust. Its location on a major fault line accounts for frequent earthquake activity, volcanic mountains, the drowned glacial valleys of Fiordland, and the string of mountain ranges, which stretches, with a few interruptions, from the alpine peaks of the South Island up to the blunted headland at Cape Runaway.

But ask any Maori and you'll get a far different story. Now, maybe this theory won't be as authentic, but it's a lot more fun.

According to Maori legend, in the days of the gods and demi-gods, the frail fifth son of a woman named Taranga was thrown into the sea by his mother, who felt the infant was too weak to survive. He was rescued, however, by Rangi, the Sky Father, who raised him through childhood, then returned him to his amazed mother, complete with a full set of magical abilities and the enchanted jawbone of his grandmother. The overjoyed mother doted on Maui, her restored offspring, to such an extent that his brothers quickly developed an oversize case of sibling jealousy, which really wasn't eased much when Maui pulled off such astonishing feats as snaring the sun in the pit from which it rose each morning, then smashing its face with that all-powerful jawbone until it was too weak to do anything but creep across the sky, thus giving all the people longer days in which to fish and eliciting buckets of gratitude and respect for Maui.

Needless to say, when Maui set out to fish, his was always the record catch, while his nonmagical brothers barely brought home enough to feed their families—much to the consternation of their wives, who duly complained to Maui. With a condescending (and irritating) wave of his hand, Maui promptly promised his sisters-in-law one load of fish so large it would go bad before they could eat it all. They were delighted; but their husbands were frustrated, angry, and determined to beat Maui to the punch with one last fishing expedition, which they launched at dawn.

The clever (and probably obnoxious) Maui, however, had hidden under the flooring mats of his brothers' canoe, armed with a special fishhook whose point was fashioned from a chip of the precious jawbone. It wasn't until they were well out to sea that he made his appearance, which sent the brothers into a rage. But their luck was running true to form, and when Maui assured them that it would turn in their favor if they'd only sail out of sight of any land, they grumpily agreed, and in fact soon filled the canoe with fish. It was so full that they began to take on water, and the brothers were all for turning back for home. To their consternation, the arrogant Maui insisted they sail still farther into the unknown waters and calmly produced his magic hook. Their protests fell on deaf ears, so—bailing and complaining—they sailed on until at last Maui struck his nose until it bled, smeared his blood on the hook as bait, and threw his line overboard while chanting an incantation for "the drawing up of the world."

Well, what he hooked turned out to be a gigantic fish, as large as the gable of a *whare runanga* (meeting house), whose very size rendered it *tapu* (sacred). With it came a large wedge of land, which we know today as New Zealand's

North Island. Maui, respectful of the *tapu,* quickly departed for home for a priest, leaving his brothers behind with strict orders not to cut up the fish until his return. He was no sooner out of sight than the brothers disobeyed that order, scaling and cutting the huge fish. Now, the gods were much angered at such flagrant disregard for *tapu,* and they set that great fish to lashing about, throwing cut-up chunks in every direction—which is a perfect explanation for the North Island's mountains and offshore islands! And while we may call it the North Island, any Maori knows it is really *Te Ika a Maui,* "the Fish of Maui."

The South Island is actually Maui's canoe, with Stewart Island as its anchor stone. And up in Hawke's Bay, that famous fishhook has been transformed into Cape Kidnappers.

So take your pick—geological fault line or magical Maori.

MAORI SETTLEMENT: When it comes to New Zealand's first inhabitants, again there is more than one belief as to how they settled here. From the mists of prehistory comes the Maori legend of Kupe, who sailed from the traditional homeland of the Polynesians, Hawaiki, around A.D. 950. Even legend doesn't tell us exactly where Hawaiki was located in the vast South Pacific, but present-day authorities believe it was one of the Society Islands group, which includes Tahiti. One version of Kupe's adventures has it that he murdered the carver Hoturapa, and with the murdered man's wife and canoe set off on a long, wandering voyage, which eventually brought the pair to the land he named Aotearoa (the "land of the long white cloud"). Another says that he was in pursuit of a mammoth octopus when he happened onto New Zealand. Both versions agree that he returned to Hawaiki, taking with him sailing instructions for reaching the uninhabited "Fish of Maui." From some historians comes another explanation—that the first Maori canoes to reach New Zealand came by accident, after having been blown off course at sea.

In the 12th century, two more Maori canoes are said to have touched the shores of Aotearoa. A young Polynesian, Whatonga, was swept out to sea during canoe races, and his grandfather, Toi, went in search of him. When the two were reunited somewhere in the Whakatane region in the Bay of Plenty, they found people already living there and the newcomers intermarried with those we know simply as moa-hunters because they hunted a meaty, wingless bird by that name, which reached heights of up to 13 feet. Nothing more is known about them, and they are sometimes referred to as the Archaic Maoris. Descendants of the two Polynesian canoes and moa-hunters now form the basis of two of today's Maori tribes.

It was not until the mid-14th century that Maoris arrived in great numbers. They came from Hawaiki because of devastating tribal wars, which had erupted in the wake of overpopulation and severe food shortages. If we are to believe Maori tradition, seven ocean-going canoes sailed in a group, which has come to be known as "the fleet." Others sailed in groups of one or two; some came singly. On making landfall, canoe groups kept together, settling in various parts of the country, and it is from these first canoes that most modern-day Maoris trace their roots.

By the time "the fleet" arrived, the moa had been hunted to extinction, along with other bird species, such as giant rails, swans, and geese. There were, however, bounteous supplies of fish and seafood to be had for the taking, as well as berries and a few other edible plants, which were supplemented by tropical plants such as taro, yams, and kumara (a kind of sweet potato) that had come in the canoes from Hawaiki. Dogs and rats had also been canoe passengers, and became an important source of protein. The cultivation of these imported vegetables and animals gradually led the Maoris to become an agricultural culture living in permanent villages centered around a central *marae* (village common, or courtyard) and *whare runanga* (meeting house). It was in these villages that the distinctive Maori art forms of carving and tattooing evolved, along with a strong sense of family loyalty and total harmony with their environment. It was this culture that thrived at the time of Capt. James Cook's first contact with New Zealand's "natives."

EUROPEAN DISCOVERY: The first recorded sighting of New Zealand by Europeans came on December 13, 1642, when Abel Tasman, scouting new trade territory for the Dutch East India Company, spied what he described as "a great high, bold land" in the Hokitika region of the South Island's west coast. Sailing north in his two tall-masted ships, the *Heemskirk* and *Zeehaen,* he entered Golden Bay on December 18, where he encountered the Maoris without ever setting foot on land. As the two ships lay at anchor in the peaceful bay, several war canoes put out from shore and shouted challenges from a safe distance. The next day, however, they were bolder and attacked a cockboat rowing from one of Tasman's ships to the other, killing four sailors in the brief battle before withdrawing. Tasman, dismayed at this hostility and disinclined to seek reprisals, fired round shot at the retreating canoes and put out to sea. For many years afterward, lovely Golden Bay was known as Murderer's Bay, as it was christened by Tasman on that December day.

As it turned out, this was his only glimpse of the Maoris since bad weather prevented his entering Cook Strait, so he proceeded up the west coast of the North Island, failed to find a suitable landing spot, and left what he charted as a vast southern continent to sail on to Tonga and Fiji. But for that bad weather and the hostile Maoris, the first European exploration of New Zealand would almost certainly have been Dutch. But that distinction was left for an Englishman more than a century later.

THE COMING OF CAPTAIN COOK: When Capt. James Cook left England in 1768 on the 368-ton bark *Endeavour,* he was under orders from King George III to sail to Tahiti to observe the transit of the planet Venus across the sun, a once-a-century happening. But the Yorkshireman carried "secret additional orders," which he opened only when his initial duty was accomplished. King George had directed him to sail southwest in search of the "continent" reported by Tasman. If he found it uninhabited, he was to plant the English flag and claim it for the king; if not, his instructions were to take possession of "convenient situations" but only with the consent of the natives. In addition, he was to study the nature of the soil, its flora and fauna, and to make charts of its coastal waters.

It was on October 7 of 1769 that New Zealand was first sighted by the surgeon's boy, Nicholas Young, from his perch in the mast. Naming the headland (in the Gisborne area) Young Nick's Head, Captain Cook sailed into a crescent-shaped bay and put down anchor. A rather kindly man, Captain Cook made every effort to cultivate Maori friendship, communicating by way of a young Tahitian chief named Tupea who had come along as guide and interpreter. The Maoris, although they understood and could converse with Tupea, remained hostile even in the face of gifts the captain offered. Nor would they permit him to put aboard the food and water his men so badly needed. Disappointed and bitter, Cook weighed anchor after claiming the country for

King George and naming the beautiful bay Poverty Bay because, as he noted in his journal, "it afforded us no one thing we wanted."

Sailing north, Captain Cook rounded the tip of the North Island and went on to circumnavigate both islands during the next six months, charting them with amazing accuracy, missing only such details as the entrance to Milford Sound (which is quite invisible from the open sea) and the fact that Stewart Island was not a part of the mainland (he mistakenly believed Foveaux Strait to be a bay). In addition, he recorded the flora and fauna as instructed and brought back sketches of the natives, who grew more friendly as word of the gift-bearing Pakehas (fair-skinned men) "who do not eat men" spread. He also recorded details of Maori customs and described the "Indians" as "a brave, open, war-like people." Even today, the journal he kept so meticulously makes fascinating reading.

Captain Cook returned to New Zealand for a month in 1773 and again in 1777. Until his death at the hands of natives in Hawaii on February 14, 1779, he ranged the length and breadth of the South Pacific, sailing as far north as the Arctic Circle and as far south as Antarctica. He and the *Endeavour* have in fact become as much a part of New Zealand legend as those early Maori chiefs and their mighty canoes.

EUROPEAN SETTLEMENT:
Organized European settlement in New Zealand did not get underway with any success until 1840, and the *un*organized settlement that preceded it was, for the most part, a disaster.

Sealers began arriving in 1792 and virtually denuded South Island waters of what had been flourishing colonies of seals through their ruthless policies of killing cows and pups and allowing no closed seasons or limit on skins (some ships carried off as many as 60,000 per year). By 1820 they had moved on to more profitable waters.

Whalers, too, discovered rich hunting grounds in New Zealand waters and arrived in droves. Oil vats soon dotted the Bay of Islands, where safe anchorage was an added attraction. Their unscrupulous methods were much like those of the sealers, and New Zealand's coastal waters were no longer a natural haven for the mammoth animals. Unlike the sealers, however, the whalers brought in their wake a multitude of land-based evils in the form of an attendant population, which Charles Darwin described after his 1835 visit as "the very refuse of Society." Consisting of escapees from Australia's penal colonies, ex-convicts, runaway sailors, and a motley collection of "beachcombers," and concentrated in the Kororareka settlement (now known as Russell), their grogeries, brothels, and lawlessness earned it the nickname "hell hole of the Pacific." Ships that would have normally called in at the port stayed away in fear of the widespread practice of shanghaing sailors for whaling vessels that were shorthanded.

Legitimate traders and merchants, attracted by the wealth of flax and trees such as the kauri, which were ideal for shipbuilding, as well as the lucrative trade in muskets and other European goods with the Maoris, while law-abiding (that is, observing such law as there was), were little better than the sealers and whalers in respecting the country's natural resources. Great forests were felled with no eye to replanting; luxuriant bushlands disappeared in flames to clear hills and valleys for man's encroachment; and when a commercial value was placed on the tattooed and preserved heads that were a part of Maori culture, even the native population was threatened for a time as chiefs eager to purchase muskets lopped off more and more heads, both friend and foe. The latter was a short-lived trade, but quite lively while it lasted.

Perhaps the greatest damage done by these early arrivals was their effect on the Maoris. Equally destructive were the introduction of liquor, muskets, and European diseases against which the natives had no immunity. Muskets in particular set off decimation of Maoris on a grand scale, for they intensified the fierce intertribal warfare, which for centuries had been a part of the Maori lifestyle—tens of thousands were killed off by the fire-spouting sticks until the availability of muskets became so general that no one tribe had superiority in firepower and chiefs began to realize that the weapon was literally destroying *all* tribes (about 1830).

Missionaries constituted the one benign group to arrive during this period, spearheaded by the Rev. Samuel Marsden, who arrived in the Bay of Islands in 1814 and preached his first sermon to the Maoris on Christmas Day with the help of a young chief he had befriended. His was a practical brand of Christianity, and when his duties as chaplain to the convict settlement in Sydney demanded his return, he left behind a carpenter, a shoemaker, and a schoolteacher to instruct the Maoris in the skills of civilization. Most of those men of the cloth who followed were of the same persuasion, and they were responsible for setting down the Maori language in writing (largely for the purpose of translating and printing the Bible), establishing mission schools (by the 1840s large numbers of Maoris could both read and write), and upgrading agricultural methods through the use of plows, windmills, etc.

On the religious front, their progress was slow—to their credit, they were determined not to baptize any native until he had a full understanding of the Christian faith—and it was some 11 years before they made the first Maori convert. Nor is it surprising that it took so long, for deeply imbedded in the native culture were such practices as cannibalism, infanticide, and the worship of gods of war. That the missionaries went about their conversions in much too Puritanical a manner is illustrated by the fate of one who admonished a chief for fishing on Sunday: "You are a wicked, bad man. . . . You have broken the Sabbath . . . you and your people will all go to hell and be burnt with fire for ever and ever." As the chief's great-grandson reported many years later, "to have put up with insult without avenging it according to its nature would have been fatal to a chief occupying a leading position and injurious to the tribe, as it would render it contemptible to its neighbors." Accordingly, "in less time than it takes to remove the feathers from a fat pigeon, the man of incantation was in an oven and prevented from creating further mischief."

By the late 1830s, however, Maoris were ready to accept the concept of a god of peace, undoubtedly influenced greatly by the vastly changed nature of warfare since the coming of the musket. They were also a literal-minded, practical people, much impressed by the missionaries' ability to cure diseases that resisted all efforts by their own healers, as well as their imperviousness to Maori witchcraft. But in embracing the doctrines of Christianity, they relinquished much of the sensual beauty embodied in their own complex, age-old religious traditions. Naked bodies must now be covered; symbolic carvings of the gods of fertility must be destroyed; the reverence and fear once accorded a tribe's chief must now be transferred to this new god. It was in fact the beginning of the end of Maori tribal society as it had existed for centuries.

As the number of British in New Zealand grew, so too did lawlessness, with many atrocities committed against both Maoris and settlers. The missionaries were foremost among those who complained to the British government, which was by no means anxious to recognize the faraway country as a full-fledged colony, having already experienced difficulties with America and Canada, and struggled through the Napoleonic Wars and revolts on various other fronts. As a substitute, in 1831 the Crown placed New Zealand under the jurisdiction of New South Wales and sent James Busby as "British Resident," with full responsibilities for enforcing law and order, but with such laughable means of meeting those responsibilities that he was nicknamed "the man-of-war without guns." Needless to say, he was completely ineffectual.

Back in Britain, the newly formed New Zealand Company began sending out ships to buy land from the Maoris and establish permanent settlements. Their methods were questionable to say the least, and caused increasing alarm in London. It must be noted, however, that between 1839 and 1843 the New Zealand Company sent out 57 ships carrying 19,000 settlers, the nucleus of a stable British population. In 1839 Capt. William Hobson was sent out by the government to sort things out, and by catering to the Maori sense of ceremony (and some mild arm-twisting), he arranged an assembly of chiefs at the Busby residence in the Bay of Islands. There, on February 6, 1840, the famous Treaty of Waitangi, after lengthy debate, was signed with much pomp.

The treaty guaranteed the Maoris "all the Rights and Privileges of British Subjects" in exchange for their acknowledgment of British sovereignty, while granting the Crown exclusive rights to buy land from the natives. The fact that many of the chiefs had no idea of the treaty's meaning is clear from one chief's later explanation that he had merely signed a receipt for a blanket sent by the Queen as a gift! Nevertheless, 45 of the Maori chiefs at the assembly did sign, and when it was circulated around the country, another 500 also signed. Instead of easing things, however, the Treaty of Waitangi ushered in one of the bloodiest periods in New Zealand's history.

The British were eager to exercise that exclusive right to purchase Maori land, and while some chiefs were just as eager to sell, others wanted only to hold on to their native soil. As pressures were brought to bear to force them to sell, revolt quickly surfaced, and when Chief Hone Heke (ironically, the first to sign the treaty) hacked down the British flagpole at Kororareka in 1844, it signaled the beginning of some 20 years of fierce fighting.

The Maoris, always outnumbered and outarmed, won the unqualified respect and admiration of the British as brave and masterful warriors. The British, on the other hand, were regarded with the same degree of respect by the chiefs, who had not expected that the Pakehas could put up any sort of real fight. At last the British emerged as victors, but out of the bloody confrontations came the basis of a relationship, which to this day is based on that mutual respect.

MATTERS OF GOVERNMENT: In 1852 the British Parliament passed the New Zealand Constitution Act, and self-government was administered through a governor appointed in London, a Legislative Council appointed by the governor, and an elected House of Representatives. Elected, that is, by Pakeha landowners who argued that the Maori communal land ownership disfranchised them, as the vote was only extended to "individual landowners." That situation was corrected in 1867, and women were granted the vote in 1893, a full quarter of a century before it happened in Britain or America!

The government thus established pioneered such social reforms as minimum-wage laws, old-age pensions, paid vacations, labor arbitration, and childwelfare programs. Thus New Zealand became in many respects a "welfare state," its economy based on exports of lamb, mutton, butter, and eggs to Mother England. Throughout the ups and downs of economic developments since, it has retained its humanitarian approach to government.

It also exercised strict control over immigration, screening applicants on the basis of ethnic background, age, health, and working skills. It managed to avoid the hodgepodge accummulation of refugees who were populating such countries as the United States and Australia—and in the process created a population base of less than 3½ million people (most of similar backgrounds) which supports *63 million* sheep and 9 million cattle!

2. Maoris and Pakehas

In today's New Zealand, brown- and white-skinned races live together more harmoniously than perhaps anywhere else in this troubled world. The route to this happy state of affairs has not been an easy one, and it is to the credit of both Maori and Pakeha that such widely differing cultures and a history encompassing long years of cruel warfare have been overcome to generate a mutually congenial environment. The difficult journey has required a great deal of restraint and willingness to put aside the past, but one has only to look at the results to see what can be achieved by men of goodwill.

Maoris have seen their numbers increase from a low of 42,000 at the turn of the century to more than 270,000 today. From a people suffering from alcoholism, disease, and widespread malnutrition (plus a strange sort of malaise that afflicted the race as a whole with a debilitating lethargy), they have become a largely urban people enjoying all the middle-class benefits of their Pakeha brethren while holding fast to as much of their traditional culture as survived the early years of European settlement.

Their climb out of the pit into which they had descended has been by way of a surprising adaptability to the ways of democracy and an acceptance of the responsibilities, as well as the securities, of "civilization." The skills acquired from mission schools have been improved and honed to expertise, with additions as industrial development moved across the country. The political arena has afforded them access to power acquired through the oratory prowess (and *all* Maoris are blessed with a skillful way with words!) of such leaders as Apirana Ngata, Peter Buck, and Maui Pomare, all of whom were knighted and served as cabinet members, and their Young Maori Party. Such are the Maori powers of oral persuasion that very often their candidates are elected by substantially Pakeha constituencies. They have been quick to take advantage of educational opportunities, with a high percentage of college graduates among the current Maori population. And they have managed to imbue the Pakeha population with such appreciation for their ancient culture that intermarriage is now quite common, with a complete absence of any social stigma.

To experience that culture in its purest form, the visitor these days must travel to Rotorua (a Maori center) or stumble upon a communal village. It is here that you'll find woodcarvers and mat weavers demonstrating the arts that adorn their great meeting houses with such stylized masterpieces and their handsome physiques with such colorful garb.

Yet even deep in the heart of New Zealand's largest cities (which are home for some 76% of the Maori population), it's easy to observe the traditional lifestyle rhythm that thumbs its nose at the white man's alarm clock. And while the old war *hakas* (complete with foot stomping and protruding tongues) and graceful *poi* dance are mainly performed in shows staged for visitors, any Maori city dweller is possessed of a uniquely sweet-toned singing voice and a large repertoire of such melodies as the world-famous "Now Is the Hour" (or, Maori Farewell) handed down by ancestors of this proud race. And in national elections, they are free to vote in the Pakeha district in which they reside or in one of the four official Maori electorates.

One sad by-product of the Maoris' move from rural to urban areas has been a gradual weakening of those tribal and family ties, which have always been at the very heart of their culture. When there is no *marae* (tribal court-yard and meeting place) in which to gather at the end of the day, youngsters tend to lose contact with their elders, and even the elders are less closely bound together. In some of the North Island cities (where the native concentration is heaviest), social problems are beginning to crop up, which can be traced directly to the feeling of isolation that has developed among a younger genera-tion adrift without strong identity support systems.

As for their language, with its colorful and vivid imagery, well, the Maoris came very close to losing it. Living in a Pakeha world, they drifted into the Pakeha tongue. It's been making a comeback in recent years, however, and is often heard on the radio, is used to begin each evening's TV newscast with the traditional Maori greeting, and is taught as a school elective.

You'll find most of New Zealand's whites living in the cities too. Or at least working in cities. More and more, as centers such as Auckland grow larger and larger, the people who work there go home at night to the same sort of small suburban satellite communities we know here in the U.S. Those miles of dual-lane express motorways leading into Auckland, and the sprawling shopping malls in the dozen or so communities that surround it, will have a surprising familiarity!

For most of us, though, there will be a fascinating unfamiliarity about the lifestyle of other Pakehas who live and work on New Zealand's farmlands (which bring in a whopping 60% of the country's export income from meat, dairy products, and wool).

From high-country "stations," which concentrate on wool production, to lower pastures, which fatten up lamb and mutton on the hoof, we'll click our cameras at lovable sheep who seem to have been born with a one-track mind—a fun game when you're traveling is to try to find the sheep that's *not* eating!

For the farmer, it's a hardworking life of comparative isolation, with socializing more or less relegated to the occasional drop-in at the local tavern. Some of your own best socializing may very well come from just such a drop-in if your timing is good enough to coincide with one or two of the farmers'. Or better yet, if you're in the tavern when a gaggle of shearers come in at the end of a busy day.

In the North Island, the cattle that supply all that rich, yummy cream and butter and milk—as well as the ten extra pounds you'll probably carry home on expanded hips and waistline—spend winters and summers in the pastures, for grass grows year round in this perfect growing climate. The New Zealand dairyman is more likely to be found in city or small-town watering holes, since his grazing lands are not so spread out and towns are more plentiful up north.

Actually, about three-quarters of all those people in the cities depend on the output of these country folk for prosperity, involved as they are in the processing and marketing of farm products.

City dweller or farmer, the average Pakeha is more likely to be found messing around in boats or out tramping in the bush than in dancing and singing in the manner of his Maori neighbors.

And how do they get on with those native neighbors? Very well, thank you. Pakehas don't really participate in Maori cultural activities very much, but you can be sure they're *proud* of that culture—it is uniquely New Zealand, and they're pretty near possessive about it! You can virtually count on being dragged off to a Maori concert, *hangi* (feast), or some other event by every other Pakeha with whom you spend any time. And you'll be very welcomed—as I said before, brown- and white-skinned New Zealanders live together in great harmony.

A MAORI GLOSSARY: While you're not very likely to overhear the soft, lilting sound of Maori voices speaking their native language on the streets in New Zealand, you *will* be surrounded by words and phrases, both in place names and names of objects always identified by their Maori names. It's a lot more fun to travel around New Zealand if you know, for example, that *roto* is the Maori word for lake and *rua* for "two;" hence, Rotorua. The following are a few of the most commonly used prefixes and suffixes for place names:

ao	cloud
ika	fish
nui	big, or plenty of
roto	lake
rua	cave, or hollow, or two (Rotorua's two lakes)
tahi	one, single
te	the
wai	water
whanga	bay, inlet, or stretch of water

Other frequently used words:

ariki	chief or priest
atua	supernatural being, such as a god or demon
haka	dance
hangi	an oven made by filling a hole with heated stones
karakia	prayer or spell
kereru	wood pigeon
kumara	sweet potato
mana	authority, prestige, psychic force
marae	courtyard, village common
mere	war club made of greenstone (jade)
pa	stockade or fortified place
Pakeha	white-skinned person; primarily used to refer to Europeans
poi	bulrush ball with string attached twirled in action song
tangi	funeral mourning or lamentation
tapu	under religious or superstitious restriction ("taboo")
tiki	grotesque human image, sometimes carved of greenstone
whare	house

If Maori legend and language catch your imagination, you may want to look for *The Caltex Book of Maori Lore* (published by A. H. & A. W. Reed Ltd.), by James Cowan, who spent much time among the Maoris; and *A Dictionary of the Maori Language,* by H. W. Williams, grandson of Bishop William Williams, who first compiled the dictionary at Pahia in 1844.

3. Flora and Fauna

New Zealand has been, in a sense, one huge botanical garden during its relatively short life. Undisturbed by the destructive influence of mankind, its forests and plant life flourished, regulated by no forces save those of Mother Nature. Luxuriant ground covering, ferns ranging in size from tiny plants attached to mossy tree trunks all the way to tree-size pongas, more than 100 species of trees, and garlands of starry white clematis and blossoms of other flowering vines created hundreds of miles of cool, dim, tree-vaulted "cathedrals."

The first humans to arrive, themselves closely attuned to nature, accorded the forests due reverence, with just the proper mix of awe and fear. As Peter Hooper, one of New Zealand's best writers and a leading conservationist, says in his excellent book *Our Forests, Ourselves* (published by John McIndoe, Ltd.), "Landscape possesses *mauri*—soul or mind—and it is the outward and visible form of an inward invisible power." And an acute awareness of that quality is inescapable when one walks the present-day forests of New Zealand. Its effect can be profound. As Mr. Hooper goes on to say, "The tonic wildness of natural spaces is essential to the physical/mental/spiritual wholeness of the individual." You have my personal promise of just such a restorative experience upon entering any one of the forests, which will never be too far away throughout your visit!

In the northern quarter of the North Island you'll find the surviving stands of tall, stately kauri trees, whose hardwood trunks—unblemished by knots or other imperfections—were so prized for shipbuilding by early settlers. During December and January, North Island cliffs and lake shores are a mass of scarlet when the pohutukawa (or Christmas tree) bursts into bloom, while its kinsman, the rata, is doing likewise down in the South Island. In early spring, the kowhai, which makes no distinction between north and south but grows almost everywhere, is a profusion of large golden blossoms. The totara has always been much loved by the Maoris, who find its light, durable timber just right for making canoes, as well as for their magnificent carvings. Then there are the pines, including the rimu (red), matai (black), kahikatea (white), and *Dacrydium laxifolium* (pigmy). And the beeches—red, black, and silver. Almost all are evergreen, and seasonal color changes are subtle.

New Zealand also has an astounding array of flowering plants, a full 80% of which are not to be found anywhere else in the world. Undisputed queen of blossoms has to be the world's largest buttercup, the Mt. Cook Lily. There are almost 60 varieties of mountain daisies, and a curious "vegetable sheep," which grows in mountainous terrain and has large, cushiony blooms which look like sheep even when you take a closeup look. Up to a dozen white, fringed, saucer-shaped blooms adorn a single flower stalk of the hinau, and the golden kumarahou bloom has been used over the years in medicinal herb mixtures.

An added joy in tramping the forests is the fact that you never have to be afraid to put your foot down—there's not one snake in the entire country! Nor are there any predatory animals. In fact there's only one poisonous spider, and it's rarely found anywhere except a few scattered sand dunes.

Most of New Zealand's animals did not originate there but were imported by various settler groups. The Maoris brought over dogs (and rats, though I can't say if *that* was intentional!). Captain Cook released a pig, whose wild descendants are still about. Other importees include the red deer, opossum, hedgehog, weasel, and rabbit (which were brought over for skins and meat but became so numerous and destructive that another animal, the stoat, had to be brought in to control the rabbit population).

As for birds, the more species you see, the curiouser and curiouser they get. The kiwi, whose name New Zealanders have adopted as their own, is one of the most curious. Wingless and about the size of a chicken, it lives in hollow trunks or holes in the ground; emerges only at night to forage for insects and worms with a long, curved beak, which has nostrils at its tip; and emits a shrill, penetrating whistle. The female lays one gigantic egg and then (smart lady!) leaves the hatching to the male. These days it's rare to see the kiwi in the wild, but you'll find them in special kiwi houses around the country, which simulate nocturnal lighting so you and I can see them during "normal" hours.

Down in the mountains of the South Island there's a comical mountain parrot which is as bold as the kiwi is shy. The kea nests among the rocks, but keeps an eye on the main roads and is quick to investigate any newcomers. It's not unusual, for instance, to see as many as three (as I once did) camped alongside the Milford Sound road—and if you stop, their antics will have you grinning in no time. But it's just as well you keep a sharp eye on them, for those cunning cut-ups are quick to steal jewelry or other shiny objects and to attack such formidable targets as automobile parts with their strong, curved beaks. Campers and trampers in the know are careful to keep their gear well beyond the reach of the flightless little kea.

If you hear a series of pure, bell-like sounds pouring through the forest air, it's likely to be the song of the lovely bellbird. Only slightly different in sound is the handsome tui. Around swampy areas, those ear-piercing screams you hear in the night will be coming from the pukeko. And the forest-dwelling morepork's call (often heard at dusk or after dark) may give you a start—it sounds just like its name. The graceful gannet is found only on offshore islands, with one exception, Cape Kidnappers near Napier.

As curious as are some New Zealand birds, however, none of them holds a candle to the tuatara, a reptilian "living fossil" whose prehistoric ancestors became extinct 100 million years ago. It is completely harmless—that is, if its looks don't scare you to death. Shaped like a miniature dinosaur, complete with spiny ridge down the back and a thick tail, it's protected by law and confined to offshore islets.

The richness of New Zealand flora and fauna will be within easy reach wherever you find yourself around the country, and if you should miss some particular species, there are excellent zoos as well. National parks and forests provide ample showcases for the primeval bush.

4. About This Book

DROP A LINE: In this book, as in all Frommer guides, I invite our readers to participate in future editions. Let me hasten to say that the judgments, opinions, and comments offered here are based on personal inspections and experiences. But change is the very nature of the travel world—accommodations and restaurants appear and disappear, change managements, ownership, and chefs, improve or go to pot. Should you find any of these conditions, please do let me know about it. And don't be shy about sharing with me any especially good discoveries or suggestions of your own—some of the best listings in this book have come from Readers' Selections that I have followed up. You have my word that each and every letter will be read by me, personally, although I find it well nigh impossible to *answer* each and every one. Be assured, however: I'm listening! Just write: Susan Poole, Frommer/Pasmantier Publishers, 1230 Avenue of the Americas, New York, NY 10020.

5. The $25-a-Day Travel Club

In the very next chapter I'll get on with a discussion of budget travel in New Zealand. There is, however, a terrific way you can keep abreast of money-saving methods for *all* your travels—it's called the $25-a-Day Travel Club. It was formed several years ago at the urging of $-a-Day and Dollarwise readers who felt that it would bring together economy-minded travelers all over the world, with benefits to everyone. That's exactly what has happened, and the benefits begin as soon as you join.

Following the budget concept of all our guides, the membership fee is low and brings immediate value far beyond the cost. Upon receipt of $14 (for U.S. residents) or $16 (for Canadian, Mexican, and other foreign residents) by check drawn on a U.S bank or via international postal money order in U.S. funds. to cover one year's membership, we will send all new members by return mail (book rate) the following items:

(1) The latest edition of *any* two of the following books (please designate in your letter which two you wish to receive):

Europe on $25 a Day
Australia on $25 a Day
England and Scotland on $25 a Day
Greece on $25 a Day
Hawaii on $35 a Day
Ireland on $25 a Day
Israel on $30 & $35 a Day
Mexico on $20 a Day
New Zealand on $20 & $25 a Day
Scandinavia on $25 a Day
South America on $25 a Day
Spain and Morocco (plus the Canary Is.) on $25 a Day
Washington, D.C. on $35 a Day

Dollarwise Guide to Canada
Dollarwise Guide to the Caribbean (including Bermuda and the Bahamas)
Dollarwise Guide to Egypt
Dollarwise Guide to England and Scotland
Dollarwise Guide to France
Dollarwise Guide to Germany
Dollarwise Guide to Italy
Dollarwise Guide to Portugal (plus Madeira and the Azores)
Dollarwise Guide to Switzerland (to be published March 1984)
Dollarwise Guide to California and Las Vegas
Dollarwise Guide to Florida
Dollarwise Guide to New England
Dollarwise Guide to the Southeast and New Orleans
(Dollarwise Guides discuss accommodations and facilities in all price ranges, with emphasis on the medium-priced.)

How to Beat the High Cost of Travel
(This practical guide details how to save money on absolutely all travel items—accommodations, transportation, dining, sightseeing, shopping, taxes, and more. Includes special budget information for seniors, students, singles, and families.)

The New York Urban Athlete
(The ultimate guide to all the sports facilities in New York City for jocks and novices.)

Museums in New York
(A complete guide to all the museums, historic houses, gardens, zoos, and more in the five boroughs. Illustrated with over 200 photographs.)

The Fast 'n' Easy Phrase Book
(The four most useful languages—French, German, Spanish, and Italian —all in one convenient, easy-to-use phrase guide.)

The Adventure Book
(From the Alps to the Arctic, from the Sahara to the southwest, this stunning four-color showcase features over 200 of the world's finest adventure travel trips.)

Where to Stay USA
(By the Council on International Educational Exchange, this extraordinary guide is the first to list accommodations in all 50 states that cost anywhere from $3 to $25 per night.)

A Guide for the Disabled Traveler
(A guide to the best destinations for wheelchair travelers and other disabled vacationers in Europe, the United States, and Canada by an experienced wheelchair traveler. Includes detailed information about accommodations, restaurants, sights, transportation, and their accessibility. [To be published March 1984.])

Marilyn Wood's Wonderful Weekends
(This very selective guide covers the best mini-vacation destinations within a 175-mile radius of New York City. It describes special country inns and other accommodations, restaurants, picnic spots, sights, and activities—all the information needed for a two- or three-day stay. [To be published May 1984.])

(2) A one-year subscription to the quarterly eight-page tabloid newspaper—**The Wonderful World of Budget Travel**—which keeps you up to date on fast-breaking developments in low-cost travel in all parts of the world bringing you the latest money-saving information—the kind of information you'd have to pay $25 a year to obtain elsewhere. This consumer-conscious publication also provides special services to readers: **The Traveler's Directory** (a list of members all over the world who are willing to provide hospitality to other members as they pass through their home cities); **Share-a-Trip** (offers and requests from members for travel companions who can share costs and help avoid the burdensome single supplement); and **Readers Ask ... Readers Reply** (travel questions from members to which other members reply with authentic firsthand information).

(3) A copy of **Arthur Frommer's Guide to New York,** a newly revised pocket-size guide to hotels, restaurants, nightspots, and sightseeing attractions in all price ranges throughout the New York area. (4) Your personal membership card, which, once received, entitles you to purchase through the Club all Arthur Frommer publications *(including* the *Adventure Book)* for a third to a half off their regular retail prices during the term of your membership.

So why not join this hardy band of international budgeteers and participate in its exchange of travel information and hospitality? Simply send your name and address, together with your membership fee of $14 (U.S. residents) or $16 (Canadian, Mexican, and other foreign residents), by check drawn on a U.S. bank or via international postal money order in U.S funds to: $25-A-Day

Travel Club, Inc., Frommer/Pasmantier Publishers, 1230 Avenue of the Americas, New York, NY 10020. And please remember to specify which *two* of the books in section (1) above you wish to receive in your initial package of members' benefits. Or, if you prefer, use the last page of this book, simply checking off the two books you select and enclosing $14 or $16 in U.S. currency.

Chapter I

NEW ZEALAND: A TOURIST SURVEY

**1. The Currency
2. Preparing for Your Trip
3. When to Come
4. How Long to Stay
5. Where to Stay
6. Where and What to Eat
7. Shopping
8. Where to Go and What to Do**

WHILE CERTAINLY NOT the most exciting words between these covers, this chapter may well be some of the most important reading you'll do before setting off on your New Zealand trip. It deals with the preplanning and "homework," which can make the difference between returning with pleasant, happy memories or with a feeling of frustration and bewilderment.

What I'll be talking about here are the details that will help you plan a trip as carefree as possible. You'll *need* to know about such things as currency, the rate of exchange, and travel documents. You'll *want* to know when to go, how long your trip should be, what sort of clothes to pack, and what you may expect in terms of accommodations, restaurants, shopping, and things to see and do.

Since finances are at the very heart of successful budget travel, let's start with a discussion of money in New Zealand.

1. The Currency

You won't have any trouble at all with New Zealand currency. It's based on the decimal system and has coins in denominations of 1, 2, 5, 10, and 50 cents—notes come in $1, $2, $5, $10, $20, and $100 amounts. From 1975 until 1982 the New Zealand dollar was at near parity with the U.S. dollar, but things have changed drastically in the past year. As a result, your U.S. money is worth (as we go to press in late 1983) very nearly 1½ times as much over there as it is at home.

What this means, of course, is that you'll be able to do more, see more, buy more, upgrade accommodations, and still stay within your *U.S.* $20 and $25 per day allowance for room and board. As I said right up front, in terms of New Zealand money those figures now amount to $29.80 and $37.25. Far be it from me to predict that this exchange rate is going to stay in effect for the entire life of this book, so my very first financial advice is to check for the current rate at the outset, *before* you do any concrete planning. Then make any necessary adjustments to the rates shown in these pages.

The exchange rate in effect as this book is written is $1 U.S. equals NZ$1.49, and all conversions listed are at that rate.

Just a word or two about the money you carry with you. There's no need, I'm sure, to say that it should be in travelers checks, *not* in cash. But I will remind you that for safety's sake, it's a good idea to keep the record of your travelers checks separate from the checks themselves, and to be sure to record each one you cash. If the worst should happen and you lose checks, replacement will depend on your having those uncashed numbers. Banks, of course, offer the best exchange rates, not hotels, department stores, etc.

You may be asked upon arrival to show that you have sufficient funds to cover your expected stay without having to get a job (they're pretty picky about things like that, although I must say I've never been questioned personally). Also, when leaving you'll not be allowed to carry more than $100 in New Zealand currency out of the country. It would be best to convert funds into the currency of your next destination before departure time.

2. Preparing for Your Trip

Good preparation makes for good travel, and in this section you'll find both the essential matters (passports, visas, etc.) and a few suggestions to make your pretravel preparations easier and better.

TRAVEL DOCUMENTS: You'll need a passport for entry to New Zealand, and it must be valid for no less than six months beyond the date you plan to depart. A travel tip about passports: It's a good idea to make two photocopies of the identification page of your passport (the one with your photo), as well as any other travel documents, then leave one copy at home and carry the other with you. You'll save yourself a lot of hassle if you and those vital papers part company and you have to have them replaced! Of course, the photocopies will not serve as valid documents, but they'll furnish the information necessary to cut through miles of red tape to get new ones.

For a stay of less than 30 days, you won't need a visa if you're a citizen of the U.S. or Japan, or if your passport is French and was issued in Tahiti or New Caledonia. Nationals of Iceland, Finland, Malta, and the German Federal Republic may stay as long as three months without a visa; those from the United Kingdom, Irish Republic, Belgium, Canada, Denmark, France, Lichtenstein, Luxembourg, Monaco, Netherlands, Norway, Sweden, and Switzerland may stay up to six months without a visa. A visa is not required for any length stay by nationals of New Zealand and Australia, or for citizens of any Commonwealth country residing in New Zealand or Australia who arrive directly from Australia.

If you wish to stay beyond the limits stated above, or if your nationality is not listed, consult your nearest New Zealand Embassy, High Commission, or consulate for information on obtaining the appropriate visa. Americans who want to stay longer than 30 days may obtain a visa application from the consular office nearest their home. The New Zealand Embassy is located at 37 Observatory Circle NW, Washington, DC 20008, and there are consular offices in Washington, DC, San Francisco, Los Angeles, and New York. Still other consulates may be found at the New Zealand Government Tourist Office addresses shown below. No fee, but you'll need a photograph. For information on working-holiday visas, inquire at one of the consulates for current regulations.

No certificate of vaccination against smallpox is currently required of any traveler arriving in New Zealand. However, officials are quick to point out that should there be an outbreak of that disease in a particular country, a certificate of vaccination will be required from travelers who had been in any part of that country within the 14 days immediately prior to their arrival in New Zealand. Infants under three months of age are normally exempt, provided the persons accompanying them comply with the requirements and the route of travel presents no appreciable risk.

Three things *all* visitors must show before entry permission is granted: a confirmed onward or round-trip ticket; enough money for their New Zealand stay; and the necessary documents to enter the next country on their itinerary or to reenter the country from which they came.

There is no Customs duty on any personal effects you bring into the country and intend to take away with you. Also duty free are 200 cigarettes or half a pound of tobacco or 50 cigars, as well as one quart of wine, one quart of spirits, and anything else with a value of up to NZ$50 for your own use or that you are bringing as a gift. If you plan to take in anything beyond those limits, best contact the New Zealand Customs Department, Head Office, Wellington, New Zealand, *before* you arrive.

TOURIST INFORMATION: One of the most useful things you can do in planning a visit to New Zealand is to contact the **New Zealand Tourist Office** nearest you in North America for their Kiwi Travel Pack. The attractive *New Zealand Mapguide* will be your constant traveling companion, and even before leaving home it's a perfect complement to your advance reading (like this book!). They'll also include helpful brochures. Travel consultants in each office will be happy to help with any specific queries you may have.

When you arrive in New Zealand, this same government department operates both an information service and a booking service (for transportation, accommodations, sightseeing—almost anything). Staffs in every office are experts and eager to help you in any way possible.

You'll find New Zealand addresses for the New Zealand Government Tourist Bureau (known as GTB) listed in each destination section. In North America, their locations are:

Alcoa Building, Suite 970
One Maritime Plaza
San Francisco, CA 94111
(tel. 415/788-7404)

10960 Wilshire Blvd., Suite 1530
Los Angeles, CA 90024
(tel. 213/477-8241)

630 Fifth Ave., Suite 530
New York, NY 10020
(tel. 212/586-0060)

2 Bloor St. East, Suite 2922
Toronto, ON M4W 1A8 Canada
(tel. 416/961-1137)

WHAT TO PACK: When planning your New Zealand wardrobe, there is one basic tenet you can hang on to, no matter when you plan to go or what you plan to do: dress in Kiwiland, for the most part, is *informal.* Men will want to take along a jacket and tie, women at least one dress or skirt for those restaurants or hotels that have a dress code at dinner. Otherwise, casual is the keynote.

When you plan to come will of course play a big part in your dress decisions, so study the next section carefully and remember that the seasons will be those of the *southern* hemisphere. There are, however, few temperature extremes either in the subtropical tip of the North Island or in the cooler South Island. Auckland, for example, has an average midsummer temperature of 73°, with 57° the midwinter average. Queenstown's summer average is 72°, with 46° about the lowest in winter. Generally, you can look for balmy days in the Bay of Islands, cool-to-cold down in the Southern Alps. That translates into layering: a warm sweater, long-sleeved blouses to be worn over short sleeves, sleeveless knit vests—that sort of thing. One item I've found useful is a pair of cotton knit "longjohns" to wear under lightweight trousers when I get down to the cooler climes. Combined with a zip-in-lining jacket, they've seen me through two fall-to-winter stays.

What you plan to do will also determine what clothes you pack. New Zealand offers some of the best tramping in the world, and if that's what you plan to do a lot of, bring along suitable clothing, sturdy boots, backpack, and the necessary utensils if you'll be camping overnight. I might add here, however, that you needn't bring along boots and heavy coats if the extent of your tramping will be an organized trek on the glaciers—both will be provided by your guide. If you travel like most people, you'll simply be moving from place to place and sightseeing, and for that just be sure the clothes you take along are comfortable, easy to pack, and washable. Incidentally, most of those great motels I'll be telling you about later in this chapter have washing and drying facilities. One item no one should omit is comfortable shoes—no place on earth is appealing when your feet hurt!

Now for one bit of advice that stems from my own experience of returning with an overstuffed suitcase that was nice and light when I left home: there's no way you're going to be able to resist those terrific natural-wool sweaters (especially the hand-knits!), and you'll save yourself oodles of packing troubles if you leave the ones you now own at home, then pick up one (I *dare* you to buy just one!) and wear it during your trip. Men will no doubt be tempted in warm weather to adopt the universal New Zealand male dress of walking shorts, high socks, and short-sleeve shirts. In other words, leave some packing room—you'll be wearing some of your nicest souvenirs.

Besides clothing, there are a few other carry-alongs: a washcloth in a plastic bag, since they're seldom furnished in New Zealand accommodations; a travel alarm clock; prescriptions for any medication or glasses that are essential to your comfort and well-being; a flashlight if you'll be driving after dark; a pen for all those postcards; and any small personal items you're just not comfortable without. *umbrellas*

Sportsmen (or women) may want to bring along favorite fishing rods, golf clubs, etc., which are allowed through Customs, but these items are readily available in New Zealand, and many fishing guides furnish equipment and clubs can be rented at most golf courses. If the hostels will be home, bring along sheet sleeping bags or sheets and a pillowcase. Blankets can be rented.

3. When to Come

Weatherwise, you're safe to visit New Zealand any time of the year. As I said earlier, temperatures are never extreme, although I've experienced days warmer than those midsummer averages and a degree or two below the midwinter averages quoted. One thing to keep in mind, however, is that on a visit that takes you to both islands, you'll be going from a subtropical climate in the north of the North Island to the coolness (sometimes coldness) of the South Island.

Nor is there a specific rainy season, although the west coast of the South Island can experience up to 100 inches or more of rain a year on its side of the Southern Alps, while just over those mountains to the east rainfall will be a moderate 20 to 30 inches. Rain is heavier in the west on the North Island as well, with precipitation on the whole ranging from 40 to 70 inches annually. Milford Sound holds the record as the wettest spot in the country (and also perhaps the most beautiful—a personal bias!) with an average annual downpour of 253 inches.

As for sunshine, you'll find more in the north and east of both islands, with the Bay of Islands and the Nelson/Marlborough Sounds area leading sun spots. Frost and snow in the North Island are mainly confined to high country such as Mount Egmont and the peaks in Tongariro National Park, so if it's snow or snow-related sports you're after, look for them in the South Island. Even there, skiing is not a year-round activity, so a little research on specific destinations is in order before you set your dates. My last trip to Queenstown, for example, was in mid-June, and local headlines announced "One More Dump and We Ski." I'll get into that in more detail later in this chapter (see "Where to Go and What to Do").

Seasons, as I've said before, as those of the *southern* hemisphere, thus the exact opposite of ours. There just isn't a bad season to travel, so your own interests will set your timing priorities. A fundamental guideline, however, is that during Kiwi holiday times, accommodations can be very tight. So if you plan to come between Christmas and February, when New Zealand families are traveling about their country on annual "hols," or during the Easter, May, or August school holidays, prebooking is an absolute must. Here's a brief season-by-season rundown:

SPRING: September, October, November. This is one of the best times to visit, since Kiwis are going about their business activities, schools are in full session, innkeepers will greet you with delight—with or without a booking—and the countryside is bright with blossoming fruit trees and brand-new baby lambs.

SUMMER: December, January, February. Beaches and boats are primary preoccupations of the natives during these months, and resorts are booked to capacity. Advance planning will let you share these sun-filled days, although you should be prepared for slightly higher accommodation rates. It's a fun time to visit if you get your bookings under way early enough.

FALL: March, April, May. In my personal opinion, this is a great time to visit New Zealand. The weather is pleasant and just cool enough in southern parts to remind you that winter is on its way, while in the Bay of Islands region midday and early afternoons are still shirt-sleeve warm. Poplars are a brilliant gold, and more subtle foliage changes can be seen in the forests. Just remember those Easter and May (two weeks) school holidays, when bookings will be tight.

WINTER: June, July, August. Okay, you ski buffs—this is the time when your ski calendar goes on a year-round basis. From about mid-June on, the slopes are a skier's dream. Booking ahead at major ski resorts is certainly advisable, but you can nearly always count on finding accommodations within an easy drive even if you arrive with nothing confirmed. Around the rest of the country, this is another season you can pretty much amble around without booking ahead—except, of course, for that aforementioned two-week school holiday in August.

4. How Long to Stay

This can be a problem, for (as I keep saying) as small as it is, New Zealand has so much to see and do you'll have a hard time fitting in everything no matter how long you plan to stay. Few of us, however, have unlimited travel time at our disposal, and it *is* possible to plan itineraries which will hit the high spots during your particular time frame. Travel counselors at New Zealand Government Travel Offices are most helpful in this respect, and here are a few sample itineraries which may be of help after you have determined just which high spots you want to hit. You'll note that for short stays, you'll have to cover some of the longer stretches by flying if you're to get in even a smattering of the outstanding sightseeing.

5 DAYS (North Island only): Day 1: Arrive Auckland, tour in afternoon. Day 2: Drive from Auckland to Waitomo (125 miles), tour caves and glowworm grotto, then drive to Rotorua (98 miles). Day 3: Full-day sightseeing in Rotorua; Maori concert or hangi in evening. Day 4: Drive from Rotorua to Auckland (149 miles), tour or sightsee on your own in afternoon. Day 5: Depart Auckland.

5 DAYS (South Island only): Day 1: Arrive Christchurch, tour in afternoon. Day 2: Fly from Christchurch to Queenstown over Canterbury Plains and along Southern Alps. Day 3: Full day at Queenstown sightseeing. Day 4: Fly from Queenstown to Mount Cook in the heart of the Southern Alps, then on to Christchurch. Day 5: Depart Christchurch.

10 DAYS (Both Islands): Day 1: Arrive Christchurch, spend afternoon touring. Day 2: Fly from Christchurch to Te Anau over Canterbury Plains and along Southern Alps. Day 3: Take day trip by tour bus to Milford Sound (151 miles round trip) for launch cruise, returning in late afternoon. Day 4: Drive or take bus from Te Anau to Queenstown (110 miles), afternoon in Queenstown for sightseeing. Day 5: Full day at Queenstown sightseeing. Day 6: Fly to Mount Cook, take excursions to icefields in afternoon. Day 7: Fly from Mount Cook to Rotorua in the North Island, crossing Southern Alps and Cook Strait. Day 8: Full-day sightseeing in Rotorua; Maori concert or hangi in evening. Day 9: Take bus, or drive, from Rotorua to Waitomo (98 miles), tour caves and glowworm grotto, then on to Auckland (125 miles)—tour buses on this route allow time for sightseeing in Waitomo. Day 10: Depart Auckland.

14 DAYS (Both Islands): Day 1: Arrive Christchurch, spend afternoon sightseeing. Day 2: Fly over Canterbury Plains to Mount Cook, in the heart of the Southern Alps. Day 3: Fly from Mount Cook to Queenstown. Day 4: Full day at Queenstown. Day 5: Drive from Queenstown to Te Anau (110 miles). Day 6: Day trip to Milford Sound (151 miles round trip, by bus or drive) for launch cruise, returning in late afternoon. Day 7: Drive from Te Anau to Dunedin (190 miles) through pleasant farming country; late afternoon for sightseeing. Day 8: Fly from Dunedin to Wellington, following coastline and crossing Cook Strait; sightseeing in afternoon. Day 9: Drive from Wellington to Napier (203 miles) through rugged Manawatu Gorge. Day 10: Sightseeing in Hawkes Bay area around Napier, then drive to Taupo (96 miles), and on to Rotorua (55 miles). Day 11: Full day in Rotorua; Maori concert or hangi in evening. Day 12: Drive from Rotorua to Waitomo (98 miles), tour caves and glowworm grotto, then on to Auckland (125 miles). Day 13: Full day sightseeing in Auckland. Day 14: Depart Auckland.

All these itineraries are possible, but I strongly recommend that if there's any way you can manage it, you plan a minimum of *three weeks* to see both islands at something like a leisurely pace. Some of New Zealand's beauty spots simply invite (almost command!) loitering, and there are several you will have to omit on a shorter visit. A month would be even better. Failing that, I personally would stick to one island per visit for the shorter time periods and take in such extras as the Bay of Islands on the North Island and Stewart Island in the south. You will have come a long way to see New Zealand, and it would be a shame to get around at too fast a trot!

5. Where to Stay

New Zealand presents a vast supermarket of accommodation choices, even in our budget range. The sheer number and variety of places to lay your weary head will add spice to your trip, and although there is no national system for inspection or grading, I have yet to come across a single one that wasn't spotlessly clean, an accomplishment of which I cannot boast in any other country in my travels!

We'll examine the variety in detail below, but first, there are some elements they all share. Check-in time is usually around 2 p.m.; check-out, 10 a.m. There's no tipping (unless you feel especially grateful for some special service) and no tax. Many hotels and motels charge an extra NZ$1 for one-night stays, and in some resort areas rates go up slightly during peak seasons. Almost all have discount rates for children based on the following: under 2 years, free; 2 to 4 years, 25% of the adult rate; 5 to 9 years, half of the adult rate; 10 and over, full rate. Even the most "budget" of budget accommodations will have an electric kettle (which goes by the name of "jug" in New Zealand), tea and coffee, sugar and milk, either in your room or in a centrally located public room—at no charge (they *know* it's too much to ask of guests to send them out for such necessities!). All have telephones either in-room or in a public room, hall, or office available to guests, except in the case of some hostels. Almost all have laundry facilities, which means electric washing machines and either a dryer or drying rooms—and there's seldom a charge for their use. With the exception of some hostels and cabins, all have good winter heating, either central or individual room heaters. There's not much air conditioning, but not much need for it either.

To the above, I'd like to add one little message from my New Zealand accommodations friends: it seems that we Americans are highly valued as guests for many reasons, including the fact that they say we always leave the premises in such good order (for once, we're the "pretty Americans"). Our one failing has to do with that "jug," and I think it's because we're so accustomed to appliances being turned on and off by thermostatic controls. Well, where the jugs are concerned, it's up to *you* to unplug it or flip the control switch on the wall socket when the water comes to a boil; otherwise, it keeps boiling away, the jug's heating element burns out, and our "highly valued" status becomes a little less so. So keep an eye on it and be sure it's turned off when you've made your tea or coffee.

I know I've told you this before, but it bears repeating: during peak travel months, *you must book ahead.* "Peak" means December through February, Easter, and the two (two-week) school holidays in May and August. New Zealanders are on the road in droves during those periods—most spend their holidays within their own country, and most are as budget-conscious as we are. They do their booking months in advance, and so should you to avoid disappointment. When you have selected the accommodations you prefer, simply write as early as possible enclosing a money order or bank draft to cover the first night's lodging and an International Reply Coupon for confirmation to be mailed back to you. If you should have to cancel and you do it within a reasonable time, you'll usually receive a prompt refund, although in some cases there will be a small service charge.

The accommodations listed in this book, I rather immodestly believe, are a pretty select group, but for a complete listing of all accommodations available around the country, the New Zealand Government Tourist and Publicity Department publishes an excellent *Accommodations Guide,* which you can obtain from all New Zealand Government Tour Offices in North America. If there's not one in your city, write the nearest office and ask for it by mail. It lists hotels, motels, bed-and-breakfast and farm accommodations, and private-home-host organizations. All price ranges are included. Also, the Automobile Association covers the subject very comprehensively in a series of accommodation guidebooks: hotels and motels in the North Island; motor camps and campgrounds in the North Island; and a "South Island Handbook." If you're an AAA member at home, you'll have reciprocal privileges in New Zealand and will have no difficulty picking up all three guides. Or contract them in advance at 166 Willis St., Wellington.

BOOKING SERVICES: The **New Zealand Government Tourist Bureau** (known throughout Kiwiland as the **GTB**) has six offices located in major visitor centers (you'll find addresses in the destination chapters of this book) that will make accommodation bookings in all price ranges and all locations throughout the country. They'll also make your transportation bookings. Those services are combined with their free, government-sponsored travel-information service with one important difference—when they handle your bookings, they're acting as full-fledged, profit-making travel agents. They list only their commission clients (i.e., they won't have every accommodation in this book on their lists), and they charge the same fees as other New Zealand agents: NZ$2 ($1.34) per accommodation booking plus long-distance or telegram charges; two free transportation bookings, after which the charge is NZ$1 (67¢). If you go to them only for travel *advice* or for help in sorting out travel schedules and then do the actual bookings yourself, their expert staffs are at your service at no charge whatsoever.

Of course, there are bound to be times when you need that kind of help and aren't anywhere near one of those six offices. Not to worry—just look for a Public Relations Office (PRO), Visitors' Bureau, or something similar. There's no standard marking (like the international "i" symbol) used in New Zealand, but there are few places in the country that do not have some central information and booking office.

YOUTH HOSTELS: You'll be way below our $20- and $25-a-day costs if you utilize New Zealand's excellent network of hostels. And aside from saving all that money, you'll be mingling with hostelers from all over the world as well as a fair few friendly natives. It's a great way to travel, and you'll find Kiwi hostels above average.

There are more than 45 hostels throughout New Zealand, many in choice scenic locations—you'll be paying hostel rates for a beachfront, lakefront, or mountainside room just down the way from a luxury hotel whose guests are paying an arm and a leg for the same view! The hostels vary both in size and style, with the smallest sleeping 10, the largest 84, and their architecture ranges from comfortable old farmhouses to slick, modern edifices.

Here's what you must do to qualify: be a Youth Hostel member (and if you're age 5 or over, "youth" has no age limitations) with a valid membership card. In the United States, you can join through **American Youth Hostels, Inc.,** National Administrative Offices, 1332 "I" St. NW, 8th Floor, Washington, DC 20005, by sending $7 if you're under 18 (Junior membership), $14 if you're over 18 (Senior). You can join in New Zealand for NZ$8 ($5.37) and NZ$15 ($10.06) for the same age groups. Either card is good internationally. If you join in New Zealand, you'll receive free the invaluable New Zealand *YHA Handbook;* overseas members pay NZ$1 (67¢). It describes each hostel in detail, with transportation, food shops, and other useful information for each location. It also sets out all hostel rules and regulations (leave things tidy, no drugs, liquor, firearms, gambling, etc.).

You'll need to bring with you a sheet sleeping bag and pillowcase, but blankets are available at a small rental fee. Also, if you plan to use the fully equipped kitchens, bring your own cup, plate, and cutlery, as well as a tea towel. Managers are called wardens, and most reside in the hostel itself, with those who don't living close by—the warden is the person to whom you show your card and pay your fee. Don't show up after 10:30 p.m., however, because that's curfew time and you can be refused entry; you'll have to vacate the premises between the hours of 10 a.m. and 5 p.m., when all hostels are closed. Your booking will be held until 7 p.m., so when you cross the Cook Strait by ferry in either direction, be *sure* it's the afternoon crossing, since the evening ferry will arrive too late for you to stay in a hostel.

New Zealanders are great hostelers within their own country—there are some 29,000 native members—which makes advance booking every bit as important at hostels during peak months as in any other type of accommodation. In fact, you'll be well advised to book ahead in all major resort areas or large cities at any time of the year. You can do so by either sending a money order or bank draft for one night's lodging, along with an International Reply Coupon, directly to the warden of each hostel, or to the **YHA National Reservations Centre,** P.O. Box 436, Christchurch. Bookings are limited to three consecutive nights in any one hostel, and fees range from NZ$3 ($2.01) to NZ$6 ($4.03), half that for Juniors.

There are a number of benefits that come along with your YHA membership, such as discounts on rail and ferry transportation, rental cars, and sightseeing attractions and activities. There's also a helpful **Travel Section** which actually offers hostel package tours. Planned with a great deal of flexibility, they're based on public transportation and the use of hostels throughout. The Travel Section issues an informative booklet entitled *YHANZ Hostelling Holidays,* which outlines services and tours, available (along with any specific information you'd like) by writing YHANZ Travel Section, P.O. Box 436, Christchurch or P.O. Box 1687, Auckland.

National headquarters for the **Youth Hostel Association of New Zealand (YHANZ)** is in the Arts Centre of Christchurch, 28 Worcester St. (tel. 799-970), just across the street from the Rolleston House Y.H. In Auckland, their office is in Australis House, 36 Customs St. East (tel. 794-224). Both are open from 8:30 a.m. to 4:40 p.m.

MOTOR CAMPS, CABINS, AND CAMPING: New Zealand is a camper's delight, whether you're toting a tent to pitch, backpacking and looking for a cabin at night, or hauling along a motor caravan. There are facilities to suit all needs, and they're all over the place. The nice thing is that you'll many times find the whole array available in a single motor camp!

On grounds that are sometimes quite extensive, and many times in prime locations (practically beachfront in Gisborne, for example), there are **campsites** for tents, which will cost as little as NZ$3 ($2.01) per person per night (NZ$4, or $2.68 U.S., if there's a power connection). Then there are the rustic "ungraded" **cabins,** or huts, which hold beds or bunks, pillows, a table, and chairs. Many times linen and blankets can be rented; otherwise you bring your own. You must also supply your own crockery and cutlery. Cabins come in two-, four-, or six-bedded sizes, and on an average cost NZ$10 ($6.71) *per cabin* per night without running water, NZ$14 ($9.40) to NZ$18 ($12.08) with. Both cabins and campsite occupants have full use of centrally located shower, laundry, and kitchen facilities. Kitchens supply a fridge and stove (usually more than one), hotplates, electric jugs, and toasters, but everything else is left for you to bring. Needless to say, the "leave it tidy" doctrine applies.

Rubbing elbows with those "bare essentials" accommodations, almost all motor camps will have at least one block of **tourist flats.** They are rustic in decor, and you still must bring the bedding, but they have one or two separate bedrooms, cooking facilities (all have running water), and private showers. Prices are in the NZ$18 ($12.08) to NZ$25 ($16.78) range for double occupancy.

In the chapters that follow, you'll find several **motor camps** listed, which I believe are outstanding, and for a complete directory, just write the Camp & Cabin Association of New Zealand for their official publication: Secretary, C.C.A., 4A Kamawa St., Waikanae, North Island (tel. 4781).

Trampers will find basic, rustic **bunkhouses** or huts in all national parks, with water and outdoor cooking areas provided. Maps of their locations are furnished by park rangers, who also collect the NZ$1 (67¢) or NZ$2 ($1.34) fee.

THE Y's: Unlike other New Zealand accommodations, both the YWCA and YMCA hostels are booked to capacity from February through November, when students fill the available space. This could be a real boon, especially in city areas, if you have trouble finding a room during those peak months of December through February.

Y rooms are, as you might expect, very basic, and in a few cases have a rather grubby aspect, while others are as light and cheerful as you wish. Beds are narrow, floors are rugless, and showers and baths are down the hall, with no water basins in rooms. There are, however, laundry rooms, TV lounges, and the usual Y facilities. Some provide full board, and all serve breakfast. You'll find YWCAs in Hamilton, Hutt Valley, New Plymouth, Whangarei, Wanganui, Wellington, and Rotorua in the North Island; Christchurch, Dunedin, and Gore in the South Island. Each has its own rate structure, but you can expect them to be in the neighborhood of NZ$5 ($3.36) or slightly higher.

Especially for the young traveler, the Ys are a pleasant travel base, since the majority of other guests are likely to be in a similar age group (although that should by no means deter those in upper age brackets). Overseas members of the YWCA will receive a 5% discount.

BED AND BREAKFAST: I have always favored B&B accommodations when traveling, both because that terrific cooked breakfast will very often see me through until dinnertime (saving the cost of lunch) and because when I'm tired of my own company, there are always other guests to get to know in the lounge (I've made some enduring friendships in just this way over the years). Also, their rates are usually by the *room*, so I'm not penalized when I'm traveling alone and become that loathsome (and so often expensive) "single."

Unfortunately, New Zealand is not blessed with a plentiful supply of the bed-and-breakfast establishments so many travelers consider the only way to travel. I have managed to ferret out some, however, which are real gems, and you'll find them described in detail in the following chapters.

When doing your scouting, you should know that B&Bs go by two names in New Zealand: **guest houses** and **private hotels.** Both provide comfortable, homey rooms with hot and cold running water (H & C), bath and shower down the hall, and a huge cooked breakfast. And both are unlicensed (serve no liquor). Guesthouses, however, are limited to bed and breakfast, with dinners sometimes served guests by special arrangement, but never to nonguests. Private hotels (which are usually much larger), on the other hand, serve all meals to both residents and nonresidents. Rates in both will run about NZ$16 ($10.74) to NZ$20 ($13.42).

MOTEL FLATS: I once wrote in a travel guide, "A motel is a motel is a motel." Well, while that may have been true for the location under discussion, it is definitely *not* true for New Zealand! If you think you've seen enough motels to know all variations, just wait until you see them in this country—they give a new definition to the word. Get set for a rave about the best budget travel value you're likely to run across anywhere.

You'll note that the heading for this section is "Motel Flats," not simply "Motels." And therein lies the difference between New Zealand's offerings and those we're accustomed to under that latter label. First, most—if not all—have been built in the last decade or so, since tourism as a full-fledged industry has been a late bloomer in New Zealand. What this means is that all modern conveniences have been incorporated in their designs. And the last five years or so have seen the addition of spa pools (we know those as Jacuzzis) in most properties. All of which is a bonus, but not the biggest bonus. That comes in the form of "flat," a fully developed, fully equipped *apartment* as opposed to the room (no matter how spacious, a room is not a flat!) and bath which comprise our motel units.

What you'll find in Kiwi motel flats are: a lounge, usually with sofas that open into beds; one or two separate bedrooms (except in the case of "bedsitters," when the lounge becomes your bedroom at night); a kitchen or kitchenette (and here's where "fully equipped" takes on special meaning, for they come with everything from pots and pans to dishes and silverware to potato peelers to the obligatory electric jug to coffee, tea, sugar, and milk in the fridge, right down to the tea towel); and a bathroom. If you're a taker of baths, I should warn you that most bathrooms have showers rather than a bathtub, although more and more places are installing both, and in some the shower rim is built up and there's a stopper for the drain, so you can fill the "shower" and proceed to bathe in a square "tub." The units are so well planned that where there are two bedrooms, the bathroom is accessible to each separately, thus providing privacy for two couples or a family traveling together. There's a TV and radio in virtually every unit, telephones in a good many, and personal touches such as plants, paintings, tablecloths, etc., in all. Heating is usually by means of individual heaters, and beds come with electric blankets or (most often) electric underblankets. You can count on a laundry room with automatic washer and dryer (or a drying room with a clothesline), many times with soap powder for guests' use, and most are available at no charge. There are few motels (or motor inns) without at least one outdoor swimming pool.

It should be noted that, just like home, you'll be expected to do such elementary household chores as make beds and wash dishes. Motel flats are *not* serviced. But everything you'll need to take care of those basic jobs will be right there—dishwashing detergent, fresh linen twice a week, clean tea towels daily, etc. Now, that's entirely to my own tastes, for I must confess to being a slow mover in the early a.m., and it's a relief to loiter leisurely, secure in the knowledge that "housekeeping" won't be pounding on the door.

A continental or cooked breakfast can be ordered the night before, with the makings brought to your room that evening so you can please yourself as to breakfast time if you're going continental, or the hot meal delivered to your unit at a prearranged time in the morning. As for other meals, many motels have frozen and canned goods in a small shop in the office so that you can cook pickup meals if you choose. Few now have restaurants, although while researching this book I found that there is a definite trend developing to add them. As a rule, however, if you don't choose to eat in, a good restaurant will be close by.

In addition to all this, there is a bonus that goes beyond monetary values. Almost all motels are owner operated, which means there's no possibility of your running into impersonal, uncaring attitudes. To the contrary, you're very likely to leave each establishment on a first-name basis with the owners and all their family. In fact, it's one of the best ways I know to get to meet and know native New Zealanders.

That, dear reader, is the description of *budget* accommodations in New Zealand! The average cost for a double in these home-like dwellings is NZ$30 ($20.13) to NZ$38 ($25.50). Singles, as I said earlier, don't fare quite as well, with an average price of NZ$20 ($13.42), although that's still well within our budget range. And, of course, the per-person cost goes down as the number of occupants goes up: you'll pay about NZ$7 ($4.70) per extra adult, bringing the individual cost for a party of four way down.

As you can clearly see, all New Zealand motel flats are a true bargain, but the Best Western chain takes things a little further and offers a bargain on top of a bargain with their **Best Western Travel Club.** If you stay in Best Westerns throughout your stay, you'll receive a 10% discount on all rates (that's for cash—it's 5% if you pay by credit card), and they have a computerized booking system to book ahead as you go, or for the entire trip if you prefer. I've found, *without exception,* that Best Westerns are tops in this type of accommodation in New Zealand, with many extras such as a higher percentage of in-house restaurants and choice locations. In some cases their rates will be slightly higher than others in the region, but generally that difference is equalized by the discount program. Incidentally, BWs are individually owned and operated, not franchised. The "chain" aspect only means that each property is rigidly inspected on a regular basis to be sure that high standards are being maintained (those copper-bottomed pots must have shiny copper bottoms!). North Americans can preplan their entire trip before leaving these shores by contacting Best Western headquarters (tel. toll free 800/528-1234) and asking for the International Desk. Or write Mrs. Lori Dahlman, Marketing Dept., Best Western, P.O. Box 102030, Phoenix, AZ 85064. They'll send you a BW directory for New Zealand to make your selections for that first night only if you're free-wheeling, or for your whole stay. In New Zealand, their address is Best Western New Zealand Ltd., C.P.O. Box 276, Auckland (tel. 792-854). Those units are at the very heart of the recommendations in this book, and I've included a large selection in every location.

SERVICED MOTELS: This term refers to motels just like those at home—one room and private bath—with one (very important to this tea and coffee drinker) difference: the ever-present electric jug plus tea bags and instant coffee. You'll find some scattered through the following pages, but because those in our price range tend to be small and sparsely furnished and not nearly as good value as motel flats, their numbers are few. Still, if you have a thing about not making the bed in the morning or you'd rather someone else flicked a dustcloth around, you may find them to your liking. I must say that the ones recommended here were quite on a par with their counterparts in the U.S.

LICENSED HOTELS: Most of the licensed hotels in New Zealand are luxury establishments and in a price range beyond our budget. And many of those that we could budget for, we wouldn't want to—they're relics of the days when sleeping accommodations had to be offered in order for drink to be served, and bedrooms invariably came off second (or third, fourth, or fifth) to the public drinking rooms. I've found a few whose rooms are clean, comfortable, and inexpensive. If, however, you are tempted by a listing in any of the accommodations guidebooks mentioned above, I strongly recommend that you insist on a personal inspection before plunking down a night's rent.

There is one important exception to the above, and that is the THC hotels. The **Tourist Hotel Corporation of New Zealand** operates about a dozen semi-luxury hotels in some of the country's remote beauty spots where commercially owned hotels would have a hard time making a go of it. The avowed purpose of the corporation is to "provide suitable accommodation in vital but remote areas." It's an admirable goal, and one that is realized in admirable style: some of the hotels have gained international recognition, such as the Château, a white-gabled, country mansion in Tongariro National Park, and the window-walled Hermitage, facing Mount Cook's majestic peak. Others of special note are at Milford Sound, Waitomo, and Franz Josef. You may well choose one of these as your "Big Splurge" indulgence spot, since budget accommodations are sparse (although there's a THC hostel at Milford Sound and motel flats at Mount Cook, Wanaka, and Waitangi run by the corporation). Whether or not you book in, you're likely to spend some time at a THC facility somewhere along the line, for they're the very center of tourist activity in their areas—that's where you'll book many sightseeing tours, find the most pleasant public bar (and often inexpensive pub grub, as well), and go for nighttime entertainment. Pricewise, they're sort of moderately expensive as compared to other luxury hotels, with doubles anywhere from NZ$50 ($33.56) to NZ$90 ($60.40), and a uniform charge of NZ$7 ($4.70) per extra adult. For full particulars and booking, contact their central headquarters (they have *no* connection with the Government Tourist Bureau): Tourist Hotel Corporation of New Zealand, 35 Albert St., Auckland (tel. 773-689). Or contact the manager of the individual THC hotel in which you wish to stay.

FARMHOUSE AND HOME STAY HOLIDAYS: In a country where agriculture reigns supreme, I can't think of a better place to feel the pulse of the people than on a working farm. A firsthand knowledge of just what it takes to raise all those sheep and cattle and kiwi fruit will give you more insight into New Zealand life than you could gain in any other way. Besides, what a joy to wake in the mornings to pastoral beauty and a charming country home in the midst of a host family who are delighted to have you as a guest and eager to show you around the farm!

Farmhouse Holidays New Zealand can give you that closeup experience on farms throughout the country. There are rugged South Island sheep stations, horse farms, farms with glowworm caves, Maori burial sites, hot springs, trout fishing, and scenery that includes magnificent mountains and coastlines. And if you want to jump in and help muster sheep on that station or groom one of the thoroughbred horses, well, you have only to let your wishes be known. On the other hand, if a day or so of quiet rusticating suits you better, that's okay too. You will have your own bedroom (sometimes with a private bath, but more often it's on a share-with-the-family basis), plus two hearty farm meals each day, which you'll take around the family dining table.

With such a widespread network of host farms, the folks at Farmhouse Holidays can book you in virtually every location you want to visit. Daily charges for bed, breakfast, and dinner, per person, are NZ$42 ($28.19) for adults, NZ$32 ($21.48) for children ages 5 to 11, NZ$24 ($16.11) for toddlers ages 2 to 4, and NZ$16 ($10.74) for infants under 2. They also operate half-day farm tours out of Auckland and tours featuring overnight farmhouse stays to several sightseeing destinations (see "Where to Go and What to Do"). In New Zealand, contact them at: **New Zealand Farmhouse and Country Home Holidays,** P.O. Box 31250, Auckland 9 (tel. 492-171); in the U.S., **Network Travel Planners, Inc.,** 202 Main St., Venice, CA 90291 (tel. toll free 800/421-9979).

Now maybe you like the idea of staying with a Kiwi family, sharing meals, etc., but aren't much drawn to country life. Then **New Zealand Home Hospitality Ltd.** may have just the package you're looking for. For NZ$252 ($169.13) per adult, they'll furnish seven vouchers, which you can use on a freewheeling basis to stay in private homes around the country. There are more than 350 from which to choose, and bedrooms can be single or double. Your vouchers will cover bed and breakfast for all seven days, plus two evening meals. Book through any of the New Zealand Government Tourist Offices in the U.S or in New Zealand.

6. Where and What to Eat

Mention New Zealand and food to almost anyone and the response is "lamb." Well, I'm told by my Kiwi friends, with a groan, that the best lamb gets shipped out to the likes of you and me on our home turf. That may well be so, but I've had very good lamb in New Zealand—as well as some that wasn't so very good. No matter what the quality, however, it's served as a roast more often than not, and a well-done roast at that. Quite frankly, I've become very fond of roast **hogget** (that's sheep a little older than lamb and a little younger than mutton), and I rather suspect that that's what comes to table many times under the "lamb" label. What's not so well known outside New Zealand is their beef, and it's superb. Steaks and roast beef are plentiful and inexpensive.

The star of Kiwi cuisine, as far as I'm concerned, however, is **seafood,** always fresh and of a wide variety. Bluff oysters are a treat on which I shamelessly gorge myself every trip—they're large and tangy, with a strong taste of the sea. Then there are the tiny whitebait, usually served in fritters, sometimes crisply fried. And the crayfish (you'll recognize the taste as that of the New Zealand rock lobster we buy frozen in the U.S.), which is more expensive than other seafood, but worth every penny. And a fish I've never encountered anywhere else but with which I'm on a first-name basis—the John Dory, as sweet and succulent as any I've ever tasted. Up in the north of the North Island, you can sometimes find toheroa soup, a delicacy made from a small shellfish much like a cockle, which is served in a rich chowder. Trout, of course, abound in the rivers and lakes of New Zealand, but they are not sold commercially (seems Kiwis adhere to the theory that for such a sporting fish, it would be a deep indignity to be eaten by anyone who didn't land him in a fair fight!). Nevertheless, it does appear on the menu (maybe when the chef is a fisherman?).

Dairy products, too, play a starring role in the New Zealand diet, and you'll know why after your first taste of rich, creamy milk and butter that reminds you of what it *used* to taste like in this country. Both are served in generous portions in restaurants and guest houses, so enjoy. Government subsidies keep prices low, so you can afford to indulge even for those meals you cook in motel flats. Cheeses are also delicious and inexpensive. A loaf of vogel bread (rich, whole-grain bread, which you'll find in almost any health-food store and many supermarkets), a selection of cheeses, and a bottle of good wine or beer makes the perfect picnic lunch on long drives.

You'll find **meat pies** everywhere, from lunch counters in rail and bus stations to pubs to take-away shops. They're thick-crusted little pies filled with chunks of meat and gravy, and can be quite delicious. That's if they're the homemade variety, with light, flaky crusts and just the right combination of mild spices and herbs. Keep an eye out for the "homemade" sign, which is more prevalent than you might imagine—and avoid whenever you can the tasteless, factory-mades.

I've been told that the traditional New Zealand **dessert** is called pavlova because it's "as light and airy as the great dancer for whom it is named," and I don't doubt that for one moment. It consists of really a large meringue made of stiffly beaten egg whites which have been baked slowly at a low temperature to form a crusty outside and soft inside. Shaped like a large cake, its top is usually filled with whipped cream and fruit (kiwi fruit when it's available)—great!

Beer is almost the national drink, and you'll have to do a bit of sampling to find your own favorite among the many brands—friends of mine spend a lot of time debating the merits of DB (Dominion Breweries), Lion, Steinlager and a few others. Be cautious, however, when testing those labeled "Export"—they're more than twice as potent as American beer! If you're a dedicated beer drinker or have a large party, you'll save money by ordering a "jug of draft," which holds about five eight-ounce glasses.

In recent years New Zealand's vineyards have been producing better and better **wines.** Labels like McWilliams, Montana, Mission, Corbans, and Penfolds are surprisingly inexpensive and varied in their offerings. Prices are even lower when you buy half-gallon flagons. Spirits have risen in price somewhat when purchased by the bottle, but are quite cheap (by U.S. standards) by the drink. You may want to stock up in Dunedin, where the bottle shop at the Gresham Hotel has the lowest prices in the country.

Alcohol is only sold in licensed premises, bottle shops, and wholesale bottle stores (the best bargains are in the latter). Wholesale does not mean they won't sell individual bottles (although some have minimum purchase requirements), so look for that name, usually in city-center shopping areas. Licensed hotels serve drinks from 11 a.m. to 10 p.m. (11 p.m. on Saturday, *never* on Sunday) in their bars and lounges, but anytime with a meal. Registered guests may be served anytime, regardless of the hour. Hotels with a Tourist House License are allowed to serve alcohol only to residents. Licensed restaurants serve drinks only with meals, and some unlicensed restaurants invite you to bring your own wine (most post a BYO notice—some don't, so it pays to inquire).

As for where to eat, the budget-wise thing to do is to breakfast at your lodging place, have pub grub at lunch (look for the "bistro" signs for pubs that serve food), and take your main meal in the evening in one of the many inexpensive and quite acceptable restaurants. A bistro lunch (which usually offers a choice of hot dishes such as pot roast, steak-and-kidney pie, stew, etc., served with potatoes and vegetables; or cold platters) will run around NZ$3.50 ($2.35), but an even better buy are the buffet lunches where you can eat your fill for no more than NZ$5 ($3.36).

For any meal, a **Cobb & Co.** restaurant will provide good food (definitely not gourmet, but very good) at really low prices. Open from 7 a.m. until 10 p.m., seven days a week, and fully licensed, they're all over New Zealand, in large cities and towns of any substantial size. You'll find them listed throughout this book, and they have my highest recommendation as dependable for both price and quality. All have the same menu, hours, and decor (colonial in nature, with much red velvet, gleaming brass hanging lamps, dark woodwork, and cozy, comfortable booths). Specialties are dishes like the old-fashioned beef-and-kidney pot pie, served with jacket potato and salad for NZ$4.20 ($2.81) and stuffed Cobb schnitzel, at NZ$5.20 ($3.45). Seafoods, grills, sandwiches, quiches, and hamburgers are also on the menu at prices of NZ$3.85 ($2.58) to NZ$6.60 ($4.43). Beer and wine are reasonably priced, and come in pitchers and carafes as well as by the glass. The restaurants are the last vestiges of the original Cobb & Co., one of New Zealand's first and largest public transport companies in the days of the coach-and-four, and placemats and menus feature interesting bits of the company's history.

New Zealand has in the last few years seen the birth of some truly fine **restaurants,** with elegant decor, polished service, and superb international cuisine. They're too pricey for budget travel, true, but—holding firmly to the belief that there comes a time in every trip when you just can't *stand* to pinch one more penny—I've listed some of the more outstanding for those "Big Splurge" dinners. Expect to pay NZ$25 ($16.78) or slightly more (without wine) at these establishments, and if you should unearth others you feel warrant that kind of expenditure, do let me know about them.

One thing that will take some getting used to is the use of "entree" to mean *not* the main course (which they call the main course), but a small serving of a hot dish immediately before the main course. Most New Zealanders will eat a five-course dinner consisting of appetizer, soup, entree, main course, and dessert. Well, I've never been able to manage that much food at one sitting, and unless the set dinner price covers all five, I save my money and my figure by sticking to an appetizer or soup, main course (which is always a generous portion and always comes with vegetables and salad), and dessert. You may want to do the same.

7. Shopping

Before we get into specifics, let me say that shopping is *fun* in New Zealand, with craft, hand-knit woolens, and souvenir shops cropping up in the most unexpected places. Prices are sometimes better in these out-of-the-way shops than in tourist centers—they're best at the duty-free shops in Auckland, Wellington, and Christchurch, but selections can be very limited in both. My own credo has been to buy something that appeals wherever I find it—price variations aren't *that* wide, and there's always the possibility of not finding it again.

New Zealand wools, leathers, and knits are sold all over both islands, as are sheepskin rugs. Really bulky purchases can be mailed home, but I've found that half the fun of buying a suede coat or woolen sweater is using it there. And look for the hand-knits rather than machine-made sweaters—one of my most prized sweaters was handmade by a lovely little lady in the Bay of Islands, the other by a talented knitter in Hokitika on the South Island. Both served me well as I traveled the country.

Souvenirs feature Maori carvings or designs, and there's a wide selection, from greenstone tiki figures on neck chains to carved wooden keychains to coasters, placemats, and small replicas of beautifully carved war canoes. Items made from paua shell are also very popular. You'll probably want to bring home at least one Maori concert record or tape, probably more—a marvelous way to trigger instant memories once you're back home. Pottery and ceramics will tempt you, especially in places like Nelson, where many are made by fine craftspeople and prices are inexpensive to moderate.

Paintings of the gorgeous scenery by New Zealand artists are on sale almost everywhere. Some are quite good, and a small oil can sometimes be found for as little as NZ$25 ($16.78). You're almost certain to find one depicting that bit of Kiwiland you fell in love with, and like the Maori music, a painting is instant mental transport back to a lovely experience.

Look for **Rehabilitation League Shops** in all large cities and major resorts. Their prices are competitive, and they offer an extensive selection of New Zealand crafts, woolens, and souvenirs. It's also gratifying to know that profits from the shops go to a program of vocational assessment and rehabilitation for the disabled. Indeed, the shops were initiated as outlets for disabled veteran craftsmen following World War II.

8. Where to Go and What to Do

The temptation in this section is simply to say "Go everywhere and do everything!" That's because New Zealand has such a wealth of sightseeing treasures and activities, especially those of an outdoor nature.

WHERE TO GO: Sightseeing highlights are pretty well covered in the sample itineraries of "How Long to Stay" above. But, given time, there are some other pretty special areas you really shouldn't miss: the Bay of Islands is one such; Gisborne and the Sunrise Coast are another; Stewart Island is a place unto itself of unspoiled scenery and rugged island people; the South Island's west coast is a sunlit panorama; and Milford Sound's mystical, primeval beauty begs more time than an afternoon launch cruise. All will be detailed in the following chapters—follow your heart in making additions or substitutions in your itinerary as you go along.

ACTIVE SPORTS: New Zealanders are water bugs! Anytime they're not slaving away in an office or some other workplace, you'll find them in the water, on the water, or fishing the waters. As a visitor, you can participate in all sorts of **water sports.** There are pleasant beaches in the Bay of Islands, the Gisborne area, the Marlborough Sound areas, and around Nelson. Surfing is especially good around the Bay of Plenty, with Tauranga offering what a Kiwi friend assures me is "the best surf of any New Zealand beach." Sailing is available to visitors in the Bay of Islands, where you can indulge in deep-sea fishing jaunts as well.

Angling for rainbow and brown trout can put dinner on the table as well as provide a day in the open. Rotorua and Taupo are trout-fishing centers, but it's hard to fish any river or lake in the country without coming up with a good catch. In Rotorua, look up Rex Forrester at the GTB—he wrote the Tourist Bureau's free booklet *Fishing New Zealand* and can point you to especially good fishing spots in the area. In Taupo, Brian Leverell (owner of the Adelphi Best Western) is one of the North Island's best fishing guides and will practically guarantee you at least one trout on a half- or full-day fishing trip. Down South, Tony Busch (of Sportsgoods Nelson Ltd.) will do the same. The season is a long one—from the first Saturday in October to the end of June (year round at Rotorua and Taupo), and you can buy a license for one day (NZ$1, or 67¢ U.S.), a week (NZ$2.75 or $1.84 U.S.), or a special Tourist Fishing License for a month (NZ$4, or $2.68 U.S., for men; NZ$2, or $1.34 U.S., for women). Any fishing tackle or sporting goods store can sell you the first two, and the Tourist License you can get through the GTB.

Tramping (hiking) is another popular sport, and as you move around the country good hikes are almost always right at hand. The ten national parks, which cover more than five million acres, all have well-defined trails, and many provide bunkhouses or huts for overnight stops. Even when you're based in a city, there will be scenic walks in the vicinity; I'll tell you about some in the chapters to come, and tourist offices can furnish brochures for their area. In fact, it's possible to hike the entire 1000-mile length of New Zealand, and if that's your inclination, contact the **New Zealand Walkways Commission,** c/o Dept. of Lands & Survey, Private Bag, Wellington, for details of connecting regional and local walks. The most famous—and one of the most splendid—is the guided five- to seven-day Milford Track walk in Fiordland National Park, which draws trampers from around the world. You can book the guided walk through the GTB or contact park rangers if you'd like to strike out on your own. Tramping is best in New Zealand from late November through April, when temperatures are their most moderate.

New Zealand has some of the best ski terrain in the world, which, for North Americans, makes year-round **skiing** possible, since the season runs from mid-July through September—just in time to take up when our season leaves off and end just prior to the beginning of ours. Major ski fields in the South Island are at Queenstown, Tekapo, Wanaka, Mount Hutt, and—for advanced skiers—famed Mount Cook, where you fly by skiplane to the 8000-foot-high head of the Tasman Glacier and ski down the 12-mile run. In the north, there's good skiing at Tongariro and Turoa.

There are over 300 registered **golf** clubs in New Zealand, and members of overseas clubs are granted guest privileges in most private clubs. Clubs and a "trundler" (don't expect motorized carts) can be rented, and greens fees are low. One of the most outstanding courses is 50 miles south of Rotorua at Wairakei.

SPECTATOR SPORTS: Rugby dominates the sports scene from Easter through September, with Saturday matches featuring Kiwi males from schoolboys to businessmen to members of the national team, the All Blacks (who are elevated to a status in national esteem approaching reverence), to senior citizens. International matches are held in Auckland's Eden Park, Wellington's Athletic Park, Dunedin's Carisbrook Park, and Lancaster Park in Christchurch. If you're a football nut at home and think our players are pretty tough hombres, be sure to take in at least one match and watch the lads rough-and-tumble around to pitch in knee pants—with nary a padded shoulder to be seen!

After rugby, it's **horse racing** that claims national affection in New Zealand. There are 271 days of licensed racing (133 of trotting) during the year, and race meets take place in informal beach settings or open fields with the same degree of enthusiasm as those at the larger tracks around the country. In January there's the New Zealand Cup, a highlight of the racing year—if you're there and are overcome by gambling fever, go ahead and indulge: betting is perfectly legal, both on and off the track.

Speaking of **gambling**, you may also want to enter the Golden Kiwi Lottery, held at regular intervals with a NZ$60,000 ($40,268) first prize. Tickets cost NZ$1 (67¢). There's also, from time to time during each year, a Mammoth Kiwi Lottery with a NZ$500,000 ($335,570) grand prize and tickets cost NZ$5 ($3.36) to NZ$20 ($13.42).

EVENING ACTIVITIES: Except in larger cities, nightlife is quiet, quiet, quiet. Quiet, that is, when it isn't totally nonexistent. New Zealand will have little appeal for jet-setters who require a swinging nightlife that goes on into the wee hours. In Auckland and Wellington, supper clubs and a very few nightspots offer revues or other entertainment, and there are theater productions on a sporadic basis. And of course there are the Maori concerts in Rotorua and nighttime visits to Waitomo's glowworm grotto. Otherwise, do as the Kiwis do—enjoy full, bracing days of outdoor activity followed by a satisfying evening meal followed by quiet visits with friends or a little time in front of the telly followed by an early bedtime. It makes a refreshing change from our frenetic pace at home, and you may be surprised to find how ready you are for those early evenings after a day or so of heavy sightseeing.

Chapter II

GETTING TO AND AROUND NEW ZEALAND

1. Getting There
2. Getting Around

WE'LL BE DEALING in this chapter with the single largest item in any budget for New Zealand travel—the cost of getting there. While not nearly as costly as it once was, transportation across the South Pacific is the first financial hurdle in your planning. Once you arrive, you'll have a number of options as to how much or how little to spend on transport around New Zealand.

1. Getting There

You *could* go by ship, of course—one of the luxury liners that sails maybe twice a year, or a freighter making stops all across the Pacific—but for most of us, the only practical way to go is by jet plane. And although air fare cannot be called cheap, it *can* be called a travel bargain if you utilize the options wisely. For example, a stopover in Hawaii, Tahiti, Fiji, or the Cook Islands is permitted at no cost (additional stops add only $50 each to your fare). Now, when you get two travel destinations for the fare you would pay just to go to New Zealand, that fare becomes a budget buy. For just a bit more, it's possible to include as many as ten destinations.

The most important part of your holiday planning begins with predeparture research on air fares. There are differences in the types of fares and seasonal charges, and there are differences in airlines. Your first task should be to study these differences, decide on the one best suited to your needs, then telephone or visit a qualified travel agent or the individual airline offices. Be forearmed with a list of the *specific* information you need so that answers to your questions can be as direct as possible.

All direct flights to New Zealand from the U.S. depart from Los Angeles, and principal airlines offering this service are Air New Zealand, Pan American, and Continental (a word about person preference later on).

FARE OPTIONS: Set out below are the basic types of fares available and their costs as this book is written. Remember, however, that these figures are far from cast in stone—nor are the fare types, for that matter. Fares can change in a matter of days as airlines rush to introduce new and more competitive fare structures. Use these as a guide, then shop around carefully.

AIR NEW ZEAL

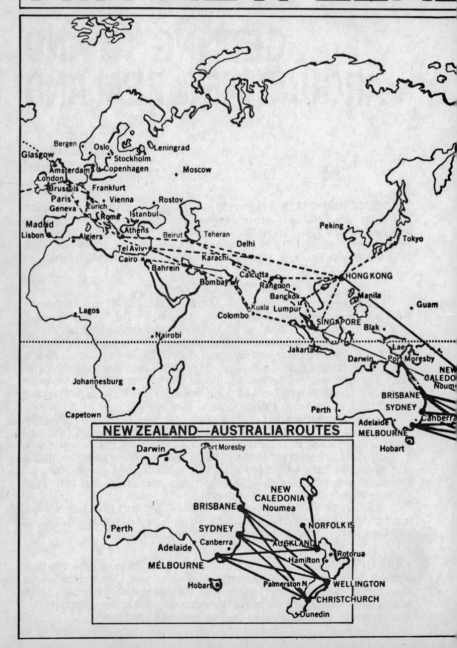

AND ROUTES

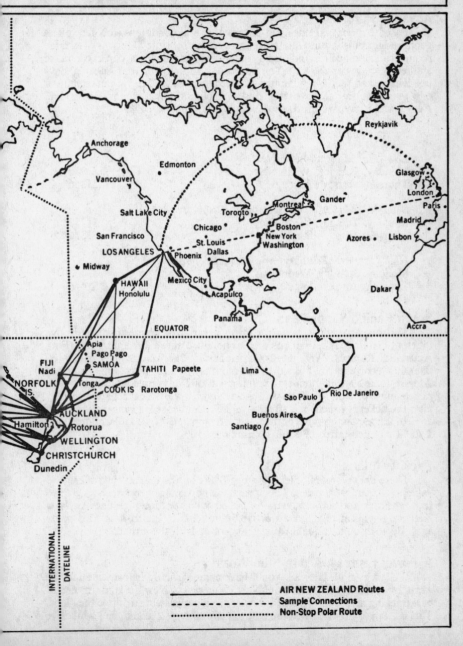

Economy Fare

This ticket is good for a maximum of one year, with unlimited stopover privileges. It offers immense flexibility. Cost: $2112. Infants fly for 10% of the adult fare, and children ages 2 to 12 are given a one-third discount.

Advance Purchase (APEX)

Based on seasonal rates and carrying several conditions, this fare offers good budget possibilities. Your departure date from the U.S. will determine round-trip seasonal fare, and the day of the week on which you depart can make a difference in what you pay. You must book and pay for your ticket 30 days in advance, and there's a minimum-stay requirement of 7 days, a maximum of one year. One free stopover is included; each additional stopover costs $50. Ages 2 to 12 pay two-thirds of the adult fare; infants, 10%.

Seasons and fares:

Low (May, June, July, August)
Monday, Tuesday, Wednesday	$ 980
Thursday through Sunday	$1056

Shoulder (March, April, September, October)
Monday, Tuesday, Wednesday	$1250
Thursday through Sunday	$1326

High (January, February, November, December)
Monday, Tuesday, Wednesday	$1400
Thursday through Sunday	$1476

South Pacific Super Pass

This one fare allows stopover at no fewer than ten destinations in five different countries. Destinations are: Honolulu, Papeete (Tahiti), Nadi (Fiji), Auckland, Rotorua, Wellington, Christchurch, Brisbane, Sydney, and Melbourne. Departures are limited to the months of April, May, June, July and August; there's a minimum-stay requirement of 7 days (maximum, one year); tickets must be paid for 30 days in advance, with a 25% cancellation penalty after the ticket is issued; and after travel has commenced, a cancellation fee of 25% of the remaining value of the ticket will apply. Cost: $1350. Children ages 2 to 12 pay two-thirds of adult fare; infants, 10%.

Package Plans

There are several excellent package plans on the market that offer good value to the budget traveler. They provide land arrangements such as ground transportation and accommodations, but *no guides or formal groups.* Air New Zealand, for instance, offers attractive fly-drive, farm holidays, and ski packages. Book through a qualified travel agent or with the airline.

A Travel Fantasy: Around the World

Well, why not! After all, you'll have come virtually halfway around the world by the time you travel from North America to New Zealand. Instead of backtracking across the Pacific, it seems like a perfect time to circle the globe. This is a fantasy that nags at me on each trip to New Zealand, and while I've not yet managed the free time, it's definitely in my future. There are several ways it could be done, of course, and one of the most economical is Air New Zealand's hookup with British Airways, which allows up to seven stopovers and is good for one year. Sections may be open-dated, and you're permitted to interline (wander off the beaten track with other airlines). You must be ticketed at least 21 days prior to departure, and there's a nonrefundable 25% cancellation penalty. Cost: $2200. Certainly worth thinking about!

TRAVEL TIPS: No matter which airline you choose, if you fly direct it's going to be a *long,* 13-hour flight during which you cross the International Dateline and lose one whole calendar day (which you gain, of course, on the return trip), go through four time zones, and turn the seasons upside down. There's no way your body is not going to suffer the pangs of jet lag! There are as many ways to minimize that malady of long-distance travel as there are long-distance travelers, but two strategies which work for me are these: first, I make it a point to get up from my seat at least once an hour when not sleeping and walk around the plane to keep my legs and feet from swelling; and second, I plan on a stopover of at least 24 hours (48 hours or more when I can manage it) en route both ways—gradually, I'm getting to know those South Pacific islands, and my body gets to make the time adjustment in easy stages. You, of course, no doubt have your own, time-tested jet-lag remedies. If they really work, drop me a line.

YOUR CHOICE OF AIRLINE: "You're in for *such* a treat—just *wait* till you fly Air New Zealand!" The elderly British couple had overheard my request to be let off at that airline's Los Angeles terminal, and having just completed the long trans-Pacific flight themselves, had rushed back to my seat on the airport shuttle bus to share their bubbling enthusiasm with someone obviously facing the same flight in the opposite direction. They sang the praises of New Zealand's national airline long and loud, which, I must confess, gave rise to my natural skepticism about the "delights" of almost any airline.

Well, that skepticism vanished before we even left the ground. A gracious attendant welcomed me with a glass of fresh juice, made sure that I was comfortably settled in the seat, which sported a lambskin covering, and introduced me to a brand of friendliness I shall forever associate with her native land. Then the intercom crackled and the captain's welcome was a surprising "Welcome aboard, ladies and gentlemen, girls and boys. We're going to do everything we can to see that you have a good flight. In the meantime, get comfortable, look around, and maybe introduce yourself to that fellow or girl sitting next to you—who knows, you may make a friend for life." Friendlier than that, it's hard to get!

From a budget standpoint, I like the idea of no extra charges once you board the plane. That's right: there is *never* any charge for drinks (alcoholic or otherwise) or for headsets to listen to the movie or music, or for anything else. Granted, these are not major expenses, but the concept of an all-inclusive fare appeals to my penny-pinching heart. From a pampered standpoint, I love the food service and friendliness of the cabin crew. Except for a plastic bread tray and salad dish, my meals were served on real crockery, not the usual dinky plastic tray. Dinners came via trolley (following the predinner drink trolley!) and consisted of lamb (which had that "home-cooked" flavor), three fresh vegetables, hot rolls, a great dessert, cheese, and fruit. Breakfasts were every bit as good, and when I commented on the fresh, sweet taste of both milk and butter, my hostess informed me that Air New Zealand flies supplies of both to departure points so that only good, native dairy products are served on all planes. Now, *that's* attention to detail! That same care and concern pervades every Air New Zealand cabin crew with whom I've ever flown—they have seemed as alert to my physical needs as I am myself, and have blanketed and pillowed me, adjusted my seat for maximum comfort, and seemed ever poised to do battle with any hunger pangs that threatened.

That first Air New Zealand flight made a confirmed fan of yours truly, and it would take a tremendous fare difference to tempt me even to try another airline. But there's more to it than simply enjoying the journey: in addition to its good food, fine service, comfort, and the character of the entire staff, Air New Zealand can boast of a history which goes back to 1940, when a 19-passenger flying boat first flew from Waitemata Harbour in Auckland to Sydney under the name of Tasman Empire Airways—and its record since that inaugural flight has included an enviable safety record as well as outstanding passenger service. Pampered you most certainly are on all Air New Zealand flights; yet even the most jaded traveler rests a little easier when there's a long tradition of getting from one place to another safely. Maybe the combination of all these factors accounts for Air New Zealand's consistently topping international passenger polls—and without doubt they account for my wholehearted and loving recommendation of the airline to readers. It's a great way to experience New Zealand before you reach New Zealand!

2. Getting Around

When it comes to getting around New Zealand, you can pick and choose, mix and match, modes of transport. As I said earlier in this book, things *work* in this country. Bus and rail transportation are both reliable, car-rental firms are dependable, and the two airlines furnishing domestic service cover longer stretches with ease. Driving, of course, affords the most flexibility, as you are tied to no one's schedule except your own. However, public transportation is an economical, pleasant way to go, and in one form or another will reach any destination within the country.

RAIL AND ROAD: Most rail and bus services are provided by the **New Zealand Railways Corporation** and the **New Zealand Railways Corporation Road Services** (referred to familiarly as **NZR** and **NZRRS**). Although there are other coach lines, these two organizations run all railways, most provincial buses, some suburban buses, ferry service between the North and South Islands, and many of the better sightseeing tours. For the budget traveler, they offer what is probably the least expensive way of getting around the country.

A personal word here: As a veteran of two, seven-week-long jaunts around New Zealand by train and bus, I can tell you that—aside from so many early-morning departures, which are a bit hard on my late-rising psyche—this method of travel has much to offer that cannot be found otherwise. Consider: You travel with New Zealanders who are not touring, but simply going about their own business—a chance to rub elbows in the most elementary way. Consider: On many of the buses (particularly in the South Island), drivers give an excellent commentary on the countryside—not for tourists, mind you, but for Kiwis who may travel the route frequently but who seem as interested as those of us who are traveling through for the first time. Consider: Trains run along coastlines and mountain gorges with fantastic views, which are completely hidden from highways that run farther inland or on higher ground. Consider: When you leave the driving to someone else, there's no need to worry about

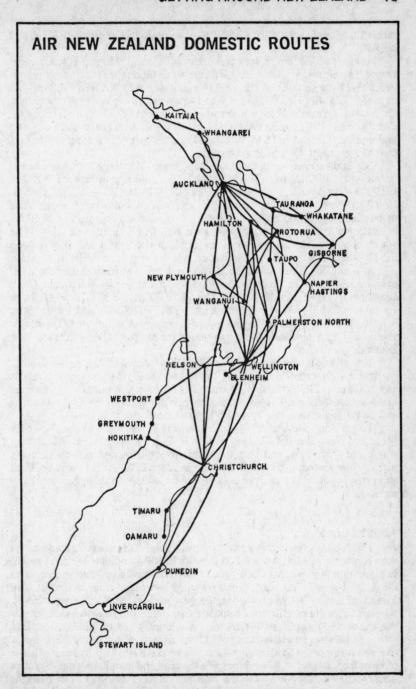

AIR NEW ZEALAND DOMESTIC ROUTES

driving on the left, keeping one eye glued to the map or looking for road signs rather than scenic splendors. I admit it—I'm positively addicted to NZR and NZRRS.

Aside from all that, a very good reason to travel this way is the money-saving **Travelpass,** available from February 1 to December 14. You get unlimited travel by both rail and bus for 15 days at a cost of NZ$180 ($120.81), 22 days for NZ$240 ($161.07). Ages 4 to 14 pay half price; under 4s travel free. Extensions are available for a maximum of 6 days at NZ$15 ($10.07) per day, and if you buy the Travelpass outside New Zealand, there are special 8-day and high-season (December 15 to January 31) passes available through New Zealand Government Tourist Bureau offices.

For high-season travel, there are **Bulk Travel Vouchers,** which are issued in multiples of NZ$100 ($67.11) with a minimum purchase of NZ$200 ($134.23) travel value, for which you pay NZ$180 ($120.80)—a 10% savings. You'll receive a book of vouchers, which you then present to any booking office to purchase tickets on any rail, road, or ferry service operated by NZR or NZRRS with the exception of suburban buses and sightseeing tours. The vouchers may be used by any or all members of your party, and they're good for 12 months. You must not, however, sell them to anyone else.

Mount Cook Lines offers the **Kiwi Coach Pass** which may be purchased only outside New Zealand and is good for coach service on Mount Cook Landlines, NZRRS, and Newmans. The cost for 7 days is NZ$79 ($53.02); for 10 days, NZ$100 ($67.11); for 15 days, NZ$131 ($87.92); and for 25 days, NZ$203 ($136.24). It may be purchased from travel agents or GTB offices; you'll be given a certificate that you trade in for the pass when you reach New Zealand.

You should know that *all bus and rail journeys must be booked*—this is particularly important during peak travel periods. Bookings may be made at any NZR or NZRRS station or through GTB offices as much as six months in advance. Of course, I've never seen anyone just show up without a booking and be refused a seat, but I wouldn't recommend chancing that.

To preplan your entire trip before leaving home, write to the Passenger Manager, New Zealand Railways, Private Bag, Wellington, and tell them where you'd like to go and your time limit—they'll respond with an itinerary planned to your requirements. In New Zealand the GTB will do the same. Both will provide you with a complete set of timetables covering rail, bus, and ferry services.

About Buses

The NZRRS service network is extensive, and there are good connections with Newmans or Mount Cook Landlines to those few points they don't reach. For example, if you cross Cook Strait from Wellington to Picton en route to the South Island's west coast, you'll travel by Newmans as far as Greymouth. Your vouchers or Travelpass will not apply on those portions of your travel.

All buses are comfortable; some are carpeted; most have individual reading lights. Frequent stops for tea or refreshments are scheduled, and as I mentioned above, on many runs you'll hear an interesting, informative narrative about the country through which you're traveling. In rural areas, buses often pull up in front of T-bars alongside the road and drivers lean out to collect mail sacks to be dropped off at the next post office. All sorts of other freight travels along with you as well—a closeup look at Kiwi life outside the cities!

About Trains

All trains in the country are operated by NZR, and all are quite comfortable, although the equipment can be anything from older suburban cars to very good overnight sleepers to sleek, modern rail cruisers. The major rail services are:

Auckland–Wellington: The *Northerner,* a part sleeper, leaves Auckland and Wellington at 7:30 p.m., arriving at the opposite terminal at 8:30 the next morning. There are twinette sleeper cars and normal seated carriages, plus a licensed buffet car where drinks and buffet food are served. Sleeper fare is NZ$69.40 ($46.58); a carriage seat, NZ$49.70 ($33.36).

The day trip is via the *Silver Fern,* and there's an informative commentary as you pass through fern forests, sacred Maori burial grounds, and volcanic peaks. Free morning and afternoon tea is served by uniformed hostesses and stewards, who also provide newspapers and magazines and will take drink orders to be served at your seat. There's a lunch stop at Taihape Station. Departure from Auckland is at 8 a.m., with arrival at Wellington at 7:02 p.m.; departure from Wellington is at 8:20 a.m., with arrival at Auckland at 7:30 p.m. Both run every day except Sunday, and the fare is NZ$55.80 ($37.45).

Christchurch–Dunedin–Invercargill: Daily except Sunday, the *Southerner* makes this run, one train in each direction. Christchurch departure is at 8:40 a.m., Dunedin at 3:05 p.m., and arrival at Invercargill is at 6:45 p.m. Going north, trains leave Invercargill at 8:40 a.m. and Dunedin at 12:21 p.m., arriving at Christchurch at 6:35 p.m. There's a buffet car which serves drinks and buffet food, and drinks may also be ordered from the hostess in your carriage. You're given an illustrated map of the route, which passes some quite spectacular coastal scenery as well as pastoral scenes of grazing sheep and wheat fields. From Christchurch to Dunedin the fare is NZ$24.60 ($16.51); from Christchurch to Invercargill, NZ$39.20 ($26.31).

The *Northerner, Silver Fern,* and *Southerner* express trains are the showpieces of the system. They're carpeted, attractive in decor, and well heated, air-conditioned, or ventilated. Comfortable trains run daily between Wellington and Gisborne (with a stop in Napier), Christchurch and Greymouth, and Christchurch and Picton. Although there are no hostesses or buffet cars on these trains, refreshment stops are made en route.

BY CAR: New Zealand is a driver's paradise. You can wander at will over roads, which (outside the larger cities) are virtually traffic-free. Better yet, you can stop at will to take a closer look at an inviting seascape or lush fern forest. When lunchtime arrives, it's picnic time at whichever scenic spot takes your fancy. Bus and train rider that I am, I usually plan to drive at least one segment of the trip just for the joy of all that freedom. And if you can possibly afford it, I highly recommend the experience.

New Zealand **roads** are exceptionally well maintained, except for a few mountainous stretches in the South Island, where you sometimes wonder how they managed to carve out a road in the first place. And speaking of mountains, let me say—as one who has driven for donkey's years in all sorts of terrain—that if you're not accustomed to mountain driving, you might consider using public transportation from Hokitika to the glaciers, Queenstown, Te Anau, and Milford Sound, then resuming your journey by car from Te Anau. I've been assured by my Kiwi friends in this area that such a plan is entirely unnecessary and that driving is not that difficult in this part of the South Island. All I can say is that I personally feel much more secure when someone else is navigating along those mountain roads.

You must be at least 21 to rent a car in New Zealand, and must possess a current **driver's license** from the U.S., Australia, Canada, the United Kingdom, or a few other countries, or an International Driving Permit. You drive on the left and must—by law—buckle that seatbelt when the car is moving. Speed limit on the open road is 50 m.p.h. (80 k.p.h.) and in congested areas, town, cities, 30 m.p.h. (50 k.p.h.). Drive with extreme caution when an area is signposted "LSZ" (Limited Speed Zone). Signposting, incidentally, is very good all through the country—there's little chance of losing your way.

You'll be given a set of **maps** when you pick up your rental car, and if you're a member of the Automobile Association in the U.S. or Australia, you'll have reciprocal privileges with the New Zealand AA, which includes their very good maps, plus "strip maps" of your itinerary and comprehensive guidebooks of accommodations (some of which give discounts to AA members). You can contact the New Zealand AA at 166 Willis St., Wellington.

Nearly all New Zealand **car-hire firms** offer unlimited-mileage rates, a decided plus for budgeteers. The best car-rental bargain I've been able to unearth is through Maui Rentals, which provides late-model Japanese cars at one low daily rate, NZ$27.50 ($18.46). That's an all-inclusive rate—even insurance. With offices in Auckland and Christchurch, they don't even charge for pickup in one island and dropoff in the other. They also have terrific rates for caravans (more about that later). You can book through GTB offices in the U.S., or contact them directly at: **Maui Rentals,** 96 New Nth Road, Auckland (tel. 793-277); or 500A Wairakei Rd., Christchurch (tel. 598-207).

Dominion Budget Rent a Car, 73 Beach Rd., Auckland (tel. 796-768), also provides Japanese cars (the Toyota Starlet or equivalent) at NZ$45 ($30.20) per day, with seasonal bargain rates often available. For a nominal fee, they'll deliver to your hotel, and there are airport dropoff privileges.

Avis (insurance is an additional charge, and you must *ask* for special unlimited-mileage rates) is at 22 Wakefield St., Auckland (tel. 792-650); **Hertz** at 154 Victoria St. West, Auckland (tel. 34-924). Insurance is extra. Airport delivery.

Motor Homes

If you want to take advantage of New Zealand's budget motor camps—or if you're simply a caravaner at heart—**Maui Rentals** offers motor homes at incredibly low rates. Their compact Budget-Sleeper accommodates two adults comfortably, includes cooking facilities and utensils as well as crockery and cutlery, and rents for NZ$60 ($40.27) per day. The Hi-Top Campa adds a third bunk plus enclosed shower and costs NZ$75 ($50.34) per day. More luxurious is the Campa, which accommodates four adults and one child at NZ$94 ($63.09) daily; and the spiffy Travelhome sleeps up to six adults at NZ$110 ($73.83) per day. They'll meet your plane and you can be installed in your motor home within two hours of landing (saving that first night's hotel bill). All rentals are on an unlimited-mileage basis, and you can pick up and drop off at either their Auckland or Christchurch office at no extra fee. There's a NZ$3 ($2.01) daily insurance charge and a NZ$100 ($67.11) deposit required when you book (the balance due 30 days prior to picking up your motor home). In New Zealand, contact them at the addresses shown above for rental cars. North Americans can also book directly through all three U.S. New Zealand Government Tourist Bureau offices listed in the Introduction.

Air New Zealand also offers motor home tour packages in connection with Newmans and Southern Cross Tours—contact a qualified travel agent or the airline for details.

The Buy-Back Plan

If you're going to be in New Zealand for as long as four months or more, the most feasible transport is your very own car. The problem is what to do with it when you leave. But a long-established auto firm in Auckland has solved that problem for you. **Letz Buy a Car Ltd.,** 55–61 Shortland St., P.O. Box 2752, Auckland (tel. 30-145) will sell you a used automobile in perfect condition (a 1979 or 1980 Honda or Datsun, for example), and give you a fixed figure at which they agree to buy it back when you leave. The buy-back price is guaranteed, barring any mechanical or body damage to the car. You're not obligated to sell to Letz if you can sell it on the open market for a higher figure. You can book from the U.S. through their office at 1448 Fifteenth St., Suite 105, Santa Monica, CA 90025 (tel. 213/393-8262 collect, or toll free 800/472-5015).

BY AIR: Both Air New Zealand and Mount Cook Lines fly internal routes in New Zealand. Schedules are frequent and convenient, and equipment is modern and comfortable on both.

Air New Zealand flies Boeing 737s and Fokker Friendships, and serves some 23 destinations. There's no meal service, since most flights are short, but on most you'll be served snacks of crackers, New Zealand cheese, and a beverage. All flights are one class. If you plan to use this domestic service often during your stay, it will pay either to have those flights included with your international air ticket or to inquire about the **ANZ Airpass**—both must be arranged *before your arrival in New Zealand.* Also, as this book is written, **Air New Zealand** has just inaugurated a discount **"Thrifty Fares" plan** for passengers who book and pay at least seven days in advance for travel on specific evening flights from Sunday through Friday between Auckland–Wellington, Wellington–Christchurch, and Christchurch–Auckland. It remains to be seen if they'll be successful enough to become a permanent fixture, but be sure to inquire.

North to south, Air New Zealand serves: Kaitaia, Whangarei, Auckland, Tauranga, Hamilton, Whakatane, Rotorua, Taupo, Gisborne, New Plymouth, Napier, Hastings, Wanganui, Palmerston North, Wellington, Nelson, Blenheim, Westport, Hokitika, Christchurch, Timaru, Oamaru, Dunedin, and Invercargill. Reservations, rental cars, and hotel accommodations may be booked through their offices.

Current sample fares are: Auckland–Rotorua, NZ$66 ($44.30); Rotorua–Wellington, NZ$88 ($59.06); Wellington–Christchurch, NZ$78 ($52.35); Christchurch–Dunedin, NZ$82 ($55.03).

Ages 14 and under pay half fare; under 2, free; and students receive a 50% discount on a standby basis if they have a valid International Student card. There are attractive domestic package tours available through Air New Zealand offices providing a rental car and accommodations.

Mount Cook Line links New Zealand's major tourist areas to each other and to Auckland and Christchurch. Schedules are designed to connect with Air New Zealand's domestic service, as well as international flights.

They also provide some of the most spectacular flight-seeing tours to be found anywhere in the world. If you splurge (as you most certainly should) on a glacier flight, you'll be flying Mount Cook Line. And if you're on one of those short-stay itineraries, it's Mount Cook Line that can get you around to the sightseeing points that top your list. In that case, you should definitely consider the **Kiwi Air Pass,** which must be purchased *before you arrive in New Zealand.* For NZ$299 ($200.67) you can take a circle trip around New Zealand, with stops at any point. Travel need not be continuous, but must be in one direction—no backtracking. The pass is also valid on Mount Cook Line's coach service if it's substituted for air travel. The Kiwi Air Pass is valid for one month following your first flight, and you can purchase it through qualified travel agents in the U.S.

Sample fares: Auckland–Bay of Islands, NZ$76 ($51); Auckland–Mount Cook, NZ$208 ($139.60); Christchurch–Mount Cook, NZ$79 ($53.02); Christchurch–Queenstown, NZ$125 ($83.89).

INTERISLAND FERRY: Even if you fly the better part of your trip, try to plan a crossing of Cook Strait on the Wellington–Picton ferry in at least one direction. You'll get a look at both islands from the water, just as those early Maoris and Europeans did, and the crossing is one of New Zealand's very best travel experiences. You'll find full details at the end of the Wellington chapter.

Chapter III

AUCKLAND

**1. The City and Surroundings
2. From Auckland to the Bay of Islands
3. The Bay of Islands
4. From Auckland to Waitomo
5. Waitomo Caves**

IT IS NEW ZEALAND'S largest city; holds a full 24% of the entire country's population (820,200); has the largest Polynesian population of any city in the world; adds another 25,000 residents each year, making it the country's fastest growing city; and its international airport is the overseas visitor's introduction to this delightful land and its people.

Straddling a narrow, pinched-in isthmus, which was created by the activity of some 60 volcanoes over a period of more than 50,000 years, Auckland is said by Maori legend to have been inhabited by a race of giants in the days before the moa hunters. Its present-day giants are those of commerce and industry, but the attraction for both ancient and latter-day Goliaths was probably the same—its excellent twin harbors. Europeans arrived in Auckland in 1839, and when the Waitangi treaty was signed in 1840, negotiations with the Maoris transferred the isthmus to British ownership. The flag was hoisted on September 18, 1840, an event marked annually by the Anniversary Day Regatta (celebrated in January because of better sailing conditions). The thriving town served as New Zealand's first capital until 1865, when the seat of government was transferred to Wellington because of its central location.

Today's Auckland is nestled among volcanic peaks, which have settled into gently rounded hills, minor mountains, and sloping craters. North Head and Bastion Point stand like sentinels on either side of Waitemata Harbour's entrance, and Rangitoto, the largest and more recently active volcano (it erupted in the 13th century), sits in majestic splendor just offshore. Mount Eden's eastern slopes are marked by Maori earthworks, and One Tree Hill has become an archeological field monument because of the large Maori *pa* that once existed there. What is possibly the world's finest collection of Maori artifacts can be seen in the Auckland War Memorial Museum, along with a display of the moa, that giant bird that stood ten feet from beak to toe and that has been extinct for centuries. Colonial-style homes are monuments to its Pakahe development. Side by side with these reminders of its history are modern Auckland's diversions—outstanding restaurants, more entertainment than you'll find in other parts of the country, and an ambience that grows more cosmopolitan every year. The city warrants a few days of your time, with much to offer which will enhance the remainder of your New Zealand visit.

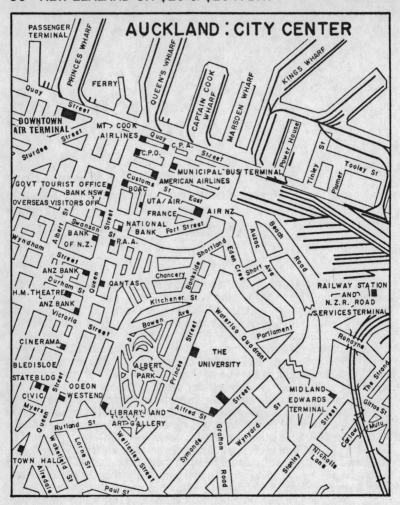

1. The City and Surroundings

ORIENTATION: You can credit the Kiwi's inborn desire for his own home and garden for the fact that central Auckland is surrounded by districts that have become cities in their own right—your man may *work* in the inner city, but when evening comes, he's off to wider spaces. And his homeward journey will take him over at least one bridge (the place is broken out with bridges: they cross the harbor, rivers, creeks, and bays) and possibly onto the speeding motorway that runs north-south through the city. That motorway can be a blessing for the visitor unfamiliar with the territory and driving on the left, for it virtually eliminates the possibility of losing your way when you set out for the Bay of Islands, Rotorua, or other major points.

The city itself is also fairly straightforward. The main street is **Queen Street,** which ends in Queen Elizabeth's Square at Quay Street. **Quay Street** runs along the Waitemata harborfront. At the other end of Queen Street is **Karangahape Road,** a mere 1¼ miles from Quay Street. Within that area you'll find most of the city's shops, restaurants, nightspots, and hotels, as well as bus, rail, and air terminals.

The city's **bus system** is quite good, reaching all districts with convenient and rather frequent schedules. You can pick up route maps and timetables from most newsagents or the Quay Street (near Commerce) bus terminal; or call the Auckland Regional Authority (tel. 797-119) for information. Fares are by zone, running from NZ$.40 (27¢) to NZ$1.20 (80¢). Children under 15 pay half fare; under 4, free; and you must have the exact change. If you're going to be using the buses a lot, you can purchase a one-day Busabout unlimited bus travel ticket for NZ$3 ($2.01) or the same ticket for two days at NZ$5 ($3.36). Buy them on the buses or through the Auckland Regional Authority. One word of caution when you're planning evening activities: Auckland buses stop running around 11:30 p.m. on weekdays, 10 p.m. on Sunday; so if your evening is going to be a late one, plan on taking a taxi home.

Auckland has a high percentage of drivers per capita, and driving in the city can be a real hassle. My best advice is to park the car and use that excellent bus system as much as possible. If you must drive into the city, you can park the car for the day in **car parks** operated by the City Council. They're on Beresford Street, just off Karangahape Road; near the waterfront on Albert Street, west of Queen; on Victoria Street, just east of Queen; Britomart, to the east of Queen Street; downtown to the east of Queen Street; downtown to the west of Queen Street, and at the rear of Travelodge and one block from the Princes Wharf Passenger Terminal; Civic Underground on Mayoral Drive; and Greys Avenue, alongside City Hall. All are open seven days a week, 24 hours a day, and rates are quite reasonable.

USEFUL INFORMATION: The **New Zealand Government Tourist Bureau** has a **Travel Office** at 99 Queen St. (tel. 798-180), open Monday through Thursday from 8:30 a.m. to 5 p.m. (until 8:30 p.m. on Friday). Go by to pick up free brochures, any specific help you may need, and a copy of the *Auckland Tourist Times* (which is also distributed free by many hotels) for a listing of current daytime and nighttime happenings. . . . NZRRS buses and NZR trains arrive and depart from the **Auckland Railway Station** east of Queen Street on Beach Road (tel. 792-500). Domestic **Air New Zealand** flights can be booked at the Government Tourist Bureau Travel Office, 99 Queen St. . . . **Mount Cook Lines** is at 101 Queen St. (tel. 778-389). . . . **Taxi ranks** are at all terminals and on the corner of Customs Street West at Queen Street. There's a NZ$.40 (27¢) surcharge if you telephone for a taxi (tel. 792-792 or 328-991). . . . The **Chief Post Office** (CPO) is between Quay and Customs Streets on Queen Street, and is open Monday through Thursday from 8 a.m. to 5:30 p.m. (until 8:30 p.m. on Friday). Dial 14 to send telegrams; 792-200 for information. . . . **Emergency** telephone number is 111 (fire, police, ambulance).

Auckland International Airport

Auckland International Airport lies 13 miles south of the city just behind Manukau Harbour. You'll find the **Downtown Airline Terminal** (tel. 796-055) at 86–94 Quay St. at the corner of Albert Street next to the Travelodge Motel. Coach fare to and from the airport is NZ$4 ($2.68), NZ$1 (67¢) for ages 5 to 15, free for under-5s. If you're staying at a city hotel on the direct bus route, the driver will drop you off upon request. A **shuttle bus** connects the International terminal to the Domestic Terminal, about a mile away for NZ$1 (67¢). **Taxi fares** to and from the airport run NZ$10 ($6.70) to NZ$18 ($12.08) on weekdays, NZ$12 ($8.05) to NZ$20 ($13.42) on weekends.

At the International terminal, there's a **Public Information Office**, coffee-shop, licensed restaurant, bar, bank, post office, rental-car desk, and rental showers. The attractive terminal building's decor is designed to showcase New Zealand's character through the use of murals, timber, stone finishes, and wool carpets.

Special Help for the Budgeteer

Otto and Joan Spinka have, since 1978, operated the small **Touristop** in Auckland's Downtown Airline Terminal, 86–94 Quay St. (tel. 775-783). This attractive and knowledgeable couple (she hails from Minnesota) specialize in offering value-for-dollar services such as bookings for accommodations, tours, rental cars, sightseeing tours, harbor cruises, and, well, just about anything else you'd like to do at the best possible price. There's never any booking fee! They're open seven days a week from 9 a.m. to 6 p.m. (until 9 p.m. on Friday), and you'll also find magazines, candies, coins, and a nice selection of New Zealand souvenirs at Touristop.

ACCOMMODATIONS: The most important thing to remember about accommodations in Auckland is that you should have booked *before you leave home*—I can think of few things worse than arriving anywhere after a 13-hour flight and having to look for a room! If you should deplane without a room already reserved, however, turn immediately to the Government Tourist Bureau. Just keep in mind that you'll be in no position to do much shopping around for budget accommodations. Another source for help is the Best Western/NZ reservation number (tel. 30-326, or 30-313 after hours). (See Chapter I for an outline of their discount Holiday Pass.) This network of high-standard, independent motels provides a 24-hour booking service through a central booking office during normal business hours (8:30 a.m. to 5 p.m.) and by the motels themselves on a rotation basis after hours. From the 500 or so motel flats they have registered, they'll do their best to get you one for under NZ$38 ($26.22) double. Remember that Best Western bookings can now be made in advance in the U.S. by calling their toll-free number (tel. 800/528-1234) and asking for the International Desk. A prebooked room is especially important on weekends, when Auckland can be very tightly booked.

Hostels

The **Percy Shieff Youth Hostel,** 7 Princes St. near Shortland Street (tel. 790-258), is in an ideal location—within walking distance of just about everything. It has 74 beds in 11 rooms, a kitchen, and a small shop. Rates are NZ$6 ($4.03) for Seniors, NZ$3 ($2.01) for Juniors.

Some 2½ miles south of the city center, but easy to reach by the Three Kings city bus, the **Mount Eden Youth Hostel,** 5a Oaklands Rd. off Mount

Eden Road (tel. 603-975), is also close to the airport coach route. Located in a residential area, the hostel has 46 beds in six rooms and a large kitchen. Shops and inexpensive restaurants are within walking distance. Seniors pay NZ$5 ($3.36); Juniors, NZ$2.50 ($1.68).

The Y

The **Auckland YMCA**—one of the best in the country—at the corner of Pitt Street and Greys Avenue (tel. 32-068), is a five-story, gray-and-white building with small, neat rooms, all singles. All are carpeted, have a window, and are fitted out with reading lamps and desks. There are an elevator, laundry, and shower on each floor, parking on the premises, two TV lounges, a gymnasium, and table tennis and health club facilities. They accept both men and women over the age of 17, and about half of their 126 rooms are filled with permanent guests, either students or working people. Rates, which include full board (breakfast, a cut lunch during the week and hot lunch on weekends, and dinner) are NZ$15 ($10.06) per night or NZ$66 ($44.30) per week.

Bed and Breakfast

The **Manor House Hotel,** 363 Queen St. (tel. 778-542), sits right at the top of Queen Street, about a two-minute walk from the heart of the city. The 23 rooms are high-ceilinged, clean, and most are somewhat spacious. All have H&C, and a few have private baths. Tea and coffee are in a centrally located hallway, and there's a TV lounge. Bed and continental breakfast rates for rooms that share a bath down the hall are: NZ$20 ($13.42) daily, NZ$80 ($53.69) weekly, for singles; NZ$30 ($20.13) daily, NZ$120 ($80.54) weekly, for doubles. Rooms with private baths cost NZ$5 ($3.36) extra per day. The Uptown Restaurant and bar is on the premises, serving inexpensive lunches and moderately priced dinners.

Another bed-and-breakfast establishment conveniently located is the **Aspen Lodge,** 62 Emily Pl. (tel. 796-698). This small, neat hotel, which has recently been refurbished, is a short walk from Queen Street and also from the main rail and coach station. The 24 rooms are on the small side, but clean and bright. Singles run NZ$17 ($11.41); doubles, NZ$25 ($16.78); and the one triple, NZ$30 ($20.13).

A long-time favorite with readers of this book is **Harbour Bridge Hotel/ Motel,** 6 Tweed St., Herne Bay, near the bridge entrance (tel. 763-489). Run by Mrs. Wilson, a seasoned traveler herself, Harbour Bridge consists of a large old cedar-wood main house set in shaded grounds, with a modern two-story block of rooms out back. The house is some 90 years old, with a TV lounge centered around a big marble fireplace and grand piano. There's a wide selection of accommodations, from rooms with H&C, which share bath facilities, to large family rooms with private bath, fridge, and stove, to 12 self-contained motel units (some are duplexes with cozy little upstairs rooms), which feature such extras as terraces or patios. Some of these units can accommodate up to seven. There's even a "honeymoon suite" filled with antiques, Persian rugs, oil paintings, and a harp! Bed and breakfast rates are NZ$16 ($10.74) per person; motel flats, NZ$26 ($17.45); and the family units, NZ$30 ($20.13) for two, NZ$6 ($4.03) for each additional person. The honeymoon suite goes for NZ$36 ($24.16)—double, of course.

Aachen House, 39 Market Rd., Remuera (tel. 502-329), sits up on a hill overlooking Hobson Park and is one of a pair of two-story residences built back in 1905, which were known as the "Two Old Ladies of Market Road." There's a decided Victorian air about the place, with its rounded turret wing off to one side and lots of gingerbread trim. Geoff and Pauline Lancaster bought the place expressly to run as a bed and breakfast, and in time they plan to acquire the "sister" house next door, as well. Rooms all have high ceilings, some have bay windows looking out onto nice views, and all share the three baths at one end of the upstairs hall. Downstairs, a cooked English breakfast is served in a quaint old dining room and there's a TV lounge with tea and coffee makings. On cool, evenings, the lounge is warmed by an open fire. Several bus lines into the city are just one block away, so there's frequent service. Bed-and-breakfast rates are NZ$18 ($12.08) single, NZ$27 ($18.12) double, and you can have an evening meal for NZ$7.50 ($5.03) if you let them know early in the day.

Centrally located (within easy walking distance from the Chief Post Office), the **Grande Vue Private Hotel,** 3 Princes St., between Bowen Avenue and Shortland Street (tel. 793-965), is another of Auckland's accommodation bargains. There are 19 rooms with H&C and one with private facilities, all high-ceilinged and cheerfully decorated. Some have good harbor views, and two have small sun porches. A full hot breakfast is served, and tea and coffee makings are yours for the taking. There's a lounge with telly and one without. Rates are NZ$19 ($12.75) single, NZ$26 ($17.45) double.

The **Rosana Travel Hotel,** 217 Ponsonby Rd. at the corner of Pember Reeves Street (tel. 766-603), serves up maps and tourist literature along with breakfast in the dining room, and tea and coffee are on hand in the upstairs lounge. The downstairs TV lounge also holds a pool table and piano, and upstairs lounge windows frame an excellent harbor view. There's a laundry room out back and a car park in front. Rooms all have H&C, and there are *five* singles—a real find for the solo traveler—as well as one double, which share bath facilities. One double and one triple have private baths. Rates for those rooms without bath are NZ$14 ($9.40) per person, NZ$16 ($10.74) per person for those with.

The Salvation Army's **Railton Travel Hotel,** 411 Queen St. (tel. 73-129), is also well supplied with single rooms and is quite handy to the city center. The four-story, gray-and-white building opens onto an alleyway to the rear of a cluster of shops, and has paneled, red-carpeted public rooms and clean, comfortable, simply furnished lodging rooms. There are 36 singles in the 130 rooms, and 94 with private bath. All have H&C. The cheerful dining room serves a three-course dinner for NZ$7 ($4.70), as well as breakfast, which comes with your room rate. Bed-and-breakfast rates for rooms without bath are NZ$20 ($13.42) single, NZ$30 ($20.13) double; with bath, it's NZ$25 ($16.78) and NZ$40 ($26.85), respectively.

A Licensed Hotel

Take a big old hotel built in the same year (1931) and style as the Auckland Railway Station, which has skidded from the "best hotel in town" to little more than a flophouse, then take a far-seeing management that recognizes the need for inexpensive hotel accommodations in Auckland and is willing to invest in resurrecting the splendid old edifice to meet those needs, and what you come up with is **Farthings Hotel,** 131 Beach Rd. (tel. 30-629). The 75 rooms have been freshly decorated and there are now over 140 comfortable beds. Some are larger than others, but small ones are not tiny; all have H&C; some share baths down the hall, others have private facilities; and there are single, double, and triple rooms available. The three bars (one of which overlooks the Waitemata Harbour and Hauraki Gulf) have been so successful they're now favorite gathering places for locals as well as guests. The lovely new restaurant, Off the

Avenue (with seating on three levels), has also caught on as a lunch spot with the business community. Special evening entertainments built around a central theme are a feature of the Fifth Avenue nightspot. All in all, the transformation is quite spectacular. Farthings is tied in with an international travel discount club by that same name for those in the 18 to 35 age group, but this hotel will have appeal to almost any age. Rates are: single without bath at NZ$26 ($17.45), with bath at NZ$32 ($21.47); double without bath at NZ$38 ($25.50), with bath at NZ$46 ($30.87); triple without bath at NZ$46 ($30.87), with bath at NZ$56 ($37.58).

Motel Flats

Located on the direct airport route, the **Ranfurly Court Motel,** 285 Manukau Rd. near Ranfurly Road (tel. 689-059), is no more than a ten-minute bus ride from the city center. Dulcie and Bruce Hobson are the owner-managers of this two-story, beige brick with wood trim Best Western member in its setting of manicured lawn, roses, hedges, and subtropical plants. There are 12 lovely one-bedroom flats, each accommodating two to four people. Each unit has one full window wall, is nicely decorated, and comes equipped with telephone, radio, color TV, and electric blankets. And unlike most motel flats, these are serviced daily. There is a guest laundry, as well as car-wash facilities, on the premises, and a shopping center is just 100 yards away. Rates are NZ$30 ($20.13) single, NZ$35 ($23.49) double, and NZ$8 ($5.37) for each additional adult, NZ$6 ($4.03) for children under 12. A continental breakfast is NZ$3 ($2.01); a cooked breakfast, NZ$5.50 ($3.69).

The **Barrycourt Motor Inn,** 10–20 Gladstone Rd., off St. Stephens Avenue (tel. 33-789), offers a wide variety of accommodations—all first rate. This is a personal favorite of mine not only because of the quality of the units, but because the staff is unfailingly pleasant, friendly, and helpful—a reflection of owner Norm Barry's business philosophy. The original part of the motor inn consists of 22 units in a modern brick building: bedsitters, one-bedroom, and two-bedroom flats sleeping two to five people, with especially well-equipped kitchens and ample closets (both features throughout the Barrycourt). The Executive Block holds 140 units. Throughout, all units have tea- and coffee-making facilities, phones, color TVs, radios, and refrigerators; many units also have complete kitchens, and two-bedroom suites have their own clothes washer and drier (worth the NZ$73—$48.99—splurge just to go home without dirty laundry!). Most rooms in the Executive Block have terraces with harbor views. Daily maid service is provided throughout. The best bet for budgeteers are five units in a lodge at the bottom of the property priced from NZ$15 ($10.06) single to NZ$27 ($18.12) double. These are both charming and spacious; some have oak paneling, beamed ceilings, stained-glass panels, leaded-glass windows, etc. On-premises facilities include four spa pools, a complete guest laundry, and a Victorian Building that houses a conference room, lovely little guest bar, and restaurant. The last, Gladstone's, is done up in turn-of-the-century motif with stained-glass panels, fabric wall coverings, tables elegantly set with crystalware, and even a working fireplace. Prices are in the NZ$8.50 ($5.70) to NZ$12.50 ($8.39) range, and the fare is excellent. The Barrycourt is conveniently located less than a mile from the CPO and in easy walking distance of Parnell Road's quaint shopping district (about which more later), a beach, boating, fishing, and tennis courts. Rates range from NZ$40 ($26.85) to NZ$46 ($30.87) single, NZ$44 ($29.53) to NZ$56 ($37.58) double. Take the Portland Road bus from the downtown bus terminal, which stops right at the door. It's a Best Western, so ask about the Holiday Pass discount.

You'll need a car for these next two listings, but each is ideal for families or anyone who doesn't want to stay in the city center. The **Green Glade Motel,** 27 Ocean View Rd., Northcote, Auckland (tel. 487-445) is eight kilometers across the Harbour Bridge on the north shore. Dawn and Ian Trott are the owner-operators of this Best Western member, which has eight one- and two-bedroom units. All have complete kitchen, color TV, radio, telephone, central heating, and electric blanket. Furnishings are modern, the decor bright and cheerful, and there's a children's playground. There's a swimming pool, spa pool, and fully automatic guest laundry; a small additional charge is made for a continental or cooked breakfast. Nearby are a licensed restaurant, municipal golf course, beaches, and shopping. The motel is backed by a lovely forested public reserve (where you're free to walk) with stands of white pines. Rates are NZ$30 ($20.13) single, NZ$38 ($25.50) double.

Farther from the city (21 kilometers, a 25-minute drive), but in a gorgeous beachfront setting, the **Beach Court Motel,** 5 The Esplanade, Eastern Beach (tel. 534-5159), may tempt you to loiter a day or two to prepare for strenuous sightseeing ahead or to rest up at the end of your trip. There are marvelous views of Hauraki Gulf with its islands, and a very good swimming beach (safe for children) just across the road. The 17 units are exceptionally spacious, all with full kitchen, lounge, and one or two bedrooms (some sleep up to seven). Diane and Don Colquhoun are the owner-operators of this pretty Best Western member, and as friendly hosts as you'll find. Like the Green Glade, this is ideal for families, with large public tennis courts immediately behind the motel and a five-acre municipal playground adjoining. Units are brightly decorated (all will sleep four to six comfortably), have color TV and ironing board and iron. There's a swimming pool, spa pool, and sunroom. Rates are NZ$30 ($20.13) single, NZ$35 ($25.50) double.

READERS' ACCOMMODATIONS SELECTIONS: "A short drive from the hustle and bustle of the city, the **Olive Tree Motel,** 24 Glencoe Rd., Browns Bay, Auckland (tel. 478-644), provides a delightful experience and an honest-to-goodness bargain. Kathy and Dave Hearne, the owner-managers, promote an atmosphere of genuine friendliness and warmth. We loved it" (Jack and Shirley Wilkerson, Walla Walla, Wash.). . . . "The gathering place for backpackers is the **Ivanhoe Lodge** (tel. 862-800), a private youth hostel with doubles and dormitories, communal kitchens, family rooms, no restrictions" (Bob and Gery Ruddick, San Diego, Calif.).

MEALS: Eating out in Auckland can be just about anything you want it to be. There are scads of small, attractive, and inexpensive coffeeshop-type eateries, a wide range of cuisine at moderate prices, and an impressive array of posh restaurants serving international dishes. They're scattered all over the city, but there are interesting concentrations along Parnell and Ponsonby Roads (a large percentage along the latter fall into a high price range, which can only have a place in any budget vacation as a Big Splurge). You'll find examples of each in these pages, but you should also pick up a copy of the free *Auckland Dining Guide,* published quarterly and available at many hotels, as well as the Government Tourist Bureau. Its listings are quite complete and there's a city map included showing restaurant locations.

In the city center, you can literally eat your way through 13 different cuisines in the "Gourmet Gallery" downstairs at the **Plaza Arcade,** 128 Queen St. Within the NZ$1 (67¢) to NZ$5 ($3.36) range, there is a carvery (beef, chiefly); a French bistro; Turkish kebabs; quiche, flans, and omelets; seafood; Indonesian satay; London fish and chips; hamburgers and hot dogs; a salad bar; Mexican cuisine; pizza; and an ice cream parlor and coffee lounge with a smörgåsbord! Everything is sparkling clean, with lots of white dotted with bright colors—it's a cheerful place for lunch or a drop-in snack anytime during the day. Hours are 10 a.m. to 5 p.m. (until 9 p.m. on Friday).

A little farther up Queen Street, the **Village Inn,** 202 Queen St., is downstairs in "The Corner," a shopping complex at the corner of Queen and Victoria. It's bright, with blond wood tables and booths, and serves very good hot meals (excellent roasts, with the usual vegetables) and cold salad plates for NZ$3 ($2.01) to NZ$7 ($4.70). It's self-service, and there's a BYO license if you want to bring along wine. Open seven days a week: 11:30 a.m. to 3 p.m. and 4:30 to 9 p.m. weekdays, 10:30 a.m. 9:30 p.m. on Saturday, and 11:30 a.m. to 8 p.m. on Sunday.

Vegetarian dishes supplemented by meat and fish are the mainstay at **Peacock's,** Norfolk House, Upper Vulcan Lane off Queen Street. It's a small, cheery place made to look larger by a mirror on the back wall and its high ceiling. Service is cafeteria style, and everything is fresh and homemade. At prices which range from NZ$1.50 ($1.01) to NZ$4.50 ($3.02), there are such dishes as fish pie, cottage pie, omelets, large salad plates, and luscious desserts featuring real New Zealand whipped cream. Open Monday to Thursday from 11 a.m. to 3 p.m., until 8 p.m. on Friday.

The name of **The Hard to Find Café,** 26 High St. (tel. 734-681), means just what it says—it *is* hard to find. But well worth the effort! And sometime during 1984, it's just possible that it will move, so if you walk up Vulcan Lane from Queen Street, turn right onto High Street, and don't see the painted sandwich-board sign outside a narrow little lane, head for the nearest telephone directory and look up its new address. Helen Bilbee, the attractive owner and chef, assures me she'll keep the name and the menu. And it's the menu—and the prices—which will make it worth your while to track it down if they *do* move. Helen serves some of the best Mexican food I've had anywhere in the world (including my favorite New York City spot). Her marvelous tacos come with all kinds of fillings, including vegetarian, and the nachos are *really* crispy. Although the enchilada salad and sour cream alone makes a good lunch, for something even more filling, try the enchilada and taco with rice and salad. There's a nice selection of desserts and several special coffees. Prices? From NZ$1.80 ($1.21) to NZ$5.30 ($3.56)! No alcohol served, but you're welcome to bring your own beer or wine. Hours are noon to 2 p.m. weekdays, 6 to 10 p.m. on Thursday and Saturday, and 5 to 10 p.m. on Friday.

The **Hungry Horse,** 33 Elliott St., near Wellesley St. (tel. 735-124), specializes in two things: value-for-money meals and a casual, rustic atmosphere. The farmyard decor and jeans-clad staff set the tone in this conveniently located, family-style restaurant. Children order from their own menu "for hungry horses under twelve," and just wait until you see the portions for hungry horses of any age! Take a look around at other diners' plates before you lose your head and order a lot of bill-raising extras—unless you have one whale of an appetite, you can stick to the mains. The best buy is the roast of the day at lunch, which might be lamb, pork, or beef, at the incredible price of NZ$2.80 ($1.88). The menu also includes steaks, chicken, fish, wienerschnitzel, mixed grill, and spaghetti bolognese. Prices range from that low daily special to NZ$8.50 ($5.70), and hours are 11:30 a.m. to 9:30 p.m. every day. It's licensed, and a glass of house wine costs NZ$.95 (64¢); a carafe, NZ$5.20 ($3.49).

You'll find the dependable **Cobb & Co.** on the first floor of the South Pacific Hotel at the corner of Queen and Customs Streets (tel. 778-920). In the usual setting of beamed ceiling, red velvet booths, and brass accents, there's the usual, good-value Cobb & Co. menu of beef-and-kidney pies, grills, seafood, hamburgers, sandwiches, and egg dishes in the NZ$3.85 ($2.58) to NZ$6.60

($4.43) price range. It's licensed, of course, and open seven days a week from 7 a.m. to 10 p.m. Other Auckland Cobb & Co. locations: the Poenamo Motor Inn, Northcote Road, Takapuna (tel. 486-109); Browns Bay Motor Inn, Beach Road, Browns Bay (tel. 479-5016); Manukau Arms, Great South Road, Wiri (tel. 278-5164); Meadowbank Shopping Centre, St. John's Road (tel. 588-003); and the White Horse Inn, Reeves Road, Pakuranga (tel. 569-079).

If the lines are long at **Déjeuner,** 1 Fort Lane (tel. 33-139), don't let that put you off—they move quickly in this large basement eatery, which is a favorite of downtown Auckland office crews. Large it may be, but there's a coziness about the room, where tables are separated with plants, screens, and display units. Self-service salad selections include as many as ten varieties, pâtés, quiches, and cold meats, as well as mouthwatering desserts. A good lunch will run somewhere between NZ$3.50 ($2.35) and NZ$5 ($3.36). It's BYO, and hours are 11 a.m. to 2:30 p.m. Monday through Friday, 5 to 9 p.m. on Friday only.

Dynasty, 28 Customs St. East (tel. 732-421), was the first licensed Chinese restaurant in Auckland when it opened in 1975, and since that time it has been a consistent favorite of locals. Food is Cantonese, and the four chefs all trained in Hong Kong. The pretty red and gold decor extends throughout all four levels of the restaurant, and there's live music every night after 8:30 p.m. Specialties include honey prawns, ginger and garlic lobster, and paradise duckling, among many others on the extensive menu. Prices are in the NZ$4 ($2.68) to NZ$8 ($5.37) range, and an especially good value is the Sunday Yum Char lunch at NZ$6.50 ($4.36). Hours are noon to 2:30 p.m. and 6 to 11 p.m., seven days a week.

Chances R, 21 Elliott St. (tel. 796-120), is a good place to eat almost anytime, but if hunger pangs strike late at night, this is the place to head for. It's open seven days a week from 4 p.m. to midnight. They specialize in hamburgers, cooked in a variety of ways, which come with french fries or jacket potato and salad (a meal, no less) at prices of NZ$5.10 ($3.42) to NZ$6.80 ($4.56). There's also a blackboard menu of hot meals such as chicken breasts stuffed with ham and asparagus topped with mushroom sauce, jambalaya, scotch filet steak, spaghetti bolognese, and Mexican shrimp enchilada, which run NZ$5.50 ($3.69) to NZ$9.50 ($6.38). Fully licensed.

Over on Parnell Road, **Fraser's Place,** 116 Parnell Rd. (tel. 774-080), is one of the special little places beloved by local residents and so seldom found by visitors. Ian Fraser left a successful business career to follow his heart into the kitchen of this sparkling deli cum restaurant. You enter through the deli, which displays such unexpected treasures as those melt-in-your-mouth Greek spinach-and-cheese pies (NZ$1, or 67¢ U.S.!) and mini-quiches, to be eaten at the pine-stool counter just back of the shop or to take away (great to take home for that late-night snack when you don't want to go out). All sorts of sausages, cheeses, salads, rolls, etc., as well. Upstairs, there are three distinctly different dining rooms: the Graffiti Room (you can leave your mark if you can find a spot on the wall), the Piaf Room, and the Conversation Room. The decor throughout is a treat, but it's the food that makes this place special. Ian was brought up in the East, and you'll find several spicy dishes on the menu like goulash, chili con carne, and mustard veal. Salad platters include smoked salmon, coppa and paw paw, shrimp and avocado, spanakopita Greek salad, and assorted cheese and fruit platters. Pâtés are homemade and out of this world. Be sure to include this stop in any Parnell Road wanderings. No wine license, but there are four special liqueur coffees, and you can bring your own wine along. Lunch can run from NZ$3.25 ($2.18) to NZ$6.50 ($4.36). Hours are noon to 3 p.m. Monday through Saturday; dinner, Thursday through Saturday, *summer only,* 6 to 9:30 p.m.

Over at Farthings Hotel (see "Accommodations"), the fully licensed **Off the Avenue,** 122 Anzac Ave. (its entrance is on the higher, back entrance to the hotel; tel. 30-629), serves breakfast, lunch, and dinner and in as pleasant a setting as you'll find in the city. Looking out over Beach Road and parts of the waterfront, the restaurant has a bright, sunny look, which is accented by the use of chrome-and-cane chairs, soft pastel colors, and lots of plants. Service is cafeteria style; there's an exceptionally good salad bar (to which you can return as many times as you wish); and you can choose from a wide variety of cold and hot meats, oysters, teriyaki steak, fish, chicken, beef, and lamb. Lunch will run around NZ$5 ($3.36); dinner, between NZ$7.50 ($5.03) and NZ$9.95 ($6.68). It's fully licensed, with a good selection of wines.

If just the thought of steak sets your mouth watering, then you should know about **Tony's,** 32 Lorne St. (tel. 732-138), one of Auckland's best steak-houses. In a setting of brick walls, rough beams, assorted antiques, high-backed booths, brass lamps, and velvet curtains, Tony's serves up such delights as Napoleon steak with brandy cream pepper sauce, steak béarnaise with tarragon and lemon butter sauce, steak Italiano, marinated in a soybean and garlic sauce, and . . . well, steak in just about any style you can imagine. The beef is always first rate, and your steak arrives with either a salad or a side dish of spaghetti bolognese. Other items on the menu include veal, scallops, ham, and chicken. There's another Tony's just around the corner at 27 Wellesley St. (tel. 374-196), with similar decor and menu (it is, in fact, the original Tony's, opened some 20 years ago). Both are great local favorites, and you may encounter a short wait (since they don't accept reservations), although a recent expansion at the Lorne Street location should allow prompt seating. On fine summer days there's also outside seating at umbrella tables. Steaks are in the NZ$8.50 ($5.70) range, with other dishes slightly lower. Both locations are fully licensed, and hours are noon to 2:15 p.m. Monday through Friday, 11 a.m. to 3 p.m. on Saturday; 5 to 10 p.m. Monday through Saturday, and 5 to 9:30 p.m. on Sunday.

Two Big Splurges

With Auckland's wealth of fine dining, it almost seems obligatory to indulge in at least one Big Splurge while you're there. Here are two that I consider worthy of that extra expenditure.

Harley's, 25 Anzac Ave. (tel. 735-801), specializes in New Zealand foods, and the only word for their preparation is exquisite! Joanna Coulter, the chef behind those culinary delights, is Cordon Bleu trained, and she has teamed up with Helen Brabazon to show New Zealanders (and lucky visitors) just how good their native foods can be. In a spacious, converted old warehouse, these two have created a relaxed, interesting dining room, with a color scheme of rose and gray on painted brick walls, polished pine furniture, and terracotta linen. Table settings are elegant, with German porcelain, crystal stemware, and French cutlery. Original paintings, framed prints, and leafy palms complete the setting. The service is as good as the food—and friendly. The menu changes almost daily, since Joanna insists on serving only the freshest foods available, but you'll usually find lamb in one form or another, sometimes chicken breasts stuffed with ginger and apricots and served with grape sauce. Seafood dishes figure prominently, featuring whatever the day's catch has to offer. Kiwi fruit makes a pretty regular appearance, as do other native fruits and vegetables. Prices run from NZ$10.95 ($7.35) to NZ$12.95 ($8.69), which includes vegetables; you bring your own wine. Hours are 6 to 10 p.m. every night except Tuesday, when it's closed, and reservations are an absolute must. You'll have spent your Big Splurge on New Zealand food at its very best in romantic, elegant showcase if you choose Harley's. It was recommended to me by transplanted Americans now living in the Bay of Islands, with the flat statement, "You really must not miss it." It's hard to top an endorsement like that!

Also very much "Kiwi" in atmosphere, and perhaps a little more posh, **Ponsonby's,** 1 Williamson Ave. (tel. 769-499), will take you back to Auckland's early days. This unique restaurant has two dining rooms in a triangular brick building erected in 1889 for Borough Council offices. At one point it housed the local fire brigade, and its official functions are well documented by mementos displayed on brick walls. There is also the original carved-wood staircase and beautiful examples of stained glass. Elegance is the only word for Ponsonby's, from menu selections to service to exquisite table settings. Among its Kiwi specialties are tua-tua chowder, smoked eel, and Bluff oysters. Main courses feature such delicacies as venison steak (one of my personal favorites); fresh mussels with tomatoes, spring onions, and chopped parsley poached in fresh orange and lemon juice; and loin of lamb, filet steak, and fresh fish. It's well nigh impossible to make a bad choice! For dessert, try the brandy snaps with cream. Ponsonby's is fully licensed, and there's an excellent wine list. Main courses will run NZ$11.50 ($7.72) to NZ$15 ($10.06), with at least one specialty priced as high as NZ$18.50 ($12.42). It's an à la carte menu, however, so count on spending more. Here, too, reservations are essential.

READERS' DINING SELECTIONS: "**Auckland University** (serves a good evening meal. Across in Devonport, the **Windsor Tea House** makes their own fresh-daily meat pies. Delicious!" (Maureen Stolliker, Dana Point, Calif.). . . . . "For excellent and inexpensive dining, try the **Quadrant Coffee Lounge** in the basement of Newman House, located next door to the Auckland Hyatt Hotel at 16 Quadrant Waterloo. Omelets that are fresh and filling, toasted sandwiches, miscellaneous savouries, and a hearty hot chocolate" (Carol Collier, Honolulu, Hawaii).

THINGS TO SEE AND DO: If your time in Auckland is going to be limited and you can't quite figure out how you'll work in everything you'd like to see, the **Guest Travel Advisory Service** of the GTB will do their best to come up with an itinerary for you. Call them at 798-180 and tell them what you want to see and how much time you have.

A visit to Auckland's **War Memorial Museum,** in the Auckland Domain (tel. 30-443), is a virtual necessity for a full appreciation of the Maori culture you'll be exposed to in other parts of the country. The imposing, gleaming-white museum, surrounded by sweeping lawns and flower gardens right in the city center, houses the world's largest collection of Maori artifacts, providing you with a rich background from which to understand the Maoris of today. Be sure to pick up a free guide map as you enter the museum.

In the Maori Court, the most impressive exhibit is probably the 82-foot war canoe chiseled from one enormous totara trunk and covered with intricate, symbolic carvings. You'll see that same artistic carving in the 85-foot meeting house, whose rafters are a wonder of red, black, and white scrollwork. Wooden panels, dyed red, also feature tribal-motif carvings interspersed with traditional woven flax patterns. The meeting house sits between two storehouses raised on stilts to protect community goods from predators. To the left of the court, the Dress and Ornament wing holds gorgeous feather cloaks (each feather knotted in by hand) worn by high-ranking males, as well as a display of jade tikis. There's also a demonstration on the making of the *piu piu* (reed skirt) from flax. In the Industrial Arts and Warfare wing on the right of the court, look for the greenstone *mere* (war club), such a lordly weapon that it was reserved for the slaying of only the highest ranking captives (who considered it an honor to meet their end with such a club). Look also for the Maori portraits, the life's work of famed New Zealand artist C. F. Goldie, a Pakeha who captured on canvas not only the ornate tattoos of chieftains and common folk, but their fierce tribal pride as well.

Elsewhere in the museum, there's a hall of South Pacific art, a hall of Asian art, a canoe hall, native bird displays (including that giant moa exhibit), and much, much more. Especially interesting is "Centennial Street," a reconstruction of an Auckland shopping street of 1866—equally interesting is a comparison of prices then and now! The Planetarium gives working demonstrations on Saturday beginning on the hour from 11 a.m. to 3 p.m. and on Sunday, also beginning on the hour, from noon to 4 p.m.

The shop near the entrance of the museum is worth a little browsing time for publications on Maori art and New Zealand flora and fauna, as well as reproductions and replicas of some of the exhibits—a good place to pick up mementos to carry home. There's also a coffee lounge (open from 10 a.m. to 3:45 p.m.), which serves sandwiches, salads, desserts, and beverages. Museum hours are 10 a.m. to 5 p.m. Monday through Saturday, 11 a.m. to 5 p.m. on Sunday. You can reach it via the 635 bus from the downtown bus terminal.

A nice ending to museum visits is a call at the nearby **Winter Garden,** on the museum grounds, to view the impressive collection of tropical and subtropical plants. Hours are 10 a.m. to noon and 1 to 4 p.m., and there's no admission charge.

And speaking of gardens, if it's rose-blooming time when you visit, plan a stop by the **Parnell Rose Gardens** on Gladstone Road (tel. 775-359). The Rose Garden Lounge serves lunches and teas on weekdays. Bus 702 from the downtown bus terminal will get you there.

The **Auckland City Art Gallery,** on the Kitchener Street side of Albert Park (tel. 792-796), is reputed to be the most up-to-date gallery in the South Pacific. Its permanent collection ranges from old masters to contemporary European art to Japanese prints and drawings, plus the most comprehensive collection of New Zealand art in the country. Also on display are fascinating sculpture, paintings, drawings, prints, and photographs dating from 1770 to the present. A coffee lounge and a bookshop are on the premises. Hours are 10 a.m. to 4:30 p.m. Monday through Thursday, to 8:30 p.m. on Friday, and 1 to 5:30 p.m. on Saturday and Sunday. No admission charge.

One of the few places to observe the kiwi, that flightless bird that has become New Zealand's national symbol, is the Nocturnal House at the **Auckland Zoo** (with entrance at Motions Road; tel. 764-785). Four birds are exhibited daily in natural bush settings, which resemble a moonlit forest floor. You can watch them foraging, their long beaks seeking food in the leaf-covered ground. Don't plan a quick run out to the zoo just to look at the kiwis, however—more than 2000 other birds, mammals, fish, and reptiles (representing some 200 species) will entice you from one area to another in the beautifully tended park surroundings. For instance, you can also take a look here at the tuatara, Earth's oldest reptile (see the Introduction). Hours are 9:30 a.m. to 5:30 p.m. (last admission is at 4:15 p.m.). Admission is NZ$3 ($2.01) for adults, NZ$1.50 ($1.01), and there's a family ticket for NZ$8.50 ($5.70), which admits two adults and up to four children. You can reach the zoo by bus 040, 044, or 045, leaving every ten minutes from Customs Street.

You can drive among African lions and watch them being fed at the **Auckland Lion Safari,** on Redhills Road, in Massey. Also in residence are camels, water buffalo, emus, and other exotic animals to observe along the three-kilometer safari. There's a miniature train ride and corkscrew water slide. It's situated about 16 kilometers from Queen Street (turn left at the end of the North Western motorway and follow the signs).

There's a fascinating collection of vehicles, trains, trams, aircraft, steam engines, pioneer artifacts—and a host of other items—at the **Museum of Transport and Technology.** MOTAT, as it is best known, is situated just five kilometers from the city center on Great North Road, Western Springs (tel. 860-198). There, you'll find New Zealand's only publically operating tramway, including Auckland's first electric tram, circa 1902. In the Pioneers of Aviation Pavilion, special tribute is paid to Richard Pearse, who on March 31, 1902, flew an aircraft in the South Island. Life in 1840–1890 New Zealand is recreated in the Pioneer Village, where the church is still used for weddings and christenings. Special events are frequently scheduled on weekends and public holidays. There are several food facilities on the grounds, but the 106-year-old Colonial Arms Restaurant is rather special, serving Devonshire teas and à la carte meals. MOTAT is open every day, except Christmas Day, from 9 a.m. to 5 p.m. Admission is NZ$3.50 ($2.35) for adults, NZ$1.60 ($1.07) for children and senior citizens. A family ticket (two adults and up to four children) costs NZ$9.50 ($6.38). Reach it via city bus 045 from Customs Street East.

The **Ewelme Cottage,** 14 Ayr St., was built by the Rev. Vicesimus Lush (somehow, I find humor in that surname for a minister!) and named for Ewelme Village in England. It has been authentically restored, right down to as much of the original wallpaper as could be salvaged and 19th-century furnishings. Open daily from 10:30 a.m. to noon and 1 to 4:30 p.m., except Good Friday and Christmas Day. Adults pay NZ$1 (67¢); children, NZ$.50 (33¢).

With or without binoculars, the view is nothing short of spectacular from the summit of **Mount Eden,** Auckland's highest point. An extinct volcano, which was fortified by Maoris, Mount Eden looks down on the city, both harbors, and Hauraki Gulf. The 274 bus from Customs Street East will get you there, or it's a lovely drive.

One Tree Hill (Cornwall Park, Mount Eden) is also an extinct volcano and was also the site of a large Maori *pa* (fort). There's an obelisk on the summit as a memorial to that race. The views are terrific, and the adjoining parkland is great for long walks.

Walks

The City Council's Parks and Recreation Department sponsors several interesting guided walks around the city at no charge, as well as furnishing maps and booklets for do-it-yourselfers. Ask at the Government Tourist Bureau for the booklets that give days and times of walks that examine arts and crafts and specialty shops, current art exhibitions, historic spaces and places, marketplaces, the Auckland Domain and a Domain nature walk. If you're a *real* walker, there's a self-guiding map for an interesting coast-to-coast walk across the nine-kilometer isthmus between the Pacific Ocean and the Tasman Sea. Allow about four hours, but since many parts of the track pass near bus routes and car parks, you don't have to do it all at once. Although, perforce, you must walk through industrialized sections, there are many wooded spots, archeological sites, parks, gardens and panoramic views of the city and harbor which are ideal for a picnic.

Note: You can also pick up at the GTB office *New Zealand Walkway* pamphlets for other interesting walks throughout the North Island.

Sports

Golfers will find themselves welcomed at any of the many fine **golf** courses in the area. For details, call 276-6149 and ask for the name of the course nearest you and current greens fees. **Tennis** players are equally welcome at the Stanley Street Tennis Stadium, which has racquets and balls for hire and charges NZ$5 ($3.36) per hour. For bookings, call 733-623.

A Ferry Ride

One of the nicest ways I know to see Auckland is from the harbor **steam ferry,** which crosses to the North Shore. As the city recedes, you're treated to a focused look at big-city growth: the old red-brick ferry building with its clock tower stands in marked contrast to streamlined skyscrapers, and the stately white War Memorial looks down on it all with the dignity born of historical perspective. As you pass the naval base, it's perfectly permissible to raise your hand in salute to New Zealand's seafarers. Then, if you plan it right and return in the evening, the sparkling city lights turn big-city sprawl into diamond-studded magic. You catch the ferry at the Queens Wharf terminal on Quay Street (its North Shore destination is Devonport), leaving every 40 minutes from 7 a.m. to 11 p.m., seven days a week. The fare is NZ$2.70 ($1.81) for adults, NZ$1.35 (91¢) for children.

If your trip is on a Saturday, you'll run into the **Old Ferry Arts and Crafts Market,** which is held on the Devonport Wharf every Saturday from 10 a.m. to 5 p.m.—a pleasant way to browse or shop for New Zealand handicrafts. The little suburb of **Devonport** is where the Maoris say their great ancestral canoe *Tainui* first touched land in this area, somewhere around the 14th century. You'll see a stone memorial to that event on the grassy strip along King Edward Parade foreshore—the bronze sculpture is an orb topped by a *korotangi* (weeping dove), one of the birds the Maoris brought with them from their homeland. There are four white-sand beaches in Devonport, as well as Mount Victoria, which sits near the business center and is now topped by a harbor signal station (great views from up there). You can also walk up to North Head and explore the old military fort with its tunnels and gun sites.

There are several good eateries in Devonport if you should decide to stay over for dinner. And if you're at all interested in an authentic working man's pub, which dishes up massive helpings of good grub at inexpensive prices, stop in at the **Masonic Tavern** on King Edward Parade. I first tasted paua fritters there, and they were delicious! Hot meals, as well as light snacks, all go for wee prices. Food is served from noon to 2 p.m. and 5:30 to 8 p.m. Monday to Saturday.

A Scenic Flight

If there's anything better than seeing Auckland and its harbor from the water, it must be to see it from the air. Well, **Sea Bee Air** has scenic flights, which can give you that very special experience, and at prices that might stretch your budget, but certainly won't break it. Over at Mechnics Bay on the Auckland waterfront, you board the four-passenger seaplane on land, it then sort of waddles down to the shoreline and into the water, and the first thing you know, you're adrift. The motors rev up, you speed across the water, and lift off for an unforgettable flight over the inner city, the harbor bridge, Hauraki Gulf, the now-overgrown crater of the once mighty Rangitoto volcano, a glimpse of other islands and the Coromandel Peninsula, then back to Mechanics Bay to settle down gently into the water once more and waddle back on to terra firma. It's a thrilling ten minutes which leaves Auckland and its surroundings indelibly stamped on your memory. The cost? NZ$25 ($16.78) per adult, NZ$15 ($10.06) per child. Rates for longer flights are: 15 minutes—NZ$30 ($20.13) and NZ$18 ($12.08); 20 minutes—NZ$35 ($23.49) and NZ$20 ($13.42). To book, call 774-406. In addition to scenic flights, Sea Bee Air also runs charter flights to almost anywhere, and regular service to the Bay of Islands and several other destinations.

Bus Tours

Through the **Government Tourist Bureau,** you can book several half- and full-day tours of the city and its environs. There's the "Town Alive" tour, which departs 9:30 a.m. daily and includes the city, Harbour Bridge, Mount Eden, War Memorial Museum, Ellerslie Garden Racecourse, St. Helliers, Kohimaramara, Mission Bay, and Savage Memorial. The fare is NZ$12 ($8.05). The "Emerald City" tour leaves daily at 1:45 p.m. and takes you to Auckland University, Albert Park, Westhaven, Lynmall, Waitakere Scenic Drive, Montana Wines (for a tasting, except on Sunday), Titirangi, Auckland Zoo and the Kiwi House, and the Museum of Transport and Technology. The NZ$14 ($9.40) fare includes admission to the Kiwi House. Children pay NZ$7 ($4.70). There are morning "Western City" and afternoon "Eastern City" tours (half day each) which cost NZ$12 ($8.05) each, and a full-day "Coast-to-Coast" minibus tour which crosses the Harbour Bridge to visit Mount Victoria's volcanic cone overlooking the city and harbor, Devonport, coastal suburbs, hot mineral pools, a country town tavern for lunch (not included in the fare), a dairy farm, a man-made pine forest, the West Coast iron sand beach, a pottery and craft center, and several spectacular lookout points. Adults pay NZ$28 ($18.79); children, NZ$14 ($9.40). There's also a launch excursion out to Rangitoto Island which operates during school holidays and from Christmas through January. Two coach excursions on the island are included, and the fare is NZ$20 ($13.42). Other special interest tours are also available; ask at the GTB for a full listing.

Sightseer Tours (tel. 770-886) operates half- and full-day tours to the Auckland Zoo, MOTAT, and Lion Safari Park. You can choose any one or all three, at prices which range from NZ$6 ($4.03) to NZ$18 ($12.08); children pay half price. These may also be booked through the GTB. This same firm runs a full-day Hunua Ranges and Botanic Gardens tour with prices of NZ$25 ($16.78) and NZ$12.50 ($8.39).

Meet the Kiwis

One of Auckland's (and indeed, New Zealand's) very best attractions is offered by the **Auckland Tourist Hospitality Scheme,** and it doesn't cost a penny. Do this at the beginning of your trip if possible—it will give more meaning to every Kiwi contact you make thereafter. This group of enthusiastic volunteers will arrange for you to spend a morning, afternoon, or evening with an Auckland family for absolutely no other reason than to have an opportunity to talk on a one-to-one basis in the informal, relaxed atmosphere of a private home. It's a terrific chance to learn about New Zealand daily life firsthand and to to exchange views from our different parts of the world. They'll try to match you by profession or hobby from among the 80 Auckland families who participate. They do *not* arrange overnight stays—just friendly visits. You can call them when you arrive, or better yet, write in advance to any one of the following: Mrs. Polly Ring, 775 Riddell Rd., Glendowie, Auckland 5 (tel.

556-655); Mrs. Jean Mahon, 129 Taylors Rd., Mount Albert, Auckland (tel. 860-342); Mrs. Eve Swanson, 170 Cook St., Howick, Auckland (tel. 53-58098); Mrs. June Colwill, 45 Richard Farrell Ave., Remuera, Auckland (tel. 544-469); Mr. Clive Kingsbeer, 43 Allenby Rd., Papatoetoe, Auckland (tel. 27-82513); and Mrs. Meryl Revell, 60 Prince Regent Dr., Half Moon Bay (tel. 53-55314).

You can spend a half day with a New Zealand farm family by contacting the **New Zealand Farmhouse Holidays** folks, P.O. Box 31250 (tel. 492-171). They'll take you to a dairy/sheep farm at Clevedon, 35 kilometers south of Auckland, to have afternoon tea with the farmer and his family, then watch as the farmer shears a sheep in the wool shed and works his sheep dog for you. The per-person cost is NZ$35 ($23.49). They can also arrange overnight farm holiday stays.

Where to Leave the Kids

Comes a time in every parent's life when it's time to strike out on your own for sightseeing, shopping, or whatever. Well, you can give the kids a break too, by leaving them (ages 2 through 7) at **Barnardo's Auckland City Creche,** on High Street in the city center (tel. 735-251). You may rest easy in the knowledge that they're in good hands and having a stimulating—and fun—time while you're off doing your thing. Hours are 9 a.m. to 3 p.m. weekdays, and charges are NZ$2 ($1.34) an hour (three hours maximum). It's ideally situated, just a two-minute walk from Queen Street.

READER'S SIGHTSEEING SUGGESTIONS: "**Waiheke Island,** an hour by ferry from Auckland, is a gorgeous place! Auckland also has some beautiful seaside resorts. We went to a 'pick your own' apple orchard with a friendly Kiwi couple and loved it!" (Maureen Stolliker, Dana Point, Calif.).

SHOPPING: There are two **Rehabilitation League Shops** in Auckland from which to buy souvenirs while supporting a worthy cause at the same time: 58 Queen St. and at the Princes Wharf Passenger Terminal. . . . A very special shopping spot for authentic New Zealand handmade products is **Brown's Mill,** in Durham Lane between Queen and Albert Streets. The century-old mill is now a cooperative marketplace for craftspeople who are skilled, friendly, and happy to demonstrate their work. Weavers, potters, jewelers, and a host of other artisans are on hand. Open Monday through Saturday from 10 a.m. to 5 p.m.

For shopping fun and maybe a bargain, don't miss Auckland's **Cook Street market** on Friday and Saturday. Patterned after London's street markets, this one offers an amazing variety of clothing, food, antiques, bric-a-brac and secondhand goods of all descriptions. You'll see people from all walks of Kiwi life browsing through the stalls, and there are even buskers plying their trade. Have your photograph taken in a Victorian costume as a reminder of your visit. You'll find the market in Aotea Square next to the City of Auckland administration building, and hours are 9 a.m. to 8 p.m. on Friday, 10 a.m. to 4 p.m. on Saturday.

When departure time arrives and you begin to think what you'll be paying for that good New Zealand lamb when you get home, hie yourself down to **R. and W. Hellaby Ltd.** on Quay Street and select your favorite cuts—they'll be individually wrapped, frozen, and packed into "Lamb-to-Go" chilly bins and delivered to the airport Farm Produce Shops for you to collect on your way out of the country. The cost is a fraction of what you'd pay on this side of the Pacific. Official documentation is required for the meat pack, and for this reason you must give them three days' notice. You can, however, purchase preselected packs containing a variety of cuts directly from the **Farm Produce Shop** at the airport at the last minute, since these packs are already documented and ready to go. Hellaby's is open from Monday to Friday, 8 a.m. to 4 p.m. (tel. 770-610).

Plan to spend at least half a day shopping or just browsing or sightseeing in **Parnell Village.** That's the stretch of Parnell Road between York Street and St. Stephens Avenue. In restored colonial homes and stores, there are boutiques, art galleries, craft shops, antique stores, restaurants, and pubs. It's great people-watching territory, and a place you just may pick up that one-of-a-kind souvenir. Most shops, restaurants, and pubs are open Monday through Saturday.

NIGHTLIFE: You couldn't really call Auckland's nightlife "swinging." Still, there are enough things to do after dark to finish off a heavy day's sightseeing or shopping. In addition to the listings here, you'll find current goings-on in the *Tourist Times.*

Several of the posh (and expensive) restaurants feature dancing along with dining, but one that isn't so expensive, serves very good food, and has dance music as well is **El Matador,** 200A Symonds St., near Khyber Pass Road (tel. 798-454). The decor motif, like the name, is veddy, veddy Spanish, with bullfight posters, copper sculptures of matadors and bulls, and red lampshades and tablecloths. But the menu is veddy, veddy Kiwi—with just a dash of European cuisine. There's thick, tasty tuatua soup, grills, steaks, roasts, beef Stroganoff, and wienerschnitzel, among other items on the menu. And Hungarian palachinka stars among desserts. The dance floor is ample size, and the band plays a nice mixture of old and new tunes (including disco music for the younger set). A three-course dinner and a bottle of wine will set you back about NZ$25 ($16.78), and closing isn't until 1 a.m., which means you can dine leisurely and dance to your heart's content. One caution: If you want to be close to the music and dance floor, be sure to ask for a table in the main room when you book—it's a large place, and you could wind up in a remote corner. There's free parking for patrons on the corner of Burleigh Street and Khyber Pass Road. Fully licensed; no cover charge; and hours are 7 p.m. to 1 a.m. every night except Sunday, when they close at midnight.

The **Victoria Room Theatre Restaurant,** in the Royal Albert Hotel on Queen Street (tel. 33-653), throws in a show with dinner for the remarkable price of NZ$12.50 ($8.39). It's usually a comedy or musical, and performances are Thursday, Friday, and Saturday nights at 7 p.m., plus Sunday at lunch (1 p.m.).

There are two major theaters in town. The **Mercury Theatre,** 9 France St. (tel. 33-869), and **Theatre Corporate,** 14 Galatos St. (tel. 774-307), both have resident companies that perform year round in everything from classics to musicals to modern plays, many of them by New Zealand playwrights. Ticket prices are in the NZ$9 ($6.04) to NZ$12 ($8.05) range. **His Majesty's Theatre,** on Queen Street (tel. 375-100), is occasionally the venue of both international and New Zealand touring companies.

WHERE TO GO FROM HERE: North or south? From Auckland, *most* tourists head south to Waitomo and its glowworms, then on to Rotorua and its concentration of Maori culture. And rightly so. Nowhere else in the world will you find anything to compare with the mystical, silent glow of Waitomo's grotto; nowhere else can you duplicate Rotorua's thermal steaminess and lakes, hills, and valleys alive with myth and legend and with a Polynesian race who revere those tales of long ago and follow an ancient lifestyle while perfectly at home in the modern culture surrounding them. If push comes to shove and it comes down to north *or* south, then by all means opt for the southern route.

Ah, but if you can work in an extra two days, which will let you go north *then* south, you're in for one of this world's travel treats. Take the long route up and experience the shady "cathedral" created by centuries-old kauri forests; cut across the northern end of the North Island to Waitangi in the Bay of Islands and walk where the British negotiated with Maori chieftans to establish their first official New Zealand foothold; relive this country's history as you visit its first Christian mission, then the splendidly carved native meeting house; discover private beaches, some on one of the many uninhabited islands that account for the naming of this lovely spot; head out to the open sea for some of the finest deep-water fishing in the world; enjoy sunny days and balmy evenings, a friendly and hospitable local populace. You can *plan* on two days, but chances are you'll alter plans to extend your stay—or leave looking over your shoulder and wishing you had!

2. From Auckland to the Bay of Islands

In your trek north, then back south, you're going to have to come back through Auckland—luckily, however, *not* over the same route. There's a long route that wanders through 234 miles of New Zealand scenic splendor and history, and that will take a full day (count on at least seven or eight hours for the trip). Then there's the direct, 150-mile State Highway 1, which can take anywhere from three to four hours. Heed the voice of experience and take the *long* way up, the short route back. There's the distinct possibility that you'll stay over an extra day up north (that's what happened to me), and even if you don't, time pressures may begin to set in and you'll skip that long drive back, thus missing out on a part of New Zealand you really *shouldn't* miss.

Most of the longer route is over well-paved roads, but the most interesting part—the part that makes this whole day's drive worthwhile—will be along about 43 miles of gravel-surfaced, winding roads through the majestic Waiopua Kauri Forest. It's a good idea to pack picnic provisions, since you could well be miles from an eatery when your lunchtime alarm goes off, and besides, there's an idyllic picnic spot right in the forest. And be sure to get an early start—you'll need the whole day.

Leave Auckland via the Harbour Bridge (NZ$.25, or 17¢ U.S., toll going north) and take the East Coast Bays Road off Route 1 to pass through North Shore residential districts, superb beaches at pleasant seaside resort towns like **Orewa** and **Waipu** (resist the urge to stop for a swim—you can do that on your way back!), and as you turn inland, hills and farmland, which lead you into **Silverdale,** where you'll rejoin Highway 1. (If you strike Warkworth at morning tea time, try the **Dome Valley Tea Rooms,** just north of town.) Just above Kaiwaka, turn into Route 12 toward Dargaville.

This was a thriving timber and gum industry area during the late 1800s, and scene of some of the most devastating kauri-forest slaughters. Other trees were felled too—totara, rimu, and kaihikatea—but the kauri was the most sought-after because of its straight, firm trunk, which made it ideal for ship masts, and its beautifully mottled grain, much prized for making furniture. You'll see remains of numerous lumber mills along your way. Kauri gum was the source of many fortunes during those days, as well as the grinding poverty of gum diggers (Maoris and Yugoslav immigrants, mostly) who dug the gum from underneath peat for criminally low wages. The gum was scraped and washed for use as a base in paint and varnish, and polished to rich, clear amber, brown, or black to be used in the making of costume jewelry. You can relive those days of forest and labor exploitation if you stop at **Matakohe** to examine the photographs, gum displays—over 1700 pieces, the largest collection in the world—and kauri furniture at the **Otamatea Kauri and Pioneer Museum** (tel. 37-417). The implements of the trade will bring it vividly alive: gum washing and digging equipment, a bush dam and whim model, a bullock wagon and the 1929 tractor that replaced them, large kauri logs, and a bushman's hut. The museum is open every day except Christmas from 8:30 a.m. to 5 p.m. (longer in the summer), and adults pay NZ$1.50 ($1.01); children, NZ$.50 (33¢).

In **Dargaville,** if time allows, plan to stop also at the **Northern Wairoa Maori, Maritime, and Pioneer Museum** in the Municipal Chambers on Hokianga Road. It was originally in the the the stables of founder Joseph Dargaville's residence on Jervois Street, a building that still holds a Maori canoe from the Pouto Peninsula. In its present location, there's memorabilia of the area's early days, much of which has been donated by local families: lovely mottled kauri furniture, antique household furnishings, photographs of early settlers and the town in its infancy, the town's first newspaper (1894), and a collection of relics of some 42 shipwrecks which occurred between 1840 and 1915 in nearby Kaipara Harbor. The museum is open every day except Saturday and holidays from 2 to 4 p.m. During summer months, it also opens from 10 a.m. to noon, including Saturday. Adults pay NZ$.50 (33¢); children, NZ$.20 (13¢).

From Dargaville, it's only 30 miles north to the kauri forest (see below), the highlight of this drive. On the other side of the forest, you pass through seaside settlements of **Omapere** and **Opononi** before heading inland to **Ohaeawai** and Route 10, which will lead you to **Paihia** on the shore of the Bay of Islands. Now, about that forest . . .

WAIPOUA KAURI FOREST: Within this 22,500-acre preserve, kauri stands account for some 9,000 acres! Tall and slender, with straight, firm trunks reaching up to branches that grow at the very top and arch into a dim, cool canopy, the kauri is such a commanding presence that you understand forthwith the Maori's imparting of diety to the mighty tree. It is *lordly!* I don't even have to caution against rushing through this awesome abode of natural treasures—you won't! Be sure, however, to stop by the **Fire Lookout,** signposted to your left near the entrance—the 1010-feet-above-sea-level observation post provides a breathtaking panorama of hills and forests and sea. Forest Headquarters are at the next left turn, where you can inspect the **Maxwell Cottage,** which utilizes kauri wood in its construction and was the 1890s home of the first forest caretaker. A 15-minute walk off the road at the sign reading "Te Matua Ngahere" will bring you to the "Father of the Forest," a 98-foot-tall tree, 58 feet 10 inches around, whose exact age is shrouded in the mists of time. A short distance away stands the unique grouping of four trunks growing from one root, known as the Four Sisters. Farther north, just off the main road, the mundane sign stating "Big Kauri Tree" hardly prepares you for **Tane Mahuta,** "God of the Forest." This immense tree soars to 169 feet, has a girth of 43 feet, and is estimated to be 1200 years old! This is where you'll find that picnic spot I mentioned, set among tall punga ferns just across the road. A place to sit, absorb the silence and peace of the forest, and ponder the fact that once these giant trees were only a small part of thousands more.

3. The Bay of Islands

For New Zealanders, this is where it all began. "Civilization" in the guise of British culture, that is. But long before Capt. James Cook anchored the *Endeavour* off Motuarohia Island in 1769, civilization of the Maori sort existed in perfect harmony with the soft forces of nature, often at considerable *disharmony* with their tribal neighbors. They tell of the arrival of Kupe and Ngahu from Hawaiki, then of Whatonga and Toi, and later of the great chiefs Ruatara, Hongi Hika, and Tamati Waaka Nene. They point to the waterfront settlement at Kororareka, already well established when Captain Cook put in an appearance and gave the region its Pakeha name. Be that as it may, New Zealand's *modern* history does begin here in the Bay of Islands.

British settlers first set foot on New Zealand soil in 1804, and a whole litany of British "firsts" follows that date: 1814, the first Christian sermon (today, you'll find a large Celtic cross memorial planted on that very spot, a stretch of beach on the north side of Rangihoua Bay); 1820, the first plow introduced; 1831, the first European marriage; 1835, the first printing press; 1839, the first bank; and 1840, a whole slew of important "first" events—post office, Customs House, and official treaty between the British and Maori chieftains. After that, the British brand of civilization was in New Zealand to stay.

The Bay of Islands you will encounter is a happy blend of all that history—pride in those important happenings—and relaxed contentment in the natural attributes, which make this (as any resident will tell you) "the best spot in the country to live—or play." And play they do, for recreation is the chief industry up here. Setting and climate combine to create about as ideal a resort area as you could wish. Imagine a deeply indented coastline whose waters hold some 150 islands, most with sandy stretches of beach. Imagine waters so filled with sporting fish like the kingfish (yellowtail) that every world record for their capture has been set here. Imagine, too, a climate with *average* temperatures of 85° (70° is considered a cooler-than-usual winter day!), *maximum* humidity of 40%, and cool bay breezes every day of the year—imagine all that and you'll know what to expect in the Bay of Islands!

All that is what you will find in the Bay of Islands. What you won't find is a local transportation system in any form other than the delightful little ferry, which delivers schoolchildren, business people, tourists, and freight from one shore to the other. Nor will you find any sort of wild nightlife. Toting up the "wills" and "won'ts," I'd have to say you come up with a balance in favor of a perfect place in which to soak up sun and sea and fresh air, and put the frenetic pleasures of big city life on hold.

ORIENTATION: There are three distinct resort areas in the Bay of Islands: Paihia (throw in adjacent Waitangi), Russell, and Kerikeri. If you've come for the fishing, you'll want to be based in **Russell,** on the eastern shore and home of most charter boats; for almost every other activity, **Pahia,** across on the western shore, is the central location; and **Kerikeri** is the center of a thriving citrus-growing industry as well as a small, interesting "don't miss" sightseeing side trip.

Actually, no matter where you settle, you're going to come to know that neat little **ferry** intimately—unless you have your own boat, that's the only inexpensive way to get from one shore to another (well, there *is* a long-way-round drive, but it's much too time-consuming). Personally, I have a real fondness for that 15-minute voyage. For that little space of time, you're in close contact with the daily lives of the locals as you cross with housewives returning from a supermarket run, school kids as rambunctious on the after-school run as on schoolbuses the world over, and all sorts of daily-living goods being transported. It runs at hourly intervals beginning at 8 a.m. (from Russell) and ending at 5:30 p.m. (from Paihia). In summer, crossings are extended to 10:30 p.m., and on Sunday there's no 8:30 a.m. service. Fares are NZ$2.70 ($1.81) round trip for adults, NZ$.70 (47¢) for children 5 to 15. You'll soon have that schedule firmly fixed in your mind—it's important to be on the same side of the water as your bed when the service shuts down! If you should find yourself stranded, however, all is not lost—just considerably more expensive. The **Bays Water Taxi** (tel. Russell 720, or prebook at Fullers) offers 24-hour service, and fares depend on the hour and number of passengers (one thing is certain: they'll far exceed those of the ferry).

Three miles south of Paihia, at **Opua,** there's a flat-bottom **car ferry** for drivers that crosses the narrow channel to Okiato Point, five miles from Russell. Crossings are 7 a.m. to 7 p.m. from March 2 through November 30, to 9 p.m. the rest of the year, and the round-trip fare for car and driver is NZ$2.85 ($1.91) plus NZ$.35 (23¢) for each additional passenger.

USEFUL INFORMATION: The Williams Road Shopping Center is where you'll find the **Public Relations Office** (mailing address: P.O. Box 70, Paihia; tel. 27-683). The friendly staff, headed by Bob Franklin, arrange accommodations bookings throughout the entire Bay of Islands—bed and breakfast, motel flats, motor camp or tent site—with no booking fee. They also keep up-to-the-minute information on all sightseeing and other activities. The office is staffed from 9 a.m. to 5 p.m., and during the hours it's closed, a telephone number is posted that will reach someone who can give you any assistance you might need. . . . **A. E. Fullers & Sons** (tel. 27-631), locally known simply as Fullers, handles all NZRRS bookings, passenger and car-ferry bookings, and original Cream Trip and launch cruise bookings. **Mount Cook Line** (tel. 27-811) operates the Tiger Lily Cruises and the coach tours to Cape Reinga, plus airline information and bookings (including international flights). All of these services, plus all marine activity offices, are in the Maritime Building on the Paihia wharf. . . . There are daily NZRRS and Mount Cook Airline flights to and from Auckland. . . . For **taxi service,** call Paihia 27-506.

ACCOMMODATIONS: The Bay of Islands is a budget traveler's dream: the area abounds in excellent, inexpensive accommodations, and more are building all the time. Most are of modest size, earning a modest-but-quite-adequate-thank-you income for couples or families who seem far more interested in their guests' having a good time than in charging "what the traffic will bear." Rates *do fluctuate according to season,* however, with a slight increase during holidays and a slightly higher jump during the peak summer months of December through February. Those are also the times it is absolutely essential to book *well in advance,* since the Bay of Islands is tops on just about every Kiwi family's holiday list, and many book from year to year. If you're planning a visit during any of these seasons, you can either write directly to one of the properties you see listed here, or write to the Public Relations Office and put yourself in their capable hands—no risk, I can assure you.

A Hostel

The **Kerikeri Youth Hostel,** on the main road just north of the village (mailing address: P.O. Box 62, Kerikeri; tel. 79-391), is set in 2½ shaded acres, with river swimming just a five-minute walk from the hostel. There are 28 beds in six dormitory rooms, as well as a communal kitchen and laundry, a lounge and recreation/games room. Many of the area's historic sites are within easy walking distance. Seniors pay NZ$5 ($3.36); Juniors, NZ$2.50 ($1.68).

Cabins

Twin Pines Motor Camp, Puketona Road, Haruru Falls (mailing address: P.O. Box 168, Paihia; tel. 27-322), was a run-down and dilapidated mess when young Gordon Putt bought it back in 1973 and transformed it into what is now one of the prettiest camps in these parts. There are five two-unit and cabin cubicle A-frame chalets set in landscaped grounds overlooking Haruru Falls. The kitchen block, laundry, and communal bathrooms are all well equipped and immaculate. You can rent blankets and linens, and Gordon will usually lend such items as pots and pans. There's a tidal estuary just below the falls that's safe for swimming, and barbecues are held some evenings on the lawn. A restaurant and turn-of-the-century tavern are right on the premises, and there's a waterski boat for hire. Rates are NZ$4.70 ($3.15) per adult, NZ$2.35 ($1.58) per child for caravan sites; NZ$9.50 ($6.38) per adult, NZ$4.75 ($3.19) per child for cabins (a minimum of NZ$24, or $16.11, applies in high season); NZ$7 ($4.70) per person per day for hostel accommodations; NZ$30 ($20.13) minimum (two people) for tourist flats.

The **Lily Pond Holiday Park,** Puketona Road, Paihia (tel. 27-646) is midway between Puketona Junction and Paihia, and sits on parklike grounds right at the Waitangi River's edge. Paul and Eileen Leamy have 250 sites, 100 caravan sites, four on-site caravans, and 11 cabins, all of a quality that has won them a four-star grading by the Camp & Cabin Association of New Zealand. You can rent linens, and there's a store on the grounds, a large, modern kitchen for campers, and a separate, fully equipped kitchen for the cabins. Rates are NZ$5 ($3.36) per adult for sites; NZ$5.25 ($3.52) per adult for caravan sites; NZ$16 ($10.47) per couple for on-site caravans; and NZ$18.50 ($12.42) per couple for cabins.

Bed and Breakfast

Most bed and breakfasts in the Bay of Islands consist of one or two rooms in private homes, and the Public Relations Office keeps a daily record of availability. They can book you in on arrival, except in high season, when you should write ahead and tell them exactly what you want and your price limit. Average charges are NZ$15 ($10.06) per person per day.

Motor Flats

In Russell: Not all good New Zealand hosts are Kiwis, and that fact is borne out by Carole and Jim Hotchkiss, native Californians who picked up, bag and baggage, to become the owner-operators of the **Motel Russell,** Matuwhi Bay Road, P.O. Box 54 (tel. 854). Jim, a Pan Am pilot, fell in love with the country during the course of frequent flights here and brought Carole over for an extended visit. She shared his enthusiasm, and now you'll find them happily ensconced in this pretty motel just a three-minute or so walk from the Russell waterfront. There are 13 units, all with complete kitchens and all reflecting Carole's good taste in decor and Jim's expertise in adding the little extras that mean so much to comfort. For example, there are two units with facilities for the handicapped. Six have one bedroom and lounge (will sleep up to four), five with two bedrooms and two double-bedded units, as well as three very pretty cabin-type units. The location is a wooded hillside, and Jim and Carole are now in the throes of installing a swimming pool and hot spa pool. I suppose the hospitality here is Kiwi-California style—however you label it, it's tops! Rates are NZ$30 ($20.13) single, NZ$35 ($23.49) double, with a slight increase during holidays and summer peak season. This is a Best Western member, so their Holiday Pass rates apply.

The hospitality at **Wairoro Park** (tel. Russell 459) could probably be labeled Kiwi-Swiss-English, since owner Jan Boerop (an ex-pilot for KLM and Swissair) is Swiss, his wife Beryl is English, and they're both now dyed-in-the-wool Kiwis. They've settled in on the Russell side of the Opua car ferry (about a mile from the ferry, then a left turn up a hilly dirt road) in an absolutely idyllic setting of some 160 acres on the shores of a sheltered bay cove. They use a great many of those acres to run cattle and sheep, and in the midst of an orchard just steps away from the beach they have three two-story A-frame chalets. The first level of each holds a large lounge, fully equipped kitchen, shower, and separate toilet. Two bedrooms occupy the upstairs, and with the three divans in the lounge, the units accommodate up to eight. There's a covered car port and decks looking out to gorgeous views. The Boerops provide a dinghy or motorboat at no charge for guests who want to fish. The "Garden of Eden" is what Jan calls this place, and I expect you'll agree. Certainly the Kiwi population does, for regulars book from one holiday season to the next—which means, of course, that unless you get your bid in very early, you stand little chance of getting in during those times. Actually, it's a good idea to write as far in advance as possible no matter when you're coming. Rates are NZ$40 ($26.85) double, NZ$6 ($4.03) per extra adult, NZ$4 ($2.68) per child. There's a Christmas holiday minimum charge of NZ$75 ($50.34) per chalet. Incidentally, there is an additional rustic, self-contained cabin that sleeps two and goes for NZ$22 ($14.77) year round.

Paul and Linda Cummuskey too came to Russell from other parts, although in their case it was only up from Auckland. Holidays in the Bay of Islands led them to buy the **Arcadia Lodge,** on Florence Avenue (tel. 756), where they have four attractive, dirt-cheap units that are spotless, comfortable, and look out onto great views of the bay. Actually they're an extension of the main house. One, a self-contained unit with kitchen, bath, and toilet, sleeps six. Two will accommodate up to four, and another sleeps six. A fridge, stove, H&C, and electric heat are in all units. Rates at the moment are NZ$10 ($6.71) single, NZ$14 ($9.40) double, and NZ$24 ($16.11) double for the self-contained unit; NZ$4 ($2.68) per extra adult, and NZ$2 ($1.34) per child under 12. The Cummuskeys plan, however, to offer hostel-type accommodations during off-seasons (June through October) at a projected charge of NZ$7 ($4.70). This is a *very* popular place with budget travelers, both in New Zealand and among overseas travelers who've heard about it by word of mouth, so it's a good idea to book ahead if you can.

In Paihia: "Making you feel at home is our business and pleasure" is the motto of Mrs. Lila Rapley, the motherly owner-manager of the **Aywon Motel,** Davis Crescent (tel. 27-684). And she goes about doing just that with such homey touches as helpful advice on sporting and sightseeing activities and providing homemade jams with her cooked or continental breakfasts. The attractive, L-shaped white-and-yellow, two-story motel offers bright, cheerful two-bedroom units, all with fully equipped separate kitchen, shower and vanity, color TV, radio, heater, and electric blanket. All are spotless, nicely furnished, and carpeted throughout; and the second-floor units have balconies overlooking the bay, complete with deckchairs. There are automatic laundry and ironing facilities, as well as two swimming pools, two hot spas, and a sauna.

At the edge of her hillside lawn, there's a bush walk leading to the top of the hill, where three lookouts give panoramic views of the islands in the bay. Mrs. Rapley also provides twin-bedded bed-and-breakfast rooms that open onto a sundeck looking out over the water. Motel flat rates are NZ$30 ($20.13) single, NZ$34 ($22.82) double, NZ$6 ($4.03) for each additional adult. Bed-and-breakfast rates are NZ$10 ($6.71) or NZ$15 ($10.06), depending on the season. This one has my highest recommendation, based on both accommodations and the gracious hostess.

Reg and Mary Dench preside over the ten self-contained colonial-style cottages set in spacious grounds at the **Bay of Islands Motel,** Tohitapu Road (mailing address: P.O. Box 131; tel. 27-348). Each cottage has a lounge, separate bedroom, full kitchen, and bath (shower and tub). Privacy is assured, since cottages are placed at angles to prevent the windows of one from facing those of another, and the whole effect is that of a charming mini-village. Other facilities include a swimming pool, spa pool, laundry, and a playground for the young fry, who will also enjoy nearby beaches (close enough to hoof it). The Denches are knowledgeable, friendly hosts, who will gladly help with your sightseeing or dining arrangements in the Bay of Islands. It's a Best Western, offering the Holiday Pass discount. Rates are NZ$30 ($20.13) to NZ$34 ($22.82) single, NZ$35 ($23.49) to NZ$39 ($26.17) double, with a NZ$7 ($4.70) charge for each extra person, adult or child. Minimum rates during holidays and summer and long-stay rates upon request.

Another attractive member of the Best Western chain is the **Averill Court Motel,** Seaview Road (tel. 27-716), set in spacious grounds lush with semitropical plantings. There are large one- and two-bedroom units, all with full kitchen facilities, color TV, radio, and electric blanket. Plus full laundry facilities, swimming pool, hot spa pool, and for fishermen, even boat-washing facilities. The Averill Court is close to shops and beaches, and Bronwyn and Ernie Taylor, the friendly owner-managers, can arrange almost any sort of holiday activity you wish. Rates are NZ$36 ($24.16) single, NZ$40 ($26.85) double. Holiday and summer minimum rates upon request.

The **Casa-Bella Motel,** McMurray Road (tel. 27-387), is a sparkling white, red-tile-roofed, Spanish-style complex close in to shops, restaurants, and the beach. There are a variety of nicely furnished units, all with full kitchen facilities, color TV, piped-in music, and electric blanket. There are some waterbeds, and one very special honeymoon suite. On the premises there's both a swimming and a hot spa pool, as well as full laundry facilities. Picnic tables and benches shaded by umbrellas are set about on the landscaped grounds. Rates are NZ$25 ($16.78) single, NZ$30 ($20.13) double, with a NZ$6 ($4.03) charge for each extra person.

A Licensed Hotel

The **Duke of Malborough Hotel,** The Strand, Russell (tel. 829), is the Grand Old Man of the Bay of Islands, having watched the comings and goings of generations of residents and visitors from its waterfront perch since it opened as New Zealand's very first hotel. It has suffered major fires three times, and three times been rebuilt. Grand it may be; stuffy it isn't. Just a few steps from the Russell wharf, its covered veranda is the natural gathering place for fishermen at the end of a day on the water in pursuit of those deep-sea fighters. The conversation tends to be lively, rather than stuffy, attracting locals as well as hotel guests. The Duke, in fact, could be called the social hub of Russell (if Russell could, in fact, be said to have a social hub!). Its public bar, across the street in the back, is also the center of community conviviality.

Regulars come back to the Duke year after year for its old-worldness, and also for the homey comfort of its rooms. Beds have wicker headboards, floors are carpeted, walls are wood paneled, and tea- and coffee-making facilities are in each room. Hall showers and toilets are squeaky clean. There's a charming dining room serving all meals (see "Meals" below), a TV lounge, and a charming guest lounge with wicker furniture, a colonial-style bar, and a working fireplace. Year-round rates are NZ$35 ($23.42) single, NZ$52 ($34.90) double —a little above budget, but bargain prices for the likes of the Duke.

READERS' ACCOMMODATIONS SELECTIONS: "We stayed at **Centabay,** on Selwyn Road in Paihia (tel. 27-466). It's open 24 hours a day, with youth-hostel atmosphere, but *much* nicer. It's small, clean, quiet, with kitchen facilities, TV, lounges. Run by a very nice married couple, Manford and Jill Manacher" (Susan Quinby, Milton, Mass.). . . . "**Whangarei Falls Motor Camp,** P.O. Box 7013, Tikipunga, Whangarei (tel. 70-609), is a small camp in rural surroundings, yet close to town and not far from good beaches. Charges were very much in the budget range and below some others in which we stayed" (Lou Howard, Little Falls, N.J.).

MEALS: As you would expect in such a popular resort area, the Bay of Islands has many good places to eat. Seafood tops the list of menu offerings (which should come as a surprise to no one), with fish coming to table just hours after they were swimming in the waters offshore.

In Russell

Freshness is something you can count on at **The Quarterdeck,** The Strand, Russell (tel. 761). In a setting of early Bay of Islands prints and photographs and high-backed booths, there's a terrific seafood salad, as well as snapper or whatever the latest catch has brought in, mixed grill, chicken, and a good selection of sandwiches and light meals. Prices run from NZ$2 ($1.34) to NZ$3 ($2.01) for the lighter fare, NZ$6 ($4.03) to NZ$8 ($5.37) for full meals. Hours are 9:30 a.m. to 3:30 p.m. and 6 to 9 p.m. (with longer openings in high season) Monday through Saturday. Closed Sunday. BYO.

A charming—and inexpensive—place for sandwiches, scones, sausage rolls, savouries, meat pies, and other snacks, as well as a limited selection of hot meals, is the **Flower Day Coffee Lounge** in Traders Mall on Yorke Street. Red-checked tablecloths and flowers create a cozy atmosphere inside, and there are outside tables in good weather. Everything is home-cooked, pastries and cakes are especially good, and prices can range anywhere from NZ$.75 (50¢) for meat pies to NZ$4.50 ($3.02) for a meal of soup and fresh fish. Next door is an ice-cream parlor. Hours are 9:30 a.m. to 3:30 p.m., later during January and February.

The **Reef Bar Bistro,** located in the Duke Tavern (tel. 831), serves delicious bistro meals in its family and garden bar. Fresh fish, oysters, scallops, shrimp (*tons* of shrimp in the shrimp cocktail!), steaks, and light snacks are all at low, family prices—in the NZ$4 ($2.68) to NZ$6 ($4.03) range. It's closed on Sunday, open other days from noon to 2 p.m. and 5:30 to 8:30 p.m. Fully licensed, of course.

Its big brother, the **Duke of Marlborough,** serves a pricier à la carte meal in its elegant dining room, daily from 6:30 to 9 p.m. Main courses are fresh seafood, roasts of lamb or sirloin, pork, and chicken. Meals are half price for children under 10. There's also a generous five-course lunch, served from noon to 1:30 p.m. Fully licensed, with an excellent wine cellar.

For a splurgy dinner, head for **The Gables,** on the Strand facing the waterfront (tel. 618). This was one of the first buildings on the waterfront, built in 1850, and was a riotous brothel in the days of the whalers. Its construction is pit-sawn kauri on whalebone foundations (in fact, there's a huge piece of whale vertebrae, discovered during renovation, now on display in the small bar). Decor is early colonial, with a kauri-paneled ceiling in the bar, kauri tables, prints, maps, photographs of early New Zealand, and the cheerful warmth of open fires. The blackboard menu changes seasonally, but owners (sisters Jenny Loosley and Barbara Farn, both Londoners who have traveled the world) emphasize seafood in the manu. There's a thick, creamy oyster chowder, garlic crayfish served in the shell, and local smoked marlin served with avocado. Beef, lamb, and game also appear periodically, and fresh vegetables and fruits are a mainstay. Main courses on the à la carte menu are in the NZ$9 ($6.04) to NZ$11 ($7.38) range, and the Gables is fully licensed, with a respectable wine list. It's open seven days a week during summer from 6:30 to 9:30 p.m. (also serves lunch in January only, from noon to 2 p.m.). Open Tuesday through Saturday other seasons (it sometimes closes from the end of May through July, so be sure to check). Bay of Islanders love this place, so book early.

On the Paihia Side

For good food at tiny prices, go into **The Pantry,** on Selwyn Road. It's a bright, cheerful eatery serving nonstop from 9 a.m. to 5 p.m. every day except Sunday. Mrs. Jean Pemberton serves a full breakfast (two eggs, bacon, grilled tomato, toast, marmalade, and coffee) for NZ$3.90 ($2.62); curry and rice, spaghetti bolognaise, or macaroni and cheese for NZ$1.50 ($1.01); full salads (chicken, ham, or beef) for NZ$2.25 ($1.51); sirloin steak and salad for NZ$5.50 ($3.69); and sandwiches for just NZ$.80 (54¢). Americans love the home-cooked food and Mrs. Pemberton loves her American guests. When I was researching this edition, I found her in the throes of experimenting with American-style pancakes because so many patrons had requested them.

The tiny **Jolly Roger,** on Kings Road (tel. 27-783), is the constant subject of letters from readers, all writing to say how much they've enjoyed the Cape Cod atmosphere of this place, the friendliness of owners and staff, and most of all, the food. Its popularity is well deserved: lightly battered, really fresh seafood comes from the kitchen deep-fried and crisp, accompanied by coleslaw, tartar sauce, and tons of chips, plus bread and butter. But if you're a devotee of the broiler, all you have to do is ask and yours will arrive broiled to perfection. There are all sorts of seafood offered—the fish of the day, oysters, scallops, shrimp, etc.—and a heaping combination platter. Steaks are on the menu as well. Prices are in the NZ$6 ($4.03) to NZ$8 ($5.37) range, with children's servings about half price. During the summer, hours are 11:30 a.m. to 2 p.m. and 5 to 10 p.m.; in winter it closes earlier. BYO. There's also a take-away service.

Also very popular with both residents and visitors is the **Bella Vista,** on the waterfront at Waitangi Bay (tel. 27-451). Its big front windows look out to bay views, which somehow make the food taste better (and cocktails here at the sunset hour are really something special!). Downstairs, it's casual all the way, with a blackboard menu of fish, oysters, omelets, etc., at moderate prices that peak at NZ$7 ($4.70). Upstairs, elegance holds sway in the lounge as well as in the dining room. Such delicacies as hapuka and whitebait are specialties, and steak is a staple. Fresh fruits, such as boysenberries or kiwi fruit, come with globs of fresh whipped cream and confectioner's sugar. Prices run NZ$7.50 ($5.03 to NZ$16.50 ($11.07), which includes french fries and salad with your main course. Downstairs hours are 9:30 a.m. to 5 p.m. (until 10 p.m. in summer) upstairs is open 5 to 10 p.m., later in summer. Both are fully licensed, and reservations are usually necessary upstairs.

Lunch will undoubtedly be your main meal of the day if you go by the **THC Waitangi Hotel** (tel. 27-411) for the gigantic poolside buffet (in the poolside restaurant when it rains). For NZ$9 ($6.04), you eat as much as you want of seafood, steak, roasts, salad bar, desserts, tea or coffee. Children under 14 pay half. Hours are noon to 2:30 p.m., and it's a good idea to book. On Sunday (when you *must* book) there's much the same, with live music thrown in—they call it the Beef & Ivory Buffet, and you're invited to bring along your musical instrument and "jam it up with the band." Over at the Waitangi's **Anchorage Bar,** in a plainer, but very pleasant, setting, lunch and dinner (everything from salads to fish and chips to seafood to roast beef) range from NZ$3 ($2.01) to NZ$6 ($4.03). Both are fully licensed, of course.

Jane's Restaurant, on State Highway 10 between Paihia and Kerikeri (tel. 78-664), looks like a roadhouse on the outside, a French provincial restaurant on the inside. The low-beamed ceiling, sideboard filled with china and knick-knacks, and fireplace in one corner make this a cozy, relaxed setting for the superb food that comes to table. It's a far-ranging menu, from omelets to crayfish mornay at prices of NZ$5 ($3.36) to NZ$15 ($10.06). It's essential to book ahead during the season and on weekends. Hours are 10 a.m. to 10 p.m. daily. Fully licensed, with a good selection of wines.

Upstairs in the Selwyn Road Shopping Center, **La Scala Restaurant** (tel. 27-031) has a pretty garden atmosphere, with window walls, green carpet, light-wood tables, cane-back chairs, and greenery everywhere. The freshest of seafood is the specialty, as are New Zealand steaks. In addition to the fish of the day, scallops, oysters, and crayfish, there are such items as honey prawns (shrimp battered, dipped in honey, and sprinkled with sesame seeds). Prices are in the upper ranges—NZ$8 ($5.37) to NZ$15 ($10.06)—and there's a children's menu for NZ$3 ($2.01) to NZ$5 ($3.36). Fully licensed. Open for dinner only, 6 to 10 p.m.; closed Monday. Reservations are a must.

THINGS TO SEE AND DO: Again, I'll issue my standard Bay of Islands caution: there's so much to see and do up here that you're going to be sorely tempted to stay over an extra day or so. For example, with just two days, you'll barely have time to take one of the cruises (which you should do if you have to skip everything else!) and do a little sightseeing, the other to see the rest of the historical sights. But then there's the day-long to Cape Reinga, swimming, fishing, boating, diving, etc., etc., etc., for which you'll have no time. So I suppose it comes down to assigning priorities to fit the length of your stay.

The very first thing on your agenda should be to go by the Public Relations Office and pick up their brochure, *What to See & What to Do in the Bay of Islands.* They can also give you brochures outlining the Cream Trip and Tiger Lily cruises and setting out schedules and prices for each. In fact, they can furnish specific information on just about any of the activities listed in this section, although you'll have to do the booking yourself.

Sporting Activities

There are beaches galore for good **swimming** from November through March. They're lined up all along the town waterfronts, and delightful little coves with curving strands are just awaiting your discovery down almost any side road along State Highway 10 headed north (if you pass through privately owned land to reach the water, you may be asked to pay a small fee, something like NZ$.20 (or 13¢ U.S.).

You can arrange to play **golf** at the beautiful 18-hole waterfront course at Waitangi Golf Course, where clubs are for hire (call 27-713).

Deep-sea fishing is at its best up here. In fact, world records for yellowtail, marlin, shark, and tuna have been set in these waters. There are several good big-game fishing charter boats operating out of Russell, but I might as well warn you that it can be an expensive proposition unless you can form your own group (or fall in with a group that has a vacancy) to share the NZ$350 ($235) cost for a full day's fishing. With a party of six (the maximum), the per-person cost becomes a more manageable $40 (U.S.). If the fact that some 600 striped, blue, and black marlin were landed in these waters makes this an irresistible expense, Fullers or Game Fishing Charters (both in the Maritime Building in Paihia) may be able to help you line something up.

Light-line fishing is much more affordable. There are a number of charter boats available, and two very good ones are the M.V. *Waimarie* and M.V. *Arline* owned by John Scott (tel. Paihia 28-025). For a party of four, John charges NZ$14 ($9.40) per person for four hours of fishing, with line and bait provided. Tea is provided too, but you bring your own lunch. Fullers also arranges light-line fishing charters.

If the idea of a few days **sailing** these waters, living on a boat and learning to handle it yourself, fishing or not fishing as the mood dictates, appeals to you, then the people to contact are Roger and Evelyn Miles, of **Rainbow Yacht Charters** (mailing address: P.O. Opua, Bay of Islands; tel. Paihia 27-081 or 27-269). Based in Opua, the Miles own or lease 17 yachts ranging in size from the Davidson M20 trailer-sailer to the new luxury 38-foot Chieftain keelers, including nine of the popular Laurie Davidson–designed 28-foot yachts. And they have a range of programs designed for everyone from experienced sea-hands to those whose boating has been confined mainly to the bathtub. Their cruises are unstructured, allowing you to follow your sense of adventure, with or without one of their crews (provided, of course, you know or take the time to learn how to handle the boat). Roger says that "encompasses over 500 miles of shoreline and something like 86 islands—every boatie's idea of paradise."

The boats are a dream, and having been a closet "boatie" all my life, this is another New Zealand treat I'm definitely budgeting time for next trip! Costs to be budgeted? They run from $190 (U.S.) to $290 per day (most can accommodate five or six people comfortably, so the per-person cost comes down with each additional person) or $1150 to $1750 per week, depending on size of boat and season. The bargain way to do it, however, is to book one of Rainbow's package deals. For $1928 you get seven days' sailing and nine days' touring in a rental car with unlimited mileage and nine nights' accommodations in Best Western motels throughout the country, *plus* round-trip airfare on Air New Zealand, with free stopovers in Hawaii and Australia! That's the price for the peak season, December 15 to February 29—the cost comes down to $1269 other months. A very good deal! There are equally good Ski & Sail packages. Rainbow has had so many Americans book with them (many for several return trips) that they've opened their own office in the U.S. You can contact them for full details at Rainbow Yacht Charters, Suite 224, Ventura Blvd., Woodland Hills, CA 91364 (tel. 213/702-0111 or 714/966-0256).

There's good **scuba-diving** in these waters, and Paihia Dive, Hire and Carters, Ltd., on Williams Road (tel. 27-551), can provide all equipment and arrange dives.

The Bay of Islands is rich in excellent **scenic walks,** and the park rangers at the following addresses can furnish details of all trails, as well as a very good booklet called *Walking in the Bay of Islands Maritime and Historic Park*. Go by Park Headquarters in Russell (P.O. Box 134; tel. 134) or Kerikeri (P.O. Box 128; tel. 78-474) for their friendly assistance.

There are also beautiful camping sites, some of them on uninhabited islands in the bay, with fees of NZ$1 (67¢) to NZ$3 ($2.01) per night. You must book with the park rangers at the above addresses—you might write ahead and ask for their useful booklet *Huts and Camping, Bay of Islands Maritime and Historic Park.*

Sightseeing

There's a wealth of sightseeing to be done on land in the Bay of Islands, but nothing compares with the bay itself. All those islands are set in a bay which is so sheltered it is known to mariners as one of the best hurricane anchorages in the South Pacific—literally, one of Mother Nature's jewels. And if you do no other sightseeing during your stay, you should take one of the **bay cruises** that circumnavigates these islands. Mount Cook Lines offers the most comprehensive cruises with its catamarans, *Tiger Lily I* and *Tiger Lily II*. Both are fully licensed, with hostess service on all cruises, and they offer solid comfort, with jet air ventilation, tinted windows, and carpeting throughout. There's the thrilling Cape Brett and Piercy Island cruise, with its breathtaking passage through the "Hole in the Rock" when the weather is right. On the return journey you'll pass the more tranquil inner islands of the bay, past playful dolphins sporting around the boat. It's a three-hour cruise, and the cost is NZ$15 ($10.06). There are three departures a day, one at 9:30 a.m., and two in the afternoon. The longer (four-hour) Cream Trip retraces the route used in years gone by to collect cream for market from the islands and inlets around the bay. This cruise also visits Cape Brett and the Hole in the Rock. Along the route, your knowledgeable skipper will point out Captain Cook's first anchorage in 1769, the spot where Dr. Samuel Marston preached the first Christian sermon on the beach, island locales of violence, murder, and cannibalism, and Otehei Bay, on Urupukapuka Island, which was the site of Zane Grey's camp so well written of in his *The Angler's Eldorado.* There are two of these super-cruises each day, one in the morning, the other an afternoon cruise. The cost is NZ$16 ($10.74). Lunch is provided on each at an additional charge, but must be ordered in advance. If you'd like to take both cruises (maybe one in the morning, another in the afternoon), there's an excellent Twin Tour discount, which saves you NZ$4 ($3.02), with a NZ$34 ($21.82) fare for both. Fullers also operates a Cream Trip cruise for NZ$14.50 ($9.73), with bar and canteen service and an optional chicken and champagne lunch at an additional charge (must be pre-ordered), as well as a Champagne Islands Cruise at NZ$13.50 ($9.06), also with the optional lunch available. Both **Mount Cook Lines** and **Fullers** have booking facilities in the Maritime Building at the Paihia Wharf, and Mount Cook also has an office on Williams Road, opposite the post office, with 24-hour telephone service (tel. 27-811).

If time permits (it will take an entire day) I heartily recommend the Mount Cook Lines trip to **Cape Reinga.** There's something intriguing about being at the very top of New Zealand (and if you work in Stewart Island down south, you'll have seen the country from stem to stern!). And besides, there's a mystical aura about the cape, since the Maoris believed that it was from a gnarled pohutukawa tree in the cliffs here that souls jumped off for the return to their Hawaiki homeland after death. Then there's the drive along hard-packed golden sands of the **Ninety-Mile Beach** (which measures a literal 52 miles!) at low tide. The tour leaves Paihia at 7:45 a.m. and returns at 6:30 p.m., for a NZ$16 ($10.74) fare.

Tainui Cruises, in Paihia (tel. 27-357), can give you seven hours of sheer laziness with its Beachcomber Cruise, with no more strenuous activity scheduled than lying on the beach working on your tan, swimming, collecting shells, or a little hiking. The cost is NZ$22 ($14.77), including lunch. They also have a three-hour Islander Cruise (with lunch available at an additional charge), as well as a Sunset Dinner cruise with a lavish buffet and after-dinner music for dancing at $NZ18 ($12.08).

On land, your sightseeing will be divided between Russell and Waitangi. At the top of your "must see" list should be the **Treaty House in Waitangi,** where the British Crown succeeded in having its first treaty with the Maoris ratified by enough native chieftains to assure its acceptance by major Maori leaders throughout the country. It's the birthplace of modern New Zealand.

The Georgian-style house was the home of James Busby from 1832 to 1840, and its broad lawn was the scene of the colorful meeting of Pakeha and Maori during those treaty negotiations. Inside, there's a museum display of a facsimile of the treaty written in Maori (you can see the original in the Alexander Turnbull Library in Wellington), other mementos of those early days, and rooms with period furnishings. On the grounds stands one of the most magnificent *whare runangas* (meeting houses) in the country, constructed for the 1940 centennial celebration, containing elaborately carved panels from all the Maori tribes in New Zealand. Just below the sweeping lawn, on Hobson's Beach, there's an impressive 117-foot-long Maori war canoe, also made for the centennial, from three giant kauri trees. The Treaty House and its grounds are open daily from 9 a.m. to 5 p.m. Adults pay NZ$1 (67¢) admission; children, NZ$.10 (7¢).

If you've an ounce of romance in your soul, you won't want to miss the **Museum of Shipwrecks,** a three-masted barque, the *Tui,* moored near the Waitangi–Paihia bridge. Kelly Tarlton, a professional diver, has made this the focus of his life's work, excavating treasure from more than 1800 ships that have perished in the waters off New Zealand. Beside each display of treasure he's brought up from the deep, there's a photograph of the ship from which it was recovered. There's a continuous slide show depicting Kelly going about his work underwater, and realistic sound effects of storms, the creaking of timbers, and the muffled chant of sea shanties. Well worth the NZ$1.50 ($1.01) admission (children, NZ$.50 or 33¢ U.S.).

Russell is a veritable concentration of historical sites. It was there that the great Maori leader Hone Heke burned everything except mission property at a time when most of what was there *should* have been burned in the interest of morality and environmental beauty, since the town seethed with all sorts of European vices, diseases, and injustices against the natives (see the Introduction). The old Anglican church and headstones of sailors buried in its graveyard bear to this day bullet holes from that long-ago battle.

Right on the waterfront, **Pompallier House** was built in 1841 by the French Bishop Pompallier for the Roman Catholic printing press used from 1842 to 1849 to print religious documents in the Maori language. You can see that press here today. There's also a collection of carved whale ivory and various other artifacts of the times. It's open every day, except Good Friday and Christmas Day, from 10 a.m. to 12:30 p.m. and 1:30 to 4:30 p.m. Adults pay NZ$1 (67¢); children, NZ$.50 (33¢).

On the highest elevation in Russell stands the flagstaff Hone Heke chopped down in defiance of British rule. It is reached by auto or on foot, and the lookout up there affords one of the best views of the bay.

You really should take time to make the 20-minute drive to **Kerikeri**, a small town that figured prominently in the country's early history. It holds the oldest European building in New Zealand, the **Kemp House**, built between 1832 and 1835 as a mission supply center, which is now a museum and general store. Kerikeri is also an arts and crafts center, and you can watch many of the artisans at their work in small shops. Look for weaving, spinning, and pottery at the Black Sheep, potters at the Red Barn Pottery. The Arts Centre presents professional music and drama performances. A direct descendant of Hongi Hike constructed the replica Maori village of **Keri Park** without hammer or nails, as his ancestors built their own dwellings. Another authentic reconstruction of a pre-European Maori settlement is **Rewa's Village.**

For a look at another side of Bay of Islands history, take the two-hour **Farm Safari** run by Roger Bayly, "Wairoa," Paihia (tel. 27-379). He's the owner of Wairoa sheep and cattle station, which was settled in 1837 by a Captain Hingston. Roger's father became the second owner, and Roger himself has devoted his adult life to further developing the large Romney sheep flock and Angus cattle herd, incorporating modern farming practices. You'll see day-to-day activities like dipping, shearing, "cutching," and whatever happens to be going on while you're there, and you'll meet the family and farm workers on a personal, one-to-one basis. The cost is NZ$8 ($5.37) per adult, half that for children.

Shopping

Do take time from all the other activities in the Bay of Islands to browse around the several very good shops in the area. I have lugged home some of my best New Zealand handcrafts from up here, including a gorgeous natural-wool, hand-knit sweater from the **House of Gifts**, The Strand, Russell, where Aline and Jim Ryan keep an assortment of good-quality gifts and souvenirs at reasonable prices. Over on the Paihia side, **Classique Souvenirs** is a good bet for good buys; you'll find exceptional craft items at **Katoa Crafts** (pottery, weaving, woodwork, paintings, etc.); and a very good selection is at **Waitangi Crafts and Souvenirs** on Williams Road. Prices, far from being resort-area-inflated, are competitive with city shops and in many cases cheaper—and it's fun to shop with the friendly Bay of Islander proprietors, who take a personal interest in seeing that you find what you want. Most are open daily during peak season, and weekdays plus Saturday mornings at other times.

For the absolute epitome in shopping pleasure, give **Suzanne MacInnes** a ring in Russell (tel. 859) to arrange a visit to her studio, which is also her home. Suzanne and her late husband arrived in New Zealand from Richmond, Virginia, in 1971 with their six children, stayed five days in Auckland, then came north and found this lovely old home perched on a high hill overlooking Russell and the bay. The children are all grown and on their own now (son Johnny is a mainstay at The Gables restaurant in Russell), and Suzanne devotes her time to the painting she's done all her life. A vibrant, enchanting woman, she paints incredible land- and seascapes, as well as all sorts of enamel costume jewelry minatures and decorative and useful items such as enamel boxes, thimbles, and the like. Her prices are reasonable, her designs are exquisite, and I can promise you a shopping experience you'll treasure for life.

AFTER DARK: Pub pickings are limited to the **Duke** in Russell (where conversation is likely to center around fishing), the **THC Waitangi pub** and **Anchorage Bar** (where you'll bend an elbow with residents of the Paihia side of the bay, including a native Maori or two, and holidaying visitors), and **Putty's Pub** at the Twin Pines Motor Camp (where campers are joined by neighborhood residents).

During summer months, the Mount Cook Line *Tiger Lily* becomes a "Night Tiger," the closest thing to a nightclub in the Bay of Islands. There's a band playing music to request as the *Tiger* cruises to a tranquil bay. Departure is just after 8 p.m., with a return after midnight. The fare is NZ$15 ($10.06), drinks extra. To book, stop by the Mount Cook desk in the Maritime Building at Paihia Wharf, or call Paihia 27-099.

SPECIAL EVENT: Lucky you if your visit coincides with the February 6 celebration of **Waitangi Day!** It's like being in the U.S. on the Fourth of July. The center of activity is the Treaty House lawn, scene of the Waitangi Treaty signing, with a recreation of that event, lots of Maori song and dance, and Pakeha officials in abundance, dressed to the nines in resplendent uniforms of yesteryear and today. The Royal New Zealand Navy is there in force, as are crowds of holidaying Kiwis. Book *way* ahead, then get set to join in the festivities.

4. From Auckland to Waitomo

If you're going from the Bay of Islands directly to Waitomo, count on a long day's drive, shortened considerably if you return to Auckland via Highway 1 (about a four-hour drive). Along the way, you might stop by the **Waiomio limestone caves,** three kilometers south of Kawakawa—they're about half a kilometer up a dirt road to the left of Highway 1, and guided tours are at 10 and 11 a.m., and 1, 2, and 3 p.m. Farther south, the town of **Warkworth** was once the center of extensive sawmilling of kauri spars to furnish masts for the Royal Navy, and there are the remains of several Maori *pas* (fortified villages) in the area. About seven kilometers away, at the coastal town of **Sandspit,** you can take a launch to Kawau Island to visit **Mansion House,** the restored home of Gov. George Grey. Then there are those beautiful beaches nearer Auckland at Waiwera and Orewa.

These are all en route possibilities, but on a one-day drive to Waitomo, you'll have to keep an eye on the clock. If you leave the Bay of Islands around 8 a.m., driving at a steady pace (with a lunch break) will get you to Waitomo not much before about 5 p.m. An alternative is a leisurely drive back to Auckland or some other intermediate spot for an overnight stop, and an early-morning start to go on to Waitomo the following day.

If you're traveling by bus, there's excellent NZZR transportation from the Bay of Islands to Auckland, and service leaving Auckland at about 9 a.m. for Waitomo, which stops for a tour of the caves, then goes on to Rotorua. You can, of course, break the journey with an overnight stay at Waitomo and continue on to Rotorua the next afternoon.

From Auckland, the 125-mile drive to Waitomo passes through rich farm country and horse and cattle farms. A good lunch stop is the Victorian **1870 Restaurant** at Ngaruawahia (tel. 8121). This is an old clapboard house, built in 1869, which has been in its day a police station, post office, and courthouse, and its atmosphere is still very much of the 19th century, with interesting antiques in the licensed dining room. The fare is simple, good, and moderately priced. Luncheons run from NZ$1.50 ($1.01) for soup and toast, to NZ$5 ($3.36) to NZ$7 ($4.70) for main meals, served from noon to 2:30 p.m. Dinner prices range from NZ$7 ($4.70) to NZ$10 ($6.71), served from 6 to 10 p.m. Closed Monday.

Hamilton is New Zealand's largest inland city and the commercial and industrial center of this agricultural area, as well as the site of the University of Waikato. Several major religions are centered here: it's the see city for the Anglican Diocese of Waikato; the Mormons have their magnificent South Pacific temple headquarters at Temple View, high on a hill at Tuhikaramea southwest of the city center; and there's a Sikh temple on the northern outskirts of town at Horotiu. Throughout the city, you'll see lovely gardens both in city parks and private lawns.

A scant ten miles before you reach Waitomo and the caves, there's a **Kiwi House** at Otorohanga, as well as an excellent youth hostel, which is open only from December 17 to January 25. The remaining distance to Waitomo runs through more farmland.

5. Waitomo Caves

Waitomo Village owes its existence to the more than 200,000 visitors who come annually to visit three remarkable limestone caves, and its main street holds a general store, post office, and tavern (which sells tickets to the caves as well as souvenirs, and has the usual bottle store, public bar, and bistro restaurant). At the top of a gracefully winding driveway stands the THC Waitomo Hotel (with not a budget-priced room under its roof). Across from the general store, a large open field is called The Domain, where cabins may be rented. Waitomo Cave, with its splendid Glowworm Grotto, is some 400 yards beyond the tavern, and about 2½ miles away are Ruakuri and Aranui Caves, both of which rival Waitomo as sightseeing attractions.

ACCOMMODATIONS: Not many from which to choose.

A Hostel, Sort of

It's the closest thing Waitomo has to a youth hostel, and hostelers, backpackers, or cavers will find the **Hamilton Tomo Group Hut,** about half a mile past the Waitomo Cave on the main road (tel. Te Kuiti 219-K), quite adequate. The bunkhouse will sleep 30 (but has been known to accommodate more in a pinch) on wooden bunks that have rubber mattresses. House rules are basic: no alcohol, guests must tidy up, and lights go out at midnight. Booking? You don't—although Mr. Dimond, the warden, lives close by, he doesn't bother with bookings; you simply go to the hut, drop NZ$2.50 ($1.68) in the Honesty Box, and claim your bunk space (if available). There's not likely to be space on a weekend, since that's when there's an invasion of great numbers of trampers and cavers who are members of the Hamilton Tomo Group. Equipment in the hut includes light, heat, hot water, showers, electric stove (plus all cooking and eating utensils), refrigerator, washing machine, drying room, and radio. There's an interesting caving display, and lots of club photos. You'll need to bring in food from the general store, since there's none closer.

Motor Camp

The **Waitomo Caravan Park,** Box 14, Waitomo Caves (tel. Te Kuiti 1234-M), has a total of ten cabins located in two blocks. Each will sleep four in two bunk beds. Furnishings are simple: cold-water sink, table, chairs, and a small hotplate. Cooking and eating utensils are not supplied, but may be rented for a small fee. Also on the premises are communal showers, laundry, and kitchen. There are also powered caravan and tent sites. You'll find the busy owners, Tony and Patty Doull, at the Mobil gas station, tea room, or general store, all of which they also run. If you've arrived without a reservation, check in at the general store. Rates are NZ$10 ($6.71) double, NZ$2 ($1.34) for each additional person. Tent space runs NZ$5 ($3.36) for two.

In nearby Otorohanga, there's the **Otorohanga Motor Camp** (c/o Otorohanga Taxis, Wahanui Crescent, Otorohanga; tel. 8279) with 20 tent sites and 24 caravan sites. Its location on Domain Drive is right next to the Kiwi House and public swimming pool. On the premises are a communal kitchen, showers, laundry with dryer, and barbecue facilities. Rates are NZ$5 ($3.36) per adult for tent sites (half that for children) and NZ$6 ($4.03) per adult (half price for children) for caravan sites.

Motel Flats

You'll find the **Waitomo Country Lodge** (tel. Otorohanga 8089) at the corner of Waitomo Caves Road and Highway 3. Jackson and Patsy Roach, owners of this Best Western motel, are both natives of the area and always happy to give expert sightseeing advice. There are 20 serviced units (one with a waterbed) and a spa pool. A great convenience is the licensed restaurant on the premises. Rates are NZ$27 ($18.12) single, NZ$32 ($21.48) double, NZ$6 ($4.03) per extra adult.

Licensed Hotel

The **Otorohanga Royal Hotel**, on Te Kanawa Street off Maniapoto Street (tel. 8129), has charming, immaculate rooms with flowered carpets, white bedspreads, and lace curtains. All have H&C, and bath and shower facilities are in the hall. The communal kitchen has tea-making facilities and a laundry. The Rangatira Room restaurant serves all meals every day (see "Meals," below). The reasonable rates are NZ$17 ($11.41) single, NZ$28 ($18.79) double.

MEALS: Picnics can be a pleasure, either at the outdoor umbrella tables at the **general store** or the facilities on the Domain. You can also buy hot and cold snacks and light meals at the general store's tea room.

There's a sort of Victorian pub air about the **Otorohanga Royal Hotel's Rangatira Room.** Dark wood paneling, padded captain's chairs, wide booths, and fringed lampshades make it cozy. A nice touch is the series of Maori chieftain portraits on restaurant and lounge walls. All three meals are served seven days a week; the food is good, and prices are quite reasonable: NZ$6.50 ($4.36) to NZ$8 ($5.37) for fish and fries, grilled sirloin steak, fried chicken, and the like.

The **THC Waitomo Hotel** offers a variety of eating possibilities, all pretty pricey (but families get a break in their "half price for children" policy). Costs for grownups' breakfast run about NZ$9 ($6.04) and it's served from 7:30 to 9 a.m. There's a generous smörgåsbord lunch from 11:30 a.m. to 1:30 p.m. at NZ$11 ($7.38), or you can pick up a picnic box lunch for NZ$7.50 ($5.03), if you call ahead with your order. You can dine at night in the elegant Glowworm Restaurant, with its coral tables and chairs, mossy green upholstery and shades of yellow-and-green linen, or in the more informal Garden Room with its white garden furniture set off by lots of green and yellow and, of course, flowers.

Prices are à la carte, and in the Glowworm Restaurant three courses will average about NZ$18 ($12.08).

There's the licensed restaurant at Waitomo Country Lodge, bistro meals at the Tavern, and in Otorohanga, Maniapoto Street has several good, inexpensive restaurants from which to choose.

THINGS TO SEE AND DO: The caves are *the* attraction at Waitomo, chief among them the Waitomo Cave with its Glowworm Grotto. But you should include the Ruakuri and Aranui caves in your sightseeing—each has its own delights, the cost is low, and they're all worth the time.

The Caves

Forty-five-minute guided tours are run on regular schedules at all three caves—tickets and tour times are available at the Tavern and at the THC Waitomo Hotel. There's a three-cave combination ticket for NZ$8.50 ($5.70), and individual rates are: Waitomo, NZ$4.50 ($3.02); Aranui and Ruakuri, each cave NZ$4 ($2.68). Children pay half price. The family package price for all three caves (two adults and two children under 15) costs NZ$20 ($13.42). Be sure to wear good walking shoes and carry a sweater if the weather is a bit cool—it'll be cooler underground.

For me, the most wonderful (and I *mean* wonder-full) time to visit the **Glowworm Grotto** in Waitomo Cave is in the evening. Crowds are smaller, for one thing, and somehow the experience just seems to be one for after dark. Sheer delight.

About 400 yards from the THC hotel, a guide greets you at Waitomo's entrance to escort you through large antechambers, pointing out limestone formations with names like "The Organ," 8 feet high with a 24-foot base. Largest cavern in any of the caves is "The Cathedral," which rises 47 feet and is an acoustically perfect auditorium that has seen performances by such recording artists as the Vienna Boys' Choir and Dame Nellie Melba.

Then it's on to a small grotto festooned with glowworms, where your guide fills you in on the glowworm's life and death cycle. Fascinating! A very *short* cycle it is, for the adult fly lives exactly four days, just long enough to produce the next generation. Having done that, it simply dies and becomes food for the next batch of glowworms.

The whole process begins with a tiny egg, which has a 21-day incubation period, then hatches into an inch-long grub. The grub then cloaks itself in a hollow mucous tube-like nest, which is pinned to the grotto roof with a multitude of slender threads, each holding minute drops of acid and suspended like fishing lines down from the roof. The bait for those lines is the hypnotic blue-green light that comes from the larva's light organs (and that, of course, is what you see as you pass through the grotto) to attract a night-flying midge, which is "caught" by the threads, paralyzed by the acid, and reeled up and eaten by the larva. After about six months, the larva pupates for about two weeks, becomes a hard, brown cocoon about half an inch long and suspended by a circle of those slender threads. The pupa's flirtatious light show attracts several males, which proceed to help the fly escape her cocoon. Four days of egg laying, then it's time to end it all by diving into the lines cast by new larvae as a main course along with the midges.

Now that you understand how and why the glowworms glow, your guide is ready to take you on an unforgettable boat ride down the underground river, which flows through the 100-foot-long, 40-foot-high, 50-foot-wide Glowworm

Grotto. As you board the large, flat-bottomed boat, he will caution you that absolute silence is required, since the glowworms will extinguish their lights at the slightest noise. I must say that warning is probably unnecessary, since the spectacle of more than 10,000 of those tiny pinpricks of light leaves one awed beyond words, and silence seems the only fitting way in which to view them. The boat glides slowly along what is called the "Milky Way," then returns to the dock, where you climb back up through the cave and are given an opportunity to question your guide on any of the things you have seen. It's a unique experience, and one that is sure to live in your memory.

Ask at the THC hotel desk if you need transportation to the other two caves, which are some 2½ miles away. Dramatic Ruakuri, with its labyrinth of caverns alive with the sound of an underground waterfall and its river, which flashes in and out of sight, is the largest of the three. The smallest is Aranui, and many people think it's the loveliest. There's an unusual delicacy about its limestone formations and ivory-colored, translucent stalactites. Light refreshments are available near these two caves.

Adventure Caving

If you're fairly fit, and have brought along warm clothes and boots, and are a spelunker at heart, write or call John Ash, P.O. Box 13, Waitomo Caves (tel. Te Kuiti 226-J) about his **Adventure Cave Tours.** These are three- to four-hour tours through "wild caves," to, as John says, "see a cave the way cavers do." Helmets, lights, overalls, and all technical equipment are provided, and no more than 12 people are allowed on any one tour. The cost is NZ$12 ($8.05) per person.

Kiwi House

While in this area, stop by the **Otorohanga Nocturnal Kiwi House** on Alex Telfer Drive, off Kakamutu Road (tel. 7391). The Otorohanga Zoological Society always has one pair of the national bird awake and on view, and there's always a knowledgeable person on hand to tell you about them and answer any questions you may have. There's also a large aviary on the grounds, which has an interesting collection of waterfowl. Hours are 10 a.m. to 5 p.m. in summer, 4 p.m. other months. Admission is NZ$1.50 ($1.01) for adults, NZ$.50 (33¢) for children.

Shopping

There are two shops in the area deserving of a browse through. The **Country Touch** is set back from the road between Otorohanga and Hangatiki, and carries an interesting, well-priced assortment of unusual Maori and Pakeha handicrafts. Owner Mary Brett seeks out local craftspeople who produce lovely pottery, mud-dyed flax skirts, Maori carvings, and hand-knits. Well worth a stop. Hours are 10 a.m. to 5 p.m.

The other shop, **Baraka Crafts** (tel. 7183), is on Otorohanga's main street. They specialize in New Zealand crafts such as basketry, woolen goods, pottery, and spinning wheels (they'll give you free lessons on how to use them). They're also the proud owners of what is recognized by the *Guinness Book of World Records* as the world's largest spinning wheel, which is proudly exhibited inside. Hours are 8:30 a.m. to 5 p.m.

It's an easy, three-hours-or-less drive from Waitomo to Rotorua, through rolling farmland and long stretches of bush. Approaching that steamy thermal town, you'll catch glimpses of its gleaming lakes and volcanic peaks. There's an "other world" aspect about Rotorua and its environs, which will begin to capture your imagination even before you roll into town.

Chapter IV

ROTORUA

1. The City and Surroundings
2. The Sunrise Coast
3. Gisborne
4. Napier
5. Napier to Taupo

THE FIRST TOURISTS to arrive in Rotorua were Maoris, members of the Arawa tribe whose seagoing canoe arrived on the shores of the Bay of Plenty sometime during the 14th century. Pushing inland to Lake Rotorua, they stayed on to become settlers, and today's tourist will find some 5000 of their descendants happily following much of the traditional tribal lifestyle in the largest area in New Zealand, which is both preserved and promoted as a showcase for pre-European culture.

Those early arrivals found the area ideally suited to settlement. Nature supplied not only everything they needed for survival, but threw in mysterious volcanic cones, large, deep lakes, and all those steaming thermal pools as natural habitats for innumerable Maori spirit gods who, of course, were unseen passengers in the Arawa canoe as it crossed the Pacific. There's a Maori legend centered on the antics of the gods to be told about almost every one of the natural wonders you'll see in Rotorua.

The Arawas are quick to tell you the one that explains in Maori terms Rotorua's awesome thermal activity around Rotorua. It seems the great navigator-priest Ngatoroirangi, having reached the summit of Mount Tongariro, suffered greatly from the cold and implored his goddess sisters back in Hawaiki to send along some of their native warmth to this frigid, windswept place. Their response was a generous one—they pitched their gobs of fire across the water, which hopped, skipped, and jumped over the land, touching down at White Island, Rotorua, Wairankei, Taupo, Tokaanu, Ketetahi, finally reaching the freezing Ngatoroirangi at Mount Tongariro. Geologists, on the other hand, simply say that underground lava or superheated rock heats underground water under pressures, which send it spouting up via any escape route it can find—natural fissures, porous rock, etc. Personally, I think the Maoris have the better story!

Whatever the explanation for the North Island's giant (150 miles long, 20 miles wide) thermal region, Rotorua sits right in the middle of the most intense activity. That overheated water will bubble up all around you in the form of geysers, mud pools, or steam bores. You'll bathe in it, see the local cooking with it, stay in guest houses that are heated with it, or simply walk carefully around the boiling mud pools waching this performance—of whatever gods—in sheer

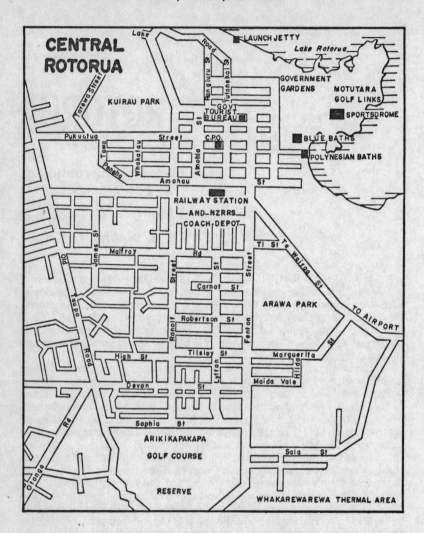

fascination.

Just as fascinating is the vast gallery of Maori culture through which you will wander. Through song and dance you'll hear some of those legends firsthand; at a hangi feast you'll taste food cooked in a centuries-old manner; in a model Maori village you'll watch the younger generation learning from their elders such age-old skills as carving and weaving. In craft shops you'll find a splendid array of "just the right gift" items.

1. The City and Surroundings

Rotorua sits in the curve of Lake Rotorua's southwestern shore, spreading inland in a neat pattern, which will have you oriented in a matter of hours. The center of town is not large: a good ten-minute walk will take you from the southside bus and rail depot (named the **Travel Centre**) northward past the those two tourist landmarks, the **post office** and **Government Tourist Bureau**, to the lovely **Government Gardens.** Older, downtown hotels are also along this route, while more modern hotels are more or less concentrated along the southern end of **Fenton Street,** which is the main street, running from the lake for two miles south to Whakarewarewa (never mind, just call it "Whaka," as the natives do), a thermal reserve owned by Maoris. There are city and suburban buses, but they are infrequent (about one an hour) during weekdays and practically nonexistent on weekends. Unless you're driving, best book an in-town room and use coach tours to reach those sights out of walking distance. Tours are numerous, well planned, and not too expensive—this is, after all, perhaps the North Island's major tourist town, and you may be sure that whatever you want to do or see, someone will have devised an easy, inexpensive way for you to do it.

USEFUL INFORMATION: There are two centers of tourist information in Rotorua: the **Government Tourist Bureau** is at 67 Fenton St. on the corner of Haupapa Street (tel. 85-179), and is open 8:30 a.m. to 5 p.m. Monday through Friday, 8:30 to 11 a.m. on Saturday, October through May. The **Public Relations Office (PRO),** on Haupapa Street (tel. 84-067), opens daily from Christmas through mid-January and on holiday weekends from 9 a.m. to 9 p.m. Both are loaded with tourist information and have helpful staffs who will make bookings. . . . Look for *This Week in Rotorua,* a free listing of current goings-on, which you'll find in many hotels and in the tourist offices; the *Official Visitors Guide* booklet at the PRO; and check the evening newspaper, the *Daily Post* for day-to-day events. . . . The **Travel Centre** (arrival and departure point for NZRRS coaches, NZR trains and most sightseeing tours) is on Amohau Street (tel. 81-039). . . . **Air New Zealand** has a ticket terminal in Amohau Street, just off Fenton Street (tel. 87-159). Buses for the airport leave 45 minutes before each flight, with a NZ$3.50 ($2.35) fare. They also meet each incoming flight. . . . **Mount Cook Lines** has an office at 33 Eruera St. (tel. 56-175). . . . You'll find **taxi ranks** at the Travel Centre, the Grand Hotel on Fenton Streets and just west of the PRO on Haupapa Street, or you can call a cab at 85-079. . . . The **Chief Post Office (CPO),** on the corner of Tutanekai and Hinemoa Streets, is open from 8:30 a.m. to 5 p.m. Monday to Thursday, until 8 p.m. on Friday.

ACCOMMODATIONS: Rotorua is replete with accommodations, and they come in all shapes, sizes and price ranges. Those in the budget range are among the best you'll find in this category anywhere in the country. Indeed, don't expect Rotorua to conform to the usual popular resort image of "charging what the traffic will bear for the least service we can get away with"—this is a resort of a different stripe, one where prices are moderate, service friendly and efficient, and accommodation standards exceptionally high.

Hostels

Just about the best buy in Rotorua is the **YHA Hostel,** 35 Tarewa Rd., off Lake Road (tel. 89-004). In fact it borders on the luxurious. Located only about a mile from the Travel Centre, it accommodates 75 in ten cheerful dormitories furnished with bunk beds. There's a well-equipped kitchen, as well as steam ovens; a provisions shop; laundry facilities and iron; recreation room; bicycle rentals; children's playground; a sauna and mineral plunge pool. Across the road there's a large, thermally heated swimming pool, and the adjacent Tarewa Tennis Club courts are available at no charge. There's even a good trout stream on the grounds—dinner straight from stream to steam oven in nothing flat! Rates are NZ$6 ($4.03) for Seniors, NZ$3 ($2.01) for Juniors.

Bargain hostel-type accommodations are also available at the **Ivanhoe Lodge,** 54 Haupapa St., off Tutanekai Street (tel. 86-985). There are both cabins and dormitory rooms, all with bunk beds. Linens are not supplied, but may be rented for a small fee. There's H&C in the rooms, thermal heating, carpeting in some rooms, and dressers with mirrors. Shared facilities include showers, toilets, kitchen and dining room, laundry, game room, and TV lounge. Rates are NZ$8 ($5.37) per person in cabins, NZ$6 ($4.03) in rooms.

Cabins

A charming setting plus first-class cabin accommodations are what you'll find at **Rainbow & Fairy Springs** (mailing address: P.O. Box 25, Rotorua; tel. 81-887). Just a little over two miles from town on State Highway 5 (the main Auckland road), the cabins are in pretty, parklike grounds, which invite relaxing walks, and all the attractions described later in this chapter are right at hand. The red wooden cabins (in sizes that will sleep from 2 to 12) nestle under big shade trees and come with varying equipment. Some have electric stoves and fridges, as well as toasters, cooking and eating utensils. Others have private shower and toilet. Bunks are in some, beds in others. Their interiors are all plain, but cheerful, with scatter rugs on the plank floors and curtains at the windows. There are communal showers, kitchen and laundry, a food shop just across the road, and a restaurant on the grounds for inexpensive lunches and teas. Linens and blankets may be rented for a small fee. Rates *per cabin* range from NZ$20 ($13.42) to NZ$42 ($28.19) in high season, as low as NZ$9.50 ($6.38) off-season.

Also set in wooded grounds through which an excellent trout stream meanders under drooping willow trees, the **Waiteti Holiday Park,** 14 Okona Crescent, Ngongotaha, Rotorua (tel. 74-749), has tent sites down near the riverbank, 24 power sites for caravans, one on-site caravan that sleeps up to eight, a bunkhouse that accommodates 32, tourist cabins that will sleep four to six people, and tourist flats that sleep five. Just as important, it has owner-managers Ian and Vicky Calvert, a friendly couple who can rent you fishing rods (and cook the trout you pull from that stream), boats (for the nearby lake), or cameras, and help with any sightseeing arrangements. You supply linens in all except the tourist flats, but they may be rented for a small fee. There's a community kitchen (fully equipped), showers, toilets, laundry, TV lounge, shop, spa pool, barbecue area, children's play area, and when I was there in mid-1983, the Calverts were in the process of finishing up a game room and indoor swimming pool. This is a convenient, attractive, and very friendly motor camp, which gets my highest recommendation. Rates range from NZ$4.50 ($3.02) for tent sites, to NZ$15 ($10.06) to NZ$20 ($13.42) double, for cabins, to NZ$30 ($20.13), double, for tourist flats.

The Y

The **YWCA,** on Te Ngae Road near Fenton Street (tel. 85-455), has 26 rooms, all nicely decorated and furnished, but with very limited vacancies for travelers since most are occupied on a residential basis. Facilities include communal showers, fully equipped kitchen, laundry, TV lounge, thermal heating, and barbecue and picnic equipment on the grounds. For those traveling with sleeping bags, there's a large dormitory room with mattresses on the floor in an area that has a small kitchen, sink, and toilet (female guests have the use of showers). Dorm space is frequently booked to capacity by local clubs, but costs only NZ$3.50 ($2.35) when there is a vacancy. Room rates are NZ$7.50 ($5.03) per person.

There is, unfortunately, no YMCA in Rotorua.

Bed and Breakfast

Two of Rotorua's best bed and breakfasts are in the same quiet, residential street just a short distance from the Travel Centre. Both maintain high standards, which prompt readers to write us about them in glowing terms year after year.

Nellie McQueen runs **Tresco Guest House,** 3 Toko St. (tel. 89-611), with seven attractive rooms. There are one, single, five twins, and one triple, all fully carpeted, with H&C and tea-making facilities. All are spotlessly clean, and there's a homey air about the place. Nellie provides a laundry, a small bathhouse with a hot mineral plunge pool, and off-the-street parking. Bed and breakfast is NZ$18 ($12.08)—and you can book for a home-cooked dinner for an additional NZ$8 ($5.37).

A flood of readers' letters led me to **Morihana Guest House,** 20 Toko St. (tel. 88-511), where Marnie and Peter Mellor proved to be just as hospitable as reported in all those letters. Like Tresco, this is a one-story bungalow with a comfortable, homey atmosphere. The Mellors provide five guest rooms (one single, two doubles, one twin, and one triple), all quite cheerful and all with H&C. There are tea- and coffee-making facilities for guests' use, a laundry and drying room, and a mineral pool. The full, cooked English breakfast here has earned high praise from our readers. Rates for bed and breakfast are NZ$18 ($12.08) single, NZ$30 ($20.13) double.

Motel Flats

Noel and Joyce Warner run the **Fernleaf Motel,** at 23 Toko St. (tel. 87-129), just across the street from the Morihana listed above. And they run it just as if every one of the six lovely units were their private home. Not only are those units kept in spit-and-polish order, but they're furnished and decorated with loving care. There are paneled walls; peaked ceilings with exposed beams; colorful, color-coordinated carpets, drapes, and sofa coverings; fully equipped kitchens; plus TV, phone, radio, and geothermal heating you control to suit your own fancy. You can swim in the outdoor freshwater swimming pool, or take a dip in the hot mineral pool (the bathhouse even has a shower—typical of the Warners' thoughtful planning). Other facilities include a laundry, drying room, and car wash. If your day includes fishing and your luck holds, Noel will cook your catch in the steam cooker out back—and non-fisher-people are treated to a steamed chicken (at market price) by request. There's a food shop close by to supply those meals you cook yourself. Further examples of the personal attention you can expect from Noel and Joyce is their willingness to arrange for babysitters and the courtesy car service they provide to the Travel Centre. All in all, the Fernleaf has to rank as one of the best value-for-money accommodations in Rotorua, with rates of NZ$24 ($16.11) single, NZ$34 ($22.82) double, NZ$9 ($6.04) per extra adult, and NZ$7 ($4.70) per child under 12. No additional charges for the use of any of the facilities on the premises.

The **Boulevard Motel**, on the corner of Fenton and Seddon Streets (tel. 82-074), is set on two acres of landscaped grounds and is a family-owned and -operated project of the Bradshaw family. The white, two-story, balconied motel also has a restaurant on the premises and is just down the street from a licensed restaurant with entertainment. Flats have separate lounge, one to three bedrooms, and are beautifully furnished, with complete kitchens, TV, telephone, and central heating. There are serviced units (sleeping two), which are smaller and have tea-making facilities, fridge, TV, and telephone. Those lovely grounds are set about with garden furniture and hold a multitude of recreational facilities: a putting green, swimming pool, four spa baths, swirl pools, sauna, and game room. There's a laundry, dryer, and steam iron for your use. Units come in sizes that accommodate from three to nine people, and rates range from NZ$32 ($21.48) single to NZ$38 ($25.50) double, NZ$8.50 ($5.70) per extra adult, NZ$5 ($3.36) per extra child.

Just a short walk from the lakefront, the **Ambassador Motel,** on the corner of Hinemaru and Whakaue Streets (mailing address: P.O. Box 1212; tel. 479-581 or 85-281) is an attractive white, three-story building with arched covered balconies and self-contained units, some of which have ceilings with exposed beams. The 19 flats come in sizes that accommodate from two to nine people. There are two private thermal pools, a swirl pool, outdoor freshwater pool, and a game room with snooker table. Restaurants and a host of attractions are within easy walking distance in this central, but quiet, location. Year-round rates are NZ$29 ($19.46) single, NZ$35 ($23.49) double.

The **Eason Court Motel,** 13 Eason St. (tel. 82-093), is a complex of brown, one-story units with thermal central heating. Each has a full kitchen, TV, telephone, and radio. All six have one bedroom and will sleep up to five. There's a swimming pool, luxury spa, steam cooker, guest laundry, and drying room. They'll send a courtesy car to pick you up at the Travel Centre or airport. Rates are NZ$26 ($17.45) single, NZ$34 ($22.82) double.

Each of the spacious units at the **Wylie Court Motor Lodge,** 345 Fenton St. (tel. 81-151), has its own private hot tub as well as full cooking facilities, TV, radio, and central heating. There's also a guest laundry. The dark-wood motel is set among willow trees and green lawns. Rates are NZ$30 ($20.13) single and NZ$38 ($25.50) double.

Mrs. Sheila Lafferty's **South Pacific Motel,** 96–98 Lake Rd. (tel. 80-153), features a lovely stream, which runs through the grounds and is crossed by an arched footbridge. Scattered over the landscaped lawns are multicolored brick units of one, two, or four bedrooms, all exceptionally well furnished and attractively decorated. All come equipped with complete kitchens, telephone, TV, radio, and central heating. Beside the stream there's a hot mineral pool; on the lawn, a boiling fountain; and inside, a large "soda" bath. A food store is conveniently located next door. High-season rates are NZ$32 ($21.48) single, NZ$37 ($24.83) double, NZ$9 ($6.04) per extra adult, NZ$6 ($4.03) per child under 12; off-season rates run a little less. The South Pacific is a Best Western, honoring the Holiday Pass discount.

Situated within comfortable walking distance of downtown Rotorua, the **Voyager Resort,** 107 Ranolf St. (tel. 479-594), is one of the area's largest accommodations complexes. Yet Clive and Elizabeth Garratt run it in such a personal manner you'll feel right at home. And as close as it is to shopping and sightseeing, the four acres of parklike grounds create an atmosphere of privacy and relaxation. The three blocks of one- and two-story structures are grouped around a large, landscaped, and grassy central plot, which holds a children's playground complete with trampoline, swings, etc., as well as a pretty, fenced-in, heated swimming pool over in one corner. There are three thermal mineral pools (you adjust the temperature to suit), each in its own private room and open 24 hours a day (the height of luxury, and an experience I'll not soon forget, was a midnight loll in those warm, swirling waters—prelude to a perfect night's sleep). There's a snooker room and nine-hole putting course. And never an extra charge for the use of any facilities (in fact, free detergent is supplied in the laundry). The Garratts can arrange same-day dry cleaning, help with sightseeing or dinner bookings, babysitting, and milk, cream and/or fruit juice delivery every morning. Units are attractively done up in soft tones of browns, golds, greens, and blues—second-floor units have sloping, beamed ceilings. Doubles can accommodate up to four people, and all units have full kitchen, color TV, telephone, radio, piped-in music, and central heating. Rates are pricey here, but since this is a Best Western, the Holiday Pass discount applies. Singles go for NZ$38 ($25.50); doubles, NZ$46 ($30.87); an extra adult, NZ$8 ($5.37); children, NZ$5 ($3.36). If you're looking for an excuse to splurge at the Voyager, just keep in mind those lovely private mineral pools (no swimsuit needed!). And if you want to make it an all-out splurge, the Garratts have a new block of luxury hotel rooms (tea-making facilities and fridge), some with their own spa bath—but prices for those *start* at NZ$53 ($35.57), and you'll have to decide just how big your splurge is going to be!

Licensed Hotels

Just across from the Government Gardens, 1 Arawa St. (tel. 81-179), **Price's Gate Hotel** began life way back in 1899—but not in Rotorua! In fact it had quite a lively life in the gold-mining town of Waihi until just before World War I, when the town voted to do away with any public drinking places. The hotel escaped the fate of many another hostelry left to decay in forgotten glory when its solid kauri boards were dismantled and the entire hotel moved—wide veranda, carved woodwork, stained-glass windows, and all—to Rotorua, where its traditional hospitality is carried on by owners Peter and Betty Jacobsen. There's a cozy, old-fashioned air about the rooms, 15 of which have H&C only, 22 of which come complete with private bathroom. Matching wallpaper and bedding in shades of pink, lilac, or green pretty up the wainscotted rooms, some of which open onto the veranda and look out to the lake. All rooms have a radio, piped-in music, and tea-making facilities. The Prince's Gate is a "tourist licensed" hotel, thus only resident guests are served at the unusual curved bar or in the large bar lounge with its pool table and darts. The attractive dining room serves reasonably priced meals, and there's a TV lounge, as well as a hot mineral pool and laundry room. Rooms with H&C only go for NZ$20 ($13.42) for bed and breakfast, NZ$29.50 ($19.80) with dinner. Others are NZ$25.50 ($17.11) for bed and breakfast, NZ$35 ($23.49) with dinner. All rates are per person; children under 12 pay half price, and under-2s are free.

This listing is—I admit it—a little sneaky. It has absolutely no place in a budget travel book. Still, I think you might like to know about it, so I'll tell you about it anyway. And if you're particularly flush when you hit Rotorua (or you're hypnotized by the thermal goings-on hereabouts), you may want to throw the budget out the window and book in. What makes the **Geyserland Motor Hotel** that special is its panoramic view of the Whaka Thermal Reserve, just outside the windows of most of its 75 rooms. From your room with a window wall facing the reserve, you can watch the Pohutu Geyser shoot up as high as 50 feet in the air, and those steaming, bubbling mud pools will keep you posted at the window. The hotel itself has the usual luxury hotel trappings, with pretty and comfortable rooms, spa pools, swimming pool, and a first-class restaurant. If you lean toward luxury hotels, this one is as good as any; but as

I said, it's all that steam out there that makes it warrant space in a budget book, so if you book, be sure to specify that you want a room overlooking the thermal reserve, *not* a poolside room. Rates are NZ$43 ($28.86) single, NZ$52 ($34.90) double; children under 12 stay free in their parents' room. *Note:* From May 1 through the end of September they frequently run two-day special or weekend rates at substantial reductions—be sure to inquire. Just thought you'd want to know!

MEALS: You'll find the ever-dependable **Cobb & Co.**, with the usual colonial decor and good, inexpensive food, in the Grand Hotel on Hinemoa Street (tel. 82-089). It's fully licensed and serves a good selection of grills, seafoods, and light meals. There's a children's menu and half portions of some items. The average cost of main courses is NZ$5.50 ($3.69). Continuous service every day of the week from 7 a.m. to 10 p.m.

Portions are enormous, prices small, at **Karl's Restaurant**, 259 Tutanekai St. (tel. 80-231). Proprietor Victor Karl takes great pride in the reputation his establishment has earned over the years for providing some of the city's best meals at reasonable prices. Roast pork served with apple sauce and four vegetables, at an amazingly low NZ$6.50 ($4.36), is typical of the menu, which includes salads and curries in addition to traditional roasts. All come with potatoes, two vegetables, bread, and beverage, and prices run from NZ$4 ($2.68) to NZ$6.50 ($4.36). Hours are noon to 2 p.m. and 5 to 7:30 p.m., Monday to Saturday.

The **Homestead Tavern**, 71–77 Fairy Springs Rd. (tel. 80-665), is a rambling, redwood-stained, colonial-style place with an inviting veranda and landscaped grounds. It's a family restaurant, with children's meals at NZ$2.60 ($1.74), sandwiches and burgers at NZ$4.10 ($2.75), and main meals of fish, scallops, steak, chicken, and ham at NZ$5.60 ($3.75) to NZ$6.50 ($4.36). Old-fashioned pot pies are NZ$5.10 ($3.42). Lunch is served Monday through Saturday from noon to 2 p.m., dinner from 6 to 9 p.m., and the lounge (with entertainment Thursday, Friday, and Saturday evenings) is open from 11 a.m. to 10 p.m., until 11 p.m. on Friday and Saturday.

A local favorite (and likely to become one of yours, as well) is the **Lake Tavern Restaurant** on Lake Road (tel. 85-585), in a century-old building overlooking the lake and Ohinemutu village. In its younger days it served as a leading hotel, but now it's content to meet the eating and imbibing needs of its clientele. The dining room has wood booths with high backs and gold velvet seats, red carpeting and drapes, and impressive Maori portraits on the walls. The large bar and lounge is fitted out with comfortable divans and easy chairs facing large windows looking out onto the lake. Menu selections include steak, lamb, ham, chicken, and several kinds of seafood, as well as heaping salad plates. Main-course prices are in the NZ$5 ($3.36) to NZ$7 ($4.70) range (including salad and vegetables). Lunch hours Monday through Friday are noon to 2:30 p.m.; dinner, Monday through Saturday, 6 to 9 p.m. (to 9:30 p.m. on Friday and Saturday). Bar hours are 11 a.m. to 10 p.m. Although the dining room is fairly large, reservations are usually in order. Fully licensed, of course.

In an Olde English tavern setting livened up with touches of Robin Hood and Sherwood Forest, the **Friar Tuck,** on the corner of Arawa and Tutanekai Streets (tel. 81-492), specializes in fish and steaks, at good value-for-dollar prices. There's a special menu for children, and it's fully licensed (for the grownups). Main courses run from NZ$6.50 ($4.36) to NZ$9 ($6.04). Lunch hours are 11:30 a.m. to 2:30 p.m. Monday through Friday. Dinner is served from 5 to 10 p.m. daily (to 10 p.m. on Friday and Saturday).

The **Voyager Resort,** 107 Ranolf St. (tel. 479-594), has opened a lovely restaurant with a warm decor of gold and brown wallpaper, rust carpeting, olive-green velvet drapes, and silver-beige chairs. The menu is mainly French, not too extensive, and moderately priced (à la carte). Main courses such as steak with café de Paris butter, chicken marinated in lemon sauce, and pork schnitzel with mustard sauce are in the NZ$8.95 ($6.01) to NZ$9.95 ($6.68) range, with choice filet steak with mushrooms flamed in brandy the most expensive item at NZ$10.95 ($7.35). Lunch (with a less expensive menu) is served from noon to 1:30 p.m.; dinner, from 6 to 9 p.m.—seven days a week.

Fast-Foods Note

On the theory that you can drop in for a Big Mac almost anywhere in the world, I don't normally send readers to **McDonald's.** In Rotorua, however, I emphatically recommend that you go by the one on the corner of Fenton and Amohau Streets to view the exquisite wall-size carvings done by the Maori Arts and Crafts Institute. Kudos to McDonald's for this recognition of native culture.

Big Splurge

I could recommend the **Aorangi Peak Restaurant** on Mountain Road (tel. 86-957) for the view alone—its mountaintop perch looks down on a dazzling array of lakes and forests and the city—but when you add the elegant octagonal-shaped, split-level dining room and upstairs lookout lounge and cocktail bar, plus meals of gourmet quality, this is *the* place to splurge! (If you're into justifying splurges, just count a part of your dinner check as a sightseeing charge.) Shirley and Bill Barry believe that personal service and quality are equally important, so you'll get a bit of pampering. The international cuisine features such specialties as rabbit in cider, venison tournedos, and sesame scallops. Entertainment is provided on some Saturday nights. An average main-course price is NZ$12 ($8.05). Reservations essential.

A Hangi Meal and Concert

Hangi ("earth oven") cooking is traditional with the Maoris in preparing their communal meal. A large pit is filled with a wood fire topped by stones; then when the stones are heated through, baskets of food are placed on top and covered with damp cloths. Earth is then shoveled over all to create a natural steam oven. After about three hours, dinner is unveiled, with intermingling flavors of the various foods lightly touched by wood smoke.

There's a hangi feast every Saturday night of the year at the **International Hotel** on Froude Street on the edge of the Whaka Reserve (tel. 81-189), and every night of the week from October through March. The NZ$16.50 ($11.07) would put this in the splurge category were it not for the fact that it includes an hour-long Maori concert featuring first-class performers.

Hangi preparations begin long before your scheduled arrival at 6 p.m. By 3 p.m. the Ngawha (natural Maori rock steamer) is being filled: meats like wild pork, lamb, chicken, and venison go in first for longer cooking; vegetables such as pumpkin, kumara, potatoes, and watercress are placed on top. Don't show up any later than 6:30 p.m. or you'll miss the opening of the Ngawha, when a costumed Maori maiden lifts the food out with all due ceremony and leads a procession of food-bearing followers into the dining room, where it is spread on a buffet table. Accompaniments like marinated mussels, smoked eel, raw marinated fish, salads, Maori bread, and tamarillos (tree tomatoes) with fresh cream complete the eat-as-much-as-you-can-hold feast. The traditional hangi would never include desserts, but the International provides sweets and Pakeha beverages (tea, coffee, and wine). By 7 p.m., all is ready for you to dig in. Enjoy!

At 8 o'clock, an outstanding troupe of Maori singers and dancers will begin an hour-long concert of Polynesian dances, action songs, and pois. By any standards, this is a "money's worth" splurge.

If for some reason you can't make one of the evening performances, it's possible to attend a sort of mini-hangi at a slightly lower cost. The International often presents a luncheon hangi and 20-minute concert at lunchtime for tour groups, especially during summer months. Less ceremony, but still a good Maori feed and experience. You don't have to be a member of the tour to join in—just call ahead to see if a luncheon hangi is scheduled and book. Lunch begins at 12:30 p.m., and the cost is NZ$14 ($9.40).

Should you find the International booked solid, there's an equally fine hangi and concert at the **Geyserland Hotel** on Fenton Street (tel. 82-039) every Wednesday at 6 p.m. The price is NZ$15 ($10.06).

READERS' RESTAURANT SELECTIONS: "**J.J.'s Restaurant,** 36 Ranolf St., has a super lunch buffet at a very reasonable price. In the evening there's another spread with a much broader selection of foods, at about twice the lunch price. But we were happy with the several casseroles, deep-fried fish, 13 salads, and beautiful desserts that came with lunch. Terrific, and very attractive!" (Bill and Madelyn Poland, Kodiak, Alaska). . . . "Mila Whitworth runs **Simply Delicious,** and serves salads and crêpes—both sweet and savoury. She also has specials each day like spaghetti bolognese, Hungarian goulash, and curries. Mila is Polish originally, was married to an Englishman, and has traveled extensively. A good place to find inexpensive food other than just Kiwi fare!" (Mrs. Stuart Bamforth, Lower Hutt, New Zealand).

THINGS TO SEE AND DO: While "budget" usually translates as "do it yourself," there are two exceptionally good **tours** in Rotorua that will save you time and inconvenience, which in the long run can mean a dollar savings. One is the City Tour, the other a full-day Waimangu Round Trip, which has been one of the area's most popular tours since it began in 1902.

NZRRS operates a wide variety of tours, all of them good value. But the half-day City Tour (a misnomer, as you'll see) is an especially good value, since it gives you a good overlook at Rotorua highlights. If you're here for a short stay, I'd say this tour is a must. The coach departs the Travel Centre every morning at 9:30 a.m., shows you around the Government Gardens, moves on to the Maori suburb of Ohinemutu, out to Rainbow and Fairy Springs, back to the Maori Arts and Crafts Institute, and winds up with an escorted tour of the Whaka Thermal Reserve. The informative tour of the springs is only given to bus groups, a decided plus. Also, rather than waiting for a group to form to tour the Thermal Reserve, bus tours are met by a Maori guide and taken right through. The fair of NZ$13 ($8.72) for adults, NZ$6 ($4.03) for children, is a good buy. The following are points covered by the tour.

The Government Gardens

Stately **Tudor Towers** (one of New Zealand's oldest buildings) reigns over this downtown city park. The gardens themselves are a lovely mix of rose gardens, which are lit at night, croquet and bowl lawns, and steaming thermal pools. They're a delightful in-town resting spot, and the Tudor Towers provide worthwhile sightseeing. Inside, you'll find the **Rotorua Art Gallery,** displaying paintings of both native and international artists (NZ$.20 or 13¢ U.S., admission) as well as the small, but interesting **City of Rotorua Museum** (admission:

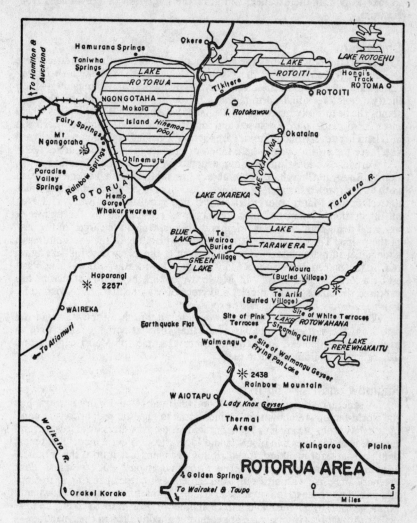

ROTORUA AREA

NZ$.50, or 33¢ U.S.). Built as a fashionable bathhouse along European spa lines, the Tudor Towers also houses a licensed restaurant.

The chief attraction at the gardens, however, is the **Polynesian Pools** (tel. 81-328) overlooking the lake. Here, for a mere pittance, you can experience the mineral pools at your leisure, for as long as you choose. There are pools open to the sky, enclosed pools, and private pools (for which you pay an additional NZ$2, or $1.34 U.S., cheap at the price for such luxury!). The soft alkaline water in the large pool maintains a constant temperature of about 100°F, while the smaller pools (reached along wooden walkways) contain waters high in sulfur and magnesium—very good for sore muscles—at temperatures of 80° to 110°F. There's a cafeteria serving light snacks and a souvenir shop. Admission is NZ$1.50 ($1.01) for adults, NZ$.50 (33¢) for children. As you enter, be sure to take a look at the excellent mural of the migration of Polynesians from Hawaiki.

Ohinemutu

This is the suburb, along the lake about half a mile north of the city, where the largest Arawa subtribe, the Ngati-whakaue, dwell. Although their residences are very much in the Pakeha style—small, everyday bungalows—their lifestyle holds to tribal custom. On a *marae* (open courtyard, or clearing) stands the beautifully hand-carved Tamatekapua meeting house. This is where most tribal matters are discussed and important decisions taken; concerts are also held here every night. Homes are thermally heated, and in every backyard you'll see the steam ovens where much of the family cooking is done.

Perhaps the most outstanding structure you'll see in Ohinemutu is **St. Faith's Anglican Church,** a remarkable representation of the Pakeha Christian faith as interpreted through Maori art. The Tudor-style church building holds a revelation of Maori color, intricate carving, exquisite scrollwork, and even an integration of ancient Maori religions, as represented by the figures of mythical demi-gods and their primitive subjects, which are carved in the base of the pulpit. There's a lovely, truly spiritual, blending of the two cultures in a magnificent plate-glass window looking out to the lake whose full-size figure of Christ is haloed, but clad in a Maori cloak of kiwi feathers. It was sandblasted by a local Pakeha artist, Mr. Mowbray, and in the figure's stance he has captured the unmistakable dignity and grace of Maori chieftains. A visit to St. Faith's is a touching, memorable experience.

Tombs of Maori tribal leaders are outside the church, all above ground and safe from the restless rumblings of all that thermal activity. Take time to explore the settlement, as there are other examples of Maori carving and decoration in buildings and statues.

Rainbow and Fairy Springs

A sanctuary—that's what you'll find at Rainbow and Fairy Springs. For the world-famous rainbow trout, which grow to gigantic proportions in complete safety from the angler's hook in these protected waters; for birds (several rare species); for trees and plants (some 135 varieties of fern, alone!); and most of all, perhaps, for mankind. As you follow the map (pick it up at the entrance) around a 350-yard path—meandering through deep bush thick with lush, dark greenery and alive with birdsong from those soaring free or resting in treetops and joined by those in the small aviary; stop to watch the antics of brown and rainbow trout, which push and butt each other in their haste to gobble up food pellets thrown by visitors; gaze at peacefully grazing deer in their paddock—there's an ease of mind that creeps in, bringing with it a sense of the harmony between man and nature, which has been achieved in this small patch of earth. Along the Fairy Springs walk, Maori myth takes on a little more reality when you see the spring from which more than five million gallons of water per day well up through the black and white sands. It isn't hard at all to credit the Maori belief that here is the home of the legendary Patupaiarehe, the fairy folk.

Rainbow and Fairy Springs are about 2½ miles from Rotorua, north of Ohinemutu. They're open every day from 8 a.m. to 5 p.m., and cost NZ$3 ($2.01) for adults, NZ$1 (67¢) for children. There's a good souvenir shop, a cafeteria for light snacks, and an attractive licensed restaurant for light, inexpensive meals. If you're not driving or on the City Tour described above, you can reach the Springs via the Ngongotaha bus that departs the Travel Centre.

New Zealand Maori Arts and Crafts Institute

On Rotorua's southern edge, just at the Whaka Reserve entrance, the Maori Arts and Crafts Institute exists for the sole purpose of keeping alive the ancient skills of Maori tribes. Youngsters are selected from all over the country to come here as apprentices to master craftspeople. Here, boys study carving for a minimum of three years, after which they may take their newly acquired skills back to their own tribes or stay on to become teachers at the institute. Girls learn to weave traditional cloaks and make the distinctive flax skirts and intricately patterned bodices. As a visitor, you are very welcome as an observer, and it's impossible not to respond to this perfect blending of beauty, myth, and spiritual symbolism as one generation passes a living heritage on to the next. Take away a lasting memento in the form of products made here and on sale in the attached shop. The institute is open every day from 8 a.m. to 5 p.m. with the exception of the carving school, which closes on Saturday, Sunday, and school holidays.

Whakarewarewa Thermal Reserve

To walk through the Whaka Thermal Reserve (one entrance is across from the institute) is to view the most dramatic concentration of Rotorua's thermal wonders. It is the home of many members of the Tuhourangi subtribe of the Arawas, and they will furnish a free Maori guide to show you through. While you're free to wander on your own, but I don't advise it for many reasons (you'll miss a *lot* of information, and you could just miss your footing and land in one of those boiling mud pools). Besides, who but a native who knows, understands, and respects this unique landscape could tell you the legends that interpret its many moods? If you must go alone, be sure to stay on the marked paths.

Inside the reserve, there's a model village patterned after Roto-whio, a pre-European village whose layout and construction has been faithfully reproduced. There are eight active geysers, which may perform for you if your timing is right (they don't operate on a fixed schedule, so it's a matter of luck). Adjoining **Prince of Wales Feathers Geyser** and **Pohutu Geyser** are particularly impressive and seem to have worked out an act that showcases them both. The Prince gets things started with a jet, which works up to 30 feet, at which time Pohutu goes into action, erupting to as much as 60 feet, with little offshoot eruptions, which sometimes more than double that height. They are, as I said unpredictable—eruptions have been clocked as little as two and as many as nine in a 24-hour period and lasting sometimes 20 minutes, sometimes only five. Whaka is open from 8:30 a.m. to 5 p.m. every day, and admission is NZ$3.50 ($2.35) for adults, NZ$1.75 ($1.17) for children.

At the Tryon Street entrance to Whaka Reserve (on the northern edge), you'll find the **Little Village,** which is, I suppose, a Pakeha answer to Whaka's Maori *pa*—it's a model of a European village of the 19th century. Around the village green are clustered colonial-style shops: a weavers cottage, newspaper office, gemstone shop, potter, and such. It's open daily.

Full-Day Waimangu Round Trip

This is the other organized tour, which has my wholehearted recommendation. And even though it entails a three-mile walk through steamy Waimangu Valley, unless you're really infirm it shouldn't be too strenuous. Just be sure to wear comfortable walking shoes. Bus departure is from the **Government Tourist Bureau,** 67 Fenton St. (tel. 85-179) at 9:30 a.m., and you'll return at 5 p.m. There are morning and afternoon tea stops, and you can bring your own lunch or purchase one from the tour operators for NZ$4 ($2.68). The fare is a hefty NZ$24 ($16.11) for adults, NZ$12 ($8.05) for children, but you'll cover 42 miles and the better portion of Rotorua's history.

Heading south past Whaka, you pass **Earthquake Flat** and a crater lake, which changes hue from green to blue every 36 hours, en route to **Waimangu Geyser.** Stilled now, it erupted regularly from 1900 to 1904, spewing rocks and earth as far as 1500 feet and claiming four lives before it fell silent. Its crater gave one gigantic, three-day-long last gasp in 1917, exploding with a violence, which flung debris as far as 1000 feet. Two weeks later the crater began to fill with water, and in a short time a six-acre boiling lake was formed, which has been aptly named **Frying Pan Lake.** Temperatures of the water from subterranean springs, which feed it average 210° at the surface, 315° in the depths.

From the lake you strike out on foot for 2½ miles to **Mount Tarawera,** which erupted in 1886 to destroy the famous pink and white silica terraces that had been a popular tourist attraction. Six European visitors lost their lives, and the 800-foot-deep hot Rotomahana Lake was formed. A launch takes you out on the lake, past steaming cliffs, which are stratified with brillant color—an incredible sight! At the end of the launch cruise, there's another half-mile walk to **Lake Tarawera,** one of the largest in the area and famed for its fishing. After a seven-mile cruise across the lake, with clear views of Mount Tarawera's blasted summit, you're met by coach to travel on to the nearby **Buried Village of Te Wairoa,** which perished in the Mount Tarawera eruption and has been excavated and well preserved. You'll also see the **Wairere Falls,** which descend 150 feet in three stages. The drive back to Rotorua passes both the Green and Blue Lakes and the Redwood Grove Forest. One suggestion: Those Polynesian Pools may be the perfect end to a full and satisfying day!

The Agrodome

Maybe it's because the shearing of sheep has been a romantic thing for me since I saw Robert Mitchum in *The Sundowners* years ago that I found the Agrodome performance so intriguing I went back for a second show! Whatever the reason, it *is* a highlight of any Rotorua visit, and I expect to be in the audience any time I'm in the neighborhood. Located four miles north of Rotorua, the Agrodome, Riverdale Park (tel. 74-350), is a huge (7000 square feet) octagonal building in a 200-acre pastureland, which displays rams of 19 different breeds of sheep in a 60-minute show that packs into an entertaining and delightful commentary more information on the engaging creatures than you probably thought existed. Each ram is released from his paddock to climb onto a pedestal while the recorded voice of champion shearer Godfrey Bowen tells you about its breed—its origins, primary uses of the wool or meat, its importance in New Zealand's sheep industry, etc. When all 19 are in place on the platform, a master shearer explains the tricks of his trade and proceeds to demonstrate his skill on a sheep you'd swear was luxuriating in the whole thing if you hadn't just been told that its relaxation is the result of one of those tricks. The shearer then whistles in his sheep dog and puts him through a few paces before inviting you to come down front, meet the dog and rams personally, and snap any photos you'd like before the entire audience adjourns outside to witness a fascinating demonstration of the dog's response to a series of a few simple commands. If you have any interest whatsoever in sheep (and even if you don't, try it—you're sure to like it!), you'll love this show.

There are Agrodome performances at 10:30 a.m. and 2:30 p.m. every day (with additional shows during heavy tourist seasons), with admissions of NZ$3 ($2.01) for adults and NZ$1 (67¢) for children. Incidentally, the shop at the

Agrodome has been the source of two of my most prized New Zealand purchases—both the selection and the prices are excellent.

Whakarewarewa State Forest Park

This popular state forest has an entrance right on the outskirts of town, a nice walk into the dark beauty of native trees and bush. Among other things, it holds a stand of fine redwoods transplanted from California and dedicated to the men of New Zealand's Forest Service who gave their lives in both world wars. The **Forestry Information and Visitor Centre** is just off Long Mile Road, and inside you'll find interesting displays on the history and management of the country's forests and forest industries, as well as a helpful staff.

AFTER DARK: Tops on any after-dark activities list would have to be the hangi feast and Maori concert described in "Meals," if one is scheduled for the night in question. Otherwise, check *This Week in Rotorua* for dine-and-dance venues or special events. Or just skip the rest and plan on a Maori concert. You won't be sorry.

A Maori Concert

In my personal opinion, one should not come to Rotorua and leave without taking in a Maori concert. It is the ultimate expression of so much of the culture that has sustained these enduring people over the centuries. There are several possibilities. Concerts are presented every night at **Tamatekapua Meeting House** in Ohinemutu at 8 p.m.—adults pay NZ$5 ($3.36); children, NZ$2.50 ($1.68)—and at various hotels on selected nights. One of the best (and most comfortable) hotel presentations is at **Tudor Towers** in the Government Gardens (tel. 81-825), where the performance is at 8:30 p.m. every night during the high season, at a cost of NZ$4 ($2.68) for adults, NZ$2 ($1.34) for children. You can come along at 7 p.m., have dinner, and stay for the cabaret show following the concert, for NZ$9 ($6.04). In either case, be sure to go early to get a good seat.

All the performers in these concerts are locals, not professionals, and they're performing for the fun of it. That fun is contagious, with the audience given a warm traditional Maori welcome and invited to join in the closing "Now Is The Hour," an authentic Maori farewell melody. By the time you join in that lifting of voices, you'll have seen intricate hand games, action songs depicting contemporary events, delicate and difficult *pois,* and earthshaking *hakas* accompanied by the ancient chants used to frighten enemies during battle.

Briefly, hand games are highly stylized sports that sharpen the reflexes of young warriors; action songs tell a story or deliver a message through Maori words (often set to popular tunes) and hand and arm movements; *poi* dances are the province of only the women, performed with small flax balls attached to a string and twirled in graceful patterns to suggest the flight of birds; and the *haka* is a posture war dance performed before battle to scare the wits out of enemies through wild leaps and ferocious facial expressions accompanied by the uniquely Maori tactic of sticking out the tongue.

Following most concerts, you'll be able to purchase records and tapes to take back home and relive a joyous occasion.

WHERE TO GO FROM HERE: Limited time will point you from Rotorua to Taupo, the Tongariro National Park, and Wanganui. For those who can spare a few days, however, there is a glorious drive awaiting around what is called New Zealand's **Sunrise Coast,** since it is the place where the sun is first seen each morning. Magnificent seascapes (some of the most exciting in the country), secluded coves and bays, deserted beaches, tiny Maori settlements, and finally the Poverty Bay town of **Gisborne** and Hawkes Bay's crowning jewel, **Napier.** It's an area alive with history, both Maori and Pakeha. You'll see where the Arawa canoe made landfall; where Capt. James Cook first saw the New Zealand mainland and where he stopped on his second voyage; where ferocious, decisive battles between Maori and Europeans were fought; and along the way there are some of the finest examples of Maori carvings in New Zealand.

This swing around the Sunrise Coast is an off-the-beaten-track digression, which I strongly urge you take if you can fit it into your timetable. It's a bit of New Zealand far too many visitors miss. If you just don't have the time, skip this section and proceed to **Taupo.**

The drive to Taupo is a short 52 miles over excellent roads. Five miles before you reach Taupo, look for the steamy **Wairakei Geothermal Project,** which harnesses all that underground energy to furnish electrical power. More about that in Chapter V.

2. The Sunrise Coast

There are two ways of commencing the splendid East Cape drive from Rotorua: head northeast on Highway 30 for Whakatane, a 57-mile drive; or drive due north for 55 miles to Tauranga, then turn east on Highway 2 for the 62-mile stretch to Whakatane. I'd say that decision rests on where your own interests lie. **Tauranga,** and its adjacent Bay of Plenty resort/port of Mount Maunganui, is now a peaceful center of citrus fruit farming, but its history is one of fierce battles, both in intertribal Maori wars and between the British and Maoris. There's a **Public Relations Office** on the Strand (tel. 88-103) that can direct you to several interesting historical spots, including "The Camp," site of a clifftop military settlement, and the **Tauranga Mission House,** built by an early missionary and one of the finest examples of colonial architecture of its time (1838). Some 12½ miles away, **Mount Maunganui** is a leading port, but is known and loved by thousands of Kiwis for its Ocean Beach, a stretch of golden sand along what is called the best surfing beach in New Zealand. Also, just off Marine Parade there's a very good aquarium, **Marineland,** where resident seals and fish are housed in pools shaped from rocks, and beyond Marineland, the Blowhole becomes a spectacular saltwater geyser in heavy seas. It is from Highway 2 (a little over 27 miles east of Tauranga) on the drive to Whakatane that you can take a short detour to the little settlement of **Maketu** and see the cairn which marks the house, a beautiful example of Maori carving. Tauranga makes an interesting prelude to the East Cape Drive if time permits.

At **Whakatane,** stop by the **Public Relations Office** on Commerce Street (tel. 60-58) for details on some of the more interesting sights in the town and nearby. This is the legendary settling place of Toi (see the Introduction) on his search for his grandson Whatonga, and the earthworks out on the road to Ohope are traditionally held to be those of his *pa*. It is also the landing place of the great Mataatua canoe, part of the Hawaiki migration fleet. A model of that canoe can be seen next to the imposing rock arch known as **Pohaturoa Rock** (once part of a sacred Maori cave and now a memorial to those who died in World War I). On Mataatua Street, right in the center of town, you'll see the beautiful **Wairere Waterfall.**

Some 37 miles east of Whakatane, Highway 2 brings you to Opotiki and State Road 35, known as the **East Cape Road,** which hugs the coastline for most of its 213-mile route up around New Zealand's most easterly point and down to Gisborne on Poverty Bay. The drive—breathtaking in any season—is a heart-stopper during the Christmas season, when hundreds of pohutukawa trees burst into brilliant scarlet blooms along the cliffs overlooking the sea. All along, you'll find lovely deserted beaches, sea views, and native bush, which combine to make this one of New Zealand's finest scenic drives. This, as you might suspect, is an area with a heavy Maori population, and most of the small villages and towns you'll pass through either still are, or once were, Maori centers. Sadly, some of the most exquisite Maori carvings from the area have been removed: the Auckland War Museum's Te Toki-a-tapiri war canoe and Wellington's National Museum's Te Hau-ki-Turanga meeting house and Nuku te Whatewha storehouse all came from this region. There are, however, still outstanding examples of the art to be seen along the drive.

Many people decide to break the long drive (about eight hours if you stay behind the wheel) with an overnight stop, and I'll tell you about accommodations possibilities. Campers will find ample facilities along the way.

Opotiki was once a large Maori settlement, but today is best known for its **Church of St. Stephen the Martyr,** scene of the particularly brutal murder of German Lutheran missionary Carl Sylvius Volkner in 1865. Blood-stained relics of that grim event are on exhibit in the church. At **Te Kaha,** Tu Kaihi meeting house in the *marae* just across from the post office has an elaborately carved lintel you'll be welcome to view if you ask permission before entering the *marae.* A little farther along, **Waihau Bay** has good views across Cape Runaway (so named by Captain Cook as he watched Maori canoes "run away" when shots were fired over their heads), as well as very good beaches. **Whangaparaoa** is where the great migration canoe *Tainui* landed—its captain's wife is credited with bringing the kumara to New Zealand. One of the many turnoffs that will tempt you is that at **Lottin Point** (it's signposted), where a 2½-mile drive through farmland leads to the coast and grasslands growing right to the water's edge.

Hicks Bay could well be your overnight stop. It's not quite midway, but has marvelous views, a modern motel, and one of the finest carved meeting houses on the East Cape. Its name comes from one of Captain Cook's officers, who first sighted it, and it was the site of a tragic Maori massacre in which one European was killed and eaten on his wedding night (after which complaints were registered that he was too tough and stringy to be tasty!). Turn left at the post office to reach the **Tuwhakairiora meeting house,** whose carvings were done in 1872. It is dedicated to local members of the Ngati Porou tribe who died in overseas wars, and its unique rafter design (found only in this region) is symbolic of the honor of death in battle for the warrior.

A little farther along, the road descends to sea level to follow the narrow bay to where the little town of **Te Araroa** nestles under the cliffs. Thirteen miles east of Te Araroa, along an all-weather road, stands the East Cape Lighthouse, in an isolated, difficult-to-reach location. There's been a light here since 1906. The track to the lighthouse must be covered by foot, and it leads up some 600 steps—perhaps a look from afar will suffice.

One of New Zealand's most ornate Maori churches is **Tikitiki's St. Mary's Church,** a memorial to Maori soldiers who died in World War I. The carved panels and rafter patterns depict Ngati Porou tribal history, and two world war hero brothers are featured in the east window. Closer to Gisborne, you can view another beautifully carved modern meeting house near the wharf at **Tokomaru Bay.** This is where a brave band of women, two warriors, and three whalers successfully defended a headland *pa* from attack by a large enemy force. **Anaura Bay,** just 43 miles from Gisborne, was Captain Cook's landing place on his second New Zealand voyage. The *Endeavour* hung around for two days trying to get watercasks beyond the surf before heading south for a better watering place. At **Whangara,** just 17 miles away from Gisborne, if you ask permission to visit the local *marae,* you can see a carved meeting house, which features a black whale with a Maori on its back. It represents the legend of *Paikea,* who arrived in New Zealand riding a whale. And Gisborne, of course, was the place Captain Cook *first* sighted the New Zealand mainland (more about that later).

It must be said that for those who simply wish to reach Gisborne from the Bay of Plenty, there's a shorter, faster way to get there than around the East Cape. Highway 2 is a pleasant, three-hour drive through green farmlands, native bush, along rushing mountain rivers, and through **Waioeka Gorge**—not a bad drive, mind you, but nothing to compare with the East Cape.

ACCOMMODATIONS EN ROUTE: Tiny Waihau Bay is where you'll find recommended accommodations in the **Waihau Bay Lodge** (tel. 804). It's been a guest house since 1914, has a licensed restaurant, and is close to a fine beach and good fishing. Rates are NZ$20 ($13.42) per person for the eight rooms (one single, four doubles, and three triples).

Be sure to book ahead at the **Hicks Bay Motor Lodge** (tel. Te Araroa 0819/880). They have self-contained kitchen units, as well as serviced rooms with tea-making facilities, a tourist-licensed restaurant and house bar, and a shop on the premises. Rates run from NZ$32 ($21.48) to NZ$38 ($25.50) for one or two people, NZ$9.50 ($6.38) per extra person. (There's a surcharge for a one-night stay.) Across from the motel there's an interesting bush walk, and there's also a glowworm grotto in back.

At Te Araroa, you will find the country's most easterly hostelry, the **Kawa Kawa Hotel** (mailing address: P.O. Box 64; tel. 809). It is licensed and is known for its restaurant. There's also a take-away food bar. Rooms are simple, with either baths or showers, and rates are NZ$20 ($13.42) single, NZ$35 ($23.49) double.

3. Gisborne

Because of its closeness to the International Date Line, Gisborne is judged to be the most easterly city in the world and the first to see the sun's rays each morning. It's also the place where New Zealand's European history began. Capt. James Cook's *Endeavour* entered these waters in early October 1769, and it fell the lot of the 12-year-old surgeon's boy, Nicholas Young, to be the first to sight land—a fact that must have caused some consternation among the rest of the crew, since the good captain had promised a gallon of rum as a reward, two if the sighting should be at night! True to another promise, Captain Cook named the white bluffs the boy had seen at the southern end of the bay's wide entrance "Young Nick's Head." As for Young Nick, he is also celebrated by a statue in Churchill Park on Awapuni Road. It was two days later, on October 9, 1769, that a party ventured forth from the ship, and after a series of misunderstandings with Maoris over the next two days (during which one native was killed when the English thought he was trying to steal a beached longboat, another when he reached toward a sword, and four more when they resisted being taken aboard the *Endeavour* from their canoe) he found it impossible to gain Maori cooperation in gathering the fresh water and provisions he needed. Small wonder! At any rate, he left in disgust, writing in his journal that he was sailing "out of the bay, which I have named *Poverty Bay* because it afforded us no one thing we wanted."

One thing is a virtual certainty: had Captain Cook gotten off on the right foot with the natives, a name incorporating the word "poverty" would never have occurred to him! Gisborne is in fact in the very center of one of New Zealand's most fertile areas, with a balmy climate that sees more than 2215 hours of bright sunshine annually. It's a gardenland of vegetable farms and orchards bearing citrus fruits, grapes, and kiwi fruit. Dairy and sheep farms prosper. That sunny climate, combined with beaches that offer ideal swimming, surfing, and fishing conditions, also make it a holiday resort that is becoming increasingly popular with Kiwis from all over the North Island.

ORIENTATION: Gisborne is situated on the northern shore of Poverty Bay where the Waimata and Taruheru Rivers come together to form the Turanganui. Riverside park areas abound, and most bridges were built for pedestrian as well as vehicular traffic. The city center is compact, with Gladstone Road a main thoroughfare.

USEFUL INFORMATION: The **Public Relations Office (PRO)** is located at 209 Grey St. (tel. 86-139), where Alison Thompson offers enthusiastic assistance to visitors from 9 a.m. to 5 p.m. Monday through Friday, and there is 24-hour telephone information service at the above number. . . . For information on suburban bus services, phone 4741 between the hours of 8 a.m. and 5 p.m. . . . A public ladies' **rest room** with a changing room for infants and child-care center is open 9:30 a.m. to 5 p.m. Monday through Friday, at the Peel Street end of Palmerston Road. . . . Gisborne is served by NZRRS and Mount Cook Line coaches, Air New Zealand flights, and NZR rail service to Napier and Wellington.

ACCOMMODATIONS: Accommodations are plentiful in Gisborne, and they include a wide variety of types and price ranges.

A Hostel

The **Gisborne YHA Hostel,** 32 Harris St., on the corner of Wainui Road (tel. 83-269), is in a relaxed urban setting close to beaches and major sightseeing. There are 38 beds in four rooms, communal showers, and kitchen. Across the street there's a food shop open seven days a week. Seniors pay NZ$4 ($2.68); Juniors, NZ$2 ($1.34).

Cabins

Gisborne has two excellent motor camps run by the City Council. Both are handy to good swimming and surfing beaches, both are kept spotless, and both provide above-average facilities. During high season (summer months), advance bookings are absolutely necessary, as both are extremely popular with Kiwis.

The **Waikanae Beach Motor Camp,** at the beach end of Grey Street (tel. 75-634), has brown-wood blocks of cabins arranged U-shape around a grassy courtyard with attractive plantings. There are tourist cabins, which sleep four in two twin-bedded rooms and have private toilet and shower, refrigerator, gas range, crockery, cutlery and cooking utensils; you supply linen and blankets. Charges: NZ$14 ($9.40) for the first two persons, NZ$3.50 ($2.35) for each additional. Double-unit cabins (both units share two gas stoves, H&C sinks, and shower) sleep five in each unit, and you must supply linen, blankets, crockery, cutlery, and cooking utensils. Charges: NZ$10 ($6.71) for the first two persons, NZ$3 ($2.01) for each additional. There's a complex of two-bedroom units, sleeping four and sharing a kitchen, dining room, and recreational building that is provided specifically for these units. Charges: NZ$6.50 ($4.36) per night for two persons, NZ$5.50 ($3.69) for one. Tent sites are NZ$4 ($2.68) for the first two; NZ$2 ($1.34) for each additional; and caravan sites with power points are NZ$4.50 ($3.02) for the first two; NZ$2 ($1.34) for each additional. On the premises is a large laundry, kitchen, showers, children's play area, and tennis courts. The beautiful and safe Waikanae Beach is just across the road, and the city center is an easy walk away.

You can book into a cell if you like, at the **Churchill Park Motor Camp,** on Salisbury Road (tel. 45-55). Well, it isn't a cell any more—just part of the converted jail building, which now holds nine cabin units and a community kitchen at this lovely beachfront motor camp. They're simply furnished with bunks, tables, and chairs. You supply linen, blankets, crockery, cutlery, and cooking utensils. Those with four bunks go for NZ$6.50 ($4.36) *per cabin;* those with six, for NZ$10 ($6.71). You supply only linens and blankets in the tourist cabins, each with two bedrooms (twin beds in each), gas range, fridge, hot and cold shower, and handbasin. Charges: NZ$14 ($9.40) for the first two persons, NZ$3.50 ($2.35) for each additional. Caravan- and tent-site charges are the same as at Waikanae Beach Motor Camp. Laundry facilities are on the premises. Churchill Park Motor Camp is immediately adjacent to the town's Olympic-size swimming pool, adventure playground, and outdoor theater, in addition to being right at Midway Beach and only three-quarters of a mile from the city center.

Bed and Breakfast

I found what is probably my favorite New Zealand bed and breakfast courtesy of one of our readers, who wrote to say, "Mrs. Atkinson is a lovely woman who is dedicated to providing good, clean, homey lodging at a reasonable price." He was writing of Mrs. Norma Atkinson, who with her husband Alf and daughter Glenda run **Greengables Travel Hotel,** 31 Rawiri St. (tel. 75-619), and she certainly lives up to our reader's rave! Greengables is an old house, set in shaded grounds and approached by a rose-bordered walk, which has been renovated (without losing one bit of its original charm) by the Atkinsons. There are nine spacious rooms (two of them singles, for you loners), all with H&C and nicely furnished, which share four baths. My own favorite is on the ground floor and has a pretty bay window. The old-fashioned lounge has a pot-bellied stove, and the attractive dining room looks out onto the lawn. This is a friendly, helpful family who provide Kiwi hospitality at its best—and one of the best breakfasts you'll find in Kiwiland. Rates are NZ$18 ($12.08) per person, and you can have the evening meal for NZ$7 ($4.70)—place your order early in the day.

Another very popular bed and breakfast is the **Aloha Travel Lodge,** 335 Childers Rd. (tel. 87-525), which has earned many return guests with its comfort and hospitality. Run by Mr. and Mrs. R. T. Ferdinando (alias Ferdy and Vera), this is also in an old home that has been modernized. It's in a central, but quiet location close to bus and rail stations and the city center. The ground floor holds rooms that can only be called luxury, with private facilities; all other rooms have H&C and share bath facilities. There's one paraplegic unit. There's a guest kitchen with tea-making facilities, a TV lounge, and car park. Rates for bed and breakfast are NZ$18 ($12.08) single, NZ$30 ($20.13) double, for rooms with H&C only; NZ$24 ($16.11) single, NZ$33 ($22.15) double, for those with private baths.

Motel Flats

My top motel recommendation in Gisborne goes to the **Best Western Gisborne Motel,** 509 Gladstone Rd. (tel. 88-899). Its spacious units all have glass window walls to let in that gorgeous sunshine, and all are nicely furnished. There's a guest laundry, heated spa pool, children's play equipment, and car wash. All units have full kitchens, but cooked and continental breakfasts are also available. But most of all, owner-operators Alison and Peter Fitzgerald are the epitome of friendly helpfulness. Relatively new to Gisborne, they love the area and set out to see that you have that same affection for it by the time you leave. The location is a short drive (longish walk) into the city center. Rates here are NZ$32 ($21.48) single, NZ$40 ($26.85) double, and of course the BW Holiday Pass discount is honored.

The **Teal Motor Lodge,** 479 Gladstone Rd. (tel. 84-019), is something a little different—it's a New Zealand motel with a decidedly Oriental flavor. Set on almost two acres of shaded and landscaped lawns, the spacious rooms have an airy look, with exposed beams and stained timber exteriors, and exciting color combinations in decor throughout. There's a restful air about the place that I especially like. Some units have full kitchens; there's one roomy unit with two bedrooms; and there are 26 serviced rooms with tea-making facilities. Units sleep from two to six. Rates for serviced rooms are NZ$26 ($17.45) to NZ$30 ($20.13); flats run NZ$33 ($22.15) single, NZ$42 ($28.19) double.

Self-Catering Flat

Alison and Eric Thompson (she's the PRO in Gisborne) have a lovely old home, high on a hill in the Whautopoka section overlooking the city and Poverty Bay, with a self-contained flat on one side of the ground floor. It has a separate entrance, its own porch overlooking green fields in the back of the house, one bedroom, lounge, and kitchen—perfect for a couple, and Alison can bring in a cot if there are children. The Thompsons raise sheep on the hills out back, and there are great walks close by. All bookings *must* be made well in advance: write Alison at 22 Hill Rd. (tel. 89-795), or reach her at the PRO during office hours. The rate is NZ$40 ($26.85) double.

MEALS: For the best in budget meals, you can't beat **Woolworths Family Restaurant,** at the corner of Gladstone Road and Bright Street. In a large, brick-walled room with deep red carpet and dark-wood booths and tables, there's a good selection of grills, sandwiches, meat pies, salad plates, and a mini-salad plate (not all that "mini," except in price—NZ$2.80 or $1.88 U.S.). Prices are as low as NZ$.45 (30¢) for some sandwiches, and go up to NZ$5.50 ($3.69) for fish, ham, chicken, and beef plates. Hours are 8:30 a.m. to 4 p.m. Monday through Thursday, open until 7:30 p.m. on Friday, and on Saturday from 9 a.m. to noon.

Out on Solander Street, near the Poverty Bay Golf Course, you'll find **The Roadhouse** (tel. 87-582), a family restaurant run by Pru and Merv Clayden. In this bright, cheerful eatery, you can find something for almost every taste, and all at bargain prices. Fish and chips; light meals of steak sandwich, quiche, or beefburger; seafoods; grills; salads, including a very good vegetarian salad plate; and luscious homemade desserts and pastries—at prices that range from NZ$2.50 ($1.34) to NZ$10 ($6.71). There's a children's menu with a top price of NZ$2.60 ($1.74), and half servings of most main meals are available. You can bring along your own wine or beer. Hours are 6:30 a.m. to 10 p.m. Monday through Thursday, till 11 p.m. on Friday, and on Saturday from 8 a.m. to 1 p.m. and 5 to 11 p.m.

Chez Julie, on Gladstone Road in the block by the town clock (tel. 84-814), is a cozy little place with red-and-white checked tablecloths, wrought-iron chairs, and tables separated by bamboo screens. The specialty here is pancakes with fillings like boysenberry, bananas, strawberries. There's also an excellent à la carte menu for all three meals, with roasts, fish, chicken, etc., main courses in the NZ$4.50 ($3.02) to NZ$7 ($4.70) range. Breakfast runs NZ$3 ($2.01) to NZ$5 ($3.36). It's open seven days a week, and hours are 7 to 9 a.m., noon to 2 p.m., and 5 to 10 p.m.

There are two good restaurants in the **Sandown Park Motor Hotel,** on Childers Street (tel. 84-134). **Longjohn's** is a fun sort of place, with a large longboat filled with seats running down the center, a bricked barbecue grill over on one side (you select your own meat and can cook it yourself if you wish), a bar on the other, and entertainment every night except Sunday, when it's closed. Prices, which include a salad bar with unlimited servings, run NZ$4.50 ($3.02) to NZ$5 ($3.36) for lamb, chicken, fish, and ham; NZ$5 ($3.36) to NZ$5.50 ($3.69) for choice steaks. Hours are noon to 2 p.m. and 5 to 9 p.m. every day except Sunday.

For more elegant dining at the Sandown, try the **Gazebo,** a pretty garden-style restaurant with a window wall overlooking the hotel's landscaped grounds. It's a warm, relaxed room, and the food is first rate. Main courses include a nice selection of seafood, beef, lamb, chicken, and veal at prices of NZ$7.50 ($5.03) to NZ$15 ($10.06). On Sunday night there's a family-night buffet from 6 to 8 p.m., and during the summer an outdoor barbecue on Sunday from 5:30 p.m.

Note: While it certainly isn't in the budget class, the Sandown has exceptionally nice accommodations in a beautiful location at rates of NZ$38 ($25.50) single, NZ$46 ($30.87) double.

THINGS TO SEE AND DO: To get a panoramic view of Poverty Bay, the city, its harbor and rivers, head for **Kaiti Hill Lookout.** It is signposted at the northern end of Gladstone Bridge, and you can drive most of the way, walking the last little bit to a brick semicircular lookout point at the very edge of the hill. There's a statue of Captain Cook there that looks suspiciously like Napoleon (notice the hand in the jacket, so characteristic of "The Little Emperor") looking out toward Young Nick's Head on the opposite side of the bay. There are three telescopes for a closer look, and a plaque identifies points of interest.

At the foot of Kaiti Hill, you'll pass one of New Zealand's largest Maori meeting houses, **Poho-o-rawiri.** It's so large that the traditional construction of a single ridgepole supported by pillars had to be abandoned in favor of more modern methods. All its carvings (which are splendid) were done in Rotorua. You'll usually find the side door open; if not, look up the caretaker, who lives just next door.

Also at the bottom of Kaiti Hill, on Kaiti Beach Road, there's a memorial on what is thought to be the spot on which Captain Cook landed, as well as a cannon, which may or may have been salvaged from the wreck of the *En-*

deavour (seems there's some dispute because it's made of iron, while Captain Cook's ship supposedly carried brass cannon).

Canadians will want to go by **Alfred Cox Park** in Grey Street to see the giant totem pole, which the Canadian government presented to New Zealand in 1969 to mark the Cook Bicentenary and to acknowledge the debt both countries owe that great explorer.

This area is filled with historic *pa* sites in the hills behind Poverty Bay Flats—ask at the PRO for information if you'd like to poke around a bit. There are also some excellent walkways in the area, and the PRO can furnish detailed trail booklets.

Swimmers and surfers will want to take advantage of the superb surf at both Waikanae and Midway Beaches. Smallfry (as well as the young at heart) will enjoy the **Adventure Park** and Young Nick's Playground (which has a commemorative statue to that enterprising young fellow).

There is excellent **fishing** in these waters, both offshore and in the rivers. You can arrange charter boats and guides through the PRO. Anglers will want to ask for the *Guide to Trout Fishing in the Gisborne Area*, compiled by the Gisborne Anglers Club.

The **Gisborne Museum & Arts Centre**, 18–22 Stout St. (tel. 83-832), has displays depicting Maori and Pakeha history along the East Coast, as well as geological and natural exhibits. The Art Gallery hosts traveling New Zealand exhibitions as well as those of local artists and craftspeople. It's open 10 a.m. to 4:30 p.m. Tuesday through Friday, 2 to 4:30 p.m. on Saturday, Sunday, and holidays. Adults pay NZ$.80 (54¢); children and students, free. There's an open-air restaurant for light snacks. No charge when you visit the **Maori Arts and Craft Centre** at the corner of Customhouse Street and Childers Road to see carving, weaving, and other crafts, and browse through the souvenir shop.

Spectacular scenic flights of the area are provided by **Air Gisborne Ltd.** at the Gisborne Airport (tel. 46-84). The 15-minute "Town and Around" flight costs NZ$11 ($7.38) per person, and there are several others, ranging upward in price to the NZ$29 ($19.46) "Captain Cook Special," a 45-minute flight, which flies over all prominent historic and sightseeing spots, as well as East Coast cattle and sheep stations. Children under 10 fly for half fare when accompanied by an adult, and there's a minimum requirement of two adults.

ON TO NAPIER: The 146-mile drive along Highway 2 from Gisborne to Napier passes through some of the most picturesque natural scenery in the country. Rugged hill-country sheep stations, lush native bush, Lake Tutira, and a breathtaking view of Poverty Bay Flats from the top of the Wharerata Hills some 23 miles outside the city. Incidentally, if you're traveling by public transport, opt for rail on this segment of your trip—the train hugs the coastline for long stretches, giving gorgeous sea views not visible from the highway farther inland.

4. Napier

Hawkes Bay has been called the "Greenhouse of New Zealand" because of its sunny climate and ideal growing conditions for all kinds of vegetables, citrus fruits, and grapes. Indeed, when you see the expanse of vineyards, you may well think of it as the "Winery of New Zealand." Its high-spirited resort center is Napier, one of the country's most delightful holiday spots. Spread around the wedge of Bluff Hill (which was virtually an island when Captain Cook described it on his voyage south from Poverty Bay), Napier was founded by whalers in the mid-1800s. You won't find any trace of those early settlers in today's city, however: in 1931 an earthquake of such violence that it was recorded as far away as Cairo and Calcutta demolished the entire city and nearby Hastings, killing hundreds of people. In its aftermath, not only did a completely new city arise, but it arose on *new ground,* for the quake had lifted the inner harbor floor, creating 10,000 acres of dry land—the present airport, for instance, was under water prior to 1931.

ORIENTATION: The pride—and showplace—of Napier is its **Marine Parade,** a beautiful stretch of waterfront lined with stately Norfolk pines. Many visitor activities center around the Marine Parade, which holds a wide variety of attractions. **Kennedy Road,** the principal thoroughfare, diagonally bisects the town. The best beach in the area is **Westshore Beach,** located in Westshore Domain, part of the new-land legacy of the 1931 disaster.

USEFUL INFORMATION: You'll find the **Information Centre and Public Relations Office** (tel. 54-949 or 57-182) at one end of the Marine Parade. Hours are 8:30 a.m. to 5 p.m. weekdays, and from Christmas to mid-February, also 9 a.m. to 4 p.m. on Saturday and Sunday. Racks are filled with helpful brochures, maps, a Visitor's Guide, and a scenic drive route. Personable Brian Cotter and his staff can also help with accommodations, and book fishing, boating, golf, and sightseeing excursions. . . . **Mount Cook Line** (tel. 435-919) has coach service to Taupo (both directions) three times daily. . . . **Newman's Coach Lines** depot is located in Thackeray Street one block from the railway station (tel. 52-009). . . . There is rail service to Wellington and Gisborne: the **railway station** is on Station Street, 2½ blocks down from the Air New Zealand office. . . . **Air New Zealand** has service to Auckland, Wellington, Gisborne, and Christchurch: office at the corner of Hastings and Stations Streets (tel. 55-588). . . . There's no airport bus into town: taxi fare is about NZ$5 ($3.36). . . . Taxi **sightseeing tours** (prearranged or your own) are available for NZ$12.50 ($8.39) an hour regardless of the number of passengers (up to five). . . . The **Chief Post Office (CPO)** is on the corner of Hastings and Dickens Streets.

ACCOMMODATIONS: As befits a leading resort, Napier is blessed with a wide variety of good accommodations: a very good hostel; bed and breakfast right on Marine Parade; a wealth of good motels out on Kennedy Road; and an outstanding motor camp right in the heart of town.

Hostels

Napier's **YHA Hostel** couldn't have a better location—it's right on the beachfront, across the street from Marineland, at 47 Marine Parade (tel. 57-039). The former guest house has 47 beds in 27 rooms. Front rooms overlook the bay; there's a pleasant kitchen and dining room; the lounge offers TV, a pool table, and piano; and there are laundry facilities. Seniors pay NZ$5 ($3.36); Juniors, NZ$2.50 ($1.68).

Halfway between Napier and Hastings, just off Highway 2 in Clive, there's another small **YHA Hostel** (19 beds in four rooms). It's not nearly as nice as the one in Napier, but all the basics are there; there's a swimming pool next door, and you can buy fresh fruits and vegetables from nearby roadside stands.

The mailing address is P.O. Box 27, Clive (tel. 662). Seniors pay NZ$3 ($2.01); Juniors, NZ$1.50 ($1.01).

Cabins

It's hard to find superlatives strong enough for Napier's **Kennedy Park Motor Camp** on Storkey Street, off Kennedy Road (tel. 439-126). If you've been impressed with Kiwi motor camps in general, just *wait* until you see this one! Set in 17 acres of trees, grass, and colorful flowers (including an acre and a half of roses!), with top-grade accommodations, this has to be the "Ritz" of New Zealand camps. Those accommodations run the gamut, from tent sites to ungraded cabins to graded (two-star) cabins to tourist flats and motel units. Ten sites with no power run NZ$4 ($2.68) per person when there's more than one, those with power just NZ$.20 (13¢) more; singles pay NZ$4.50 ($3.02) and NZ$6.50 ($4.36). Ungraded cabins come with beds, tables, and chairs, and you supply cooking and eating utensils, linen and blankets, and use the communal toilet and shower facilities. Rates are NZ$12 ($8.05) for two. The 16 graded cabins sleep four (plus rollaway bed if needed), have easy chairs, and are furnished with H&C sinks, fridge, range, electric jug, toaster, crockery, cutlery, frying pan, pots, and utensils. You supply linen and blanket, and use the communal toilet and shower facilities. Doubles pay NZ$18 ($12.08). Tourist flats fill that gap between cabins and motel units—they're actually of motel quality, but lack such extras as a TV, telephone, etc., and they're not serviced. You supply linen and blankets (which can be rented from the camp *for this type accommodation only*). These 20 units cost NZ$26 ($17.45) for two, NZ$24 ($16.11) single. Finally, motel units come in varying sizes: bedsitters, one-, and two-bedrooms. Many have peaked, pine-beamed ceilings, a window wall and stucco and wood-paneled walls. All are of superior quality, and well-chosen furnishings, look out over lawn and gardens, and run from NZ$26 ($17.45) single to NZ$35 ($23.49) double.

Bed and Breakfast

The **Pinehaven Private Hotel,** 42 Marine Parade (tel. 57-039), is just down the street from the YHA Hostel, just across from Marineland. Evelyn and Bill Dennis run the large old house, which has three family rooms, four twins, and one double. Rooms are spotless, and although they're not heated, you are furnished electric blankets. Downstairs there's a comfortable TV lounge, and the Dennises have plans to add a spa pool. Bed-and-breakfast rates are NZ$18 ($12.08) per adult, NZ$12 ($8.05) per child under 10; and there's a surcharge of NZ$2 ($1.34) for a one-night stay.

Also on the waterfront, the **Beach House,** 36 Marine Parade (tel. 53-429), is presided over by friendly Betty and Rex Reid. There's a nice lounge, a game room, and a tea- and coffee-making alcove. And you can take your pick from three room rates: NZ$14 ($9.40) per person for bed and breakfast; NZ$12 ($8.05) for bed only; and if you have your own sleeping bag, you can spread it for just NZ$7 ($4.70)—the last is reduced rate simply because Betty saves the cost of laundering linens, but the rooms are not reduced in quality.

Motel Flats

Some of the best motel flats are at Kennedy Park Motor Camp, described above.

You park outside your own unit at the **Snowgoose Lodge Motel,** 376 Kennedy Rd. (tel. 436-083). Ray and Pierrine Cooper keep things shining at the Snowgoose, outside as well as in, and the front lawn has even won an award for the best motel garden in Napier. The one- and two-bedroom units are all nicely furnished and have TV, phone, radio, and electric blankets. Most also are brightened with one or two of Pierrine's growing plants. There's a new block of executive suites that have their own spa bath (sheer luxury, that!). On-premises facilities include a laundry, car wash, children's play area, game room, outdoor swimming pool, and private spa pool—no charge for the use of any. Shops are nearby, and the Coopers can arrange babysitting. Rates at this Best Western (where your Holiday Pass discount applies): NZ$29 ($19.46) single and NZ$35 ($23.49) double for bedsitters; NZ$33 ($22.15) single, NZ$40 ($26.85) double for full-kitchen units; and NZ$37 ($24.83) single, NZ$46 ($30.87) double for executive units with waterbeds and/or spa bath.

Just across the road, the **Blue Dolphin Motel,** 371–373 Kennedy Rd. (tel. 439-129), has nine brightly furnished, *serviced,* one-bedroom units, each with TV, phone, radio, electric blanket, and heater. There are complete laundry facilities, a game room, barbecue, outdoor heated spa pool, and a babysitting service. Owner-managers David and Christine Mintrom will send a courtesy car to the airport and all coach and rail depots. They also offer a discount of 10% for stays of more than one night to readers who show this book. Rates are NZ$30 ($20.13) to NZ$34 ($22.82) single, NZ$39 ($26.17) to NZ$43 ($28.86) double.

The **Marewa Lodge,** 22 Taradale Rd. (tel. 435-839), has 20 attractive units ranged in an L-shape around a large lawn and children's playground. All are equipped with TV, phone, radio, electric blanket, and electric heater. Each unit opens up to a terrace furnished with garden chairs for sunbathing. Bedsitters have rangettes for cooking; other units have full stoves and ovens. There's plenty of parking space, a spa pool, car wash, and laundry facilities. Babysitters are available, and there's a shopping area close by. Rates are NZ$25 ($16.78) single, NZ$36 ($24.16) double.

McLean Park Lodge, 117 Wellesley Rd. (tel. 54-422), has 11 units within easy walking distance of most Napier attractions. Its colonial decor makes for a warm, welcoming atmosphere, and each unit is nicely furnished, with such extras as TV, radio, and telephone. The laundry and children's play area are added conveniences, and colorful flower beds on a well-tended lawn set the pleasant tone of the place. Rates are NZ$32 ($21.48) single, NZ$40 ($26.85) double, for both bedsitters and one-bedroom units.

MEALS: Paxies Restaurant, 92 Hastings St., opposite the post office (tel. 58-065), gets my vote as the premier budget eatery in Napier. It's a pleasant, not-too-large place that's been in business nearly 30 years. Best of all, the food is fresh, home-cooked, delicious—and bargain priced! There is seating in a cozy front room separated from a larger one in back by a dark-wood partition. My first meal at Paxies was one of of their "mini-meals" of fish, chips, and salad—a light lunch, I thought. Well, an *enormous,* very fresh flounder arrived—fried to a delicate, crisp turn—on a platter with a ton of french fries and accompanied by a good-size salad. It turned out to be my main meal of the day. Cost? A whopping NZ$3.50 ($2.35)! Other mini-meals feature sausages, ham, and a slightly less expensive vegetarian salad. Their "light" meals (hamburgers, steakburgers, toasted sandwiches, etc.) cost NZ$1.50 ($1.01) to NZ$3 ($2.01). Lest I mislead you, let me hasten to add that the extensive menu also includes full meals of steak, ham, mixed grill, seafoods, and salad plates that are in the NZ$5.60 ($3.76) to NZ$8 ($5.37) range, which includes vegetables, salad, and french fries. Add the friendliness of the Paxies themselves (this is a family-owned and -operated place), and you can see why I believe this may possibly be one of New Zealand's top value-for-money restaurants. Not licensed, but BYO (there is, however, a nice selection of liqueur coffees). Hours are 10 a.m. to 2:30 p.m. and 5 to 8 p.m. every day except Sunday, when it's open from 11 a.m. to 6 p.m.

Everything is fresh, homemade, and inexpensive too, at the **Napier Cafeteria** on Hastings Street just off Tennyson Street. Whether you go for breakfast (scones, tea, and pikelet for about NZ$1, or 67¢ U.S.) or a hot lunch of a roast, shepherd's pie, meat pie, savory, or whatnot (at prices of NZ$1, or 67¢ U.S., to NZ$3.50 or $2.35 U.S.) you can count on quality food served in cheerful surroundings. Hours are 7:30 a.m. to 4 p.m.

Ye Old Coffee House, 33 Marine Parade, is in a pleasant cottage with a bay window, pretty floral wallpaper, lace cloths on the tables, and tables out on a small enclosed porch to hold the overflow from inside. It's a wee place, with the freshest of homemade pastries, cakes, etc., as well as excellent sandwiches, homemade soup, meat pies, and salad plates. Almost everything is priced under NZ$1 (67¢) except salad plates, which are NZ$3.50 ($2.35). Open seven days a week from 9 a.m. to 4:30 p.m.

There's a **Cobb & Co.** in the Masonic Hotel on Tennyson Street (tel. 58-689), with its usual good family fare. There are daily specials, as well as the beef-and-kidney pot pie, grills, seafoods, and other menu offerings you can expect in this excellent chain. It's licensed, and open seven days a week from 7:30 a.m. to 10 p.m. Nice colonial decor. Prices average NZ$5.50 ($3.69).

Mabel's, 102 Hastings St. (tel. 55-655), is Napier's whole-food restaurant, which caters to those whose tastes run to vegetarian dishes, although on Friday night (the only day they're open for evening meals) a fish or meat course is also served. Managed by Cathy Boyce, a natural-food and outdoors enthusiast, this warm, pink-colored restaurant caters mainly to the lunchtime crowd, serving whole-meal sandwiches, quiche, carrot cake, muffins, stuffed potatoes, soup, salads of the day, and cakes—all made on the premises. Prices are under NZ$1 (67¢) for everything except evening meals, when main courses range from NZ$5 ($3.36) to NZ$6 ($4.03). Hours are 9 a.m. to 4 p.m. Monday through Thursday, to 9 p.m. on Friday. P.S. If you're wondering why a restaurant owned by a Cathy is named "Mabel's," it was named for her pet canary!

La Ronde, in the War Memorial Hall (tel. 58-180) right on Marine Parade, looks out over the water. If you can, go at night when candlelight adds to the general air of elegance created by red carpeting and curtains, gold-and-black wallpaper, art prints, and of course, Hawkes Bay just outside. At lunch, expect main courses to be in the NZ$5.50 ($3.69) to NZ$9 ($6.04) range. They start at NZ$6.50 ($4.36) and go to NZ$11.50 ($7.72) in the evening, when the menu is quite extensive, with specialties such as crayfish, escargots, veal Cordon Bleu, and even frog legs. Steak, seafoods, and chicken are also featured. It's fully licensed, and open weekdays for lunch from noon to 2 p.m., Tuesday through Saturday for dinner from 6 to 9 p.m. (until midnight for drinks), and on Saturday a combo plays for dancing. Reservations for dinner are strongly advised.

Special Note: I'm not sure this entry belongs under "Meals," but because New Zealand budget travel is so closely tied to those wonderful motel flats and their kitchens, I thought you should know about **Chantal Wholefoods,** 11 Hastings St. (tel. 58-036). Even if you're not a strict vegetarian, I think you'll love this store—all sorts of natural foods, dried fruits, nuts, tofu, etc., and in addition, marvelous whole-grain breads to make any sandwich taste its best. Alan and Carol Burke run Chantal's like an old-fashioned grocery store. The foods are all in open drums and you package them yourself—it's lots of fun, and prices come out cheaper than those in supermarkets.

THINGS TO SEE AND DO: Plan to spend most of your time along the **Marine Parade's Golden Mile.** Down at the southern end, there's the **Aquarium** (tel. 58-493), one of New Zealand's best. Stop for a moment to view the bronze sculpture showing two trawler fishermen hauling a net full of fish. It's so masterfully executed that fishermen have been known to stand and point out each species of fish in the net. The Aquarium's central feature is a huge saltwater oceanarium, which holds over 25 species of ocean-dwelling fish, ranging in size from crayfish to sharks. Feeding time is 3:15 p.m., which can get pretty exciting. You'll also get to see a crocodile, turtles, vividly colored tropical fish, seahorses, the lethal piranha, and octopi. The Vivarium, on the top floor, holds lizards, geckos, tree frogs, and the like. The Aquarium is open every day except Christmas from 9 a.m. to 5 p.m. (until 9 p.m. from December 26 to mid-February). Adults pay NZ$3 ($2.01); children under 15, NZ$1.50 ($1.01); under-3s, free.

Walking north, you'll come to the **Boating Lake,** with paddle boats for children and adult-size bumper boats, as well as the children's train ride, which are open 10 a.m. to 9:30 p.m. every day during the summer, on holidays, and for limited hours other times.

Next comes **Marineland** (tel. 57-429), where a 45-minute show puts dolphins, leopard seals, and sea lions through their paces in sports competitions and other antics much like those we see in the States. Also on hand are blue penguins, fur seals, otters, and gannets. Marineland is open from 9 a.m. to 4:30 p.m. (until 5:30 p.m. during the summer), and show times are 10 a.m. and 2 p.m., with an additional 4 p.m. performance from December 26 through January. Admissions: NZ$2.50 ($1.68) for adults, NZ$1 (67¢) for children under 15, free for those under 3.

Other amusements include children's bumper boats, radio boats, putt-putt golf, and roller skating. Stop for a while and soak in the beauty of the **Sunken Gardens,** with their waterwheel and floating white lotus sculpture. Then, on past the PRO, there's the **Sound Shell,** which is used on summer weekends for an arts and crafts market.

Across Marine Parade, opposite the Colonnade, you'll find **Lilliput Village and Model Railway** (tel. 58-566), a real delight. If you're a model train fancier, you'll love this one; and even if you're not, you'll likely be intrigued by the automated cops chasing crooks, gas station attendant washing car windows, farmer plowing, a drive-in movie with a show on the screen, and a nude bather in a stream. Call, or inquire at the PRO for the times the train is currently in operation. The **Holt Planetarium** in the village gives 45-minute shows periodically (call for exact times) for an additional small fee, and you can take a 20-minute journey aboard the starship *Nova* for another small fee. There are dolls from around the globe; military models of ships, tanks, and soldiers; animated nursery rhymes; a tiny dollhouse with over 300 pieces of furniture and electric lights; and an international display of egg decorating. It's all open every day except Christmas, and admission to the complex is NZ$1.50 ($1.01) for adults, NZ$.50 (33¢) for those 14 and under.

Next, there is the **Hawke's Bay Art Gallery and Museum** (tel. 57-781), with Maori and other Polynesian artifacts and exhibits depicting the lives of early settlers around the bay. Antiques, painting, sculpture, and earthquake memorabilia are also here. Open weekdays and school holidays from 10:30 a.m.

to 4:30 p.m., weekends from 2 to 4:30 p.m. Admission is a tiny NZ$.50 (33¢) for adults, NZ$.20 (13¢) for those under 16; and families pay NZ$1 (67¢).

The **Nocturnal Wildlife Centre** (tel. 57-553) is at the end of the Golden Mile, and here's where you can see the kiwi in a naturalistic setting. Also wetas, lizards, opossums, and other wildlife. Hours are 9 a.m. to 4:30 p.m. December to Easter, plus all public and school holidays. Admission: NZ$1 (67¢) for adults, NZ$.50 (33¢) for children 14 and under.

Swimming

Westshore Domain is Napier's most popular swimming beach, with a beach of gray sand and pebbles that stretches about a mile and a half. Surf at the **Marine Parade** beach is a bit too rough for good swimming, but it's a good place to get a little sun. There is, however, a saltwater pool at Marine Parade featuring the "Wild Rampage Ride." **Onekawa Park** at Maadi Road and Flanders Avenue, has two Olympic-size pools, one indoor, the other outdoor. Small fee.

Gannets

This is the only place in New Zealand where gannets are known to nest on the mainland (they are commonly found on offshore islands). There's a colony of some 6000 out at **Cape Kidnappers,** that dramatic line of cliffs that form Hawke Bay's southern end some 17 miles south of Napier. The gannet sanctuary is open to the public from late October to June, and the graceful, colorful birds are worth a visit. To reach them, drive 13 miles south to Clifton Domain; then it's a little less than a two-hour walk along four or five miles of sandy beach. That walk *must* be made at low tide, since high tides come right up to the base of the steep cliffs, which is why private vehicles may not be taken out to the sanctuary. Be sure to check before you go with the PRO in Napier (tel. 57-182) or in Hastings (tel. 69-001) or the Department of Lands and Survey (tel. 57-369 in Napier).

There are two options to going on your own: **Burden's Motor Camp in** Te Awanga (tel. Hastings 750-400 or 750-334) runs organized trips at moderate prices; and there's a Land Rover trip operated by **Gannet Safaris** (tel. Hastings 777-597) at considerably higher prices.

Other Activities

There are two important **wineries** you can visit in the Napier vicinity, the Mission Vineyards and McWilliams Winery. Ask at the PRO for brochures about tours and directions for reaching them. Also, Napier is where you can see how all those sheep get transformed into car seatcovers, coats, etc. You can take a free 25-minute tour through the **Classic Decor Tannery** on Thames Street off Pandora Road (tel. 59-662), weekdays at 11 a.m. The shop there sells sheepskin products at factory prices, and they have a fully insured, worldwide mailing service.

AFTER DARK: Napier is pretty lively after dark during the summer months, with more limited activity during other months. Several of the pubs and hotels have live music for dancing from midweek through Saturday. The **Travelodge** on Marine Parade (tel. 53-237) usually has entertainment Friday, Saturday, and Sunday evening. . . . The **Rafters Room,** upstairs at the Jolly Fisherman, attracts a young crowd with rock music. . . . The **Onekawa,** on Taradale Road, near Maadi Road (tel. 436-036), offers mostly country music. . . . The **Ahuriri Tavern** features mellow rock. **NiteSite**, on Dickens Street (tel. 55-710), is an actual nightclub, open Tuesday through Saturday until the wee hours, and **Banana's**, above NiteSite, features a giant disco and light show, also open until around 3 a.m. on Friday and Saturday night.

A SIDE TRIP TO HASTINGS: Hastings is just 12 miles from Napier on Highway 2, a town of lovely parks and gardens, well worth a visit. If you're not driving, there is regular bus service between the two towns. Go by the **PRO** on Russell Street North (tel. 69-001) for maps, brochures, information, and a scenic drive guide. Hours are 8:30 a.m. to 5 p.m. on weekdays, and from November to the end of February they're also open 8:30 a.m. to 1 p.m. on Saturday. Taxis charge NZ$12.50 ($8.39) per hour (up to five passengers) for sightseeing tours. The scenic drive, incidentally, is one you really shouldn't miss.

Pick up the *Tread the Wine Trail* brochure from the PRO for directions on visiting the local wineries. One of the best is the **Vidal Winery**, 913 St. Aubyn St., near Sylvan Road (tel. 68-105). Vidal has a lot to offer, including the Vineyard Bar and Barrel Room Restaurant right on the premises. They have a rustic, wine-cellar setting, with beamed ceiling, old oak casks lining the walls, and candlelight. There's also a barbecue area outside with umbrella trees and a grape arbor. The menu includes delicious homemade soup, quiche, baked potato and salad, honeyed chicken, and a variety of steaks. A basket of hot bread and butter accompanies all meals, and need I say you can order wine? Prices are in the NZ$5 ($3.36) to NZ$9 ($6.04) range; wine is NZ$.90 (60¢) per glass, NZ$6 ($4.03) to NZ$7 ($4.70) a bottle. The Vineyard Bar is open from 10 a.m. to 9 p.m. Monday through Saturday; the Barrel room from noon to 2 p.m. and 6 to 9 p.m. Monday through Saturday; drinks and light snacks are available in the Vineyard Bar from 10 a.m. to 9 p.m.

Try to plan one meal when you drive (as you *must*) up to **Te Mata Peak,** about seven miles from Hastings PRO. The view is spectacular, and ask locals or the PRO about the lovely Maori legend that gave it its name. Take Havelock Road to Te Mata Road to Simla Avenue to Te Mata Peak Road and ascend the 1310-foot-high peak for a stunning 360-degree panoramic view. On the way up or down, stop at the **Peak House Restaurant,** a pine-paneled, peaked-beam-ceilinged restaurant whose many windows show off magnificent views. Even if you can't make one of their à la carte or smörgåsbord meals, stop by for a full Devonshire tea with fresh-baked scones at NZ$2.50 ($1.68). Menu offerings include roast chicken, porterhouse steak, and Nelson scallops, all with salad and french fries, at NZ$5.50 ($3.69) to NZ$7 ($4.70). There's a generous smörg åsbord on Sunday at lunch for NZ$9 ($6.04) and one on Friday evening with dancing for NZ$13.50 ($9.06). À la carte dinner main courses run NZ$7.50 ($5.03) to NZ$9 ($6.04). Peak House is open for lunch every day, except Monday, from 10:30 a.m. to 4:30 p.m. Dinners are served Wednesday through Saturday from 6 to 9 p.m. Incidentally, there's a picnic table right at the peak.

Within the five acres that make up **Fantasyland** (in Windsor Park, entered via Grove Road, tel. 69-856) are enought assorted attractions and amusements to delight any child and all but the most hardened of his or her elders. Each time I go there are new additions, all elaborately but tastefully executed. Who wouldn't be intrigued by a pirate ship complete with cannons, a turreted castle, a spaceship parked on its moon base! The tree house (open to any and all climbers) draws me every time, as does the little village with its firehouse, jail, stores, etc. A terrific array of playground equipment is available for active youngsters, and for those of us not so active, there's a miniature train ride around the park. Canoes and rowboats compete with swans and ducks on the pretty pond, and the shady, landscaped grounds invite an extended spell of just plain loafing—spreading a picnic on the handy tables set about (easily arranged with food from the take-away bar). The tea shop is a refreshment alternative. Adults pay NZ$1 (67¢) and children under 12 go in free (some of the rides charge a minimal fare). Open daily from 9 a.m. to 5 p.m.

5. Napier to Taupo

Your drive from Napier to Taupo via Highway 5 will take less than five hours, but there was a time when it took two days. That was when stagecoach service was first initiated over a route that had been used by Maoris in pre-European days on forages to collect seafood from Hawkes Bay.

The landscape you'll be passing through changes from lush vineyards to cultivated farm fields to rugged mountain ranges—it doesn't take much imagination to know why in the early days the journey was so arduous. About 3½ miles before you reach Taupo, look for the lonely peak of **Mount Tauhara,** an extinct volcanic cone rising from the plains.

LAKE TAUPO AND BEYOND

WHETHER YOU COME into Taupo from Rotorua past Wairakei's steamy thermal power complex or from Napier under the lonely eye of Mount Tauhara, it is the lake on whose shores the town sits that will draw you like a magnet. Lake Taupo, New Zealand's largest (238 square miles), opens before you in a broad, shimmering expanse, with its far shores a misty suggestion of cliffs, coves, and wooded hills. There's a bit of magic at work in Taupo—and it's easy to see its immediate attraction to descendants of the *Arawa* canoe. Perhaps that's because the great lake was created, so present-day Maoris will tell you, by the magic of Ngatoroirangi, the legendary navigator of that migrating canoe, when he stood on Mount Tauhara and flung a gigantic tree from its summit, which landed here, leaving a vast trough as it plowed through the earth. When water welled up to fill the trough, Lake Taupo was born. Its very name is linked to legend—the Maoris called it Taupo-nui-a-Tia, or "the great cloak of Tia," after one of the *Arawa* chiefs who explored much of this region, naming and claiming choice spots for his tribe. If you're not a believer in magic, you'll accept the Pakeha explanation of its origin: that it lies in a series of volcanic craters created in the aftermath of some of the most violent eruptions in the country's history.

1. Taupo

What you'll find today is a pleasant, medium-size town dedicated to welcoming and nurturing visitors. Lake Taupo itself is as much the central attraction today as it was in those far-off times—lake activities preoccupy residents and visitors alike, although there is an abundant supply of land-based attractions as well. Water-skiing has gained such popularity that there are now specified ski lanes along the shoreline. Pleasure boating is a never-ending diversion in these parts. And the fishing on which the Maori settlers so depended has changed only in the addition of two imported trout species to enhance the native fish population. It was in 1868 that brown trout eggs were introduced from Tasmania, followed by California rainbow trout in 1884. Ironically, Lake Taupo rainbows are now considered the only *pure* strain in the world, and every year millions of young trout and ova are exported back to California and to new homes all over the world.

It is the trout that draw anglers here in such numbers that those on shore have been so tightly packed as to be likened to a human picket fence. And there is seldom a time when the lake's surface is not alive with boats trolling lines in their wake. Landlubbers have been coming in nearly equal numbers since the late 1870s to visit the thermal pools and view the natural wonders of the lake's environs.

ORIENTATION: Taupo is spread along the northeastern tip of the lake, just where the Waikato River empties into Lake Taupo's Tapuaeharuru Bay. Its main street is **Tongariro Street,** named after the largest river flowing into the lake. The small settlements of **Acacia Bay** and **Jerusalem Bay** are just across on the western shore of the bay. Highway 1 leads south along the lake's eastern shore.

USEFUL INFORMATION: The **Public Relations Office (PRO)** is just off the lakefront on Tongariro Street, (tel. 88-940), and can book accommodations, tours, and other activities (no charge), as well as provide a wide range of informative brochures on area attractions. Hours are 8:30 a.m. to 5 p.m. Monday through Friday, 10 a.m. to noon on Saturday; closed Sunday; extended hours during holiday periods. . . . **Fishing licenses** and information can be obtained from the PRO. . . . Fishing **guides** may be booked through the PRO. . . . There is regular **bus service** to Taupo from Napier and Rotorua.

ACCOMMODATIONS: Taupo's main industry is tourism, and only during holiday season should it be necessary to book very far in advance, since there are over 3000 beds available in the immediate vicinity. The efficient, well-run PRO can furnish a complete list of area accommodations, complete with current prices. There's no hostel as such, but good, inexpensive cabins fill that category more than adequately.

Cabins

Taupo Cabins are conveniently located right in town at 50 Tonga St. (mailing address: P.O. Box 795; tel. 84-346), and offer one of the best accommodations bargains in the area. There are two-, four-, and five-berth cabins furnished with two-tier bunks (you supply linen, blankets, crockery, cutlery, cooking utensils, and use the communal kitchen); two- and four-berth "flatettes," with H&C, cooking facilities, and utensils (you supply linen, blankets, and cutlery); four-berth mini-motel units with a double bed and bunks, H&C, fridge, range, cooking utensils, and heater (you supply linen, blankets, and cutlery); and four-berth tourist flats with cooking facilities plus toilet and shower (you supply only linen and blankets). There's a large community kitchen, communal showers and toilets, a store, and a laundry with iron and ironing board (metered for a small fee). Rates run NZ$5 ($3.36) to NZ$11 ($7.38) per person, depending on type of accommodation.

In a quiet rural setting overlooking the lake, **Acacia Holiday Park,** Acacia Bay Road (mailing address: P.O. Box 171; tel. 85-159 or 86-830), is one of the newest motor camps in the Taupo area and offers caravan and tent and caravan sites, cabins, and self-contained tourist flats. There are outboard motorboats and canoes for hire, as well as bikes. On the premises there's a hot spa pool and recreation room with a pool table. Rates are NZ$6 ($4.03) to NZ$8 ($5.37) per couple for tent and caravan sites; NZ$18 ($12.08) double for cabins, and NZ$23 ($15.44) double for tourist flats.

Bed and Breakfast

Muriel and Ivan Mapson have run **Bradshaw's Guest House,** 130 Heu Heu St. (mailing address: P.O. Box 210; tel. 88-288) with such friendly graciousness that it has elicited scores of letters from readers, and on my research trip for this book I ran into enthusiastic budgeteers singing their praises long before I reached Taupo. Bradshaw's is a homey, white two-story house set on a quiet residential street very close to the center of town. Rooms are nicely done up, with attractive furnishings and lots of wood paneling. There's a cozy TV lounge (with books for non-tube addicts), a tea and coffee room, laundry, and a dining room that faces the lake. Best of all, Muriel (she's from Scotland) and Ivan (he's English) are the perfect hosts—interested in their guests and concerned that they enjoy their stay in Taupo. There are 12 bedrooms, three of them singles. A few have private baths. Rates for bed and breakfast are NZ$15 ($10.06) per person for rooms with shared facilities; NZ$19 ($12.75) single, NZ$35 ($23.49) double, for those with private baths. The evening meal, if ordered ahead, costs NZ$6 ($4.03).

Motel Flats

On the corner of Kaimanawa and Heu Heu Streets you'll find Jan and Brian Leverell and their attractive **Adelphi Motel** (mailing address: P.O. Box 1091; tel. 87-594), another Taupo establishment, which has prompted letters from readers. The Leverells, their two teenage daughters, and Honey (their affectionate golden retriever) have that special knack of making the traveler feel at home—it is obvious in the well-kept premises, the friendliness of their greeting, and their availability to help with your holiday plans. The ten units include one on the top floor (the only second-floor unit) with marvelous views of the lake and mountains, and one especially designed for the physically handicapped. There are one- and two-bedrooms units, sleeping two to six, all with fully equipped kitchen, TV, radio, and electric blanket. There are two private spa pools on the premises as well as car-washing facilities and a trampoline. Contrary to most motels, the Adelphi welcomes pets (must be Honey's influence!). Continental breakfast is available for a small charge, and the Leverells can arrange babysitting. Best Western Holiday Pass discounts apply for the rates of NZ$33 ($22.15) single, NZ$40 ($26.85) double, at this member of the chain. Rates increase during holiday periods. Incidentally, Brian is a highly respected trout fishing guide (see "What to See and Do") who takes special pleasure in helping his guests land that big one. Highly recommended.

The **Spa Road Motel,** on Spa Road (tel. 89-292), throws in a travel experience with your accommodations. You'll be literally immersed in Taupo's early history at this interesting place, for it was the site of the Armed Constabulary during the Maori Wars. It's also the site of hot thermal pools. Rooms are of a rustic-cabin nature, and each is named for a member of the Constabulary stationed here. They're not large, but are quite comfortably furnished, with H&C, shower, and toilet. There's no telly or telephone, but the grounds feature a hot stream crossed by a wooden footbridge (good walking territory). The lounge is actually the only privately owned Maori meeting house in New

Zealand, and was carved by a master Maori carver about 1810. It also houses the licensed Constabulary Restaurant, where a three-course dinner will run about NZ$10 ($6.71). Also on the premises are a bottle shop and public bar. It's a longish walk, very short drive, from the town center. Rates (which include breakfast) are NZ$20 ($13.42) single, NZ$30 ($20.13) double.

Dunrovin Motel, 140 Heu Heu St. (mailing address: P.O. Box 647; tel. 87-384), is right next door to Bradshaw's on the same quiet street, yet very central to the town. There are one- and two-bedroom units, with twin and double beds, sleeping from two to eight. All have complete kitchen, radio, and TV. A children's play area is on the premises, and continental breakfasts are available for an additional charge. Rates are NZ$25 ($16.78) single, NZ$32 ($21.48) double.

Cedar Park Motel, at Two Mile Bay (mailing address: P.O. Box 852; tel. 86-325), is across Highway 1 on the lakefront, just four kilometers from the center of town. It's a Best Western, and one of the most attractive accommodations in Taupo, with some two-story units, which feature peaked ceilings and picture windows looking out over the lake. Each unit has a separate lounge, two bedrooms, complete kitchen, TV, radio, telephone, and electric blankets. There's a heated swimming pool, children's play area, barbecue, laundry, and car-wash facilities. Also, a very good BYO restaurant right on the premises (patronized by the locals as well as guests). Rates are NZ$30 ($20.13) single, NZ$45 ($30.20) double, except during holiday periods when charges are higher.

MEALS: There's a **Cobb & Co.** in the Lake Establishment Hotel on the corner of Tongariro and Tuwharetoa Streets (tel. 86-165), just across the street from the PRO. In addition to the very good standard fare of the chain, the Taupo Cobb & Co. adds local specials daily on a blackboard menu. Another special feature here: the chef will cook that trout you caught in the lake—talk about fresh! Hours, as usual, are 7:30 a.m. to 10 p.m. seven days a week. It's fully licensed, and main courses average about NZ$5.50 ($3.69).

A very special place for lunch is the **Huka Village Eating House** at the Historic Village (a sightseeing must) on Huka Falls Road (tel. 85-286). You'll love the farmhouse atmosphere, and the smörgåsbord table offers a wealth of homemade breads, scones, soups, salads, cheeses, and desserts. You can lunch exceedingly well for about NZ$5 ($3.36) and get in some of the best sightseeing hereabouts at the same time. Hours are 10 a.m. to 4 p.m., seven days a week.

There's very good value in pleasant, Oriental surroundings at **Chinatown,** 25 Tongariro St. (tel. 87-026). The à la carte menu offers an extensive list of Chinese dishes, which are very good and a break from Kiwi food, with some European selections (beef, chicken, etc.) as well. It's fully licensed (in fact, the attractive lounge bar is open until midnight) and prices are quite reasonable. Also, it is convenient, both in location (it's at the lake end of Tongariro Street) and in hours—service is continuous from noon until 10 p.m., seven days a week. Lunch will run around NZ$5 ($3.36), dinner without wine about NZ$7 ($4.70).

Kipps, located above the Real Estate House on Heu Heu Street (tel. 86-396 or 87-159), specializes in seafoods, and the menu is quite extensive. Almost anything you select will arrive prepared to perfection, and the reasonable prices will surprise you. Fully licensed. Hours are 6:30 to 9:30 p.m. Tuesday to Sunday, with prices in the NZ$6 ($4.03) to NZ$9 ($6.04) range. Children's portions are less.

The **Constabulary,** out at historic Spa Motel on Spa Road (tel. 84-120), offers good, solid Kiwi dishes plus fresh seafood selections in the restaurant adjoining the Maori meeting house, which also serves as a lounge. It's an à la carte menu with prices in the NZ$10 ($6.71) range for three courses, fully licensed, and the kids eat for half price. Hours are 6:30 to 9:30 p.m., seven days a week.

Ben's Echo Cliff, 5 Tongariro St. (tel. 88-539), is right at the lake, upstairs over Sullivan's Sports. Good value here, with a menu that includes all the New Zealand standards (lamb, veal, chicken, beef, etc.), plus Dutch Indonesian and continental dishes, all at prices which let you lunch for around NZ$5 ($3.36), dine for about NZ$7 ($4.70). BYO. Lunch is served from 11:30 a.m. to 1 p.m., dinner from 5 to 9 p.m.

Definitely a splurge in atmosphere, and not-quite-a-big-splurge in the price department, is a meal at the **Colonial Goose,** 94 Heu Heu St. (tel. 89-312). Located in one of the oldest colonial houses in Taupo, it's very European in style, with candles on tables, open fires, an intimate atmosphere, and a menu that features nouveau cuisine (no heavy sauces). The dessert trolley is a work of art and guaranteed to add an inch to your waistline. Lunch is served Monday to Friday from 11:30 a.m. to 2:30 p.m.; dinner, Wednesday through Saturday from 6:30 to 10 p.m.. Main courses at lunch are NZ$4.50 ($3.02) to NZ$6 ($4.03), those at dinner from NZ$7 ($4.70) to NZ$9 ($6.04).

You'll find numerous attractive, inexpensive coffee lounges in Taupo—the one I favor is the **Copper Kettle,** on Heu Heu Street (tel. 89-936)—but most are more than adequate.

THINGS TO SEE AND DO: Well, there's fishing. And even if you've never cast a line, this may be the very time to join that "picket fence" and experience the singular thrill of feeling a nibble and pulling in a big one. And they do grow big in Lake Taupo—the *average* trout size is 4½ pounds, with 8 and 10 pounds not unheard of. Just remember that there's a limit of eight rainbow trout and five brook trout per person per day. The PRO can fix you up with a license (you can get one for just one day if you like) and fill you in on rules and regulations, as well as help you find a guide if you'd just rather not be a "picket." **Brian Leverell,** at the Adelphi Motel (see "Accommodations" tel. 87-594) is one of the best in the area and charges about NZ$20 ($13.42) an hour, which includes transport, all fishing equipment, and lunch if you're fishing when that time rolls around.

There are **lake cruises** aboard the steamer *Ernest Kemp* every morning and afternoon, seven days a week. It's a two-hour-and-fifteen-minute sail, well worth the fare of NZ$5 ($3.36) per person (there are special family prices on holidays)—a great way to experience the lake itself and get a very different look at its shoreline. Check at the PRO for exact sailing times and booking, or go along to the Boat Harbour.

Scenic flights leave the lakefront by Taupo Boat Harbour, ranging from a ten-minute flight over Wairakei's steaming valley, Huka Falls, and Taupo, to one-hour forays as far away as Tongariro National Park, to a two-hour excursion, which takes you even farther afield. Prices begin at NZ$12 ($8.05) to NZ$42 ($28.29)—children pay half. You'll find the **Float Plane Office** (ARK Aviation Limited, P.O. Box 238) at the Boat Harbour (tel. 87-500).

At the PRO office, look for the *Taupo Town Tour* published by the Taupo Lions Club. It's a self-guiding **auto tour** that leads you by the hand to everything there is to see in Taupo and its environs. Easy to follow, with informative notes on most stops.

The PRO puts out an excellent booklet, *Walking Trails,* outlining city and near-city walks as well as tramping trails in the area. There are long walks and short walks; walks close to town and others as far away as Tongariro National Park. What a peaceful interlude to take the 45-minute forest walk, and for sheer scenery excitement, there's the contrast of thrilling thermal activity and serene pine plantations along the Craters of the Moon track. The booklet gives clear, concise directions (with maps for most tracks), as well as estimated times and such helpful information as the fact that all of Mount Tauhara is a Maori Reserve and its trustees must give permission to use the marked walking track (the current trustee telephone numbers are listed in the booklet). A terrific idea is to intersperse sightseeing or other sports activities with a walk into the very soul and being of New Zealand, its forests, mountains, and rivers.

To see firsthand the awesome power of all that steam you've only glimpsed in Rotorua, take the five-mile drive out to the **Wairakei Geothermal Project.** When work began in 1950 to harness all that power, this was the second largest such project in the world and the first to use wet steam. Scientists from around the globe came to observe. Using some 60 bores and over 12 miles of pipeline, the project now supplies a great deal of the North Island's electricity requirements. Stop by the Information Centre (on the left as you drive into the valley), which is open 9 a.m. to noon and 1 to 4 p.m. every day of the year, including holidays. The display gives a compelling overview of local geothermal activity and furnishes answers to all the obvious questions that spring to mind (look for the board titled "Questions Often Asked"). Study the excellent borefield model and drilling process diagram, then leave the center and follow the marked road, which crosses the borefield itself, to a lookout from which you can view the entire site. You can also visit the power station itself during the hours listed above.

Just in front of the De Brett Thermal Hotel, a short way out of town on Highway 5, a cut has been made through the pumice on the south side of the road and pumice strata has been marked and dated showing **volcanic debris** dating as far back as 1480 B.C. and as "recently" as A.D. 131. It's an eerie feeling to gaze on physical evidence of the earth's history! The De Brett, itself, is worth a short visit, since its grounds incorporate the fabulous **Onekeneke Valley of Hot Pools.**

Be sure to visit **Huka Village,** a replica pioneer village in which authentic buildings from New Zealand's days of early European settlement have been restored and brought back to life with working exhibits of village life as it was then. One cottage holds a shop stocked with handcrafts. There are picnic facilities in this lovely, shaded site, but I strongly recommend that you time your visit to include lunch at the pioneer tea and lunch room (see "Meals"). The village is out the Huka Falls Road about a mile and a half from the center of town.

2. Taupo to Tongariro

The 58-mile drive from Taupo to Tongariro National Park is an easy one—good roads with changing scenery as you follow Highway 1 along the eastern shore of Lake Taupo through small towns and fishing settlements, around charming bays, always with that vast lake on your right. Look for **Motutaiko Island** (the only one in the lake) as you approach Hatepe. As you near the southern end of the lake, you'll begin to catch glimpses of volcanic cones, which are at the heart of the park. Highway 47 cuts off from Highway 1 to lead you through plateau-like tussocklands across to Highway 48 and the entrance to park headquarters and the elegant Château. It's clearly signposted, and as you leave Lake Taupo behind, the volcanic nature of this terrain begins to dominate the landscape. By the time you reach the Château, you've entered another world from that of the lakeside you've just left.

READERS' FISHING TIP: "Bruce and Elizabeth Rountree operate the **Gamekeeper's Loft** in the town of Turangi (Town Centre Shopping Mall; tel. 8821) at the south end of Lake Taupo. Turangi is right in the middle of the best Taupo-area fishing, and **Bruce Rountree** has to be one of the world's best trout cooks. Take your fresh-caught trout to Bruce in the late afternoon, then get ready for a feast you'll never forget at a ridiculously low price" (John and Betty Jean Sager, Seattle, Wash.).

3. Tongariro National Park

This was New Zealand's first national park (the world's second, after Yellowstone), and the original 1887 deed from Te Heuheu Tukino IV and other Tuwharetoa tribal chiefs transferred only some 6500 acres (all the land within a one-mile radius of the volcanic peaks), an area that has now been expanded to 30,453 acres. It's a dramatic landscape, dominated by the three active volcanoes, which rise with stark beauty from heath-like plains. Drama-loving Maoris considered the volcanoes to be sacred *(tapu),* found mythical explanations for their origins, and chose caves on their slopes as burial sites for their chiefs.

Ruapehu, with its 9175-foot snow-capped summit, is the highest mountain on the North Island and provides its principal skiing facilities while holding in its basin the simmering, ice-ringed Crater Lake. Its most recent eruption was in 1971. **Ngauruhoe,** rising 7515 feet, smoulders constantly and from time to time sends showers of ash and lava spilling from its crater (the last in 1954) to alter its shape once again. **Tongariro,** lowest of the three (6458 feet), is also the most northerly and the center of an engaging Maori legend. There were once, so the story goes, many mountains in the North Island's center, all male with the exception of Pihanga, who was wed to Tongariro and the object of the other mountains' lustful fantasies. According to one version of the legend, Pihanga's heart belonged only to Tongariro, who defeated the other mountains and exiled them from the region. Another version has Pihanga discovered by Tongariro dallying with Taranaki, which resulted in a fierce fight ended by a swift, hard kick to Taranaki's backside and his hasty retreat to the west coast, where he stands in solitary splendor today as Mount Egmont, an almost perfect replica of Japan's Mount Fuji. You can follow his trail, which became the Wanganui River, and still see the enormous depression under Mount Egmont's Fantham's Peak put there by Tongariro's kick. When mists surround Egmont today, Maoris will tell you he is weeping for his lost love.

For non-legend-believers, there is the nonlegendary fact that these are at the end of a volcanic chain that extends all the way to the islands of Tonga, 1000 miles away. Their origin is fairly recent, as these things go, dating back only about two million years.

ORIENTATION: You'll find the **THC Château Tongariro** and the **National Park Headquarters** in the little village of **Whakapapa** at the end of Highway 48. The Château is the center of visitor activities such as booking ski and tour trips, dining, and drinking; the Visitors' Centre of the Park Headquarters is the center of information and assistance in planning tramps through the park. They keep up-to-date weather-conditions data, and provide detailed maps, guiding services, camping permission, and hunting permits. The popular ski fields (used by as many as 6000 visitors per day during season) are 4½ miles above the village.

ACCOMMODATIONS: Accommodations are as scarce as the proverbial hen's teeth! There is, of course, the elegant **THC Château Tongariro** (mailing address: Mount Ruapehu, Tongariro National Park; tel. Ruapehu 809), and if this is a big stop on your itinerary, you might consider a night or two at Big Splurge prices, ranging seasonally from NZ$40 ($26.85) to NZ$87 ($58.39) single, NZ$48 ($32.24) to NZ$95 ($63.75) double. It's a grand hotel in the manner of years gone by, but with a 1930s deco-style lounge. Rooms and suites are elegant, and there are such additional comforts as a heated pool and sauna. The Château justifies its listing in a budget travel guide on two counts: it's an outstanding hotel, internationally famous; and it's one of those scarce hen's teeth in this neighborhood!

Now, on to accommodations more in our budget range, few though they may be. Need I say that *early* bookings are absolutely necessary during the skiing season? Actually, it's a good idea to book as far in advance as possible in any season, what with accommodations being so scanty.

Cabins

Whakapapa Motor Camp (mailing address: c/o Mount Ruapehu Post Office; tel. Ruapehu 897) is down the first right turn after you pass park headquarters. Set on the banks of Whakapapanui Stream, it's surrounded by lush bushland. There are tent and caravan sites (all nicely screened by foliage), four six-berth cabins, and two four-berth cabins. Cabins come with two-tier bunks, table and chairs, and electric heating. On the premises are toilets and showers, electric stoves, a laundry with drying room, and a small camp store. Rates (which vary seasonally): NZ$5 ($3.36) for tent sites, NZ$7 ($4.70) for caravan sites, NZ$10 ($6.71) to NZ$15 ($10.06) for cabins.

Trampers on the mountain slopes can arrange through the Park Headquarters rangers to use rustic, strategically placed **huts,** which are equipped with bunks and coal stoves, and cost a mere NZ$3 ($2.01) per person.

Lodges

The rustic **Ruapehu Skotel** (mailing address: c/o Mount Ruapehu Post Office; tel. Ruapehu 819), located on the lower slopes of Mount Ruapehu above the Château, offers both self-contained chalets and lodge accommodations. The attractive, paneled, slant-roofed lodge rooms can accommodate two, three, or four; most have H&C and many have shower and toilet. There's a large, bright guest kitchen with individual food lockers, stoves, fridge, plus cooking and eating utensils. Also on the premises are a laundry with washers and dryers, a sauna, private spas, a gym, a shop selling food, and a large game room. The lounge invites conviviality with a dance deck and fireplace, and a new restaurant was under construction when I was there. Chalets sleep six (four bunks and a double bed); kitchens are completely equipped; and there's a TV. Outside, views of Ngauruhoe's cone are spectacular. All buildings are centrally heated and have piped-in music. This is a lively place, where manager Melvyn Lee and his family keep things humming with planned get-togethers before the fire, movies, lectures, hikes, fishing and botany expeditions. Seasonal rates begin at NZ$32 ($21.48) double with H&C, NZ$38 ($25.50) double with private facilities, NZ$42 ($28.29) double in chalet, and NZ$4 ($2.68) per extra person. Expect them to be higher during ski season.

There is also a combination of facilities at **Mountain Heights** (mailing address: P.O. Box 7, National Park; tel. 833), located on Highway 4. The 14 lodge rooms sleep up to seven and are comfortably furnished. Three self-contained units have complete kitchens and one bedroom that sleeps four. In each, there's electric heating, electric blankets, TV, and toilet and shower. No kitchen facilities for lodge rooms, but the dining room serves breakfast and dinner. There is a laundry and drying room, and ski hire is available. Winter rates begin at NZ$25 ($16.78) per adult (children, half price); in summer, rates are NZ$40 ($26.85) per unit.

A Motel

The **Buttercup Alpine Motel** (mailing address: P.O. Box 45, National Park; tel. 702) sits at the junction of Highways 4 and 47 at National Park township. This friendly place provides a host of planned activities such as white-water rafting, skiing, horse treks, and hiking expeditions, as well as a nice selection of accommodations. There are Manorhouse units sleeping up to six, with private plumbing, tea and coffee facilities, TV and piped-in music; Greenhouse units have combined lounge and other facilities per each three bedrooms; and Honeymoon Lofts (not limited to newlyweds, however) are up under the roof, with gorgeous views added to all those facilities listed for other units. There's an attractive Butternut Farmhouse Restaurant and Den with a potbellied stove, and evening movies, sing-alongs around the fire, gluhwein parties, and occasional fancy-dress dances. Also on the premises are four outdoor hot-water Jacuzzis. Rates all include bed, breakfast, and dinner: NZ$45 ($30.20) per person for Manorhouse and Greenhouse, NZ$55 ($36.91) per person for Honeymoon Lofts (children pay half; infants are free).

MEALS: You can eat at any price range at the **Château.** For the truly budget-minded, there's the paneled, no-frills **Cafeteria,** open every day from 8 a.m. to 5 p.m., where you'll find meat pies, sandwiches, salads, and such at inexpensive prices. The cozy, pub-like **Carvery** serves a quite nice NZ$11 ($7.38) evening meal with a choice of roasts, fish, grills, and salads. For an elegant—and expensive—dinner, it's the high-ceilinged, chandeliered **Ruapehu Room,** from 6:30 to 9 p.m. The à la carte menu features New Zealand specialties, as well as many exotic dishes, which are prepared or flamed at your table.

The Château can also supply you with box lunches for a day on the slopes, and during ski season there are kiosks and snackbars open at the ski fields.

THINGS TO SEE AND DO: Skiing is *the* activity during the season, which normally lasts from June 15 to the end of October, with three well-developed fields inside the park. The most popular is Whakapapa Skifield, on the northwestern side of Mount Ruapehu just 4½ miles beyond the Château. The Château can also rent you ski equipment, provide instruction and a current brochure detailing all charges. If you have your own equipment with you, expect to spend about NZ$15 ($10.06) for lifts and tows for a full day. All facilities operate from 8:30 a.m. to 4:30 p.m. unless weather conditions interfere, and there's public transportation via coach to the ski field from the Château, which I heartily recommend you use, since driving and parking can be a real problem.

In any other season, there are fascinating **walks** to view and more than 500 plant species, the giant rimu trees (some well over 600 years old), and 30 bird species within the park's boundaries. Then there's that hot **Crater Lake** on Mount Ruapehu, the **Ketetahi Hot Springs,** and a pleasant, 20-minute **Ridge Track.** Ambitious trackers can take a whack at climbing all three volcanoes in one day—but believe me, it takes a *lot* of ambition, with a healthy dose of stamina thrown in! Check with the Park Headquarters for details on all park possibilities.

4. Tongariro to Wanganui

The 89 miles from Tongariro National Park to Wanganui pass through some of the most scenic countryside in the North Island. Indeed, the 32 miles of winding road between Raetihi and Wanganui has been labeled the "Valley of a Thousand Hills." These are the **Parapara Hills,** formed from volcanic ash, with shellrock seams and great walls of "papa" rock (a blue clay), which can, incidentally, be quite slippery when landslides put it across the highway. This entire drive, however, is one to be done at a leisurely pace (with an eye out, especially in winter, for patches of that clay across the road) so as to enjoy the spectacular scenery. Sheep farms line your way, with at least one deer farm visible from the highway. There are numerous rest areas en route, offering delightful panoramic views, and in autumn, silver birches dot the landscape with brilliant golds and oranges.

You'll pass the beautiful **Raukawa Falls,** skirt three small lakes whose waters shade from green into red into black over the course of the year and are held sacred by the Maoris, then cross the Wanganui River over the Dublin Street Bridge to enter Wanganui.

5. Wanganui

Wanganui is one of New Zealand's oldest cities and was settled amid much controversy over just how title to the land was obtained by Col. William Wakefield on behalf of the New Zealand Company in 1840. It seems he took ashore an assortment of mirrors, blankets, pipes, and other trinkets and piled them on the site of the present-day Moutoa Gardens. With this offering, he "bought" some 40,000 acres of Maori land. The Maoris, however, replaced Wakefield's gifts with 30 pigs and nearly ten tons of potatoes—their customary "gift for gift"—and had no idea they had transferred title to their lands. Despite the dispute, settlers began arriving and the town prospered, even though constantly caught up in Maori-Pakeha conflicts. It wasn't until 1848 that land problems were laid to rest with the payment of £1000 for about 80,000 acres clearly defined in a bill of sale from the Maoris, which ended with the words "Now all the land contained within these boundaries . . . we have wept and signed over, bid farewell to and delivered up forever to the Europeans."

It was, of course, the Wanganui River (whose riverbed was carved out by Taranaki in his wild flight from Tongariro's wrath) that made this site such a desirable one for the Europeans. It had long served as an important waterway to the interior, as well as affording an excellent coastal harbor. It was said by the Maoris that the great explorer Kupe sailed the river. Pakehas soon established regular steamer service between the town and Taumarunui, and because of the magnificent scenery along the riverbank, the three-day journey quickly became an important sightseeing trip for tourists from all over the world. The steamer plied the river until 1934, and it's a pity that fire destroyed the wonderful old hotel and houseboat, which provided overnight accommodations to those travelers. Plans have now been completed to make a large portion of the Wanganui River a national park early in 1984.

ORIENTATION: Today's Wanganui has every bit as much friendly hospitality as it has age and history. Indeed, its slogan is "The Friendly City," and **Hospitality Wanganui** (a volunteer group of enthusiastic residents) operates a

Host Panel to squire overseas visitors around. They provide a personal guide who will devote as much time as necessary to seeing that you get to see and do everything there is to see and do in Wanganui. There's never a charge, and in the process of making arrangements, you'll get a bonus in the form of City Information Officer Gerald Weekes. You'll find him at the **Information Office** in the forecourt of the Municipal Chambers on the corner of Guyton and St. Hill Streets (tel. 53-286), eager to tell you about his town and to make certain you enjoy your stay. Gerald was, in my humble opinion, *born* for this job—you'll leave claiming him as a new friend and filled with as much affection for Wanganui as he is himself! Just let him know how you'd like to spend your time there and he'll take care of all the details. Your guide will furnish transportation and often steer you to special events you might not have known about otherwise. Every volunteer is knowledgeable about the area, so if you have a special interest (history, archeology, botany), they'll happily take you to spots most likely to fit in with that interest.

The Information Office can also furnish interesting brochures, book river tours, and provide maps.

ACCOMMODATIONS: That famed Wanganui hospitality extends to virtually every owner or manager of accommodations I have met, and you can be sure of a friendly reception no matter where you end up staying. There are good digs both in town and in the Castlecliff seaside suburb, which is where you'll find the hostel.

A Hostel

You can reach Wanganui's **YHA Hostel,** 3 Tregenna St., Castlecliff (tel. 44-111), by city bus (ask for the Morgan Street stop). The small hostel, which sleeps 12 in two rooms, is just 300 yards from the beach on the Tasman Sea. Rates are NZ$4 ($2.68) for Seniors, NZ$2 ($1.34) for Juniors.

The Y

A big old gracious house right in the city center serves as Wanganui's **YWCA,** 232 Wicksteed St., parallel with Victoria Avenue (tel. 57-480). There are only nine rooms available, and it's necessary to write or call as far in advance as possible. Rooms are simple, but homey and comfortable. Those on the top story have marvelous views. Only a light breakfast is served, but there is a guest kitchen, laundry, and TV lounge. There's no age limit, but an 11 p.m. curfew. Bed-and-breakfast rates are NZ$6.50 ($4.36) per person, NZ$3.50 ($2.35) if you have your own sleeping bag.

Cabins

The **Alwyn Motor Court and Motel Flats,** 65 Karaka St., Castlecliff (tel. 44-500), offers excellent value-for-money under the auspices of Jeff and Audrey Dabbs, who bought this business because they love to meet people from overseas. Just four miles from the city center, and close to a city bus line, the Alwyn is only a short walk through the bush from Castlecliff Beach. All units face a concrete courtyard and swimming pool, and all are bright, freshly painted, and have linoleum flooring. Each has either two two-tier bunks or two sleeping divans, with a curtain for privacy. Five have H&C and a stove, but share the communal shower and toilet. Rates for these units are NZ$13 ($8.72) double, NZ$4 ($2.68) per extra adult, NZ$3 ($2.01) per extra child. Three have shower and toilet as well as a stove, and cost NZ$20 ($13.42) double. All cabins have electric heaters, fridge, cooking pots, toasters, dishes, and cutlery. You must supply linen and blankets, but the Dabbs have them for rent at a small charge. Off the courtyard there's a laundry and TV-games room, with table tennis, pool table, and darts. In addition to the cabins, there are four lovely two-bedroom motel flats, nicely decorated. All have full kitchens, showers, TV, and all bedding. The one on the top floor has a marvelous sea view. These rent for NZ$30 ($20.13) double, NZ$6 ($4.03) per extra adult, NZ$4 ($2.68) for children under 12. The Dabbs are friendly and extremely cooperative when it comes to working out weekly and off-season rates.

Four miles east of town, on the city side of the river, the **Aramoho Motor Camp** (mailing address: Custodian, Somme Parade, Wanganui; tel. 38-402) has spacious, shady grounds. There are bunk cabins, each with four bunks; graded cabins that sleep two to six people, with H&C, small electric stoves, cooking utensils, and heaters; and chalets that sleep up to seven people, with complete kitchen, china, cutlery, pots, toaster, electric jug, and private toilet and shower. One chalet sleeps nine, has a bath, and is equipped for paraplegics. You can rent linen, blankets, irons, TV, and radio. The communal kitchen has gas stoves and fridge; the laundry includes dryers and an ironing board; and toilets and showers are stainless steel and Formica. Very near the river, there are two family barbecues, and there's a seven-day grocery store just across the road. Tent and caravan sites are also available in tree-shaded spots. Rates run from NZ$4 ($2.68) per person for tent sites to NZ$6 ($4.03) for bunks to NZ$12 ($8.05), double, for cabins to NZ$25 ($16.78), double, for chalets.

See also the caravan and camping facilities at both the Lake Wiritoa and Avro Motels (see "Motel Flats," below).

An Inn

It is seldom that I run across an inn in the old-fashioned sense of the word, but in Wanganui, the **Riverside Inn**, 2 Plymouth St. (tel. 32-529), fits that category admirably. Set back from the street in a flower garden, the rambling white wooden house (which dates from the early 1900s) has been lovingly brought up to date through renovation, which has shown due respect for its age and character. Its convenient location is just a short walk from the center of town. Accommodations consist of 12 rooms, only two with private shower and toilet. The charming decor features lace-curtained windows, potted plants, and fringed lampshades. The parlor, which serves as TV and breakfast room, is furnished in wicker and cane (on fine days, you may elect to breakfast out on the columned veranda; on not-so-fine days, in your room). There's a billards room with tea and coffee facilities, and in summer afternoon teas and barbecues are served in the garden. Breakfast is à la carte, with selections such as croissants and yogurt costing less than NZ$1 (67¢); cheese omelets and other egg dishes, less than NZ$2 ($1.34). Room rates are NZ$19 ($12.75) single, NZ$25 ($16.78) double. Book as far in advance as possible through Gerald Weekes at the Information Office, and send a one-night charge deposit.

Bed and Breakfast

Kay and Ken Savell preserve oldtime graciousness in the delightful **Cairn-brae**, 24 Somme Parade (tel. 57-918), with such touches as roses in the guest rooms. The lovely dining room looks out over the river, and the lounge holds a piano as well as a TV. Rooms are furnished in traditional style with an eclectic array of antiques. There's a small upstairs room for tea and toasted sandwiches from a vending machine kept freshly stocked. Not all bedrooms have H&C, but some of the upstairs rooms have terrific views. There are tubs and showers in the shared baths, and there's a guest laundry. Rates for bed and breakfast are NZ$18 ($12.08) single, NZ$29 ($19.46) double, and the evening meal is NZ$7 ($4.70).

Motel Flats

Lake Wiritoa Motel, Main South Road (tel. 56-179), is a mere three-minute drive from the center of Wanganui, yet in that three minutes you cross into a charming rural environment where serviced motel units look out onto rolling hills peopled with sheep, goats, horses, and even guinea pigs. Free pony rides will probably have the greatest appeal for children, but it was mostly adults I saw walking or sitting outdoors drinking in the pastoral scene with evident enjoyment. Karen and Jans Bukholt, the Danish-born owner-managers, run the place with a keen sense of what matters most to weary travelers— every unit is spotless, there's a small shop in the office with frozen meals and canned goods, and their charming little restaurant serves delicious home-cooked meals for an all-inclusive price of about NZ$7.50 ($5.03). In addition, there are outdoor barbecue facilities, as well as a swimming pool and spa, all overlooking those peaceful hills. Units, although a little on the small side, all have tea- and coffee-making facilities, TV, radio, and electric blanket. One unit has a waterbed. Those with full kitchens cost just NZ$2 ($1.34) more. Basic rates are NZ$20 ($13.42) single, NZ$24 ($16.11) double, with a NZ$1 (67¢) per-person surcharge for one-night stays and on holidays. There are also tent and caravan sites, with communal kitchen, showers, and toilets, which rent for NZ$5 ($3.36) double, NZ$2.50 ($1.68) per additional person.

There's much to choose from at the **Avro Motel,** 36 Alma Rd. (tel. 55-279). The garden-like grounds hold bedsitters, one-, two-, and three-bedroom units, all with wide windows overlooking the lawns, TV, and telephone. There's an outdoor swimming pool, two spa pools, a children's play area, and a laundry. Jackie and Tony Segat are the hosts at this nice motel, just about a mile from the city center and on a city bus line. Rates start at NZ$28 ($18.79) single, NZ$36 ($24.16) double. During the winter months, weekly rates can be arranged. Incidentally, the Avro has marvelous caravan facilities: 14 hookups, each with a small cabin enclosing a shower, toilet, and dressing room. Caravan guests may also use the laundry. Rates are NZ$10.50 ($7.05) double.

One of Wanganui's prettiest motels is the **Acacia Park Motel,** 140 Anzac Parade, Wanganui East (tel. 39-093), set in two acres of parkland overlooking the river, with units spread among magnificent old trees. The attractive brown wooden units have TV, radio, electric blanket, electric heating, and telephone. Eight are fully self-contained, sleeping from four to six, with shower, toilet, fridge, electric range, and full kitchen. Five serviced units sleep up to three and have a fridge, tea and coffee facilities, toaster, and electric fry pan. There's a guest laundry with dryer and drying room, a spa pool, game room with a pool table, children's play area, and a trampoline. Rates begin at NZ$26 ($17.45) single, NZ$28 ($18.79) double, for serviced units; and NZ$30 ($20.13) single, NZ$34 ($22.82) double, for kitchen units. The Acacia is about a mile from the city center, on a bus line and directly across the road from the Wanganui River Jet Tours.

Another motel with an especially attractive setting is the **River City Motel,** 59 Halswell St. (tel. 39-107), just across from the Peat Park Deer Reserve. The grounds are planted with flowering bushes and trees, with views of wooded hills and fields filled with grazing sheep. This rural-type setting is just one mile from the center of town, and about a two-minute walk from a city bus stop. The eight two-bedroom units can sleep up to six (one will accommodate eight), and they come with a full kitchen, electric heater, electric blanket, phone, radio, and TV. On the premises are a swimming pool, spa pool, putting green, trampoline, children's swings, and a barbecue, as well as a laundry and car-wash facilities. Rates are NZ$30 ($20.13) single, $40 ($26.85) double.

One of Wanganui's newest and prettiest motels is a Best Western. The **Gateway Motor Lodge,** on the corner of the Southern Motorway and Heads Road (mailing address: P.O. Box 970; tel. 58-164), has attractive units with vaulted, beamed ceilings. Serviced units have TV, radio, telephone, and tea- and coffee-making facilities. Two-bedroom family units add a full kitchen. Rates are NZ$30 ($20.13) single, NZ$36 ($24.16) double, for serviced units; NZ$38 ($25.50) double for family units.

There are 15 nicely furnished units at the **Astral Motel,** 45 Somme Parade (tel. 39-065). Sizes vary from bedsitters to one-bedrooms, to family units (which sleep up to six) with two bedrooms, and nine have full kitchen facilities, while the other six are serviced units with tea and coffee makings, fridge, and toaster. All have electric blankets, heaters, color TV, radio, and telephone. Wynne and Jack Brown, the obliging managers, will gladly deliver cooked or continental breakfasts at a small charge, and Wynne doesn't add any charge for cooking up the frozen dinners, which are on sale in a small shop in the office. The Astral is a Best Western, featuring the Holiday Pass discount, and a distinct advantage is its convenient location at the foot of the Dublin Street Bridge (on the city side of the river), just a short walk from the city center. Rates are NZ$31 ($20.80) single, NZ$35 ($23.49) double.

A Very Special Licensed Hotel

You should know right up front that what follows is the exact opposite of an objective viewpoint: it is an unabashedly subjective, totally in-love-with report from yours truly of one of those great old hotels, which has managed to survive with all the spirit and character of the "grand" hotels of yesteryear. **Hurley's Grand Hotel,** on the corner of Guyton and St. Hill Streets (mailing address: P.O. Box 364; tel. 50-955), was owned and operated by Tim Hurley's father for many years before Tim took over, and now as in the past, guests receive all the care and attention of friends who have come for a family visit. Modernization has been limited strictly to facilities and furnishings, with such lovely holdovers from its beginnings as dark-wood paneling and fireplaces in the spacious public rooms, oil paintings in gold-leafed frames, the marvelous old carved-wood staircase, and a bar crammed full of excellent carvings by local Maoris (see "After Dark"). Modern the furniture may be (like huge, comfortable chairs grouped around low tables in the lounge), yet the decor (upholstering, draperies, etc.) retains a period look in keeping with Hurley's origins. The 60 guest rooms range in size from those accommodating just one to those sleeping up to five comfortably. Each is individually decorated, a nice departure from the standardized look of most present-day hotel rooms. A two-family suite features two bedrooms, one on each side of the central lounge (at just NZ$5, or $3.36 U.S. per person above the regular rate). One luxurious suite is furnished entirely with antiques (at a top rate of NZ$40 or $26.85 U.S. single; NZ$50, or $33.56 U.S. double). Regular rates are a low NZ$25 ($16.78) to NZ$37 ($24.82) single, NZ$39 ($26.17) to NZ$43 ($28.86) double, and since this is a Best Western member, the Holiday Pass discount brings them even lower. In addition to the Tiki Bar (a great local favorite), there's piano music in the guest lounge and a beautiful restaurant serving outstanding food (see "Meals").

MEALS: My favorite small, inexpensive eatery in Wanganui is the **Top-o-Town Coffee Shop,** 194 Victoria Ave. (tel. 58-400), where everything is fresh and homemade. It's a cozy place with friendly people behind the self-service counter. They serve morning and afternoon teas, as well as breakfasts and light meals. There are savouries, meat pies, sandwiches, pies, and some of the best homemade cakes and pastries you're likely to find anywhere. Breakfast runs NZ$2 ($1.34) to NZ$3 ($2.01) and is served from 7 to 9 a.m.; light meals are in the NZ$3 ($2.01) to NZ$4 ($2.68) range; pastries are under NZ$1 (67¢). Hours are 7 a.m. to 4 p.m. Monday through Thursday; to 5 p.m. on Friday, and 9 a.m. to noon on Saturday.

   Hurley's Grand Hotel, at corner of Guyton and St. Hill Streets (tel. 50-955), merits a rave in the food department as well as for its superb accommodations (see above). No matter what your price or appetite range, that grand old hotel comes up with just the right place to eat. For inexpensive hot meals or bar snacks, there's **The Strand,** a bistro-bar combining the same rich dark woods as other hotel public rooms with a friendly, relaxed pub atmosphere. The same menu is served for lunch (noon to 2 p.m.) and dinner (6 to 9 p.m.), and features steaks, fish, chicken, and roasts for prices of NZ$2.50 ($1.68) to NZ$6 ($4.03). The Strand is open every day. **Timothy's Restaurant,** on the other hand, can only be described as elegant, with lovely old chandeliers, flocked wallpaper, and a beautiful embossed ceiling, which will draw your eyes upward throughout any meal. Breakfast, lunch, and dinner are all served, but it's dinner that deserves special mention. Both the menu and service match the elegance of the room, yet there's not the slightest hint of stuffiness (which so often afflicts elegant restaurants). Dishes such as beef schnitzel Cordon Bleu, flounder meunière, duckling, and a variety of roasts are perfection, yet reasonably priced from NZ$5.50 ($3.69) to NZ$9.50 ($6.38) on the à la carte menu. An excellent wine list complements your choice of entree. Since the restaurant is open to the lounge, you dine to the accompaniment of piano music. Timothy's is open seven days a week and dinner is served from 6 to 9:30 p.m. On weekends, best reserve.

   The **Garden Bistro Family Restaurant and Bar,** 33 Somme Parade (tel. 38-656), is a licensed restaurant set on the riverbank. There are three or four Chinese dishes on every night's menu (try the stir-fried lamb), although the chef is Italian. In addition, you can order fish, steaks, roasts, and salad plates. But no matter what you choose, it will come in *huge* portions. The price, however, is anything but huge—an average meal will run about NZ$4.50 ($3.02). There's a special Kids' Menu for even less. Hours are 5 to 9 p.m. every night except Sunday, and noon to 2 p.m. on Saturday, when it gets very crowded.

   Meals are home-cooked, very nearly gourmet, and easy on the budget at the **Shangri-La** on St. Johns Hill (tel. 53-654). And they're served in a lovely setting, with a window wall overlooking Virginia Lake and the winter gardens. Maurice Vige, the French owner-chef, took his training in Paris and is quite meticulous in the preparation of all the food appearing on his tables. As a result, everything from European specialties to basic Kiwi dishes to homemade pies is culinary perfection. The morning and afternoon Devonshire teas are a real treat—under NZ$2 ($1.34), served 11:30 a.m. to 2 p.m. Not licensed, but BYO. Hours are 9 a.m. to 5 p.m., seven days a week; dinners served on summer weekends.

Note: Mr. Vige also rents a guest room in his home at 59 Bell St. (tel. 53-634), for NZ$15 ($10.06) double. Breakfast is NZ$2.50 ($1.68)—no charge for the chance to brush up on your French over coffee.

The **Riverina Restaurant,** 33 Somme Parade (tel. 38-656), is a large, attractive and very popular place specializing in steaks and seafood. The adjacent lounge bar, entered through swinging doors, is pubby with dark wood and black leather seating. There's an arbor room, with growing vines and grapes, which patrons often reach up and pick. The fireplace is aglow on cool evenings. Lunch prices range from NZ$4 ($2.68) to NZ$5.50 ($3.69), and dinners run from NZ$6 ($4.03) to NZ$8 ($5.37). It's fully licensed and open seven days a week from noon to 2:30 p.m. and 5 to 9 p.m., with a special menu for children between 5 and 7 p.m.

Note: There's an excellent deli and bottle store next door to the Riverina, the **Riverside Cellars,** with all sorts of cheeses, cold cuts, salads, frozen meals, and other deli items for eating in your motel flat.

I'd list **Liffiton Castle,** 26 Liffiton St. (tel. 57-864), under a "Big Splurge" heading, except that prices aren't really *that* astronomical—so let's just call it a "Big Treat." This is a century-old house, which over the last five years has been renovated with loving care spiced up with a dollop of humor. You enter over a moat into a bar whose centerpice is the bar itself, a renovated theater box from the old Majestic Theatre—notice the three jesters behind the bar (no, *not* the bartenders!), also from the Majestic. There are pressed-tin ceilings from the Wangani Girls College; a dance floor from the Boys Technical College; a handsome, hand-carved 17th-century mantel; arched windows from a local church; an antique English sideboard; and so many suits of armor that there's an Armoury Room. All that (plus a good bit more) creates an interesting, warm, inviting—and fun—atmosphere. And there's music for dancing most evenings. The food? Superb! Steaks are a specialty, all of superior grades and beautifully cooked. Seafood, chicken, weinerschnitzel, and roast beef are also on the menu, and there's a good wine list, reasonably priced. Main courses are in the NZ$7 $4.70) to NZ$10 ($6.71) range. Hours are 6 to 10 p.m. every day except Sunday, and it's a good idea to book, especially on weekends—the locals love this place!

THINGS TO SEE AND DO: To put first things first, take a look at Wanganui and its environs, which will bring everything else you see into perspective—it's the look you get from **Durie Hill,** at the south end of the Wanganui Bridge at Victoria Avenue. Pick up the souvenir booklet that tells you the history of this place, then go through a 672-foot tunnel to reach a unique elevator, which takes you to the summit, 216 feet up. From the platform at the top, Wanganui is spread before you: the historic river's winding path is clear; to the west stretches the Tasman Sea; and to the north rises Mount Egmont (that unlucky lover, Taranaki). Of course, if you're game to walk up 176 steps, the top of the nearby **War Memorial** will give you a view, which extends from Mount Ruapehu all the way to the South Island (you'll have to take that on faith—as yet, I haven't summoned up the stamina to make the climb!). Even from the ground, the War Memorial is worth a few minutes of your time. It's constructed of shell rock from the riverbanks, which holds two-million-year-old fossils that prove conclusively Wanganui was once a part of the sea.

There are delightful **walks** in and around Wanganui. The *Scenic Walks* brochure you can get at the PRO guides you around six, which are short and easy and cover most of the things you'll want to visit. Another, the **Atene**

Skyline Walk, takes a full day (about eight hours), but rewards you with stunning views of the area and a "meander" around what was once seabed.

Children will enjoy the romp, grownups the respite, at the **Kowhai Park Playground** on Anzac Parade near the Dublin Street Bridge. The Jaycees of Wanganui built it, and its four acres now hold a Tot Town Railway (complete with station, tunnel, and overhead bridge), a huge whale, brontosaurus, clock tower, sea-serpent swings, all sorts of storybook characters, and even a mini-volcano to explore. And speaking of parks, save time for a leisurely stroll through the one at **Virginia Lake** (adjacent to Great North Road and St. John's Hill), whose grounds are a serene haven of trees, flowers, water lilies, ducks, swans, an aviary, and beautiful winter gardens.

You won't want to miss the **Wanganui Regional Museum,** in the Civic Center one block east of Victoria Avenue at the end of Maria Place. There's a large Maori collection, a settler's cottage, natural history exhibits, and a 75-foot war canoe built in 1810, which is one of the largest in the country and still has bullets from the Maori wars imbedded in its hull.

The riverside **Moutoa Gardens** historic reserve is where Maori-Pakeha contact was first made and the first controversial "purchase" of Maori land was transacted. There are memorials to Maori war dead, statues, and the city courthouse there now. It's down at Taupo Quay, off Victoria Quay (beside the huge computer center, a vivid contrast between yesterday and today).

Not quite—but almost—a sightseeing spot is **Victoria Court,** a new shopping courtyard off Victoria Avenue near Guyton Street. Interesting crafts and antiques are in the shop, and there's a very good art gallery featuring the works of New Zealand artists. About a mile from the city center, on Tawa Street, **Gonville Cottage Industries** holds a Craft Market the first Saturday of each month from March to December, with stalls held by local craftspeople.

The suburb of Putiki is the setting for **St. Paul's Anglican Memorial Church,** built in 1936 by Maoris and Pakehas working together. The stained-glass Williams Memorial Window features the figure of Christ wearing robes with Maori-design border, and there is fine carving in the church's interior. It's open every day from 9 a.m. to 6 p.m.

Plan to spend an hour or two at **Holly Lodge Estate,** Papeete Road, Upper Aramoho, Wanganui (tel. 39-344), where owners Norman and Alza Garrett will show you around the vineyards and outbuildings where wines are produced, explaining every step of the process as you go. The Wine Shop and Tasting Bar give you a chance to test several of the wines and buy at wholesale prices. Be sure to step into the small craft shop, where most items have been made locally, and the interesting Antique Porcelain Doll Emporium, to see how dolls are made entirely on the premises, from the pouring of porcelain clay to the sewing of their lovely period clothing (they go to retail outlets all over the country, but can be bought here at very reasonable prices). Another "don't miss" is Geraldo's, a small museum of memorabilia of early Wanganui assembled by PRO Gerald Weekes (and, of course, named for him). The Garretts also run a very good jet-boat river trip (see below) from their wharf across the road from the vineyards.

Two nearby scenic reserves warrant a visit. **Bushy Park** is 15 miles north of Wanganui (turn off Highway 3 at Kai Iwi and drive five miles to the park), and was originally the homestead of James Moore, who came to Wanganui in the mid-1860s. The fine old home was occupied by his descendants until 1962. It stands in spacious lawns and gardens planted with a large variety of native plants, with a backdrop of some 220 acres of native bush. The park is open every day except Monday and Tuesday, and admission is NZ$1 (67¢) for adults, half that for children. Incidentally, there are limited accommodations available in the house itself at rates of NZ$14 ($9.40) single, NZ$18 ($12.08) double, NZ$6 ($4.03) for children. Write or call: The Custodian, Bushy Park, Kai Iwi, RD 8, Wanganui (tel. 879).

The **Bason Botanical Reserve** is on Rapanui Road, and its Homestead Garden is a delightful place for a stroll among more than 100 camellias and a wide assortment of shrubs, vines, annuals, bulbs, and perennials. The ultra-modern conservatory holds the interesting display center and tropical plant house. Open daily from 9:30 a.m. until dusk (conservatory hours are 10 a.m. to 4 p.m. weekdays, 2 to 4 p.m. weekends and holidays).

Exploring the River

Exploring the river by jet boat takes top priority for most visitors to Wanganui, and there are several options for doing it. But let me suggest that before you set out, drop by the PRO and purchase the excellent Wanganui River map published by the Department of Lands and Survey (be sure you get #NZMS 258, Edition 2)—it's an excellent NZ$1.50 ($1.01) investment, showing the river and its banks in detail, with historical notes on each point of interest. I further suggest that you study the map *before* you book your river trip—while there is certainly no *un*interesting part of the river, there may be some portion you'd particularly like to see, and you'll want to be certain you choose a jet boat that will take you there. The PRO can also give you current details on which jet-boat tours are operating, departure and return times, and prices in effect at the time of your visit (I try, but you know what can happen to prices!).

Wanganui River Jet Tours (mailing address: P.O. Box 6036; tel. 36-346) has its terminal on Anzac Parade and offers a variety of good river tours. There are two all-day trips: one to the intriguing "Bridge to Nowhere" (240 kilometers; fare, NZ$90, or $60.40 U.S.) and one to Pipiriki and the "Drop Scene" (210 kilometers; fare NZ$70, or $46.98 U.S.). Shorter trips range from a 35-minute boating tour around the bridges at NZ$10 ($6.71) to a 1½-hour, 52-kilometer ride for NZ$18 ($12.08), to the 4-hour, 120-kilometer ride to Koroniti Marae for NZ$38 ($25.50). Children 12 and under pay half. You'll be treated to a first-rate narrative all the way on points along the river, and the scenery is breathtaking, as are some of the rapids encountered (and easily overcome by your expert guides). They supply protective wet-weather gear, and on the longer trips, hot drinks and tea and coffee are furnished—you're asked to bring a packed lunch on the all-day jaunts. *Note:* You should carry a light sweater no matter what the weather, and be sure to wear comfortable clothing and shoes.

There's a lovely two-hour jet-boat tour from the terminal at Holly Lodge Vineyards (see above), which takes you out to Hipango Park, with a tea, coffee, or sherry stop before returning. Your guide is not only informative, but entertaining as well, with interesting anecdotes about the river and the country through which you are passing. Fares are NZ$14.50 ($9.73) for adults, NZ$7 ($4.70) for children.

Another excellent way to explore the river is with **John Hammond's River Road Tours** (tel. 54-635). As either a substitute or supplement to the jet-boat tours, these minibus road tours are highly recommended. Coachmaster Hammond knows the river and the people who live along its banks. All along your route, he'll be dropping off mail and provisions to river dwellers, and many times will pick up locals along the way. All River Road Tours feature a stop in the Maori village of Jerusalem for tea, where you can meet and talk to the residents in a relaxed atmosphere. There are several options, some including a jet-boat trip to the famous "Drop Scene." Prices range from NZ$18 ($12.08) to NZ$22 ($14.77), with children paying half.

Following Highway 3 south from Wanganui until it joins Highway 1, you're in for an easy three-hour, 122-mile drive along excellent roads: pastoral scenes of grazing sheep and cultivated fields at first, smashing sea views later, then a four-lane expressway leading into the beautiful harbor and splendid hills of Wonderful, Windy Wellington.

Chapter VI

WELLINGTON

1. The City and Surroundings
2. Across to the South Island

"WONDERFUL, WINDY WELLINGTON" it is called—with derision by Kiwis who don't live here, with affection by those who do. Well, there's no denying that it *is* windy: 60-mile-per-hour winds sweep through what is the only substantial gap in New Zealand's mountain chain on an average of 40 days each year. Winds notwithstanding, however, Wellington is easily one of New Zealand's most beautiful cities. Indeed, its magnificent harbor rivals any in the world. Your first view of that harbor, with the city curved around its western and southwestern shoreline and surrounding hills abloom with what appear from a distance to be tiny dollhouses spilling down their sides, is likely to make you catch your breath, even if that view should happen to be in the rain (which is a distant possibility!). On a fine day, there are few city views anywhere to equal it.

This gorgeous place was discovered in A.D. 950 by Kupe, the great Polynesian explorer, and by the time Captain Cook stopped by (but didn't land) in 1773, the harbor was lined with Maori settlements. When New Zealand Company representative Col. William Wakefield's good ship *Tory* arrived on the scene in September of 1839, warring between the Maori tribes had become so fierce, and the local tribes were so fearful of their more powerful enemies, that (after a bit of negotiating back and forth, and a few of the usual misunderstandings about land transfers, etc.), they accepted the Pakeha as the lesser of two evils. By January 1840 settlers began coming in goodly numbers, and after a rather rowdy beginning (when, according to contemporary reports, meetings were held to try to determine how the citizenry could protect themselves from the lawless police force!), the town began a growth that has never really stopped. A tug-of-war with Auckland finally resulted in Wellington's being named the colony's capital on the basis of its central location and the belief that the "middle island" (that's the South Island's claim to being the "mainland," one you'll hear often after crossing Cook Strait) might well pull out and establish a separate colony altogether if it were not afforded better access to the capital than faraway Auckland provided.

Wellington today, while peopled mainly by civil servants, diplomats, and corporate home-office staffs, maintains a conservative—but far from stuffy—air. There is perhaps more sheer diversity here than in any other of New Zealand's cities: narrow streets and Edwardian buildings nudge modern edifices of concrete and glass; massive office buildings embrace continental-style restaurants; fashionable boutiques are housed in psuedo-colonial-style complexes while craft shops hold sway in avant garde structures; and the after-dark scene

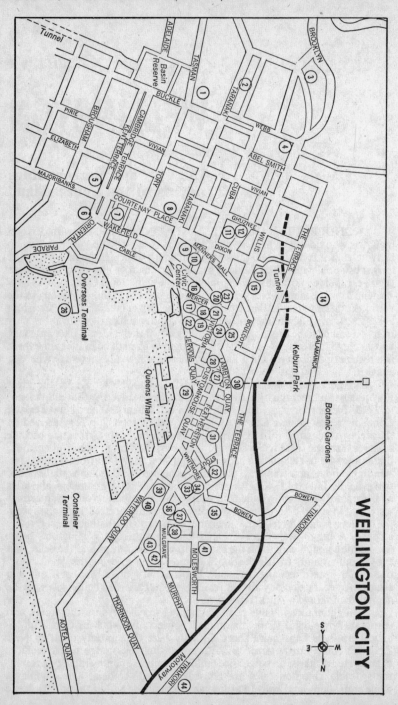

is one of Kiwiland's liveliest. Wellington is a *cosmopolitan* city, with an ever-changing skyline, a population that habitually dwindles on weekends when government workers desert the city for visits "home," and a constant influx of high-powered international visitors.

It's also your port of embarkation for the South Island's wonders—but pray don't embark until you've explored this hub around which New Zealand's government revolves. And from a practical point of view, plan your explorations for a weekend when rooms are more easily come by and special rates are offered to fill rooms vacated by that disappearing weekday population.

1. The City and Surroundings

ORIENTATION: The main point of reference in the city is, of course, the harbor. **Willis Street** is the main street; for shopping, try Lambton Quay, Manners Street, Cuba Street, and Courtenay Place. There is good city **bus service,** with most lines beginning at the railway station or **Courtenay Place.** Newsstands sell a good timetable with a small map, or you can call 856-579 during office hours (873-169 after hours and weekends) for route information. Fares are based on distance traveled, and you can purchase ten-trip concession tickets. NZR runs **commuter trains** to suburbs on fairly frequent schedules; tel. 725-399 for timetable information. If you're driving, avoid downtown Wellington traffic by parking in one of the center-city car parks. They're on Boulcott Street, under the James Cook Hotel; on Bond Street in the Lombard Parking Centre; and on Clifton Terrace, between Aurora and Everton Terraces. The best lookout for a panoramic view of the city is 648-foot **Mount Victoria** in the southern end of the city; the easiest lookout to reach is **Kelburn,** with its cable car.

USEFUL INFORMATION: The **New Zealand Government Tourist Bureau** (GTB) is at 26–31 Mercer St. (tel. 739-269), just one block away from the Town Hall. Hours are 8 a.m. to 5 p.m. Monday through Thursday, to 8 p.m. on Friday, and 9:30 a.m. to 12:30 p.m. on Saturday. . . . You'll find the **PRO Visitors Centre** at 2 Mercer St. (tel. 735-063), with the same hours as the GTB. . . . The free *Capital Visitor* is published weekly by the PRO giving information on current activities. It's distributed in most hotels as well as by the GTB and PRO. . . . **Wellington Railway Station** is on Waterloo Quay, and long-distance buses (except Newmans) depart platform 9 at that station (tel. 725-399 for bus and rail information). . . . **Newmans buses** leave from 260 Taranaki St. . . . The **Air New Zealand** office for domestic and international booking and information is at 179 Fetherston St. (tel. 859-911). . . . The **Central Post Office (CPO)** is in Chews Lane off Willis Street, open 8 a.m. to 5 p.m. Monday to Friday, with a philatelic bureau on the premises for stamp collectors. . . . **Taxi ranks** are in front of the railway station, in the Lambton Quay shopping area between Gray and Hunter Streets, and in various other street locations around the city. There's a small surcharge if you telephone for a taxi (tel. 859-900, 893-023, or 859-888), and on weekends and holidays. . . . For a 24-hour gas (petrol) station, try **Central Service Station Ltd.** on Jervois Quay.

Wellington Airport

Guthreys Coachlines runs a coach service every 20 minutes on weekdays, 30 minutes on weekends, to the Wellington Airport, which is six miles south of the city center. Coaches depart from Bunny Street (close to the railway station), and there are several pickup points in the city. Airport bus stops have a special red marking; fares are NZ$2.10 ($1.41) for adults, NZ $.80 (54¢) for children. Domestic flights and flights between New Zealand and Australia arrive and depart at the airport.

There's a good medium-priced restaurant at the airport, which serves generous portions from 10 a.m. to 8 p.m. every day, and a modern cafeteria serving light meals and snacks, open from 6 a.m. to 9 p.m. every day. Also, a bar, post office, nursery, bank, small duty-free shop, and car-rental desks. A GTB desk in the overseas lounge provides directions and information to incoming international passengers, but does not book accommodations. The bank is open one hour before any overseas departure and for each overseas arrival. There are ample luggage carts provided at no charge.

ACCOMMODATIONS: There are two things that must be said right up front about accommodations in Wellington: you should book as far in advance as possible; and you'll stand a much better chance of finding budget accommodations on weekends than during the week. It all has to do with the city's resident population tide—in on Monday, out on Friday evening. It is true that there are a lot of bed-and-breakfast listings, but the majority cater to their permanent guests and few are interested in transients like you and me. That tidal flow does, however, create one unique situation in the capital city: many superior hotels and motels cut prices drastically over the weekends when they have a surplus of rooms, and that means a little shopping around may well net you a budget price in a "splurge" location. More and more restaurants, shops, and sightseeing attractions are remaining open for the weekend, making it quite possible to take advantage of those special rates without sacrificing your usual holiday activities.

Hostels

The **YHA Hostel** is at 40 Tinakori Rd. (tel. 736-271), only about a ten-minute walk from the railway station and the Picton ferry terminal. Eight rooms hold 48 beds, and there are overflow accommodations available. Advance booking is especially advisable from December to February. Sightseeing attractions such as the Parliament buildings, Dominion Museum, and cable car are all handy to the hostel. Seniors pay NZ$6 ($4.03); Juniors, NZ$3 ($2.01).

The **Ivanhoe Inn,** 52 Ellice St., Mount Victoria (tel. 842-264), is perched on one of Wellington's picturesque hillsides in a row of small colonial houses. The red-and-white wooden house has been recently renovated, and most rooms are quite spacious. There are singles, twins, and doubles, all with H&C. Other facilities include a fully equipped kitchen, dining room, and TV lounge. Breakfast is available at a small charge. Rates start at NZ$8 ($5.37).

The Y

Unfortunately, there is neither a YMCA nor YWCA in operation in Wellington at present.

Cabins

The Lower Hutt City Council recently took over operation of the **Hutt Park Motor Camp** at 95 Hutt Park Rd., Moera, Lower Hutt (tel. 685-913), some nine miles northeast of the city, and is making great improvements to both grounds and cabins. It's a large, shaded camp with some 59 cabins, one of which is equipped for wheelchairs. They range in size from a two-berth cabin with only basic furnishings, dishes, and an electric jug, to a two-bedroom cottage with private bath and cooking facilities. You must supply linen, blankets, and cutlery, none of which are available for rent. There's a 15-hole golf course on the 92-acre premises, which is available to guests at half price. Other facilities include laundry (coin-operated), kitchens, shower rooms, TV lounge, children's wading pool, and play area. There are grocery stores nearby, as well as a racetrack for trotters. Rates run from NZ$10 ($6.71) for two to NZ$30 ($20.13) for six, with weekly rates that begin at NZ$70 ($46.98) for two. Caravan sites are NZ$6.50 ($4.36) for two; tent sites, NZ$6 ($4.03) for two. There's frequent bus service into Wellington via the Eastbourne bus.

Bed and Breakfast

The center-city **Railton Travel Hotel,** 213 Cuba St. (mailing address: P.O. Box 6421; tel. 851-632), is Wellington's largest B&B accommodation. The three-story, 170-room hotel is run by the Salvation Army and standards are high. Cleanliness is obviously next to godliness here—everything is spotless—and amenities include two TV lounges (one for nonsmokers), a reading room, luggage room, laundry with dryer and irons, and tea-making facilities in the guest lounges. Rooms are fully carpeted, with H&C in most, and there are ample showers and baths. There are around 100 single rooms, and although some are quite small, those of us who travel in ones instead of twos count that a decided blessing. Doubles, family rooms (two with private facilities), and motel units that sleep four or five (with lounge, kitchen, and private facilities) make up the remainder. The pleasant dining room is open to the public as well as guests for all three meals, all at moderate prices (dinner runs about NZ$5.50, or $3.69 U.S.). Bed-and-breakfast rates (shared facilities) are NZ$20 ($13.42) single, NZ$31 ($20.80) double; with private facilities, NZ$23 ($15.44) single, NZ$34 ($22.82) double. Motel flats (without breakfast) cost NZ$27 ($18.12) single, NZ$32 ($21.48) double, NZ$6 ($4.03) for each additional person. And there are reduced rates for children.

I fell in love with the charming **Harbour View Motor Lodge,** 33 Thompson St. (tel. 848-795), although it was a bit hard to find—down a driveway between nos. 29 and 35 Thompson St. The rambling, two-story white house sits halfway up one of Wellington's hills, well off the street, and has a magnificent view of the city and harbor. Inside, Sue and Kerry Simpson have furnished the rooms (most of which are quite spacious) attractively and comfortably, and the large guest lounge is inviting, with a fireplace, TV, and an adjoining tea and coffee room. The dining room is light and cheerful, and you can order the evening meal if you like. All rooms have H&C and share toilet and shower facilities. The Simpsons also have three motel flats, which can sleep up to six in two bedrooms. Bed-and-breakfast rates are NZ$18 ($12.08) per person; bed, breakfast, and dinner, NZ$24 ($16.11). Motel flats are NZ$36 ($24.16) double, NZ$6 ($4.03) for each additional person. City bus transportation is only one block away.

Facing Thompson Street, just in front of the Horbour View and high up enough so that some rooms have good views of the city and harbor, is the **Clinton Private Hotel,** 35 Thompson (tel. 859-515). The two-story house is well kept, with moderate-size, comfortably furnished rooms. H&C in all rooms, shared baths and toilets. There's a bright, airy lounge and a large, pleasant dining room. Mr. and Mrs. Rippin are hosts here. Bed-and-breakfast rates are

NZ$20 ($13.42) single, NZ$30 ($20.13) double, and an evening meal is NZ$5.50 ($3.69).

The ornate old **Fairview Lodge,** 8 Church St. (tel. 726-248), began life as a nightclub and commands terrific views of the city and harbor in its choice site just 300 yards off Willis Street. That hilltop location means a steep climb to reach the Fairview, but it's more than worth the effort. Lots of character here, in homey, comfortable rooms (all with H&C, some with stained-glass windows or window seats), a lobby presided over by mounted deer and boar heads, a spacious lounge downstairs, a cozy tea and coffee lounge upstairs, and a large dining room featuring those marvelous C. F. Goldie paintings, which capture so accurately the nobility of early Maori faces. There are laundry facilities and off-the-street parking, as well as courtesy-car pickup service from transportation terminals. Bed-and-breakfast rates are NZ$17 ($11.41) single, NZ$26 ($17.45) double; including dinner, NZ$22 ($14.76) and NZ$36 ($24.16). Lower rates are available for longer stays.

In the northern suburb of Lower Hutt, the **Pharazyn House Private Hotel,** 23 Pharazyn St., Lower Hutt (tel. 663-271), is a large, gracious old residence set in a half acre of lawn and conifers. It's just five minutes from the Lower Hutt and Melling railway stations. Peter and Lesley Icke, your hosts here, are English and well-seasoned travelers, whose eighteen years' experience in what they call the "hospitality industry" have given them keen insight into seeing to their guests' comfort. The seven bedrooms are bright and spacious, and all have H&C and tea-making facilities. There are two singles, five twins or doubles, and the Ickes will put in extra beds if required. In what used to be the lounge, there's now a small, intimate restaurant where Peter Icke rules as chef and takes pride in his international cuisine dishes (not licensed, BYO). Bed-and-breakfast (it's a continental breakfast) rates are NZ$22 ($14.77) to NZ$25 ($16.78) per person, NZ$10 ($6.71) for each additional.

Motel Flats

Of the very few motels, which could be considered "budget" in Wellington, one of the best is the **Wellington Luxury Motel,** 14 Hobson St. (tel. 726-825), near Davis Street at the northern edge of the city center and about a five-minute walk from the railway station. It's a large white house built back in 1912, surrounded by hedges, which has been renovated to create five nice units with such charming extras as bay windows, beamed ceilings, and small leaded window panes. Pamela and Lloyd Barnard are the gracious hosts who especially welcome American guests. Three of the spacious units are bedsitters, and two have one bedroom and can sleep up to six. All are attractively furnished and have color TV and telephones. There's limited off-street parking, and city bus transportation half a block away. Rates are NZ$36 ($24.16) double, NZ$7 ($4.70) for each additional adult.

The three motel flats at **Harbour View Motor Lodge** (see "Bed and Breakfast") are exceptionally nice if you can book far enough in advance to get one.

About seven minutes away from the city center, **Oakley's Motels,** 331 Willis St. (tel. 842-881), is a white clapboard house with flowers and shrubs out front, which has four comfortable units. Three are bedsitters, the other a one-bedroom. Furnishings are simple, but more than adequate, and the place is well maintained. All units have TV, phone, radio, and heater, and there is city bus transportation right out front. There's an outdoor swing for children, babysitters available, and parking in the rear. Rates are NZ$34 ($22.19) to NZ$36 ($24.16) for one or two people, NZ$5 ($3.36) for each additional adult.

A Licensed Hotel Discount

As I said in the beginning of this section, many of the pricier hotels offer special weekend rates. And while it's a good idea to shop around for the best of these, I want to tell you about my own favorite.

The **Abel Tasman Courtesy Inn,** corner of Willis and Dixon Streets (tel. 851-304), just couldn't be any more conveniently located. It's right in the heart of everything, with easy walking to just about any shopping or sightseeing you have planned. Its Upstairs at the Tas restaurant is elegant, relaxing, and just a tad above moderate in price. Furthermore, this is a Best Western, meeting the high standards that make this chain outstanding. Its 70 rooms, all with private bath, are exceptionally well furnished and come with either king-size beds or twins, tea and coffee facilities, complimentary morning newspaper, ironing facilities, same-day laundry service on weekdays—and a weekend accommodation bargain rate of two people for the price of one every Friday, Saturday, and Sunday! I hasten to add that you may well be able to better the rates, even at that, but this may be the only place in New Zealand where you'll have a shot at such choice accommodations at prices of NZ$45 ($30.20) to NZ$65 ($43.69). When booking, be sure to ask for the lowest weekend special currently offered—there is ongoing competition between the city's hotels these days, and the Abel Tasman is constantly revising its specials to meet it. If you can manage it, this one gets my heartiest recommendation.

READERS' ACCOMMODATIONS SELECTIONS: "A pleasant place to stay in Wellington is the **Ambassador Travel Lodge,** 287 The Terrace (tel. 845-687). It's clean and quiet, and rates are quite reasonable. Another place you might consider is the **DeBrett Hotel,** smack in the middle of town at 101 Lambton Quay (tel. 725-376). It's a bit more expensive than a bed and breakfast, but a good hotel for a businessman" (Stevan Galante, New York, N.Y.). . . . "The **Parkview Lodge** was quaint, with very low bed-and-breakfast rates and a good evening meal" (Paula Adams, Denver, Colo.).

MEALS: You'll find good, inexpensive places to eat along almost any Wellington Street. And there's an interesting diversity of cuisine offered in the city's restaurants. Space limitations necessarily mean that my listings will omit many that are worthy of note. Drop me a line if you find that special eatery you think other budgeteers should know about, and I'll include as many as possible in future editions.

For meals at absolutely rock-bottom prices, in an atmosphere especially created to alleviate the loneliness a traveler sometimes encounters in a strange city, the place to go is the **Friendship Centre,** 54–56 Boulcott St., just off Willis Street (tel. 725-571). The cafeteria is in a modern building, which holds a variety of recreational facilities, and serves home-cooked meals at prices which average NZ$3 ($2.01) for dinner, served from 5:15 to 6:30 p.m. Snacks, coffee, and tea are available throughout the day. Based on the theory that "A city can be a lonely place," the center prides itself on being "people-related. . . . where everybody is welcome, where visitors become friends, without pressure or organized programme." And although the stated concept is "The Christian faith is seen in action through genuine friendship," there is absolutely no religious pressure. Instead, friendship takes the form of such practicalities as facilities for taking a hot shower while you're there; a counselor on call if you feel the need; a reading and TV room; table tennis and billiards; and an opportunity to meet other students, clerical workers, or travelers on a relaxed, informal basis. Hours are 10 a.m. to 6:30 p.m. Monday through Friday, closed Saturday, on Sunday from 12:15 p.m. It stays open until 10 p.m. on Monday for a free games night.

The aforementioned **Railton Travel Hotel** (see "Accommodations," above), at 213 Cuba St. (tel. 851-632), serves reliably good meals at prices that average about NZ$5 ($3.36) for dinner. Roasts, chicken, beef, and lamb are regulars on the menu, as are a good selection of vegetables and sweets (which are always served with that good New Zealand cream). Breakfast and dinner are served Monday to Saturday, breakfast and the midday meal on Sunday.

There's not a **Cobb & Co.** in Wellington proper, but if you happen to be staying out in Lower Hutt, you'll find one in the Kings Cross Establishment, Queens Drive (tel. 661-947), and there's another in the Totara Lodge Hotel on Ararino Street in Upper Hutt (tel. 285-937). Both are in the chain's traditional decor and offer the standard menu (main courses average NZ$5, or $3.36 U.S.), with hours of 7:30 a.m. to 10 p.m. seven days a week, and both are fully licensed.

Jumbos is an elephant-size restaurant in the ultramodern Oaks Shopping Complex in Cuba Mall (tel. 850-583). It's as modern as its setting, with a fresh, green-and-white garden decor and a serving staff spiffed up in crisp uniforms of the same colors. Tables are set with crystal stemware and German crockery, and there are two bars for pre- or after-meal libations. The interesting menu includes such varied items as Raju's Katmandu curry (with chicken, beef, or smoked fish), deep-fried squid rings, deviled kidneys, chili con carne, and deep-fried terakihi—with a solid base of more mundane offerings like hamburgers, steak sandwiches, salad plates, and steaks. Main courses on the à la carte menu run about NZ$8 ($5.37); hamburgers and sandwiches, NZ$6 ($4.03); salad plates, NZ$7 ($4.70). Jumbos is a bright, lively place, a favorite of the young business and pretheater crowds. Hours are 11:30 a.m. to midnight on weeknights (last dinner orders taken at 10 p.m.), until 1 a.m. on weekends. Open seven days.

Sweet Sultana, in the James Cook Arcade on Lambton Quay (tel. 726-048), is a small, very clean and bright restaurant, which features Lebanese sweets, hot pies, savouries, and sandwiches for under NZ$1 (67¢), stews, spaghetti, and chili for under NZ$5 ($3.36). It, too, is very popular with the working crowd, but service is continuous from 7:30 a.m. to 9:30 p.m., every day except Sunday, so if you go before or after regular eating times you'll avoid the rush. A very pleasant place for a meal or just a drop-in for one of those luscious sweets.

Glossops, 149 Willis St., is a cozy little place with green-and-white tablecloths, and a blackboard menu featuring all home-cooked meals. And they are delicious! Salad plates, sandwiches (they're open and hearty-appetite size), seafood, quiche, and crêpes all come with salad, and the waist-expanding desserts include an absolutely sinful Black Forest cherry cake and a great carrot cake. You can opt for a light lunch of French bread and homemade soup for only NZ$4 ($2.68), the daily crêpe special at NZ$5.50 ($3.69) or go for top-priced items at NZ$6.50 ($4.36). Not licensed, but you're welcome to BYO. Hours are 10:30 a.m. to 3 p.m. Monday through Saturday, and on Friday additional dinner service from 5:30 to 8:30 p.m.

Tall, pretty Suzy van der Kwast has made her cozy **Suzy's Coffee Lounge,** 108 Willis St., between Mercer and Manners Streets (tel. 720-686), a veritable Wellington institution. The pleasant eatery is a local favorite and is always abuzz with the hum of contented conversation, although it never reaches an objectionable noise level. Suzy's Dutch, and among the many homemade goodies you'll find Dutch outsmyter and schnitzel. There are also delicious fresh croissants, hot and cold sandwiches on French bread, an array of fresh salads, and one daily hot dish, such as curry and rice. The homemade desserts draw a devoted following. Prices range from under NZ$1 (67¢) to NZ$5 ($3.36), and hours are 6:30 a.m. to 9 p.m. weekdays, 9 a.m. to 9 p.m. on weekends. If nothing else, I urge you to drop by for one of those croissants or a piece of Dutch apple cake.

The **Green Giraffe,** at Quay Point on Lambton Quay (tel. 738-916), is a light, airy, and thoroughly modern French café, perfect for lunch or a mid-morning snack. It's a place popular with shoppers in the area, but not usually overcrowded. The menu features quiches, pâtés, sandwiches, and salads, plus fresh-squeezed orange juice. Prices are moderate, under NZ$5 ($3.36), and hours are 8:30 a.m. to 4 p.m. Monday through Saturday.

A charming—and very much a New Zealand—restaurant is the **Woolshed Eating House** on Plimmer Steps, which climb steeply up from Lambton Quay (tel. 728-024). The woolshed theme is set by bales of wool, beamed ceilings lined in burlap bags from various sheep stations (all stamped with station names), wooden booths softened by sheepskins, and pine and exposed brick walls. Chairs, bar stools, and banquettes in the lounge are all upholstered with sheepskin. Rack of lamb (what else!) is featured on the menu, with mint sauce, of course. Other entrees include fresh fish grilled in parsley butter, and a nice choice of steaks and seafood. Every main course includes as many trips to the help-yourself salad bar as you wish. Prices in this atmospheric restaurant are in the NZ$7 ($4.70) to NZ$10 ($6.71) range, and hours are noon to 2:30 p.m. for lunch and 5 to 11:30 p.m. for dinner, Monday through Saturday. Fully licensed.

If you're driving, or happen to find yourself out in the lovely Evans Bay area (difficult to reach by public transportation), plan on one meal at the **Greta Point Tavern,** 467 Evans Bay Parade (tel. 861-066). The large black building with rose trim sits right on the waterfront, and has windows the entire length of its south side, looking out to sweeping views of the bay (often filled with sailboats) and a nearby marina with its forest of masts. The large, high-ceilinged room, which once housed a commercial laundry, now has a wooden lifeboat suspended from the overhead pipes. There's a nice upstairs Anchorage Lounge; the Promenade Deck bar; the Soda Fountain Café for take-aways, sandwiches, coffee, and ice cream; and the Gallery Restaurant, featuring fresh seafoods. The restaurant is self-service and fully licensed, and the long counter will have you drooling while trying to decide between Bluff oysters, roast baron of beef, marinated mussels, baked leg of ham, and a host of other tempting dishes on display. All main courses come with vegetables or a salad, and prices are in the NZ$6 ($4.03) to NZ$10 ($6.71) range. It's open for lunch Monday through Saturday from noon to 2:30 p.m., Sunday from 11:30 a.m. to 2:30 p.m.; for dinner, Monday through Saturday from 5:30 to 9:30 p.m., until 9 p.m. on Sunday.

A Big Splurge

My vote for a Wellington big splurge goes to **Upstairs at the Tas,** in the Abel Tasman Courtesy Inn, on the corner of Willis and Dixon Streets (tel. 851-304). In a beautiful room with soft lighting, luxurious carpeting, and many mirrors, that splurgy yen is satisfied even before you order. But it's the food that justifies going all out—cooked and served to utter perfection. My personal favorite on the menu is a concoction called Davy Jones, which consists of choice seafoods sauteed in white wine with tomatoes, mushrooms, onions, and sweet peppers in a creamy sauce seasoned with some magical ingredient that puts the finishing touch on an already-superb blend of flavors. There are other main courses just as inviting: suprême Véronique (breast of chicken flamed in wine and served in a cream sauce garnished with peeled white grapes); veal

Cordon Bleu, Nelson scallops, choice steaks, and lamb and pork chops. The wine selection is as fine as the menu, and desserts include a marvelous apple strudel and the traditional pavlova. There's also a good New Zealand cheese board, and several liqueur coffees. From Thursday to Saturday there's dancing and entertainment. Prices are definitely in the splurge range—NZ$11 ($7.38) to NZ$15 ($10.06) for main courses. Hours are 6:30 to 11 p.m. every day. Hint: If a splurge is just out of the question, treat yourself to a drink in the lounge, which is open from noon until midnight.

READERS' DINING SELECTIONS: "Oodles, on Level 4 of the Williams Centre, serves delightful luncheons—quiche, small pizza, open sandwiches, and delicious boysenberry pie" (Deborah Onley and Carol Morris, Perth, Australia). . . . "We had our best New Zealand meal at **Lavelles,** 291 Willis St. Prices were slightly less than Ponsonby's in Auckland, but the food far exceeded it" (Ernest Collins, Greencastle, Ind.). . . . "Just north of Wellington, in Paekakariki, we had an excellent seafood dinner at the **Fisherman's Table.** This is a very popular spot, as it is right on the main highway into Wellington" (Sandra Vargo, St. Petersburg, Fla.).

THINGS TO SEE AND DO: For the fullest appreciation of Wellington's spectacular setting, take the **cable car** at Lambton Quay opposite Grey Street. It's a marvelous 4½-minute ride in sleek red cars, which climb to an elevation of 400 feet. Fares are NZ$.40 (27¢) for adults, half that for children. The beautiful harbor lies at your feet, and it's a great loitering spot to drink in the curving shoreline backed by jagged hills. If you should be there on a Tuesday night from March to October between 7:30 and 9:30 p.m., you can visit the **Carter Observatory** (tel. 728-167) and take a telescopic look at the heavens above—NZ$.50 (33¢) for adults, NZ$.30 (20¢) for children. The **Botanic Gardens** entrance is also at the top of the cable car ride, open from dawn to dusk, and the downhill stroll through its lush greenery can be broken by a stop at the Begonia House in the Lady Norwood Rose Gardens (open from 10 a.m. to 4 p.m.) for a look at hundreds of begonias, bush foliage, and ferns. From the foot of the gardens, you can get back to the city on a no. 12 bus.

The best possible way to get an in-depth look at the city itself and its immediate environs is to take the escorted **bus tour,** which leaves from the PRO building on Mercer Street every day at 2 p.m. For the bargain price of NZ$8 ($5.37) for adults (children ride for half), you'll be driven some 30 miles, with 2½ hours of informative narrative as you see the financial and commercial center, take a look at government buildings and Parliament's unique Beehive building, visit the lookout on Mount Victoria (with a stop for picture taking), skirt the bays, stop for afternoon tea, then reenter the city via View Road, a scenic drive, which does full justice to Wellington's headlands, hills, bays, and beaches. For information and booking, telephone 724-599, ext. 719.

If you prefer a do-it-yourself tour of much the same territory, pick up the PRO's *Scenic Drive* booklet and map. Three routes are outlined, and they're color coordinated with discs on lampposts along each route so you won't go astray. They cover Wellington from top to bottom, traveling southeast on one route, west on another, and north on the third.

For those who prefer to hoof it, the PRO has a series of *Wellington Walks* brochures (small charge) outlining accessible walks, which will put you squarely in the middle of all that gorgeous scenery.

You can tour **Parliament** any weekday free of charge. Just telephone 749-199 for tour times. And if by this time you're hooked on New Zealand history and culture, spend some time at the **Alexander Turnbull Library,** 44 The Terrace. It's a research wing of the National Library, specializing in New

Zealand and the South Pacific. There are fascinating records of early explorations and discoveries, old books, pamphlets, newspapers, drawings, paintings, photographs, manuscripts, maps, and microfilm. Hours are 9 a.m. to 5 p.m. weekdays, to noon on Saturday.

And speaking of Kiwi history, keep an eye out for **12 shoreline plaques,** which have been embedded in footpaths to show the sites of early Wellington: you'll find them at Pipitea Point, on the south side of Davis Street and Thorndon Quay; at the top of the steps leading to Rutherford House; in Mason's Lane on the north side; on Lambton Quay, north of Woodward Street; on the Lambton Quay footpath near Cable Car Lane; at Steward Dawson's on the west side of the Lambton Quay corner; at Chews Lane on the east side of the Willis Street footpath; on Mercer Street outside George Harrison Ltd. on the Willis Street corner; on Farish Street on the southeast side of Farish and Lombard Streets; on Cuba Street outside Smith and Smith Ltd., on Taranaki Street outside the Caltex Service Station; and on Wakefield Street next to the Schaffer Street bus stop.

The **Antrim House,** 63 Boulcott St. (tel. 724-341), is headquarters of the New Zealand Historic Places Trust, and its information room has displays of its properties and the organization's work. There's also a gift shop with interesting items for sale. Open Monday through Friday from noon to 3 p.m.

The **National Art Gallery** and adjoining **National Museum** are on Buckle Street. The art gallery emphasizes New Zealand paintings, and on Sunday at 2:30 p.m. there's a free music recital or lecture. Artifacts of South Pacific, New Zealand, and Maori history are featured at the museum. No admission charges at either, and hours are 10 a.m. to 4:45 p.m. daily. Buses 1 and 3 run to Basin Reserve, and Buckle Street is about a five-minute walk.

Those interested in things of the sea will want to visit the **Maritime Museum** on Queens Wharf, where Wellington's close association with seafarers and their vessels is well documented. No admission charge, and hours are 10 a.m. to 4 pm. on weekdays, 2 to 5 p.m. on Saturday.

The **Wellington Zoo,** at Newtown (tel. 898-130), dates back to 1906 and its collection includes kangaroos, wallabies, monkeys, elephants, flightless birds (there's a nocturnal **Kiwi House** open from 10 a.m. to 4 p.m.). In fine weather on weekends and holidays there are elephant rides from 2 to 3 p.m. and miniature railway rides from 1 to 4 p.m., for minimal charges. You can watch them feed the cheetahs, tigers, leopards, lions, and pumas at 3:20 p.m. (except on Monday and Friday). Zoo hours are 8:30 a.m. to 4:30 p.m., and you can get there on the Newton Park bus (no. 11) from the railway station. Buses to Houghton Bay, View Road, and Melrose also pass the zoo. Admission is NZ$1.80 ($1.21) for adults, NZ$.85 (57¢) for children.

READERS' SIGHTSEEING SUGGESTIONS: "From Old St. Paul's in Mulgrave Street you can get a map for the **Town and Gown Walk,** which starts near the Skyline and ends near 12 Boulcott St." (Paula Adams, Denver, Colo.). . . . "Len Southward (Main Road North, Paraparaumu) near Wellington has built what is now known as the largest and most complete **Antique Car Museum** in the southern hemisphere, and you can bus up there, drive, or go by train. The museum includes a gift shop, restaurant, and theater" (Bob Huxtable, Lansing, Mich.). . . . "I'd like to put in a plug for some tourist attractions in the Wellington area. **Kapiti Island:** the Forest and Bird Society runs irregular trips; write them in advance at their Wellington office, or get a permit from the Department of Internal Affairs and find a boat owner in Plimmerton, Titahi Bay, or Paraparaumu to take you across. It's a slice of New Zealand before the Pakeha arrived—primeval bush and tame birds. Most spectacular are the wekas (flightless rails) and kakas (arboreal cousins of keas), both quite unashamed about sharing your lunch! The boat trip will cost a few dollars only. There's a spectacular beach at **Castlepoint,** east of Masterton. The cliffs here are made entirely of fossil shells cemented together, and the presence of a lighthouse adds to the grandeur" (Raymond Goldie, Toronto, Canada).

SHOPPING: John Bull & Co. Ltd., 8 Bond St. (near Town Hall), has good New Zealand wines at prices very close to wholesale. You can make your choices after tasting directly from large wooden casks and your wine will be bottled for you right there.

The **duty-free shop** in central Wellington is at the DFC Centre, on Grey Street, with a branch out at the airport.

For good-quality souvenirs (with profits going to disabled veterans), shop at the **Rehabilitation League NZ** (Inc.), with shops at 29 Willis St. and in the Overseas Passenger Terminal at the airport.

Sheepskin goods, knitwear, leather coats, boots, etc., are reasonably priced at the **Bo-Peep Sheepskin Shop,** 52 Manners St. (tel. 736-449). Look for their sales. They gladly mail overseas.

Handcrafted wares, leather goods, pottery, silver, and a host of other items are on sale by independent craftsmen and concessionaires at **Victoria Market,** held every Friday from 10 a.m. to 8 p.m and Saturday from 10 a.m. to 3 p.m. in a building at 188 Willis St. Look for the red flag adorned by a pig!

READERS' SHOPPING TIP: "The camping shop **Simple Living,** in the Williams Centre off Lambton Quay, offers a 10% discount to Youth Hostel members and has a wide range of goods, including packs, wool socks, hiking gear, etc." (Deborah Only and Carol Morris, Perth, Australia).

AFTER DARK: Chips, in Willis Street Village, between Dixon and Boulcott Streets (tel. 844-335), is a sophisticated nightclub upstairs in the brick-paved plaza. Music can vary from rock to jazz to smooth dance tunes. There's a very good dinner menu if you want to dine as well as dance. No formal dress code, but the rules are no jeans or T-shirts. It's an upmarket sort of place, but the mood changes according to the entertainment and the crowd. Friday night attracts a young crowd; Saturday is more sedate; midweek appeals to twosomes and handholders. There's a NZ$5 ($3.36) cover charge. Open 7:30 p.m. to 3 a.m. Wednesday through Saturday.

There's mainly rock and new wave music at the **Majestic Cabaret,** Willis Street (tel. 727-722).

Sophisticated music and entertainment is Thursday through Saturday at **Upstairs at the Tas** (see "Meals," above; tel. 851-304), in the Abel Tasman Courtesy Inn, corner of Willis and Dixon Streets. Reservations advised.

You don't have to be a member of the younger set to enjoy Saturday and Sunday nights at the **South Pacific Motel's Quarterdeck.** Located out in Lower Hutt at 15 Pharazyn St. (tel. 698-064), this fine restaurant sports a bar constructed from the side of a sailing ship, which went aground in the Marlborough Sounds, and a huge mural of Hemingway's *Old Man and the Sea.* On Saturday the menu is á la carte at NZ$7 ($4.70) to NZ$9 ($6.04) for main courses of seafood, duckling, steaks, pork chops, and the roast of the day. At 8 p.m. there's a NZ$2 ($1.34) cover charge for a top-notch cabaret. On Sunday, dinner is a NZ$9.50 ($6.38) smörgåsbord (NZ$5, or $3.36 U.S., for children) with more seafood than you've ever known existed, and from 8 to 11:30 p.m. there's country and western music with a singing group and music for dancing.

Special Note: The South Pacific is one of the Wellington area's most outstanding motels, and is in fact a resort complex, with deluxe hotel rooms in addition to top-grade motel units and such facilities as a swimming pool, spa pool, laundry, etc. While its rates average NZ$43 ($28.86) single and NZ$47 ($31.54) double—well out of the budget range—it *is* a Best Western member, honoring the Holiday Pass discount, and owners Larry and Loreen Williams are two of the friendliest hosts you'll find, all of which may make this your "splurge" spot. Bus and rail transportation into Wellington are both handy.

The **Downstage Theatre** in the Hannah Playhouse on Cambridge Terrace (tel. 849-639) presents first-rate theater in an exciting theater structure, which provides for flexibility in staging while offering wining and dining in the same space. The Downstage is a year-round enterprise, staging classics and contemporary drama, musicals and comedies. Last year (1983) they presented a varied program, which included the musical *Cabaret, Richard III, Lysistrata,* and *Educating Rita.* Check the newspapers for current showings. Theatre Society members have first choice on tickets, but the manager assures me that tourists who call for tickets will be given every possible assistance. Book as far in advance as you possibly can, however, for Downstage productions are very popular. Evenings begin with a simple dinner, which costs NZ$12 ($8.05) in addition to ticket prices. You can, however, opt to skip dinner and just come along for the performance. Ticket prices are NZ$12 ($8.05) for the theater floor, NZ$9 ($6.04) for the balcony; students (you must show ID) pay NZ$9 ($6.04) and NZ$6.50 ($4.36).

Check the newspapers to see what's doing at the new **Town Hall,** an exciting contemporary structure which has been added to Wellington's old Town Hall to enlarge auditorium space. There are concerts and other events scheduled there throughout the year.

2. Across to the South Island

A special tip to those who won't be going on to the South Island (poor souls!): A marvelous day trip is the round trip on the ferry. You can take either of the morning departures, enjoy a sea voyage and have five full hours in Picton before returning on the 6:40 p.m. ferry from Picton. I highly recommend it.

From Wellington's Aotea Quay (north of the city center), the Cook Strait ferries depart four times daily for Picton, across on the South Island. Earliest sailing is 7:20 a.m.; the latest, 6:40 p.m. Be *sure,* however, to check current sailing times by calling 725-399. City buses for the terminal leave from Platform 9 at the railway station 25 minutes before sailing time and meet arriving vessels between 3 p.m. and 5:40 p.m. Also, since crossings can become quite crowded during summer months and holiday periods, it's a good idea to make your booking as early as possible (perhaps through NZRR offices at your point of arrival). Fares for the three-hour-and-20-minute, 52-nautical-mile trip are NZ$16.70 ($11.21) for adults, NZ$7 ($4.70) for children. If you're going on to Christchurch, an express train leaves for Christchurch at 2:10 p.m. (connects with the 10 a.m. sailing from Wellington), and for a small charge your luggage can be through-checked at the ferry terminal on the Wellington side. Also, buses to and from Blenheim, Nelson, and Christchurch connect with some ferry arrivals and departures.

You'll travel on either the *Aranui* or *Aratika,* each of which has a licensed bar, cafeteria, television lounge, information bureau, and shop. The *Aranui* has a coffee lounge; the *Aratika* has a family lounge with toys to keep young children amused during the voyage and a discotheque for the young at heart. Crossings generally take on a jovial air, with passengers strolling the decks (whatever you do, don't go inside until you've viewed the departure from Wellington's lovely harbor from the rail—a sight you'll long remember) or congregating happily in the lounges, passing the time over friendly conversation and mugs of beer. A warning: Someone once spoke of Cook Strait's "vexed waters," and in truth the swells can be a little unsettling. If you're subject to queasy stomach at sea, best pick up something from the pharmacy before embarking. Another tip: If you don't want to miss one minute of the magnificent views, take along a picnic lunch to eat outside under the sky and the curious glances of seagulls wheeling overhead.

As you approach the Marlborough Sound, its green waters lap shorelines (more than 600 miles in all!) of wooded hills, sheer cliffs, sandy beaches in sheltered coves, and tidy little hideaway cottages, some of which may only be approached by water. Most of the islands and native bush reserves are a part of the Marlborough Sound Maritime Park, and there are picnic grounds, lookouts, and forest walks, as well as scenic roads, scattered throughout. The Maoris knew these waters as rich fishing grounds, and today they are still fished for blue cod, snapper, terakihi, grouper, kingfish, and butterfish. Protected sea fish like dolphins (and the occasional seal) romp playfully around the ferries. If you're crossing in the summer, you'll pass scores of pleasure and fishing launches and wave to happy bathers on the beaches.

Picton, your South Island debarkation point, is at the head of Queen Charlotte South, named by Captain Cook in 1770 for King George III's wife. He found it "a very safe and convenient cove," and indeed used it as an anchorage for much of his later Pacific exploration. He can also be credited for bringing the first sheep to New Zealand, when he put ashore a ram and an ewe in 1773—prophetic, even though that particular pair survived only a few days and thus the good captain cannot lay claim to having furnished the fountainhead of today's millions of wooly creatures.

Most travelers scurry from ferry to train, bus, or rental car and are then off to explore an island so different from the one they've just left that there have been times in the past when there was great agitation for its independence as a separate colony. However, if time permits and the Marlborough Sound tempt you beyond resistance, you might consider staying over for some time on the water aboard one of the several launches, which offer several-hours-long or day-long cruises. You'll find a cluster of launch operators at the corner of London Quay and Wellington Street near the marina in Picton, or you can make arrangements in advance through **Red Funnel Launches** (tel. 104K), **Friendship Launch Services** (tel. 255), or **The Cream Run** (tel. 887M).

Note: If you're making this crossing south to north and weather should cause a cancellation or delay in your scheduled voyage (as has been known to happen in these fickle waters), you could be looking for a place to spend the night. During school holidays only, there's a youth hostel one kilometer from the ferry in the **Catholic school** on Auckland Street adjacent to Main Road South. Also, a good Best Western motel, the **Koromiki Park** (mailing address: P.O. Box 86, Picton; tel. 1350), is six kilometers from the ferry on Highway 1, with rates of NZ$30 ($20.13) single and NZ$36 ($24.16) double.

Chapter VII

NELSON AND THE WEST COAST

1. Nelson
2. Nelson to Greymouth
3. Greymouth
4. Hokitika
5. The Glaciers
6. Queenstown via Haast Pass and Wanaka

CROSSING THE COOK STRAIT is something akin to crossing an international boundary, so different are New Zealand's two islands. That's not really surprising, because both geography and history are quite different on the two sides of that stretch of water.

It is in the South Island that the majestic Southern Alps raise their snowy heads along the diagonal Alpine Fault that forms its craggy backbone. Along its West Coast are the lush, mysterious rain forests, while to the east of the Alps the broad Canterbury plains stretch to the sea. It was on those plains that prehistoric moa hunters lived in the greatest numbers, roaming the tussock-lands in search of the giant birds that grazed there. When waves of Maoris began arriving, it was to the North Island that they gravitated, since its climate was more suitable for the growing of *kumara* and their agrarian lifestyle, leaving relatively few Polynesian settlements along the fringes of the South Island. It was the waters of the South Island that first lured sealers and whalers, although whalers found the northern Bay of Islands a more hospitable base for their land operations. Then when Europeans began arriving in great numbers and fierce land wars raged in the more populated North Island, South Island Maoris faced those conflicts only when tribes pushed from their lands in the north crossed the strait to battle southern tribes for territory. Because one tribe after another obliterated those who came before them, little evidence was left of South Island Maori culture, legend, and tradition.

It was the discovery of gold in Central Otago and on the West Coast that finally brought the white man pouring into the South Island in vast numbers. They came from Australia, from Europe, and from the goldfields of California to this new "promised land," and the South Island's tranquility and isolation gave way to a booming economy, which for a time saw it leading the country in terms of both population and prosperity. Inevitably, the goldfields were mined beyond profitability, but then came the advent of refrigeration, which meant that meat could be exported on a large scale. The South Island's grass-lands became goldmines of a different sort, and it is on this side of the strait that you'll see the most of these wooly four-legged nuggets busily eating their way to the butcher. As a tourist, you can give them a tip of the hat as you pass, for it is their need for widespread grazing land that accounts for the fact that today only a little more than one-quarter of New Zealand's population lives on the South Island. That means that you'll find uncrowded roadways, unhurried city lifestyles, and unspoiled scenic grandeur.

Newmans Coaches meet all daylight ferries in Picton, and they'll have you off to Nelson to begin your South Island odyssey for a fare of NZ$10.15 ($6.81). It's a two-hour trip—70 miles along Route 6—filled with clifftop views, sea-scapes glimpsed from bush-lined stretches of the road, and rolling farmlands: a pleasant, picturesque journey you may want to break with a stop by the giant totara tree in picnic grounds near Pelorus Bridge (Newmans Coaches also stop at the tea room here).

1. Nelson

Nelson sits on the shores of Nelson Haven, sheltered by the unique seven-mile natural wall of Boulder Bank. Its 2500 hours of annual sunshine, its tranquil waters, and its golden sand beaches make it perhaps the South Island's most popular summer resort. That wonderful climate, combined with the fertile land hereabouts, also makes it an important center of fruit, grapes, hops, and tobacco growing. And maybe all that sunshine has something to do with the easy-going, tolerant outlook, which makes it a haven for a those of an artistic bent. Potters are here in abundance, drawn by a plentiful supply of fine clay and the minerals needed for glazing; weavers raise sheep and create natural-wool works of art; artists spend hours on end trying to capture on canvas the splendors of a Nelson sunset or the shifting light on sparkling water.

Col. William Wakefield hoisted the New Zealand Company flag on Bri-tannia Heights in December of 1841 and placed a nine-pound cannon there as a signal gun (it's there today for you to see), and settlers began arriving on February 1, 1842, a day still celebrated annually in Nelson. They named the new town Nelson to honor the great British seafaring hero, since the company's first New Zealand settlement had been named for Britain's most famous soldier. Lord Nelson's victories, ships, and fellow admirals are commemorated in street names like Trafalgar, Vanguard, and Collingwood. Graves of some of those early settlers lie under the trees at Fairfield Park (at the corner of Trafalgar Street South and Brougham Street), and many of the gabled wooden houses they built still cling to Nelson's hillsides and nestle among more modern structures on midtown streets. Some have become the homes and studios of the artistic community.

Nelson has two distinctions of which it is equally proud: it is known as the "cradle of rugby" in New Zealand—first played here in 1870, and although Christchurch's Football Club is older than Nelson's, it didn't adopt the na-tional sport until some five years after its introduction at Nelson's Botanical Reserve; and a native son, Baron Rutherford, has been called the "father of nuclear physics" because it was he who first discovered the secret of splitting the atom (along with other scientific achievements, which brought him interna-tional renown), and his name is perpetuated in place names like Rutherford Park, Street, and Hotel.

Come harvest time, as many as 3000 workers—many of them students—come trouping into town to stay until the millions of apples, pears, hops, and tobacco leaf have been brought in from the surrounding fields. With its characteristic openness of spirit, Nelson assimilates them as quickly and easily as it does the hordes of tourists who descend on its beaches year after year. There's a refreshing brand of hospitality afoot in this town, which makes it a fitting introduction to the South Island.

ORIENTATION: Two landmarks will keep you oriented in Nelson: its main street, **Trafalgar Street,** and **Church Hill,** crowned by Christ Church Cathedral and surrounded by lush lawns and plantings, which are a local gathering point. You'll find the **Public Relations Office (PRO)** on the corner of Trafalgar and Halifax Streets (tel. 82-304). Hours are 8:30 a.m. to 5:30 p.m. Monday through Friday.

ACCOMMODATIONS: It is true of Nelson, as of most beach resorts, that accommodations are hard to come by during summer months (December through January), and many Kiwi families book here from year to year. While it's not impossible to arrive roomless and find a place to lay your head, it is very, very chancey. Book early. Or plan to come in late fall (April and May) or early spring (September or October) when things are not so crowded and the weather is still fine.

As is also true of most resorts, Nelson has a wide variety of accommodations. You'll find them in the city proper and at the beachside suburb of **Tahunanui,** which is four miles away, but served by city buses. The PRO is not set up to handle bookings, but will refer you to the **Nelson District Motel Association,** where members serve on a rotating basis as a central booking agency for all members. They are very accommodating and will do their best to find a vacancy for you in the price range you require. If you come into town when the PRO is not open, there will be a sign posted in their window giving the name, address, and telephone number of the "on duty" motel.

A Hostel

The **YHA Hostel** at 42 Weka St. (tel. 88-817) has 32 beds in five rooms, hot showers, a kitchen, and a food shop. Buses from Blenheim will stop if you ask at the corner of Milton and Weka Streets. Rates for Seniors are NZ$6 ($4.03); for Juniors, NZ$3 ($2.01).

Cabins

The **Tahuna Beach Holiday Camp,** Beach Road, Tahunanui (tel. 85-159), is one of the largest motor camps in New Zealand, regularly handling as many as 4500 travelers per night during summer months and even more at Christmas. Spread over 55 acres, the camp is a short three-minute walk to the beach. On the well-kept grounds are lodges, cabins, tourist flats, and tent and trailer sites. There are seven shower and toilet blocks, six kitchens, a laundry, ironing boards, heated drying room, car wash, TV lounge, a children's playground, and miniature golf. A large food shop on the grounds is open every day. It's a beautifully maintained place, with all accommodations kept freshly painted, carpeted, and comfortably furnished. Lodges come with electric jugs and toasters; cabins (which will sleep up to five) have a lounge and kitchen with fridge, hotplates, cookware, and panel heating; and tourist flats (sleeping up to five) have kitchens, heaters, toilets, and showers. Linens can be rented. Rates for lodges are NZ$10 ($6.71) for one or two, NZ$5 ($3.36) per extra adult; for cabins, NZ$12 ($8.05) single or double, NZ$6 ($4.03) per additional adult; and tourist flats, NZ$14 ($9.40) single or double, NZ$7 ($4.70) per additional adult. Campsites cost NZ$6 ($4.03) double. On all units there's a surcharge for one-night stays. Local bus service is a quarter of a mile away.

Bed and Breakfast

The lovely **Willow Bank** guest house, 71 Golf Rd., Tahunanui (tel. 85-041), is a gracious, two-story house set back from the road on shaded lawns and just a short walk from the beach. There's a pretty outdoor swimming pool, a spacious TV lounge, a recreation room with pool table, laundry facilities, off-street parking, and a courtesy car to all terminals. Rooms are attractively done up, comfortable, and have H&C, electric blankets, and thermostatic heaters. You can have a full, cooked breakfast or continental breakfast in the spacious dining room, as well as a three-course evening meal if ordered in advance. Jean and Frank Thomas are the hosts here and have a devoted following, many of whom come back again and again. Rates for bed and breakfast are NZ$18 ($12.08) single, NZ$30 ($20.13) double. Dinner is NZ$7 ($4.70).

You'll know the **Palm Grove Guest House**, 52 Cambria St. (tel. 84-645), by the two gigantic palms, which tower above the two-story white house. And you'll remember it for the friendly hospitality of Mrs. Devlin, your hostess. The house is bright, cheerful, and sunny throughout, with comfortably furnished rooms, some of which look out to nice mountain views. There's a tea and coffee room off the guest lounge, and a light and airy dining room. Only three of the six rooms have H&C, but all are convenient to baths. There are two singles, two with twin beds, one with three single beds, and one family room that sleeps four. Bed-and-breakfast rates are NZ$12 ($8.05) per person, and there's a surcharge for a one-night stay. Highly recommended.

There are two good guest houses on Grove Street. **Seafield Guesthouse,** 36 Grove St. (tel. 83-502), is a lovely old six-bedroom house, which has been lovingly done up by Mary and Vic Hague. All rooms are carpeted and decorated in a style that fits the rustic tone of the house, and all have H&C and panel heaters. There's a TV lounge, where you can enjoy a cuppa if you wish, and a flower-filled veranda on which to sunbathe or just daydream. The large cooked breakfasts feature delicious home-preserved fruits and jams. Laundry facilities are available. Bed-and-breakfast rates are NZ$20 ($13.42) single, NZ$35 ($23.49) twin.

Linda and Ernie Becker were busy with renovations and redecorating at **Lindern Lodge,** 84 Grove St. (tel. 88-816), when I called in, and even in the confusion, rooms were inviting, with bright colors and comfortable furnishings. There's a large, old-fashioned lounge with a lovely old native New Zealand timber mantel at the fireplace and a telephone available for guests' use. No charge for laundry. Of the eight rooms, two are large family rooms that can sleep four; the other six are twins or doubles. Breakfast menus (from which you order the night before) are the most extensive I've run into, with such choices as flounder, baked beans on toast, spaghetti on toast, and boiled, poached, or fried eggs with bacon or sausage. For a NZ$1 (67¢) surcharge, you can have steak and eggs, lambs fry and bacon, or kidneys on toast. That's fancy eating for a guest house! Bed-and-breakfast rates are NZ$15 ($10.06) per person.

Trafalgar Lodge, 46 Trafalgar St. (tel. 83-980), is another old two-story home, which has been restored with loving care. Betty and Harry Loose take great pride not only in their facilities, but in the hospitality they offer their guests. There's an attractive dining room and lounge with TV and radio, tea-and coffee-making facilities, laundry facilities, and off-street parking. All rooms have H&C, are fully carpeted, and are nicely furnished. Bed-and-breakfast rates are NZ$12 ($8.05) single, NZ$20 ($13.42) double, and there's no surcharge. A homey, friendly place to stay and only a one-minute walk from the city center. The Looses also have two motel units (see below), which are quite nice.

Motel Flats

Those motel flats at the **Trafalgar Lodge** (see above) sleep four, are bright, clean, and attractively furnished, and have fully equipped kitchens, TV, radio, telephone, electric blankets, and private shower and bath. Off-street parking, and laundry facilities are available. Rates are NZ$18 ($12.08) single, NZ$22 ($14.76) double, and no surcharge.

One of my favorite Best Western motels in New Zealand is the **Courtesy Court Motel**, 30 Golf Rd., Tahunanui, Nelson (tel. 85-114). That's partly because of its pretty grounds (with well-tended, colorful flower beds) and comfortable accommodations, but mostly because of Doris and Wally Cheesman, who own and operate the place. Friendlier, more helpful hosts you just won't find anywhere. And I like the arrangements of the units around an inner court away from street noises and facing the attractive heated swimming pool. There are bedsitters, one-bedroom units that sleep as many as four, and two-bedroom units that will sleep six; all have complete kitchen, electric blankets and heaters, color TV, radio, and telephone—one has a waterbed. A luxury "executive suite" is also available, with space for six. A guest laundry, spa pool, and children's play area are additional conveniences, and the beach is just a short walk away. Doris and Wally welcome children and will gladly provide a cot and highchair, as well as arrange for babysitters. Rates (which are, of course, subject to Holiday Pass discounts) are NZ$32 ($21.48) single, NZ$38 ($25.50) double. The entrance to Golf Road is just at the Kentucky Fried Chicken stand in the Tahunanui shopping area.

"Cozy, quiet, and convenient," says Vera Luty, who with her husband Hector runs the **Mid-City Motel**, 218 Trafalgar St. (tel. 83-595 or 84-399), right smack in the center of the city center. Well, I have to agree with her, and I have to add that you might walk right past it without realizing it was a motel. You see, this one is located on the second and third floors of a modern, five-story office building! Each unit is smartly done up in shades of brown and gold or turquoise, and has TV, phone, large shower room, and cooking facilities. There's a laundry room, and off-street parking for a minimal charge. There are ten units on the two floors, and a family unit up on the rooftop. Mr. and Mrs. Luty are warm, friendly hosts, and are especially fond of American guests—in fact, they'll give a NZ$2 ($1.34) discount to any Yank who arrives clutching this book. Rates begin at NZ$28 ($18.79) single, NZ$32 ($21.48) double.

All five of the family units at the **Stella Maris Motel**, 72 Grove St. (tel. 84-518), are two-story, with lounge and full kitchen downstairs, bedrooms and bath upstairs. The pretty white and reddish-brown motel stands on a quiet corner, and there's off-street parking right at your door. All units are spacious —they'll sleep up to six—and have radio, TV, telephone, central heat, and electric blankets. In addition there's a modern laundry available, and Margaret and Godfrey McHardy, the cordial owner-managers, will arrange babysitters. Just a short walk from the city center. Rates are NZ$36 ($24.16) double, NZ$9 ($6.04) for each additional adult, NZ$7 ($4.70) per additional child.

A Licensed Hotel

There's nothing fancy about the **Wakatu Hotel,** Collingwood and Bridge Streets (tel. 84-299), but there's a certain old-fashioned charm in the old, two-story structure, which has been updated with modern comforts. Rooms vary in size, and some are rather small, but all are comfortable, clean, and homey. All have H&C as well as toilet and shower. None has TV or a telephone, but there's a TV lounge and a public phone for guests to use, as well as a tea and coffee room. The location is about as central as you can get, and Nelson's branch of the Cobb & Co. restaurant chain is on the ground floor. Rates are NZ$20 ($13.42) single, NZ$28 ($18.79) double.

Free Room and Board

Well, it isn't exactly "free"—it's room and board in exchange for daily farm and domestic work averaging four or more hours a day. For that, you'll be getting three healthy meals, rather basic accommodations, and a rich learning experience in the practice of conservation. If that has an appealing ring, read on.

Todd's Valley Farm (mailing address: R.D. 1, Nelson; tel. 520-553) is the home, farm, dream, and ecological laboratory of G. R. (Dick) Roberts, a graduate of Cambridge University, teacher of biology and geography, and documentary photographer. After some few years of teaching, Dick decided in 1969 that the time had come to translate ideas into action, and he bought a beautiful, but uneconomical, 350-acre valley farm six miles north of Nelson. Only about 15 acres are flat land—the rest rise as high as 1400 feet above the valley floor. Dick does not claim to be 100% "organic" in his farming methods, but he has nurtured the flourishing vegetable garden with none of the dubious benefits of insecticides. On the slopes, he is working out an integrated approach to biological control by mixing many species of fruit and nut trees. Rough hill pastures are grazed by about 500 sheep.

Dick welcomes visitors who are genuinely interested in conservation, willing to work at it, and ready to take instruction and suggestion. Although the farm is not by any means a commune, Dick believes that the cooperative efforts of like-minded people contributing toward a constructive alternative way of life provide an important contribution to society as a whole. "Dropouts, unproductive people, and those not willing to accept responsibility," he says, "are not part of that plan." Please do not apply unless you can stay a minimum of two weeks (brief visits may be arranged, however, for those with an avid interest in ecological land use). At Todd's Valley, conservation is a way of life: you are expected to recycle all wastes, to refrain from smoking in the house or using drugs. You are heartily invited, however, to enjoy the warm, sunny valley two miles from the sea in all its natural beauty, gorge yourself on the fresh vegetables, and become intimately involved with the land and its problems. When you've contributed what you can and are ready to move on, Dick may be able to put you in touch with others with similar concerns in New Zealand—an entree into a circle of involved, concerned, and vitally interesting people.

If you'd like to stay at Todd's Valley, write or telephone Dick in advance. He can only give beds to a few persons at a time, although those who wish to camp are also welcome. Note: Occasionally, the farm is closed to visitors.

READER'S B&B SELECTION: "We are writing to compliment Nelson on having the most gracious and charming B&B accommodation we discovered on our trip—the **California Guest House** at 29 Collingwood St. In fact, it was the major attraction in causing us to triple the length of our stay in Nelson. The proprietor, Carol Glen, always made tea or sherry available to brighten the afternoon and shared some of her excellent wine with us in the evening. Breakfasts were delightful and varied each morning" (Edward A. Everts, Charlotte, Vt.).

MEALS There's a **Cobb & Co.** in the Wakatu Hotel, Collingwood and Bridge Streets (tel. 84-299), with that chain's dependable family menu at reasonable prices. Main courses average NZ$5.50 ($3.69). It's fully licensed, and hours are 7:30 a.m. to 10 p.m.

One of my favorite places in Nelson for good, home-cooked light meals in pleasant surroundings is the **Manhattan Coffee Lounge,** 206 Trafalgar St., between Hardy and Bridge Streets. Framed art prints line the walls, the staff behind the self-service counter is friendly and helpful, and all baking is done right on the premises. A full cooked breakfast runs NZ$3.50 ($2.35), and light, inexpensive fare—savouries, pies, sandwiches, etc.—is served throughout the day. Hours are 7:30 a.m. to 5 p.m. Monday through Thursday, until 9 p.m. on Friday.

La Gondola, 65 Bridge St. (tel. 81-270), is the place for outstanding Italian food. The decor is charming, with attractive table linen and fresh flowers on each table. Displays of local pottery are a window feature. Homemade pastas include cannelloni Sorrentino, ravioli con pollo, lasagne verdi, fettucine bolognese, and spaghetti. Fresh local seafood, steak, and chicken are also on the menu, as are homemade sweets. Prices for main courses start at NZ$4.50 ($3.02), at NZ$2.50 ($1.68) for entree-size portions. Lunch hours are 11:30 a.m. to 2 p.m., dinner from 5 to 9 p.m. (book ahead for dinner), seven days a week. BYO.

More than just an eating place, **Chez Eelco Coffee House,** 296 Trafalgar St. (tel. 87-595), is just about the most popular meeting place in town for students, artists, craftspeople, townspeople, and tourists. In fine weather, there are bright umbrella tables on the sidewalk out front. Inside, there are red-and-white café curtains, matching ruffled lampshades, and candles in wine bottles after dark. Eelco Boswick (a Dutchman who came to New Zealand over 30 years ago) owns the high-ceilinged, cavernous place and runs it much like one of New York City's Greenwich Village coffeehouses. There's the buzz of contented conversation, table-hopping regulars, a back room whose walls are a virtual art gallery, a piano for the occasional pianist, and paper placemats, which give names and addresses of local artists. The extensive menu includes toasted sandwiches, savouries, meat pies, hamburgers, scones, omelets, yogurt, salad plates, steaks, fried chicken, native cheeses, and sweets that include fresh cream cakes. In short, it's a place to drop in for coffee or tea and a snack, enjoy a light meal, or order your main meal of the day. Then sit back and dine at your leisure. Prices run from under NZ$1 (67¢) to NZ$6.80 ($4.56) for a porterhouse steak, the most expensive item on the menu. Open from 8 a.m. to 11 p.m. Monday through Saturday, 5 to 9 p.m. on Sunday. Bring your own wine.

The **Hitching Post,** 145 Bridge St. (tel. 87-374), sports an old hitching ring on its front door and a pot-bellied iron stove inside. Pizzas, salads, and steaks share the menu here in a price range of NZ$3.20 ($2.15) to NZ$8 ($5.37). The dining room is rustic and cozy, but I must confess to a weakness for the courtyard out back, where a brick barbecue is provided for those who want to cook their own steak or ham. In a setting of Kiwi vines and other native plantings, you dine on white garden-type furniture, and for before- or after-meal entertainment, a giant backgammon board adorns the cement tile floor (even if you don't play, it's fun to watch others while you dine). You can reach the courtyard either through the main dining room or by way of a small wooden door out front, which opens to a narrow pathway leading to the back. The Hitching Post is a good dropping-in place, since service is continuous from 8 a.m. to 10 p.m. Monday through Friday and from 5 to 10 p.m. on Saturday. It's closed Sunday. BYO.

Out in Tahunanui, the Ocean Lodge Motor Hotel, on Muritai Street (tel. 85-179), has **Saucy Sals,** an attractive family restaurant, which serves excellent food, with generous portions and reasonable prices. Fresh local seafoods are featured, but the extensive menu also includes steaks, ham, and chicken dishes, and all main courses come with a side salad and french fries or a cottage potato. The room has a nautical decor, as does the adjoining public bar. Service is knowledgeable and friendly. Prices average about NZ$8.50 ($5.70) for seafood, less for other main courses. There's an exceptionally good Sunday smörgåsbord on Sunday evenings at NZ$9 ($6.04) for adults, NZ$5 (3.36) for children. Hours are 5 to 9:30 p.m. for dinner, seven days a week. Fully licensed.

A Big Splurge

The **Brown House,** 52 Rutherford St. (tel. 89-039), is one of those very special places that provides a satisfying experience along with fine food. Built over 100 years ago, it's a steep-roofed, two-story colonial house, very cozy and homey inside, with candles on the tables, paintings on the walls highlighted by soft spotlights, and open log fires in cool weather. Judith Alexander Neill does all the cooking—she's Cordon Bleu trained—and husband Hugh (he swears he's "Fawlty Towers" trained) takes care of the dining room. Judith's menu changes daily, with emphasis on fresh local seafoods, but with international specialties like moussaka, venison, duckling, pheasant, French casseroles, and home roasts of lamb, beef, or pork. Dinner prices are in the NZ$9 ($6.04) to NZ$12 ($8.05) range. Bring your own wine. Dinner hours are 6 to 9 p.m. Monday through Saturday; lunch from noon to 2 p.m. Monday through Friday.

READER'S DINING SELECTION: "A gustatorial delight was the **Capistrano Restaurant** in Nelson, where we had cocktails, Stroganoff, scallops, and oysters for an unbelievably low price" (R. B. Hilts, Las Cruces, N.M.).

THINGS TO SEE AND DO: There's no way you're going to miss seeing the outside of **Christ Church Cathedral,** sitting as it does on a splendid elevation at the end of Trafalgar Street. And chances are good that you'll find yourself, at some point during your Nelson stay, stopping for a rest in its beautiful grounds—if you follow the lead of the locals, you'll bypass the handy benches to stretch out on the grass. That site, now known as **Church Hill,** has in the past held an early Maori *pa,* the New Zealand Company's depot, a small fort, and a tent church. The present Gothic cathedral is made of local Takaka marble, and above its misnamed "west door" are the carved heads of five bishops, one archbishop, and King George V. Inside, there are various interesting memorials and a memorial window to Dr. Thomas Renwick, prominent Nelson doctor and politician. Open to the public from 8 a.m. to 4 p.m. Between Christmas and Easter, congregation members will show you around from 10 a.m. to noon and from 2 to 4 p.m.

Nelson's affection for the arts is exemplified in the excellent **Suter Art Gallery,** on Bridge Street by Queen's Gardens. Works by a bevy of important New Zealand painters are on display—look for the marvelous Ship Cove view painted by James Webber, who sailed on Captain Cook's third voyage as official artist. There's also an outstanding collection of works by master painter John

Gully, who lived here for a time—if they're not on display, ask to see them. The gallery also has a craft shop selling prints, pottery, and weaving, and a nice restaurant overlooking Queen's Gardens. Hours are Tuesday to Sunday from 10:30 a.m. to 4:30 p.m. (also on Monday during school holidays).

Walkers will be in their element in Nelson and the immediate vicinity. Good walks abound, both in-city and in the environs, varying from an hour to a full-day's tramp. The PRO has detailed guide pamphlets from which to select those you'll have time to enjoy.

Arts and Crafts

One of the great pleasures of a stop in Nelson is visiting some of its many resident artists and artisans. The PRO can give you names and addresses of those who welcome visitors to their studios, and it will be a rewarding experience to talk with painters, weavers, potters, and other craftspeople about the subject dearest to their hearts—rewarding, too, perhaps in that very special memento or gift you may find for sale.

Actually, even without the PRO's list, you can spend a marvelous hour or two along **South Street** with its artistic population. It's lined with small colonial homes, which have been creatively restored, and imparts something of what early Nelson must have been like. The house at no. 12, which was a military cottage in the 19th century, now holds changing exhibitions and has a lovely wee garden in the rear. At the corner of Nile and South Streets, visit the **South Street Gallery** in an old, two-story brown house to see some of Nelson's finest pottery. It's open from 10 a.m. to 5 p.m., even on weekends.

Nancy Mason's **Fo'c'sle Weavers**, just back of 300 Trafalgar St., is both shop and workshop. Her six-foot woven rugs are masterpieces (current prices start at NZ$120, or $80.54 U.S.), and if you'd like to learn how to weave, Nancy enjoys instructing beginners almost as much as turning out her own beautiful work. A full day's instruction will cost something like NZ$15 ($10.06)—a bargain indeed for a skill that will bring lifelong pleasure! Open every day from 9:30 a.m. to 4:30 p.m. More very good woven articles can be seen at **7 Weavers,** 36 Collingwood St., which is open daily from 10 a.m. to 4 p.m.

Other interesting craft shops are **The Woolstore,** 14 Nile St.; the **Glass Studio,** 276 Hardy St.; and **Jens Hansen,** silversmith, 320 Trafalgar Square.

Out at Tahunanui, Elly and Neils Maas run the **Tahuna Craft Centre,** 13 Beach Rd., Tahunanui (tel. 86-502), where you can see works made locally. Included are pottery, candles, copperware, wooden articles, hand-knit woolen garments, and Elly's own colorful weaving. The Maases are planning a coffeehouse addition to the center, so by the time you read this you can probably begin or end your inspection of the shop with something refreshing.

Still farther south, on Salisbury Road in Richmond (tel. 47-481), Jack and Peggy Laird and their son Paul run **Waimea Pottery Ltd.** Their ovenproof stoneware is sold throughout New Zealand and Australia. The small showroom is open 9 a.m. to 5 p.m. Monday through Friday, and "seconds" with no visible defects are tagged with a red label and priced considerably below "firsts." If you'd like to go back into the workrooms and watch the potters at work, an appointment can be arranged by telephone.

In the Vicinity

A map detailing **scenic drives** from Nelson is available at the PRO, all past points of historical significance as well as natural beauty. There are two national parks within driving distance, sheltered sandy beaches all along the coast (one of the best is **Tahuna Beach,** three miles to the south), and several wineries open to the public (ask at the PRO for *A Guide to Nelson's Wineries*). If you don't relish being behind the wheel yourself, several coach tours and scenic flights are available. The PRO can give you current details.

One place you should definitely plan to visit is the suburb of **Stoke.** That's where you'll find the **Provincial Museum,** filled with pioneer artifacts and displays depicting the area's natural history and *pre*history. The museum sits directly behind an elegant 19th-century stone house with dormer windows and an ornate veranda, which is known as Isel House, situated in manicured grounds (called Isel Park) set back from the Main Road. The house, with its collections of early porcelain, pottery, and furniture, is only open weekends from 2 to 4 p.m., but the park itself is well worth a stroll to relax beneath mature trees, which came to New Zealand from Europe as mere saplings many years ago. The museum is open Tuesday through Friday from 10 a.m. to 4 p.m., 2 to 4 p.m. on weekends and holidays.

Also in Stoke is **Broadgreen House** on Nayland Road, a cob house (thick walls made of packed earth) built in 1855, which has been authentically restored and furnished completely by dedicated volunteers. Their care and attention to detail is evident all through the house, from the drawing room with its slate mantelpiece and original French wallpaper (if you feel you just *must* reach out to touch that rich red-flocked wallpaper, don't—the committee in charge here knows how you feel and have thoughtfully provided a special "touching piece") to the upstairs nursery with wicker carriages and antique dolls. Outside, the rose garden holds more than 2500 plants, with some 250 varieties represented. Broadgreen has rather uncertain opening hours, so be sure to check with the PRO before setting out to see it.

Fishing

If you've ever cast a line or dropped a hook, the South Island's marvelous fishing waters are bound to be a temptation to tarry long enough to try your luck. The only problem is knowing just where, when, and how to fish all those rivers, lakes, and streams. Well, in Nelson take yourself off to **Sportsgoods (Nelson) Ltd.** on the CML Corner (tel. 89-899) to see Tony Busch. He knows these waters well and has guided fishermen from all over the world who come here just to fish with him. Tony has also written the definitive *Sportsman's Outdoor Guide,* a beautiful (and expensive) volume with detailed information on South Island fishing grounds, what kinds of fish to find where, how to reach each one, and what sort of equipment to use. No matter what your time or budget requirements, he can put together a fishing expedition to fit them, and you may be certain you'll carry home many a "fish story" as a result—no one *ever* fishes with Tony and returns empty-handed!

2. Nelson to Greymouth

A full day's driving—6½ to 7 hours—means an early start. This trip is ideal for picnicking, or you might stop for lunch in **Murchison** (the bus depot tea room is your best bet—turn left at the Hampton Hotel) or in Westport if you can hold out that long, where there's a wider choice of eateries.

If you're traveling by Newmans Coach, your driver's interesting narrative will fill you in on the history of most of the terrain you'll be covering along a road, which is steep and winding at times, drops through heavily wooded mountain gorges at others, touches the sea, then turns south along a dramatic coastline, sometimes seen from high bluffs along which the road passes. If you're driving, keep an eye out for the following.

Between Murchison and Westport, you'll be following the **Buller River** much of the way. Those jagged gaps and high scarped bluffs above the wall of the gorge between Murchison and Lyell are the legacy of a disastrous earthquake in June 1929. Passing through the ghost mining town of **Lyell,** there is little left to suggest the thriving, bustling town it was during goldrush days. Its last surviving building, the Lyell Hotel, burned in 1963, leaving only a few faint vestiges of those turbulent times. Descending to the lower gorge, you'll be driving through flatlands, then under **Hawkes Crag,** where the road has been hewn from a sheer face of solid rock above the river, and on to a stretch of road between bush-clad walls and rocky ravines.

Westport's history is that of the rise and fall of gold mining, followed by relative prosperity as a coal-mining center. If there's time and you're interested, stop by **Coaltown,** a museum detailing that industry in this area. Turning sharply south at Westport to follow the coastline, you'll pass through **Charleston,** where gold was discovered in 1866, leading to a population boom, with dancehalls, stores, and some 92 hotels—of which little remains today.

About halfway between Westport and Greymouth, you'll come to one of the West Coast's most unusual natural formations, the **Punakaiki Pancake Rocks.** (*Note:* Newmans buses stop here long enough to allow passengers time to make the walk down to see them.) At the top of a steep headland, a simple tea room, restroom, and shop are on the inland side of the road along with space for parking to allow you to leave your car and follow the track across the road through native bush to the sea, where limestone structures, which look for all the world like a gigantic stack of pancakes, jut out into the water. When the seas are high and rough, water comes surging into the deep caverns below and is spouted up some 20 to 30 feet into the air, accompanied by a tremendous whoosh of sound. The surrounding area has been kept as a scenic reserve.

From the Punakaiki Rocks, the road is almost continually within sight of the sea until you turn to cross the **Grey River** and drive into Greymouth.

3. Greymouth

At Greymouth, it's decision-making time: whether to stop here or push on another 25 miles to Hokitika. Greymouth offers a wider choice of accommodations; Hokitika has more attractions. The one Greymouth attraction you will surely not want to miss is Shantytown, a reconstructed gold mining town, but it's quite possible to double back to see it from a Hokitika base. In the final analysis, your decision may rest chiefly on just how tired and hungry you are when you reach Greymouth, erstwhile "Heart of the Coast."

New Zealand's West Coast is a rugged stretch of country whose incomparable beauty has been molded and shaped by the elements—and its inhabitants are perhaps the most rugged and individualistic of a nation of individuals. Lured by Mother Nature's treasures, they have from the beginning seemed to revel in her challenges, and along with a resilient toughness have developed a rollicking sense of fun, a relaxed acceptance of the vicissitudes of West Coast life, and a brand of hospitality, which is recognized (and even boasted of) by Kiwis in every other part of the country. "Coasters" are a hardy and good-hearted breed who will welcome you warmly to this unique region.

The Coast's beauty and hidden wealth were entirely lost on Captain Cook when he sighted it from the sea, remained offshore, and described it in his journal as "wild and desolate and unworthy of observation." Of course, his sea-based observation could not possibly reveal the presence of nuggets of gold strewn about those "unworthy" beaches—that discovery was left for 1864, when it precipitated an influx of prospectors and miners from as far afield as California (along with a goodly number from Australia), many of whom would remain after the goldfields played out in 1867 to form the basis of a permanent population who take fierce pride in their particular part of New Zealand.

Greystone these days keeps busy with coal and timber exports and the import of tourists who come to roam the beaches in search of gemstones and greenstone, fish in the clear streams nearby, and perhaps do a little panning for gold.

USEFUL INFORMATION: The helpful and efficient **Public Relations Office (PRO),** is in the Regent Theatre Building on Mackay Street (tel. 51-01; after hours, 63-40), on the corner of Herbert and Mackay Streets. Hours are 9 a.m. to 5 p.m. Monday to Friday. They can furnish detailed information about the area, book accommodations, etc. . . . NZR coaches depart for Shantytown Monday through Saturday at 11 a.m., with the return departure from Shantytown at 1:40 p.m.

ACCOMMODATIONS: In addition to Greymouth's many good accommodations at inexpensive rates, the PRO keeps a list of residents who take guests in private homes on a B&B basis. Motel and guest-house operators are also very cooperative, helping you find a vacancy if your choice is filed.

A Hostel

The **YHA Hostel, "Kainga-Ra,"** (mailing address: P.O. Box 299; tel. 70-15), is just off Cowper Street, about a 20-minute walk from the town center. There are 43 beds in eight bunkrooms. This is a modern, very well-maintained hostel with a large, fully equipped kitchen and game room. Book ahead if at all possible. Rates for Seniors are NZ$5 ($3.36); for Juniors, NZ$2.50 ($1.68).

Cabins

Greymouth Seaside Motor Camp, Chesterfield Street (tel. 66-18), is, as its name implies, situated by the sea. On level, sheltered sites on the beachfront at the southern edge of town there are 150 tent sites, 72 caravan sites, six on-site caravans, 23 cabins, 15 tourist cabins, and 1 tourist flat. Chesterfield Street is just off the Main South Road, and the camp is signposted from the Main Road. There's a modern TV lounge, kitchen, washing machines and dryers, hot showers, linen for hire, and a camp store. Grounds and all accommodations are well kept. Per-person rates are NZ$5 ($3.36) for tent sites, NZ$5.50 ($3.69) for caravan sites, NZ$12 ($8.05) for the on-site caravans. Rates for double-occupancy cabins run NZ$10 ($6.71) to NZ$12 ($8.05), NZ$18.50 ($12.42) for tourist cabins, and NZ$23 ($15.44) for the tourist flat. Children pay half price in each case.

Bed and Breakfast

Unfortunately, most of the B&Bs in Greymouth do not have H&C in the rooms. They are, however, homey, comfortable, and inexpensive.

Gladys Roche is the hostess at the **Golden Coast Guest House,** 10 Smith St. (tel. 78-39), just back of the railway station. The red-roofed house is set in a sloping, flower-bordered lawn. The four guest rooms are bright and clean, and have heaters and electric blankets. There's a TV lounge with a pretty rock fireplace, where you're welcome to make tea and coffee whenever you wish. Bed-and-breakfast rates are NZ$17 ($11.41) per person.

The **West Haven Tourist Lodge,** 62 Albert St. (tel. 56-05), is run by Mrs. Collins and is handy to the post office, NZZR, and Newmans bus stations. The eight bedrooms (all twin or double beds, except for one large family room) have electric blankets, and there's a nice TV lounge. The evening meal is available if ordered in advance. Bed-and-breakfast rates are NZ$12 ($8.05) for adults, NZ$7 ($4.70) for children.

The **Gilmer Motel,** Grisson Street (tel. 50-14), is spotlessly clean, and run by Mr. and Mrs. Williams, a friendly couple who really care about guests' comfort. The twin-bedded rooms all have H&C, and tea- and coffee-making facilities are provided. There's a TV lounge upstairs, a lounge bar and public bar also on the premises. Bed-and-breakfast rates are NZ$15 ($10.06) per person.

Motel Flats

There are five modern, attractive suites at the **Willowbank Motel,** on the Greymouth–Westport Highway (mailing address: P.O. Box 260; tel. 53-39), all nicely furnished right down to potted plants. All units have been given old West Coast hotel names like Welcome Nugget, Diggers Home, and Plough Inn. Two-bedroom units are spacious and airy, with slanted roofs and paneled walls. Bedsitters are more modest in size, but all have full kitchens, TV, and electric blankets. There's an outdoor swimming pool and a free private spa pool. Rates are NZ$20 ($13.42) single, NZ$25 ($16.78) double, and there's a surcharge for one-night stays.

There are two Best Westerns in Greymouth, both of course honoring the Holiday Pass discount. The two-story **DB Greymouth Hotel,** 68 High St. (tel. 51-54), is just off the main coastal road (Highway 6), about one kilometer from the post office. There are 30 modern, nicely decorated units, which come in all sizes: single, twin, double, and family. All have private plumbing, telephone, tea- and coffee-making facilities (fresh milk is delivered to your unit each day), TV, and radio. Parking is outside the door for downstairs units, off-street for those upstairs. There's an excellent fully licensed family restaurant, serving all three meals at moderate prices, and pub lunches in the lounge bar. On Friday and Saturday night there's disco in the lounge. A decided plus here is the terrific sunset view each evening—not quite in sight of the sea, but just a short walk away, and the skies are magnificent when seen from the hotel. Rates are NZ$28 ($18.79) single, NZ$36 ($24.16) double.

Aachen Place Motel, 50 High St. (tel. 69-01), has ten self-contained bedsitter units, double or twin, all with full kitchen facilities. All have TV, radio, and telephone, and there are guest laundry facilities. It's quite handy to the DB Greymouth licensed restaurant, and there are grocery stores and butchers nearby. Rates are NZ$34 ($22.82) single, NZ$36 ($24.16) double. It's the other Best Western, so the discount applies.

A Licensed Hotel

Greymouth has several centrally located budget hotels, but the **Kings' Motor Hotel,** 44 Mawhera Quay (tel. 50-85), is outstanding. Its surprisingly sophisticated decor is the work of Russell King, one of the owners, who is a graduate architect. Public rooms are especially attractive. There are two restaurants, a bistro, hot pool and sauna, hairdresser, gift shop, self-service laundry, and two color TV lounges. The 25 rooms in the budget range run in size from singles to family rooms sleeping five. All are nicely furnished, with New Zealand bird prints on the walls, and all have electric heater and blankets, shower, toilet, and H&C. Rates are NZ$35 ($23.49) double.

MEALS: One of the best budget eateries in town is the **Raceway Carvery** at the Union Hotel, on Herbert Street (tel. 40-13). Breakfast is served from 7:30 to 9 a.m., lunch from noon to 2 p.m., dinner from 5 to 8 p.m. Monday through Thursday, to 9 p.m. on Friday, Saturday, and Sunday. Roasts, chicken, fish, and salads are featured. Lunch prices are in the NZ$3.50 ($2.35) to NZ$4 ($2.68) range, dinner might run up to NZ$5 ($3.36). Fully licensed.

The **Albion Bistro,** in the Kings' Motor Hotel, 44 Mawhera Quay (tel. 50-85), is as charming as the rest of that hotel. It's small, cozy, and serves good meals at inexpensive prices. Vegetables, baked potato, and salad come with all main courses, and the menu features selections such as fried chicken, porterhouse steak, ham and fish filets, with prices in the NZ$4.50 ($3.02) to NZ$5 ($3.36) range. There's also a children's menu. If you go for the full table d'hôte lunch, the tab will be NZ$6 ($4.03), and a glass of wine to go with it, NZ$.95 (64¢).

The **Caribbean Coffee Lounge,** 115 Mackay St. (tel. 54-97), is upstairs, and the walls of its spacious dining room hold murals of New Zealand landscapes. The fare consists of reasonably priced sandwiches, cakes, pies, grills, and salads. They'll deliver for an additional charge. Hours, Monday to Thursday, are 7:30 a.m. to 5 p.m., on Friday till 8:30 p.m.

The **Steak Bar,** 8 Tainui St. (tel. 57-51), has counter service in a long, narrow room with a beamed ceiling. Steaks, fish, chicken, and oyster meals are in the NZ$5 ($3.36) to NZ$7 ($4.70) range, and there's take-away service. They'll deliver for a small fee. Hours are 10 a.m. to midnight Monday through Thursday and Sunday, until 1 a.m. on Friday and Saturday.

The **J. B. Restaurant** at the DB Greymouth Hotel, 68 High St. (tel. 43-61), serves all three meals at reasonable prices (see "Accommodations").

At **Cobden Takeaways,** Bright Street (tel. 67-48), the choice ranges from toasted sandwiches to hamburgers to fish and chips to chicken with chips and coleslaw, all at very low prices—none over NZ$4.50 ($3.02). You can also order by telephone and they'll deliver for a small extra charge.

THINGS TO SEE AND DO: The star attraction at Greymouth is **Shantytown,** a reconstructed goldrush mining town. To reach it, drive five miles south to Paroa, make a left turn, and drive another two miles inland, following a well-signposted route.

Shantytown owes its existence essentially to California, for it was there that Mr. Sutherland, now the "mayor" of Shantytown, visited Knott's Berry Farm and was convinced that the West Coast needed its own living monument. On his return to New Zealand, his inspiration met with enthusiastic support from the citizens of Greymouth, and its construction is the result of a community volunteer effort. It is now operated by the nonprofit West Coast Historical and Mechanical Society.

The colorful town, which has been built with a keen eye to detail, contains several replicas of well-known structures like the Cameron & Co. livery stables from Hokitika in the 1860s and the Beehive store, which has been in business continually in Greymouth since 1865. Then there are true restorations, like the little wooden church with its slender bell tower, which was moved here from No Town, where it was constructed in 1866. There's also a 25-ton steam locomotive, dating from 1897, which you can ride for NZ$.50 (33¢), bumping along in the wooden passenger cars, which were the latest thing back then. For the same fare, a stagecoach will rattle you over an old bush road. The town is amazingly complete—sharpened razors of the era lie ready for use in the barbershop; authentic tins of the times are on grocery shelves; and the 150-year-old green-and-gold newspaper press in still in working condition.

Stop by to see the excellent display of the **West Coast Gem and Mineral Club** in Shantytown Hall, where souvenir gemstones may be purchased. Visit the gold claim and watch it in operation—if you want to try your luck, you can pan for gold for a NZ$2 ($1.34) charge. Lunch and light refreshments are available on the premises.

Shantytown is open every day from 8:30 a.m. to 5 p.m, with an admission of NZ$2 ($1.34) for adults, NZ$.50 (33¢) for children. An NZRRS bus leaves the bus depot for Shantytown every day except Sunday at 11 a.m., returning at 1:35 p.m. Round-trip fare is NZ$2.10 ($1.41).

If you'd like to visit a **working coal mine,** you can ride the train up to **Rewanui** with the miners themselves—all rugged Coasters who'll be glad of the company. The latter part of the trip is up a sharp incline with spectacular scenery. You'll have about 35 minutes before the return journey, and although it isn't possible to go down into the mine, you can see the main buildings (lamphouse and bathhouse), conveyor belt and coal bins, Rail Ambulance shed, and the air extractor. The train leaves Greymouth shortly after noon and returns before 4 p.m. Ask at the PRO for exact times and fare.

GREYMOUTH TO HOKITIKA: The 25-mile drive south follows the coastline closely along mostly flat land. But look to your left, and the snow-capped tips of the Southern Alps become clearer and clearer, sharply defined against the sky, as though painted on the horizon, a teasing glimpse of the mountain splendor that awaits in a few days when you turn away from the Tasman Sea.

About 20 miles from Greymouth you'll cross the **Arahura River.** This is where Maoris found a great quantity of the greenstone they so highly prized for making weapons, ornaments, and tools. Another five miles and you reach Hokitika, where you can see artisans still working that gemstone into a multitude of items, some of which you'll no doubt take along when you depart.

Special Note: If your time in the South Island is limited, you can drive from Greymouth to Christchurch (allow the better part of a day in order to enjoy the drive to its fullest) by way of Arthur's Pass and some of New Zealand's most spectacular scenery. Just south of Greymouth, turn left onto Highway 73. Opened in 1866, this road was one of the last in the country to be used by horse-drawn Cobb & Co. coaches. If you come in winter, Mount Temple Basin offers a full range of winter sports; in summer, the wild mountain landscape is a marvel of alpine flowers. Regular coach service is also available from Greymouth to Christchurch.

4. Hokitika

As you drive into quiet, peaceful little Hokitika, you'll find it hard to believe that this was once the boisterous, rowdy "Goldfields Capital," where more than 35,000 miners and prospectors kept the dancehalls roaring and filled some 102 hotels. And because it was more accessible by sea than overland, ships poured into its harbor, even though the entrance was so hazardous that people would gather on the shore to watch unlucky ships go aground. Even so, there were as many as 80 at one time tied up at Hokitika wharfs, many of them waiting to transport the gold that poured out of the area at the rate of half a million ounces a year. It turned out not to be the endless supply they all dreamed of, and when the gold was gone, Hokitika's fortunes took another turn.

Today, you'll see only rotting remnants of those once-busy wharfs, and almost no vestiges of all those hotels. Still, Hokitika has the most attractions of any West Coast town, and its present-day prosperity rests on farming, forestry, and tourism—likely to be much more lasting than the glittering gold. The major airport of the West Coast is located here; there's good coach service; and you'll find it an ideal base for exploring this part of the South Island.

Make your first order of business a stop by the **Public Relations Office,** located in the Hokitika Tourist Centre, 29 Weld St. (tel. 11-15), where John White is an enthusiastic booster of the area, always keen to help visitors make the most of their time here. He will, incidentally, do all he can to arrange a visit or overnight accommodations with a local family if you'd like to get to know New Zealanders on a one-to-one basis. John says, with typical Coaster hospitality, that it's usually as easy as ringing up a neighbor!

ACCOMMODATIONS: Hokitika has no youth hostel—the nearest one is in Greymouth.

Cabins

Claridges Motor Camp is on the Main South Road at Livingstone Street (tel. 172) in grounds that cover some 11 acres. There are ungraded cabins with two to four berths, at NZ$4 ($2.68) per person; graded cabins (with electric fry pans, tea and coffee facilities, and H&C), which sleep up to five, at NZ$10 ($6.71) double; tourist cabins (with H&C, crockery and cutlery, limited cooking facilities, fridge, and toilet), which sleep up to five, at NZ$15 ($10.06) double; and fully self-contained tourist flats (with full kitchens, toilets, showers, and TV), which sleep up to six, at NZ$18 ($12.08) double. Additional adults pay NZ$2.50 ($1.68) and children 14 and under pay NZ$1.50 ($1.01) in all cases. Linens can be rented, and camp amenities include two kitchens, laundry, color TV room, children's playground, and a well-stocked shop, which is open every day of the week. There are also caravan and tent sites on the grounds.

Bed and Breakfast

John and Elizabeth White run the **Central Guesthouse,** 20 Hamilton St. (tel. 12-32)—he's the PRO chief I told you about—and they are gracious hosts indeed. It is, as the name implies, centrally located, and the eight rooms are centrally heated, have electric blankets, and are nicely decorated. There's a color TV in the lounge, as well as a pool table and tea and coffee facilities. That's where you'll have your breakfast, and if you want to bring in dinner, you're welcome to eat it there. You'll be given a free daily newspaper and have the use of laundry facilities. Rates are NZ$15 ($10.06) per person for bed and breakfast.

Motel Flats

Top billing in Hokitika's motels goes to the **Goldsborough Motel,** 252 Revell St. (tel. 772). It's just across from the Tasman Sea and a short walk from the glowworm dell. Best of all, this Best Western member is run by Brian and Rosemarie Macpherson, two of the most genial hosts in New Zealand. Rosemarie is quite a golfer, and has the trophies to prove it. All units, bedsitters and two-bedrooms, have fully equipped kitchens, color TV, central heating, and electric heaters. They're all spacious and have parking at the door. The morning newspaper is delivered free to your door. There's a guest laundry, a swimming pool, spa pool, and children's playground. A seven-day food store is within walking distance. Rates are NZ$29 ($19.46) single, NZ$38 ($25.50) double. Best Western discounts apply.

Also within easy walking distance of the glowworm dell is the **Hokitika Motel,** 221 Fitzherbert St. (tel. 292). There are bedsitters, one-bedroom units, and two-bedroom units with full kitchens, as well as three bedsitters with only electric jug, toaster, teapot, crockery, and fridge. All units have central and electric heating, electric blanket, radio, TV, and telephone. There's a mini-store for essential provisions, car wash, laundry, and a courtesy car to the airport. Rates range from NZ$30 ($20.13) to NZ$36 ($24.16) single, NZ$34 ($22.82) to NZ$38 ($25.50) double.

A Licensed Hotel

There's something very homey about the **DB Westland Hotel,** 2 Weld St. (tel. 411), and its location right in the heart of town makes it an ideal place to stay, especially if you're a bit tired of hotels that have been "glitzed" to death! Rooms here are clean, comfortable, and nicely furnished—but not fancy. And you can save a penny or two by opting for a room without private facilities. Public rooms include a lounge, dining room, and lounge bar, which serves bistro meals (see "Meals," below). Rooms with facilities down the hall are NZ$14 ($9.40) single, NZ$24 ($16.11) double; those with private facilities are N$20 ($13.42) single, NZ$30 ($20.13) double.

MEALS: You'll want to go by the **Gold Strike Arcade,** 89 Revell St., just to see what an engaging young couple have managed to accomplish with an old building, doors and windows salvaged from one of those long-gone hotels (the Red Lion), and tons of imagination and hard work. Monica came from England to Hokitika, where she joined forces with Kim, who grew up here, to create from the derelict structure a bright complex of shops, which feature everything from gift items to babyware to garden supplies. But right at the entrance of the Arcade is its main attraction—a small eatery, which specializes in light meals and luscious ice creams (in 16 flavors!). There's always a brisk business at the ice-cream bar, but take my advice and sample at least one of their unusual and very good sandwiches. All come on hearty, freshly baked bread, and I'm positively addicted to the venison (which, with a bowl of homemade soup, makes a lovely light meal). A local favorite is the honey, walnuts, and raisins combination, with cheese and corn also very popular. Pork, salami, and beef are also available. Sandwiches like these you won't get at home! Prices are all under NZ$2 ($1.34).

The **Westland Hotel,** 2 Weld St. (tel. 411), serves terrific bistro meals in an attractive lounge bar flanked by twin stone fireplaces, with comfortable booths and table groupings. Hot plates include steak, scallops, fish, oysters, chicken, and ham, and there's a daily special for NZ$3.50 ($2.35). Salad plates are fresh and delicious. Prices run from NZ$3.50 ($2.35) to NZ$5 ($3.36), and hours are noon to 1:45 p.m. and 6 to 9 p.m.

In the Westland's main dining room, you can "splurge" on atmosphere while going "budget" in the pocketbook department. Lace curtains are framed by brown drapes, set off by gold-and-brown carpet, and there's a silver flower vase on each table. And on Sunday there's a smörgåsbord dinner with soup, hot and cold dishes, salads, desserts, and beverage for the grand sum of NZ$7.50 ($5.03) for grownups, NZ$4.50 ($3.02) for children. Prices are just as moderate on other nights, when the menu is á la carte.

THINGS TO SEE AND DO: One of the primary reasons for making Hokitika your base on the West Coast is to be there after dark so you can see the **glowworms**—this is the largest outdoor group in the country—in a charming dell at the edge of town, right on the main road. The 40-foot-and-higher wooded banks are filled with sparkling clusters of thousands of glowworms, a truly awe-inspiring sight. And as interesting as are the Waitomo displays, there is something about walking down a dirt path under a natural archway of treetops and standing alone in absolute silence that makes for a mystical personal experience. There's no charge, but there's a donation box at the entrance and all are appreciated by the town, which keeps this wondrous place available for us all. Best bring a flashlight for the first part of the path, but remember to turn it off when you begin to see the glowworms or they'll turn their lights off.

The **West Coast Historical Museum,** on Tancred Street between Hamilton and Camp Streets (tel. 11-18), will bring goldrush days in this area vividly alive with such exhibits as a recreated typical gold miner's shack, tent, cooking gear, forge, and prospecting equipment; a working model of a gold dredge; all kinds of mining and surveying equipment; a reconstructed mining-area bar, church altar, barbership, jail; and a vast collection of photographs, old newspapers, and personal mementos of mining families. Shipping artifacts, scrimsaw, Hokitika's first fire engine (acquired back in 1870), and a host of other interesting items are also on display. A recent addition is the 20-minute audio-visual show on the early West Coast depicting both the gold-mining and forestry industries. There are also some excellent Maori relics such as spears, clubs, fishhooks, feather boxes, and the like. It's open weekdays from 9:30 a.m. to 4:30 p.m., on Saturday and Sunday from 9:30 a.m. to noon and 2 to 4:40 p.m. Adults pay NZ$1.50 ($1.01); children, NZ$.50 (33¢).

You can do a little panning for gold yourself at the **Blue Spur Gold Mine,** four miles from town. It's a 42-acre working gold claim at which you can watch sluicing operations, see a real miner's cottage, and inspect the tunnels and shafts of the mine. Not much output these days, but every panner is guaranteed at least a trace. Open every day from 9 a.m. to 4 p.m., with longer hours in summer. Adults pay NZ$2 ($1.34); children, NZ$.50 (33¢).

The larger of the two greenstone factories in town is **Westland Greenstone Company Ltd.,** on Tancred Street between Weld and Hamilton Streets. The piles of rocks you see show their true color (and value) as the diamond-tipped wheels spin, cutting off slices. The workroom is open for you to wander through, watching talented workmen carving tikis and meres, fitting earrings and pins, and shaping a hundred other souvenirs from the gemstone. Then back to the showroom to consider which of their handiwork you will buy (but let me stress you're under no obligation to make a purchase). Monday through Thursday, hours are 8 a.m. to 5 p.m.; Friday to Sunday, from 9 a.m. **West Coast Jade Ltd.,** at 110 Revell St. (tel. 363), has much the same operation and is open Monday through Friday from 8 a.m. to 5 p.m.

The **Free Form Glass Blowing Company,** 130 Revell St. (tel. 12-61), lets you watch the glassblowers as they create their works of art and put them into cooling ovens. A showroom, where you can make purchases, adjoins the workroom. Hours are 7:30 a.m. to 4 p.m. Monday through Friday, and the showroom is open on weekends from 9:30 a.m. to 12:30 p.m. and 1:30 to 5 p.m.

A Dutch couple, Hans and Lida Schouten, display their considerable talents at **Genesis Creation,** 75 Revell St. (tel. 629). Hans works with wood in creating and restoring furniture. A specialty is spinning wheels (which are shipped all over the world). A weaver, Lida creates lovely woolens to sell in the small shop. They also feature the work of other craftspeople in the area, and you'll find hand-knit sweaters of natural wool (I've picked up one on every trip and treasure them all), shawls, leather goods, and pottery. The Schoutens are happy to mail packages overseas to lighten your load. The shop is open from 9 a.m. to 5 p.m. weekdays and on Saturday mornings by request.

Hokitika is an excellent place to do some of that souvenir and gift shopping that's a "must" on every trip. At the **Tourist Centre** in the main street, you can browse through a real Aladdin's cave of varied New Zealand goods, from sheepskin products to woodware, leather, pottery, paua-shell items, and linen goods. The staff are helpful in answering questions on travel and accommodation (this is, after all, where the PRO is located!), so you might combine sightseeing queries with shopping.

Some of the best paintings of the South Islands west coast are done right here in Hokitika by **Brent Trolle,** whose work is known throughout the country. You can visit him at his home, 13 Whitcombe Terrace (which also serves as gallery and studio), by calling for an appointment (tel. 12-50S). I can't think of a nicer way to keep New Zealand memories alive than with one of Brent's paintings.

Hokitika's Rotary Club has provided an excellent orientation base at the **lookout point** just off the road to the airport. From there you look over valley farmland to the towering peaks of the Southern Alps (each one identified by a revolving bronze pointer, which stands on a stone base) or across the town to the glistening Tasman Sea. It's a spectacular view, within easy walking distance from the center of town.

There are excellent **scenic flights** from Hokitika over the glaciers—no landing on them as some others do, but the flight is longer. The plane flies south from Hokitika to the Main Divide, over the Tasman Glacier, skirts Mount Cook, over Fox and Franz Josef Glaciers, over Okarito Lagoon (nesting place of the white heron) and large stands of New Zealand native timber. It's quite a flight. There's no regular schedule at this writing, but you can contact **Westland Flying Services,** Hokitika Airport (tel. 12-87K), or inquire at the PRO about times and current prices.

ROSS: Nineteen miles south of Hokitika is the little town of Ross, well worth a drive over from Hokitika or a stop on your way to Franz Joseph Glacier.

The **Westland Wild Life Museum** is on Moorhouse Street, the town's main thoroughfare, and it is the creation of Basil Detlaff, a skilled taxidermist, who hopes eventually to have all West Coast wildlife represented. At present there are displays of chamois, keas, and thar, as well as a live opossum, some geckos, and a working beehive. You can buy honey from that hive in the gift shop on the ground floor. Hours are 9 a.m. to 5 p.m. daily, and admissions are NZ$1 (67¢) and NZ$.50 (33¢).

Down the street, you'll find **Ross Furs** (tel. 6), where Mrs. and Mrs. Peter Gray will show you through the workshop in which bush-tailed opossum skins are worked into coats, bedspreads, purses, and a host of other items. Prices in their showroom are often considerably below those in shops. Hours are 9 a.m.

to 5 p.m. weekdays, and weekends in the summer. They will, however, open other times upon request.

Next stop is Franz Josef, 73 miles down the road.

5. The Glaciers

Glaciers are pretty impressive no matter where in the world you encounter them—tons and tons of snow crystals, which have, over thousands and thousands of years, been subjected to such enormous pressures that they fuse into a solid mass of clear ice, which even greater pressures cause to move at an invisible, but inexorable, rate. What makes the Fox and Franz Josef Glaciers so unforgettable (sure to be one of your most memorable New Zealand experiences) is their descent well below 1000 feet above sea level, framed by valley walls of deep-green bush, until they reach their terminal in luxuriant rain forests. Nowhere in the world outside arctic regions do glaciers reach such low altitudes. Fox is the longer of the two glaciers and has a more gradual slope.

On equal footing with your memories of these giant rivers of ice, however, will be those of the sunsets in these parts. From your motel lawn or window, you'll be treated to a show of great beauty. Julius von Haast, the great explorer who was the first European to explore this region, wrote of the sunsets, "New changes were every moment effected, the shades grew longer and darker, and whilst the lower portion already lay in the deep purple shade, the summits were still shining with an intense rosy hue."

ORIENTATION: The small townships of Franz Josef and Fox Glacier are only 24 kilometers apart, yet you should allow a full 45 minutes for the drive (or better yet, in my opinion, let NZZRS do the driving from here on to Queenstown, leaving your eyes free to drink in some of the world's most spectacular natural beauty). Tall trees line the road, which twists from one breathtaking view to the next. If you're driving, exercise caution all the way.

The two glaciers are only a small part of the 115,000-hectare **Westland National Park,** an impressive reserve of high mountain peaks, glacial lakes, and rushing rivers. It includes a fair bit of the Southern Alps, which cover more territory than the entire country of Switzerland! The park is much used for tramping, glacier walks, mountain climbing, fishing, canoeing, and hunting for red deer, thar, and chamois, as well as for scenic flights offered from several points.

Park rangers run **Visitor Centres** at both glacier townships, and their displays, literature on the park, and visitor activities are essential to a full appreciation of the area. Throughout holiday periods, a program of free nature lectures, slide presentations, and guided walks makes it possible for budgeteers to enjoy all the park has to offer with a minimal effect on the pocketbook. They also administer the four alpine huts and three tramping huts available for overnight hikers, and keep track of trampers and mountain climbers (you must check conditions and register your intentions with the rangers before setting out).

The only local transportation is by taxi, but for travel between the two townships, NZZRS coaches provide drop-off service.

ACCOMMODATIONS: During peak season, accommodations are woefully short, with a greater choice at Franz Josef than at Fox Glacier. Each township has a licensed hotel; however, both are out of reach of budget travelers (the one in Franz Josef is an excellent THC and books many of the glacier walks and flightseeing trips, and sometimes has off-season special rates—see below). There's no central booking service, but the Visitor Centres can furnish a list of accommodations with current prices.

Hostels

The **Franz Josef YHA Hostel** is on Cron Street (mailing address: P.O. Box 12; tel. 754). It's modern; has a kitchen, hot showers, and 48 beds in eight rooms; and is convenient to shops and tea rooms. Rates for Seniors are NZ$4 ($2.68); for Juniors, NZ$2 ($1.34). Advance booking is always advisable, especially during summer months and holiday periods. Note: There's a rather basic (canvas beds, open-fire cooking, no electricity) YHA shelter hostel at Okarito, 26 kilometers away—no telephone, no advance booking, and you're advised to take food in with you.

The privately run **Forks Lodge and Motorcamp** is 12 miles north of Franz Josef (one mile from a signposted turnoff from Highway 6; tel. Whataroa 351) in beautiful forest surroundings. There are two units sleeping four to six people, one unit sleeping up to ten. Facilities include cooking rings and other kitchen fittings, H&C, and showers. It's close to good fishing and forest walks. Rates are NZ$5 ($3.36) per adult, NZ$2.50 ($1.68) per child.

Cabins

In Franz Josef: The **Franz Joseph Motor Camp,** on the main road (tel. 766), is set in attractive grounds of bush and hills. There are 26 basic cabins sleeping two to four persons on beds or bunks, all with good, comfortable mattresses. All are exceptionally clean, and have tables and chairs and electric heaters. No cooking in cabins, but there's a kitchen, as well as showers and a coin-operated laundry. Six family cottages, sleeping up to eight, have H&C, stoves, crockery, cutlery, cookware, blankets, and heaters. Bedding can be rented. There's a large camp store, which sells groceries, snacks, and frozen meats. NZZRS coaches stop at the entrance. Cabins rent for NZ$5.50 ($3.69) per person, family cottages start at NZ$17.50 ($11.75) double, and campsites are NZ$6 ($4.03) for two.

The **Forks Lodge** (see "Hostels," above) has caravan sites in a beautiful, wooded location at NZ$6 ($4.03) for two; children pay half price.

In Fox Glacier: About a quarter mile from Fox Glacier township, you'll find **Fox Glacier Motor Park** (tel. 821), with clean, comfortable cabins, some with two bunks, others with four. There are two kitchen blocks with dining rooms, three shower blocks, and a coin-operated laundry. Linen may be rented, and canned and frozen goods are available at the camp store. Rates are from NZ$5.50 ($3.69) per person for cabins, NZ$3.50 ($2.35) per adult for caravan sites.

Bed and Breakfast

Just one block off the main street in Franz Josef, the **Callery Lodge** (tel. 738) has twin or double rooms, which, although a bit on the small side, are comfortably furnished. No H&C, and the bathroom is down the hall. There's a sauna, TV lounge, and laundry, and tea and coffee are free any time of the day. Bed-and-breakfast rates are NZ$30 ($20.13) for two. The Callery also has motel flats (see below).

The **Al Motel** (see "Motel Flats," below, for a full description) has a serviced lodge with comfortable rooms, a large kitchen, TV lounge, and tea and coffee facilities. A continental breakfast is included in the NZ$15 ($10.06) per-person rate.

Serviced Motel

By far the prettiest motel in Franz Josef township is the **Westland Motor Inn** (tel. 728 or 729), a member of the Best Western chain. Centrally located on the main street, it has a licensed restaurant (see "Meals") and lounge bar, and a beautiful guest lounge with huge glass windows and one entire wall covered by a native-stone fireplace. Grounds are beautifully planted (back lawns have lounge chairs—a perfect place from which to watch those dazzling sunsets), and just at the entrance there's an old cobble cart planted with native ferns. Dawn and Ray Eldershaw and their family run the Westland with friendly, gracious hospitality—Ray is a retired Newmans Coach driver, knows the South Island intimately, and loves to share his knowledge with guests as well as accompany them on evening walks to the glowworm dells in back of the motel. The 47 serviced rooms all have color TV (with video), tea and coffee facilities, private bath, and central heating. Two luxury suites have spa baths, and there are two spa pools, a game room, and a guest laundry. From time to time big-screen movies are shown in the conference room. Rates are seasonal (lowest are June through August) and range from NZ$32 ($21.48) to NZ$35.50 ($23.83) single, NZ$36 ($24.16) to NZ$46 ($30.87) double. Highly recommended if the budget can stretch. Best Western discounts apply.

Motel Flats

In Franz Josef: The **Bushland Court Motel,** on Cron Street (mailing address: P.O. Box 41; tel. 757), has four attractive units with high, beamed ceilings. Sleeping two to six people, all are immaculate and have central heating, color TV, radio, and covered car ports. There's a laundry and a children's playground on the premises. Rates start at NZ$30 ($20.13) double, NZ$8 ($5.37) per additional person.

Just next door, the **Callery Lodge,** Cron Street (tel. 738), offers two motel flats, which are centrally heated. Both have one bedroom, full kitchen, electric blanket, radio, TV, clock, and record player. There's a sauna, laundry, and TV lounge. Rates are NZ$34 ($22.82) double, NZ$6 ($4.03) for each additional adult.

The **Motel Franz Josef** (mailing address: Private Bag, Hokitika; tel. 742) is on the main road three miles north of the village. There are eight one- and two-bedroom units, all with private patios facing a view of distant low hills and private car ports. All are centrally heated and have TV and radio. Mrs. and Mrs. Trevor Gibb, the friendly owners, also have a small canteen with canned and frozen foods. Rates are NZ$34 ($22.82) single or double, NZ$9 ($6.04) per additional adult.

In Fox Glacier: The **Al Motel** (mailing address: P.O. Box 29; tel. 833) sits in a valley about a mile from the township and is owned by a charming young couple, Mike and Cheryl Riley. Mike, who built the entire complex himself, also worked wonders with a dilapidated old woodshed, which he has transformed into their lovely home right next to the motel. Every rock in their living room fireplace is from the fields outside; wooden furniture was built by Mike; and Cheryl's handiwork may be seen in the paintings of local scenes, which hang on the office walls. Both the Rileys know the area well, and Mike has built a model of both glaciers to use in talking to guests about them. There are seven nicely designed and attractively furnished units, one of which has one bedroom; the others, two. There are barbecue facilities, a swimming pool, a nine-hole putting green, squash court, spa pool, children's playground, and laundry on the premises. Rates are NZ$25 ($16.78) single, NZ$32 ($21.48) double, NZ$8 ($5.37) for each additional adult. There's a surcharge for one-night stays, but a reduction after three nights.

The THC

The **THC Franz Josef** (mailing address: Private Bag, Hokitika; tel. 819) has in-season rates in the neighborhood of NZ$62 ($41.61) and up—out of the question for those of us on a budget. However, they frequently have off-season specials, which are a real bargain. On my last trip (in June), they were offering a Friday-until-Sunday rate of NZ$36 ($24.16), which is budget indeed. The trick is to know when and what they're offering. These rates are not highly publicized, but it will pay you to call ahead and inquire about current offerings if you're interested in luxury accommodations within a budget range. You just might hit at the right time.

MEALS: There are not a great many places to eat in either township, and this may be where you do more home-cooking than anywhere else in New Zealand. However, some of the following are quite good.

In Franz Josef: The **Glacier Store and Tearooms** are in a beautifully designed building right on the main street and serve light fare for lunches and teas. It's self-service, and you can lunch well for NZ$2 ($1.34) and under. The upstairs tea rooms offer fantastic views of the snow-capped Southern Alps, the Croz Glacier, and the luxuriant West Coast rain forest. Within the same building you can shop for food, hardware, and clothing, and adjacent to the new building is the Fern Grove Souvenir Shop, which carries a wide range of quality souvenirs, film, and a wide selection of woolen knitwear. Open every day from 8 a.m. to 6 p.m., later in summer months.

The **Westland Motor Inn,** at the northern end of the main street (tel. 729), has the very attractive Clematis Room, with slanted-beam ceiling and gaslight-style fixtures overhead. Wide windows look out to the mountains. The à la carte menu lists such specialties as venison marinated in red wine (a personal favorite of mine), roast beef, chicken, and a lovely entree of marinated mussels, which can be ordered in portions ample for two (NZ$5, or $3.36 U.S.), as well as a number of other dishes, all superbly prepared and served. Once a week they have a Coaster's night, when all local foods are served: venison soup, whitebait, rigg (that's a local fish—I know, I hadn't heard of it, either), homemade apple pie, and whatever else happens to be available in the area. All main courses come with fresh vegetables and potato. It's fully licensed, and has a nice lounge bar for before or after meals, where you're likely to meet a local or two, all glad of a chat. Dinner prices run from NZ$8 ($5.37) to NZ$11.50 ($7.72), and hours are 6 to 9 p.m. in summer, until 7:30 p.m. in winter. You'll need to book in summer.

In Fox Glacier: The **grocery store** sells foodstuffs, hot meat pies, and sandwiches right along with camping supplies, hardware, boots, heavy jackets, and polyester shirts. The **Tea Rooms** have inexpensive grills and snacks, and **Grandma's Grub Shop,** next door, has full, inexpensive meals at inexpensive prices. All are open daily, and hours vary,

The **Fox Glacier Hotel** (tel. 839) serves soup, savoury, grill (a cold main course at lunch), and dessert for NZ$6.50 ($4.36) at lunch, NZ$10 ($6.71) at dinner.

Note: For **picnics** while you're in the area, or the day-long drive to Queenstown, both the Fox Glacier Hotel and the THC Franz Josef will pack a picnic box if ordered the night before.

THINGS TO SEE AND DO: Your sightseeing at the Glaciers can be as costly or as inexpensive as your budget dictates. There are, it must be said, several sightseeing experiences that can put a large hole in that budget—and they are among the most spectacular travel experiences in the world, worth every cent of their cost. Yet it's quite possible to enjoy Mother Nature's free display and leave with an equally soul-satisfying experience that has cost you nothing. Either Visitor Centre can give you literature outlining self-guided walks, and for just pennies you can buy detailed information sheets on each. For less than a dollar there are booklets, which give you a complete rundown on how the glaciers were formed, the movement of the ice, the mountains, the history of the region, and much, much more. If the do-it-yourself approach has no appeal, there are (during certain months) free guided walks conducted by park rangers, as well as free nature lectures and slide shows. If you're a biker instead of a hiker, ten-speed bikes are available from Bushland Court (tel. 757) for NZ$8 ($5.37) per day.

Glacier Trips

Now, about those expensive glacier experiences. You can do three very special things at the Glaciers: take a skiplane ride, take a helicopter ride, and go for a glacier walk.

If this is where you decide to go all out and splurge on one of the finest of all international travel experiences, take the **Mount Cook Lines skiplane flight** from Franz Josef to the top of the Tasman Glacier. The six-seater Cessna 185 whisks you over the lush forests, between the peaks of the Main Divide (you're then 9000 feet above sea level), and settles its skis on the surface of the 18-mile-long, 2000-foot-deep glacier. Then you're out to walk about in the snow, perhaps have a Polaroid snapshot taken by your pilot (NZ$4, or $2.68 U.S.) before returning through the jagged peaks, over ribbon-like rivers and rain forests below, back to the shining sea (all the more magnificent if you return as the sun is beginning to set over the sea). Admittedly, it *is* expensive—but it's an experience that will live with you the rest of your days. The 40-minute flight is NZ$55 ($36.91) for adults, NZ$41 ($27.52) for children 14 and under.

There are shorter flights for less. They don't cross the Main Divide, but do land on Fox or Franz Josef Glacier, and adults pay NZ$39 ($26.17); children, NZ$29 ($19.46).

The choice may not be as agonizing as you think—weather can make it for you. It's very unpredictable, and especially if your time is short, my best advice is to take the first one available. Of course, if the weather is fine, it's agonizing time again. But even if weather really closes in and neither is available, not to worry—you'll have another opportunity at Mount Cook.

Mount Cook Line also runs several **helicopter flights,** whose prices run from NZ$26 ($17.45) to NZ$64 ($42.95).

There are Mount Cook Line offices at both townships: at Franz Joseph, phone 714; at Fox, dial 812. You can also book flights through both the THC Franz Joseph and the Fox Glacier Hotel.

There is another great way to experience the Franz Josef glacier, which is far less expensive than the flights and which, in my opinion, actually complements them. That is the **glacier walk,** with an expert guiding you along the surface of the ice. If you're in reasonably good shape you'll be able to do the walk, regardless of age. Guides chip steps in the ice, which during warm weather is granular instead of glass-slick. You'll go up into the ice fall, walk among the crevasses, listen to the deep-throated grumble of the moving glacier. A minibus will pick you up at the THC Franz Josef, where hobnailed boots, waterproof parka, heavy socks, and walking stick are provided, and will take you to the glacier track at 9:30 a.m. and 2 p.m. in summer, mornings only at other times. And the walk goes regardless of the weather! The cost for adults is NZ$11 ($7.38); for children, NZ$6 ($4.03). Book through reception at the hotel.

At Fox, in addition to a glacier walk like the above, there's a half-day **helihike,** when you fly by helicopter to about one kilometer up the glacier and walk back down. It's about the same length as the glacier walk (2½ hours), but you're on the ice longer. All equipment is provided, and the cost is NZ$40 ($26.85) per adult, NZ$22 ($14.77) for children. A longer, full-day helihike goes all the way to Victoria Falls, and you spend the entire day walking down the glacier (you leave at 9:30 a.m. and get back around 4:30 p.m.). You'd want to be reasonably fit for this outing, but if you really want to get to know that river of ice, this is the walk to take. Groups are small and there's time to really explore things (this is the one the guides themselves like best). The cost is NZ$55 ($36.91).

If you're reading this book at home and the glaciers have you hooked, or if you were hooked already and are coming to New Zealand primarily to spend time at the glaciers, you might like to know that **Alpine Guides (Westland) Ltd.,** P.O. Box 38, Fox Glacier (tel. 825), offers several mountaineering courses, varying in length from seven days to two weeks. These are the guides who conduct the walks just described, and their experience covers mountain and ice climbing from the Himalayas to Antarctica. Write ahead for details on physical requirements, enrollment, and prices.

Other Sights

Other scenic spots abound in this wonderland of Mother Nature's. One is **Lake Mapourika,** nine kilometers north of Franz Josef on Highway 6. It is the park's largest lake, formed by glacier ice eons ago. There's good trout and salmon fishing in its waters, a view of Mount Tasman up the glacier gorge, and picnic areas as well as a small beach. It's a thoroughly delightful place, one frequented by such birds as the crested grebe, white-throated shag, and on occasion the white heron. Then there's **Lake Matheson,** three miles from the Fox Glacier Hotel, whose likeness you will have seen all over the country—it's famed for the mirror-like reflections of Mounts Cook and Tasman in its still waters. In Franz Josef, take a few minutes to visit **St. James Anglican Church,** the Tudor-style church whose east window frames a spectacular alpine view behind the altar. It's just south of the Visitors Centre.

6. Queenstown via Haast Pass and Wanaka

This is a day-long drive along a 256-mile route, which takes you through some of New Zealand's most striking terrain: cool green ferns; secluded sea coves; deep-walled gorges; high, steep bluffs; alpine lakes; lagoons alive with white herons; and valleys filled with grazing sheep. Before this road was built, the only passage from east to west was an old bridle path, and at the very top of the Haast Pass, there's a signpost that will point you to that path, a pretty walk back into the past. The road itself took 40 years to build, and in fact work still goes on in sections as rock slides occur. Some portions are gravel, though most are sealed and a good surface. There are steep climbs and sharp descents, hairpin curves and stretches of one-lane travel. Haast Pass is actually the lowest pass through the Southern Alps, very seldom blocked by snow, but peaks on either side rise as high as 10,000 feet.

A picnic lunch is ideal, as there are any number of places to stop and let your senses ramble as you eat. It's a good excuse, too, to loiter at a scenic spot, which especially takes your fancy. There are roofed outdoor tables (and restrooms) at a public picnic area about 122 miles into the journey at **Pleasant Flat Bridge.** Otherwise, the **DB Haast Hotel** (tel. Haast 827) serves a good lunch at reasonable prices (this is where NZZRS and most tour coaches break the trip). Incidentally, if you are meandering and would like to see more along the way, the hotel has serviced units which go for NZ$25 ($16.78) single, NZ$36 ($24.16) double. If you're picnicking, save a bit for a tea break when you reach Lake Wanaka—the view, with 9975-foot Mount Aspiring in the distance, begs a lingering look.

WANAKA: A popular resort with New Zealanders, Wanaka offers many sports activities, as well as smashing scenery. If you arrive there utterly exhausted, it makes a good overnight stopping place before going on to Queenstown.

Mount Aspiring National Park has its park headquarters in Wanaka, although the park is some 30 miles to the northwest. If you plan to spend time here, drop by the Park Headquarters on the corner of Ballantyne Road and Highway 89 (tel. 660) for information on park activities. For accommodation booking in the Wanaka area, it's the **Wanaka Tourist-Craft Ltd.,** 17-19 Helwick St. (tel. 78-04). They handle a full range of services for travelers and can tell you about scenic flights, raft cruises, launch trips, and other activities.

Accommodations

The **YHA Hostel** is at 181 Upton St. (tel. 74-05), a very central location. There are 42 beds in six rooms, and Seniors pay NZ$4 ($2.68); Juniors, NZ$2 ($1.34).

Wanaka Motor Camp, 212 Brownston St. (tel. 883), is also centrally located and has cabins sleeping up to five, as well as caravan sites. Cabin rates are NZ$12 ($8.05) double.

The **Alpine Motel,** 7 Ardmore St. (tel. 819), has well-equipped, attractive units and laundry facilities. Rates for singles are NZ$25 ($16.78); for doubles, NZ$34 ($22.82).

The **Best Western Manuka Crescent Motel,** 51 Manuka Crescent (tel. 77-73), if off Beacon Point Road about a mile from town, with seven homey units fully equipped. Rates are NZ$38 ($25.50) single, NZ$39 ($26.17) double. BW Holiday Pass discounts apply.

The **THC Wanaka,** on Ardmore Street (tel. 78-26), has a few well-equipped and spacious two-bedroom motel units, which cost NZ$41 ($27.52) double or single, NZ$7 ($4.70) per additional adult, no charge for children.

READER'S MOTEL SELECTION: "Wanaka is a resort almost as beautiful as Queenstown, but with fewer shops. We looked all around for a good motel and found several with high prices and/or limited facilities. Finally, we found the **All Seasons Motel** (mailing address: P.O. Box 112, Wanaka) five kilometers out of Wanaka on the Haast Pass road. Not rock-bottom, but much cheaper than the others, and with a very helpful manager" (John Cronquist, Fullerton, Calif.).

Meals

Aspiring Takeaways, 68 Ardmore St. (tel. 78-03), has hamburgers, ice cream, milkshakes, and sandwiches at low prices and is open seven days from 8 a.m. to 9 p.m.

The **Kingsway Tea Lounge,** 21 Helwick St., has sandwiches, soups, salads, and one hot meal daily at lunch and dinner (meat, two vegetables, and potato) at budget prices. Open every day from 9 a.m. to 5:30 p.m., with extended hours in season.

The best place for meals is the THC's **Storehouse Restaurant and Family Bar,** on Ardmore Street (tel. 78-26). It's a rustic place featuring a brick fireplace, rough-hewn crossbeams, cushioned brick booths, and photomurals of the early-1900s Wanaka Hotel. The menu includes such main courses as fish, steak, pork, lamb, and chicken, and prices are in the NZ$9 ($6.04) to NZ$11 ($7.38) range. In ski season the bar has live music for the après-ski crowd. Open Monday to Saturday for lunch, dinner, and drinks. The THC also has the wood-paneled Sundowner Bar overlooking lake and mountains, with a pianist from the dinner hour until late.

READER'S MEALS SELECTIONS: "In the Pembroke Village Mall, directly across from the lake we found the **Pizza Shop,** serving all varieties of pizza. The pizza was good and good value, and there are picnic tables outside, or you can take away. Next door, the same owner has the **Dough Shop**—the best homebaked bread, rolls, croissants, hot-cross buns, and apple shortcake I've ever tasted! In the same mini-mall, there's **Suzanne's,** a health-food, salad, and sandwich bar. Good prices and healthy food" (Linda Abbott, San Diego, Calif.).

Sights

How to get lost and found in Wanaka? Head for the **Wanaka Maze,** on the Main Highway (tel. 489). Behind tall fences, there are pathways that lead somewhere and passageways that lead nowhere. The fun comes in finding your way through without becoming hopelessly lost. Most people take about 20 minutes to do that, and they do so to the tune of peals of laughter. The cost is NZ$1.50 ($1.01) for adults, NZ$.50 (33¢) for children. On the same grounds, you can play croquet or mini-golf, browse through a puzzle shop, and visit the refreshment bar.

WANAKA TO QUEENSTOWN: There are two routes you could follow, one not open to trailers and not recommended to inexpert drivers. That 44-mile stretch of Highway 89 crosses the **Crown Range** and opens up fantastic panoramic views of the entire **Wakatipu Valley,** then descends into the valley in a series of sharp curves until it reaches the aptly named "Foot of Zig Zag," where you make a sharp right turn and level out to drive through farmlands all the way to **Lake Wakatipu** and Queenstown. The other route (the one I strongly recommend unless you're stout of heart and a whale of a driver) is via Highway 6 and is good driving all the way. You'll see road and earthmoving works en route where the gigantic **Clyde Dam** is under construction. When you reach the town of **Cromwell,** take a good look, for a good portion of it will be under water in about five years when the huge hydroelectric project is completed.

Whichever route you choose, you may want to stop in historic **Arrowtown,** although it's just a short drive back from Queenstown (and there are good coach tours from there to Arrowtown) if you're ready to push on to dinner and bed after a long day behind the wheel.

Chapter VIII

QUEENSTOWN

1. In and Around the Town
2. Te Anau
3. Milford Sound
4. Te Anau to Invercargill or Dunedin

QUEENSTOWN IS THE JEWEL of South Island resorts—pronounced by gold prospectors to be "fit for any queen," after which they promptly christened it with the present name on a very unqueenly blacksmith's anvil. It sits, nestled at the foot of mountains called the Remarkables, on the northeastern shore of Lake Wakatipu, a 53-mile-long, 1280 foot-deep beauty encased in a glacial bed. Its shape vaguely resembles that of a reclining figure with its knees drawn up. Maoris will tell you that's because at the bottom of the lake lies a great giant, slain by a lover avenging his lady love's kidnapping, who drew up his knees in pain as his body sank into the gigantic chasm that became the lake. And that, they say, explains the fact that the surface of the lake rises and falls three inches every five minutes—it's the giant's heartbeat from far below. Scientists call the phenomenon seiche action, but what do *they* know!

Sheepherders were the first settlers in this district, and endured the onslaught of hundreds of goldminers when the Shotover River, which feeds Lake Wakatipu, was proclaimed "the richest river in the world." The claim was well founded, for as much as £4000 was dredged by the discoverer of gold in his first two months. When the gold played out in fairly short order the sheep men came into their own once more, and today the Wakatipu district is filled with vast high-country sheep stations, a source of less spectacular, but certainly more reliable, riches.

1. In and Around the Town

As for Queenstown, its lifesblood is tourism, and no matter what time of year you come, you'll find visitors from all over the world here to enjoy the lake, the river, and the mountains. From late June through September an international skiing crowd flocks to ski the slopes of Coronet Peak, whose dry, powdery snows are said to be the best in Australasia. Thus the pretty little town, far from being provincial, has a decidedly cosmopolitan air.

ORIENTATION: The lakefront is the hub of Queenstown, and the street fronting the sheltered, horseshoe bay is **Marine Parade**. On the northern edge, at **Beach Street**, are the jetty, pier, and wharf. To the south are lovely public gardens. **The Mall**, reserved for pedestrians only, runs from Marine Parade for

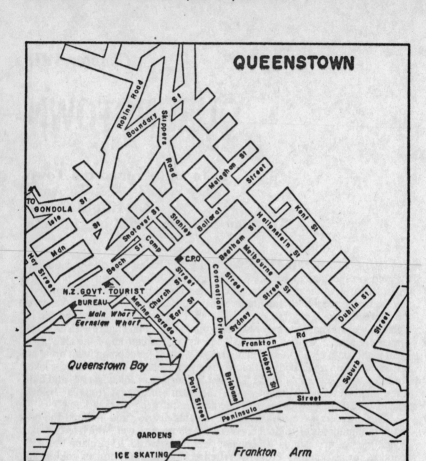

one bustling block. It is a busy concentration of activity: shops, information and booking agencies for major attractions, restaurants, the post office, and departure points for most tours. There is no local bus transportation.

USEFUL INFORMATION: The New Zealand Government Tourist Bureau, 49 Shotover St. (tel. 143), is just back of the Mountaineer Hotel in the Stage Post Building. Open 8:30 a.m. to 5 p.m. Monday through Friday on weekends in high season. . . . NZRRS buses arrive and depart opposite the Travelodge (tel. 420 for information). . . . Buses leave for the airport 40 minutes before flight times, and the fare is NZ$4 ($2.68). . . . **Mount Cook Travel Office** is at the corner of Rees and Ballarat Streets (tel. 366). . . . The **post office** is on the corner of Camp and Ballarat Streets. . . . To call a **taxi,** phone 428.

ACCOMMODATIONS: Queenstown is filled with accommodations, many of them in the budget range, despite the fact that on the whole prices are higher here than in other places, as you would expect in a major resort area. However, it's also filled with visitors vying for these lower-cost lodgings. That means you should always book before you come, be it winter, summer, spring, or fall. Between its lake attractions, river activities, and skiing, Queenstown simply doesn't have a season you can come unannounced and find a room easily. Having said that, let me add a bit of consolation if you should arrive without a booking: the GTB is very helpful, and almost every information office keeps a current list of accommodations and prices, and will help you find a place to lay your head if there is one to be had. But I repeat: far better to book as far in advance as possible. One more caution: Most Queenstown rates go up during holiday periods.

A Hostel

The **YHA Hostel,** 80 Esplanade (tel. 352), is in a beautiful location just across the street from the lake, a ten-minute walk from the Mall. The two-story, lodge-type building is designed with many windows to take advantage of the view. There are 84 beds in 12 rooms on the second floor, and there are two nicely equipped kitchens and a dining room. The game room has a pool table, there's a laundry and drying room, and you can rent blankets. This is, in fact, one of the best hostels in the country. Seniors pay NZ$6 ($4.03); Juniors, NZ$3 ($2.01).

Cabins

The **Queenstown Motor Park,** Man Street (tel. 164), is about half a mile from the post office and set on well-kept, wooded grounds overlooking the lake. Mountain and lake views greet the eye on every path, and the camp itself sparkles with fresh paint on its bright, airy kitchen, dining, and recreation blocks. There's a TV Lounge, a provision shop, a coin-operated laundry with dryers and irons, and a children's playground. Basic cabins sleep three to four in beds or bunks, and have table and chairs. Others have kitchens with rangette, H&C, and toilet, and seven have fully equipped kitchens and showers. All are carpeted and heated; you supply bedding and cooking utensils. Rates for basic cabins are NZ$6 ($4.03) for adults, half that for children; for cabins with rangette, H&C, and toilet, NZ$7.50 ($5.03) for adults, NZ$4 ($2.68) for children; for those with complete kitchens and showers, NZ$9 ($6.04) for adults, NZ$4.50 ($3.02) for children. There's a surcharge for one-night stays. The 200 campsites and 350 caravan sites are NZ$3 ($2.01) for adults, NZ$1.50 ($1.01) for children. It is especially important to book ahead from December 24 to January 10.

Motel Flats and Cabins

In a wooded, hillside setting about a ten-minute walk from town, **Mountain View Lodge,** on Frankton Road (tel. 153), offers a wide range of accommodations, all of which overlook stunning lake and mountain views. There are exceptionally nice motel flats, with full kitchens, TV, radio, heater, and electric blankets, which sleep from two to four. Rates for these are NZ$29 ($19.46) single, NZ$31 ($20.81) to NZ$36 ($24.16) double. Others, with everything except the kitchens (tea and coffee facilities only) rent for NZ$18 ($12.08) to NZ$23 ($15.44) single, NZ$25 ($16.78) to NZ$30 ($20.13) double. Then there's a two-story building farther up the hill, which houses ten rooms with heaters, but no H&C, each room with four bunks, carpeting, and a table and four chairs in front of a window with a lovely view. A fully equipped kitchen is shared by all, and there's a TV lounge bar, laundry, and children's playground. You supply bedding, plus cooking and eating utensils. Rates are NZ$10 ($6.71) double, NZ$15 ($10.06) for three, NZ$20 ($13.42) for four.

Mountain View Lodge also has a licensed family-style restaurant on the premises. There are candles at night, windows look out to mountains and lakes, and main-course prices are in the NZ$6 ($4.03) to NZ$9 ($6.04) range.

One of Mountain View's structures, the **Bottle House,** is known throughout New Zealand. Constructed entirely of 14,720 glass bottles set in sand and cement mortar, it serves as the motel office. The builder (whose identity is not revealed) avers that there's not a single beer bottle included, that he got the bottles from a dealer, and that he emptied not one himself. Cabin 7 also has bottle walls and is much in demand, especially by honeymoon couples—the unusual walls let in light, but are completely opaque.

Bed and Breakfast

Queenstown's's top guest house is **Melbourne House,** 35 Melbourne St. (tel. 378). It's a lovely white one-story, slate-roofed house set back on a lawn and approached through a small rock garden. Melbourne Street is a quiet residential street, very centrally located, and climbs steeply to give gorgeous views of the lake. The friendly owners, Les and Celia Walker, offer six single rooms and six twins. All have modern furnishings, are nicely decorated, and include, electric blankets (there's central heat as well); there are laundry facilities and off-street parking. Right next door is a little stone church, adding to the charm of Melbourne House's setting. Rates for B&B are NZ$18 ($12.08) per person. There's a courtesy car to the bus depot. Note: The Walkers also have motel units (see below).

Goldfields Motel and Guest House, 41 Frankton Rd. (tel. 221), has six rooms in a white stucco house adjacent to a block of motel units, all with H&C, and one cabin without H&C but with electric blankets and heater. There are also four chalet-type units, which sleep up to three and have balconies in the front and back, tea and coffee facilities, toaster, and private bath. Breakfast is served family style at a large wooden table, and the dining room doubles as a TV lounge. Bed-and-breakfast rates are NZ$18 ($12.08) per person for rooms in the house, NZ$15 ($10.06) to NZ$18 ($12.08) in the cabin, and NZ$17 ($11.41) to NZ$20 ($13.42) in the chalets.

A Licensed Hotel/Motel

The **Alpine Village Motor Inn** (mailing address: P.O. Box 211; tel. 795) is two miles from the center of Queenstown on the Frankton Road, but its scenic setting more than makes up for the drive. And if you're not driving, Dennis and Louise Winchester operate a courtesy coach to and from town several times a day and will always arrange to collect you at the bus station or airport. Set right on the lake in wooded grounds, Alpine Village offers A-frame chalets with breathtaking views of the lake and mountains on the far shore. They're furnished with tea and coffee makings, color TV, and fridge, and have central heating, and there are electric blankets for those extra-cold nights. In the main building there are ten standard hotel rooms with the same amenities. Provided for guests are a laundry, children's playground, and barbecue.

One feature that accounts for the high rate of returnees here is the lakeside complex of heated spa pools, which are open to the lake but enclosed for privacy on all three land sides. They are entered through heated shower rooms, which provide ample dressing space. It's absolutely heavenly to emerge from the warmth into crisp lake air and sink into the soothing hot water of the pools. The spa pools are very popular with locals, especially on star-studded nights. Equally popular are the lounge bar, where a large brick fireplace warms body and spirit, and the licensed restaurant, with its superior menu and lovely lake view. On the second floor of the main building there's the intimate, aptly named Hideaway Bar. Except during holiday periods (when they're slightly higher), rates at the Alpine Village begin at NZ$25 ($16.78) for singles, NZ$34 ($22.82) for doubles. And it's a Best Western, so Holiday Pass discounts apply, bringing the rates even lower. As is true of many others, I return again and again to this special New Zealand hostelry, always with pleasant anticipation.

Motel Flats

Melbourne House, 35 Melbourne St. (see "Bed and Breakfast," above, for complete description; tel. 378), has three family motel units, all fully equipped with kitchens and private bath. All will sleep up to five, and if you wish, a cooked breakfast is just NZ$4 ($2.68) additional. The **Autoline Motel,** on the corner of Frankton Road and Dublin Street (mailing address: P.O. Box 183; tel. 735), is a Best Western member, offering the usual Holiday Pass discount. Sandra and Bob Holdom are the gracious, friendly hosts here, who know Queenstown well and are always eager to help their guests with sightseeing plans. The two-story motel has exceptionally spacious units (one family size, which accommodates up to six, the others either bedsitters or one-bedroom), all attractively decorated in shades of gold and brown. All have nice views from their sundeck, but the end unit, no. 6, has the best lake view. Kitchens are fully equipped and have complete ranges. There's color TV, radio, central heating, and electric blankets in each unit, and a guest telephone is available in units. Additional facilities include an automatic laundry with dryer, hot spa pool, children's play area, car wash, and covered off-street parking. Units are serviced daily. The Autoline is a short walk from shopping and even closer to the gardens and public swimming pool; there's courtesy car service to the bus depot by arrangement. Rates are NZ$34 ($22.82) single, NZ$38 ($25.50) double.

The **A-1 Queenstown Motel,** 13 Frankton Rd. (tel. 289), is a pretty, two-story building with covered porches upstairs and down, most with good views of the lake and mountains. John Bax, the proprietor is a councillor of the Motel Association of New Zealand, and his wife, Glenys, is secretary—both are exceptionally interested in seeing to guests' comfort and enjoyment of the area. Units are spacious and well furnished, and all were refurbished in 1982. They come in sizes that sleep from three to five, and all have full kitchens, TV, and central heating. Skiers will appreciate the separate drying area and racks for skis and poles, and children will enjoy the swings and heated swimming pool. There's also a private spa pool and family video movies nightly, all at no extra charge. Covered car parking protects from frost, which can be quite heavy at times. Rates are NZ$38 ($25.50) single, NZ$42 ($28.19) double. *Note:* The Baxes give a 10% discount on presentation of this book!

On a hillside site not far from the town center, the **Four Seasons Motel,** 12 Stanley St. (tel. 888), is a Best Western run by hostess Jackie Davidson. All units have complete kitchens, color TV, and radio, and all but one (which will sleep four) accommodate three comfortably in well-decorated surroundings. On the premises are a swimming pool and hot-spa pool. For a small charge Jackie will provide a continental breakfast. Rates are NZ$37 ($24.83) single,

NZ$39 ($26.17) double, rising a little during holiday periods. It's a member of Best Western, honoring the discount plan.

The **Arawata Motel,** on the corner of Beach and Shotover Streets (tel. 773), is about as central as you can get. It's right on the lake in the heart of town, opposite the bus depot and adjacent to shops and restaurants. Ruth and Russell McGrouther have 13 pleasantly furnished one- and two-bedroom units with great lake and mountain views. All have TV, radio, and central heating, and there are a spa pool, car park, and laundry on the premises. Rates for singles are NZ$38 ($25.50); for doubles, NZ$40 ($26.85).

Some of the most attractively decorated units in Queenstown are at the **Alpine Sun Motel,** 14 Hallenstein St. (mailing address: P.O. Box 204; tel. 457). Many are wood paneled, with leather—upholstered furniture; all have complete kitchens, TV, piped-in music and a radio, telephone, and electric blankets. There's a hot spa pool and an automatic laundry and dryer, and you can order a cooked or continental breakfast at a small additional charge. Ken Chisholm, the friendly owner, offers courtesy car service on arrival and departure. He'll also provide cots and highchairs if needed. Rates are NZ$36 ($24.16) single, NZ$42 ($28.19) double. This is a Best Western, honoring the discount.

In Arrowtown

If you're driving, you might consider staying in quaint, historic Arrowtown, 12½ miles away. Best choice in Arrowtown is actually three miles from the town, eight from Queenstown—an ideal location from which to visit both.

The **Lake Hayes Motel** (mailing address: P.O. Box 12, Queenstown; tel. Arrowtown 705) is on the quiet, peaceful shores of beautiful Lake Hayes. Kinsie and Jim Rose are the hosts, offering eight units with full kitchens, color TV, radio, and both electric and down blankets. Laundry facilities are free to guests, and there's a guest lounge with billiard table, and office shop with foodstuffs. In the garden there's a children's playground with trampoline and barbecue. The lake is at the bottom of the garden, good for swimming and brown trout fishing. The Roses provide free boating and fishing, and will give you a free gold pan to try your luck in the local river. Parking is in car ports. This is a Best Western member offering the Holiday Pass discount, and highly recommended for those who are driving. Rates are NZ$30 ($20.13) single, NZ$36 ($24.16) double.

In town, the **Mace Motel** is on Arrowtown's famous Oak Avenue (tel. 825), with six units on lawns planted with pretty shrubs. Units have two or three bedrooms, with convertible divans in the wood-paneled lounges. They will accommodate two to eight. All have kitchens, TV, electric blankets, central heating, and radio. There's a heated spa pool, children's play area, laundry, and provision store on the premises. Rates are NZ$35 ($23.49) double.

MEALS: You won't lack for a place to eat in Queenstown, and in any price range you choose. There are some very good, inexpensive restaurants, many of them in the Mall. Moderate prices for full meals are easy to come by, and I'll tell you about just one of the several places that qualify for a Big Splurge.

For snacks and light meals, there's the **Down to Earth,** 5 Beach St., just off Camp Street. It's take-away only, featuring buttered pineapple bran muffins, banana and honey milkshakes, sandwiches, fresh salads, and wheat-germ cookies at prices that range from NZ$.25 (17¢) for the cookies to NZ$2.50 ($1.68). Hours are 8 a.m. to 5 p.m. weekdays, to 2 p.m. on Saturday and Sunday, with extended hours in summer.

The **Cadrona Coffee Lounge** is in the Mall, and its pancakes with maple syrup (among several tasty toppings) makes breakfast something special. Omelets, burgers, sandwiches, and other light fare are available. The goldmining area for which it was named is depicted in an oil mural on the wall. Highest price on the menu is NZ$3.60 ($2.41); most are less.

Downstairs in the Rees Arcade, you'll find the **Rees Café**, a homey little restaurant with friendly staff behind the self-service counter. There are red-and-white checked curtains at the front window, an awning over the counter, wooden booths and tables, and a relaxed atmosphere in which to eat. Everything is baked right on the premises, and choices include homemade soups, meat pies, sausage rolls, sandwiches, cakes, and pastries. Prices are in the NZ$1 (67¢) to NZ$1.50 ($1.01) range.

A very attractive member of the always-reliable **Cobb & Co.** chain is located in the Mountaineer Hotel on Rees Street just off Shotover Street (tel. 307). Menu selections are the same as in others, with main courses averaging NZ$5.50 ($3.69), less for sandwiches and snacks.

The **Gourmet Express,** in Bay Centre on Shotover Street (tel. 14-07), bills itself as an American-style restaurant and coffeeshop, and indeed you'll find a very Americanized menu. Hamburgers, cheeseburgers, baconburgers, club sandwiches, and omelets are among the lighter fare, with heartier offerings of steak (in several varieties), fish, chicken-in-the-basket, and lamb chops. It's a large, bright, and cheerful place with blond-wood tables and chairs, and counter as well as table service. Prices range from NZ$1.95 ($1.31) to NZ$8 ($5.37). It's open from 7 a.m. to 9 p.m. every day.

Queenstown's popular Mexican restuarant is the **Saguaro,** at the lake end of the Mall just next to Eichardts Tavern (tel. 306). Lots of south-of-the-border decor, and modern progressive music in the background (to quote young Mike Madigan, proprietor, that's because "too much Mexican music comes a lot sooner than enough Mexican food!"). A full Mexican meal—choice of two from burritos, enchiladas, tacos, or tostadas, plus rice and beans—runs NZ$8 ($5.37), and there's an interesting jalapeño milkshake offered, as well as Mexican coffee with kahlua and tequila. Hours are 11 a.m. to 2 p.m. and 6 to 9:30 or 10:30 p.m., with extended hours in high season. BYO.

Upstairs Downstairs, in Bay Centre on Shotover Street (tel. 203), is pretty pricey at night, but the charming restaurant has a blackboard lunch menu that changes daily and always features reasonable prices. Hot open-faced sandwiches, as well as such dishes as sauteed chicken livers, are typical, and prices are under NZ$6 ($4.03). Lunch hours are noon to 2:30 p.m. Monday through Friday.

Alpine Village Motor Inn on Frankton Road (tel. 795), described under "Accommodations," is as well known locally for its fine **Village Restaurant** as for those inviting spa pools. Seafood dishes here are superb, as are prime steaks and the venison, which comes topped with a marvelous tangy sauce. Owner Dennis Winchester calls on his expertise gained from leading restaurants in European countries to create and present food in exciting ways. When Fiordland crayfish is available, or those lovely Bluff oysters, yours truly can't get beyond those two items on the menu, but I have friends who feel the same devotion to Dennis's beautifully prepared lamb chops. À la carte prices range from NZ$8 ($5.37) up. Or you might opt for the gorgeous Carvery dinner, where massive roasts of lamb, beef, or chicken are carved to your order and the NZ$12.50 ($8.39) all-inclusive price buys four full courses. There's candlelight and a terrific view from lakefront windows. Hours are 6:30 to 10 p.m. daily, and to avoid disappointment, book ahead. Fully licensed.

Meal from on High

At least one of your Queenstown meals should be at the restaurant-with-a-view **Skyline Chalet Restaurant** (tel. 123). You reach it by gondola, and once inside, the wrap-around windows will give you a fantastic panoramic view of the town and lake. Food service ranges from light snacks (until 4:30 p.m. only, from the pine-paneled snackbar) to full meals, but the star attraction is the evening smörgåsbord. The NZ$16 ($10.74) tariff includes your gondola round trip, meal, and entertainment (usually a band which plays for dancing). Lunch hours are noon to 2 p.m., dinner from 6:30 p.m. to midnight Tuesday through Sunday. Closed Monday.

Big Splurge

For a "shoot-the-works" meal that's worth the shot, you couldn't do better than **Roaring Meg's,** 57 Shotover St. (tel. 968). For one thing, it's in an old Queenstown house whose rooms (other than refurbished Victorian-style dining rooms) look just as they probably did 90 years ago. There are open fires, and there's even an old coal range in what was the original kitchen. As for the menu, it's strictly Kiwi, prepared by chefs who trained at the Cordon Bleu school in London. Specialties like venison pie and whole takaka salmon and fresh New Zealand vegetables are a wonderful revelation as to what can be done with native foods. In the evenings there's candlelight; in fine weather there's outdoor garden lunching. Prices at lunch are in the NZ$8 ($5.37) to NZ$9 ($6.04) range; at dinner, a three-course meal from the à la carte menu will run about NZ$16 ($10.74). BYO.

READERS' MEALS SELECTION: "We had a very good dinner at **Westy's in the Trading Post,** the Mall (tel. 609), for a moderate price. It's open from noon to 2 p.m. for lunch and 6 to 10 p.m. for dinner" (Ann and Bill O'Brien, Whittier, Calif.).

THINGS TO SEE AND DO: There is always so much going on in Queenstown, and so many things to see and do, that your first order of business should be to go by the GTB office and pick up their *Queenstown Sightseeing* folder, which lists all current attractions, prices, hours, and booking details. Some activities are seasonal, others are in full swing year round.

One thing you won't want to miss, no matter what time of year you come, is the **gondola ride** up to Skyline Point, and don't forget your camera. The view is breathtaking, and if you go at lunch or dinner you can stretch your viewing time by eating at the restaurant or snackbar (see "Meals"). The gondola operates from 10 a.m. to 5 p.m. and from 6:30 p.m. until the restaurant closes at midnight.

One of the nicest ways to view this area from on high is to visit **Deer Park Heights** (tel. 220), a private animal sanctuary across the Frankton Arm from Queenstown. You pay NZ$4 ($2.68) per car, then drive along a well-packed gravel road for three miles, climbing steadily upward. The view at the top is truly breathtaking, perhaps even more so on the descent. And there's the bonus of deer, chamois, thar, wapiti, and lovable baby mountain goats who follow and surround your car in the hope of a hug or a handout. Animal feed is available in very inexpensive dispensers; as for the hug, you'll have to supply that, but you'll be hard pressed to resist.

Another trip to the heights is the mile-long ride 1500 feet up **Coronet Peak** aboard a twin-seat chair lift. Coronet Peak is 12 miles north of town and the center of Queenstown skiing. During the season, there are an additional three-seater lift and two Poma Button lifts. The viewing platform is actually 5400 feet above sea level, and the view is incredible—many times you look down on clouds, with peaks of the Remarkables poking through fluffy cloud layers. There are quick-food restaurants at the summit and at the base. The lift operates year round, and fares are NZ$4 ($2.68) for adults, NZ$2 ($1.34) for children, for the round trip.

From the end of October through Easter, another "don't miss" is a **lake cruise** aboard the T.S.S. *Earnslaw,* a 1912 steamship, which makes a one-hour lunch cruise at 12:30 p.m. (adults pay a boarding fee of NZ$8, or $5.37 U.S.; children pay half; lunch is extra, at moderate prices) and a three-hour cruise at 2 p.m. (boarding fee of NZ$14.50, or $9.73 U.S.; children, half that). It's a leisurely, relaxing way to see the lake and mountains during lunch. The longer cruise explores the lake from Mount Nicholas to White Point, taking a 40-minute land break at **Walter Peak Homestead,** a working sheep station. There are also smaller launches, operated privately by Walter Peak, which will take you out for a guided tour, sheepdog demonstrations, and tea. They run at 9:30 a.m. and 2 p.m., and the fare for adults is NZ$14 ($9.40); for children, NZ$7 ($4.70). The jetty at the foot of Beach Street is the departure point for all lake trips. You can book and purchase tickets at the GTB or any of the local tourist agencies.

Or take the ten-mile, 20-minute **hydrofoil** spin around the lake at 35 m.p.h. on the *Meteor III.* Fares are NZ$5 ($3.36) for adults, NZ$3 ($2.01) for children, and there's no need to book—just show up at the Main Tower Pier. Check locally for departure times.

In summer, the Shotover River's white-water rapids are the scene of **jet-boat trips** guaranteed to give you a thrill as expert drivers send you flying between huge boulders amid the rushing waters. They'll point out traces of goldmining along the river as you go along. Adults pay NZ$20 ($13.42); children, half that. You can drive out to the river (allow an hour), or there's courtesy coach service from the Mount Cook World Travel Office. For a quieter ride, board the U.S. military ten-man assault raft *Kon Tiki* and float down the river for fares of NZ$10 ($6.71) and NZ$5 ($3.36). Then there's the exciting **Heli-Jet trip,** which takes you by coach out to the airport, where you board a helicopter for the trip to the river, jet-boat through the rapids, then fly back to the airport. Fare is NZ$36 ($24.16) per person.

If you're a motoring enthusiast, go by the **Queenstown Motor Museum,** on Brecon Street just below the gondola (tel. 752). Opened in 1971, the modern museum houses 50 changing exhibits in two hangar-like wings, and is managed by Brian Middlemass, one of New Zealand's foremost automobile restorers. Brian is happy to chat away about any of the displays, all of which are in perfect road condition and burnished to a smart gleam. There's a 1922 Rolls-Royce Silver Ghost, which once belonged to the lord mayor of London, an 1885 gentlewoman's tricycle, a 12-horsepower 1903 De Dion, and other fascinating reminders of automobile travel as it has evolved over the years. Admission is NZ$2 ($1.34) for adults, NZ$.75 (50¢) for children.

Train buffs (count me one) are in for a real treat at Queenstown. From the first of October to mid-May, the **Kingston Flyer** makes three runs a day from Kingston (a 45-minute drive from Queenstown) to Fairlight and back. It's a 1915 AB Class steam locomotive, designed and built in New Zealand—a real beauty! Carriages range from an elegant 1900 gallery car to passenger cars of 1917. If you've ever fantasized about stepping into those cozy little compartments we know only from the movies, those fantasies will materialize on the *Flyer,* where each carriage has tufted leather seats, working gas lamps, and all sorts of other little touches to transport you back to early rail travel. Colonial teas are sold in the refreshment car by staff dressed in costumes of the early

1900s, and you'll puff along through rolling hills, past grazing sheep, always with the snow-capped mountains in the distance on either side. Fare for the 28-kilometer round trip is NZ$8 ($5.37) for adults, NZ$2 ($1.34) for children. Departures are 9:45 a.m., 11:15 a.m., and 2:30 p.m. Phone Kingston 553 for details and any schedule changes (mailing address: P.O. Box 23, Kingston).

Brothers Trevor and Rex Woodbury have assembled old structures and mining equipment from all over the district to reproduce a **Mining Town** two miles from Queenstown, which you can wander around for admissions of NZ$2.50 ($1.68) for adults, NZ$1 (67¢) for children. If the sight gives you a touch of gold fever, gold pans may be hired from the Fur'n Wood souvenir shop on Beach Street, and they'll point you in the right direction to seek your fortune. They also rent bicycles for NZ$1.50 ($1.01) per hour, NZ$7 ($4.70) per day.

The lake is great for **fishing**, and the GTB can help you get gear and guides together. The same holds true for those hardy souls eager for back country exploring.

Right in town—and free for everyone—is the **Government Tourist Department Park**, across from the Travelodge, with 11 acres of botanical gardens. There are tennis courts and lawn bowls to use at no charge, and the park is always open.

A marvelous day trip is a drive to **Arrowtown**, 12½ miles to the northeast. It was a boom town of the goldmining days, back in the 1860s, when the Arrow River coughed up a lot of the glittery stuff. There are many of the original stone buildings and a stunning avenue of trees, which were planted back in 1867. Go by the Lake District Centennial Museum on the main street for a detailed look at those days. Other places to look for are the Royal Oak Hotel, the oldest licensed hotel in Central Otago (you can still have a drink there); the General Store; the Old Gaol; and St. John's Presbyterian Church (dating from 1873). There's good craft shopping at High Country Crafts, and the Gold Nugget souvenir shop has very good prices.

Believe it or not, all the above is just a sample of things to do and see in Queenstown! There are scads of tours taking in many of the above and a whole lot more. A four-day **walking tour** follows the Routeburn Track, which international trampers hold second only to the Milford Track in affection. And there's **horse trekking** at Moonlight Stables, and . . . but go by the GTB and check over the complete list. They can make any bookings you require, and they'll also assist with onward accommodation and transportation arrangements.

AFTER DARK: The two pubs favored by locals are **Eichard's,** on the Mall, and the **Mountaineer** on Beach Street. Also on Beach Street is **"Wicked Willie's,"** the unofficial name for the pub at the Hotel Queenstown.

Above Eichard's tavern, **Albert's** nightclub has entertainment, which might be cabaret, disco, local bands, or even classical music. Closes at 3 a.m.

There's jazz on Sunday night at **The Cellar** in O'Connell's Hotel on Beach Street, dancing at the **Skyline Chalet** Tuesday through Sunday night.

During ski season, private parties go on all over town in almost every hotel and motel, with friendly strangers becoming invited guests at the drop of a smile.

As I mentioned in the "Accommodations" section, an after-dark activity much favored by Queenstown natives is a starlight loll in those lakeside spa pools out at the **Alpine Village Motor Inn** on Frankton Road (tel. 795) for half an hour or so. After a day on the slopes or trotting around sightseeing, it's hard to imagine anything happier!

QUEENSTOWN TO TE ANAU: It's a 116-mile drive, on good roads all the way. You'll follow Highway 6 as far as the grass-seed-producing **Lumsden,** then take Highway 94 over the summit of **Gorge Hill,** along the **Mararoa River** and through sheep and cattle country to Te Anau, the largest lake in the South Island.

2. Te Anau

Lake Te Anau spreads its south, middle, and north branches like long fingers poking deep into the mountains, which mark the beginning of rugged and grand three-million-acre **Fiordland National Park,** New Zealand's largest and one of the largest in the world. Within its boundaries, which enclose the whole of the South Island's southwest corner, lie incredibly steep mountain ranges, lakes, sounds, rivers, magnificent fiords, and huge chunks of mountainous terrain even now unexplored. In fact, one large section has been closed off from exploration after the discovery there in 1948 of one of the world's rarest birds, the wingless takahe. It had not been seen for nearly a century before, seldom even then, and was thought to be extinct. When a colony was found in the Murchison Mountains, the decision was made to protect them from human disturbance. What other wonders remain to be discovered within the vast park, one can only speculate.

Lake Te Anau itself presents a wonder of a sort, with its eastern shoreline (that's where Te Anau township is located) virtually treeless, its western banks covered by dense rain forest. To visitors, however, this second-largest-lake-in-New Zealand's attractions consist of a variety of water sports and its proximity to **Milford Sound,** 74 miles away. That sound (which is actually a fiord) reaches 14 miles in from the Tasman Sea, flanked by sheer granite peaks traced by playful waterfalls that appear and disappear depending on the amount of rainfall. Its waters and the surrounding land have been kept in as nearly a primeval state as man could possibly manage without leaving it totally untouched. In fine weather or pouring rain, Milford Sound exudes a powerful sense of nature's pristine harmony and beauty—a visit there is balm to this 20th-century soul, the highlight of every New Zealand trip.

ORIENTATION: Te Anau's main street is actually **Highway 94** (called **Milford Road** within the township). Stretched along each side you'll find the post office, Wildlife Museum, restaurants, grocery stores, and most of the township's shops. At the lake end of Milford Road sits **Fiordland Travel's booking office,** where all launch trips may be booked. Across the road and to the left from Fiordland Travel is the new Waterfront Merchants Complex, with a coffee bar/restaurant, souvenir and gift shop, craft shop, and clothing boutique. Just opposite the lake, on Highway 94 before it turns westward to become Milford Road, are the THC Te Anau and the **Park Headquarters** (open 8 a.m. to noon and 1 to 5 p.m. every day). **Mount Cook Lines** office is on the THC grounds (tel. 494).

The Milford Track

The world-famous Milford Track is considered by most dedicated trampers to be the finest anywhere in the world. Four days are required to walk the

32 miles from Glade Jetty at Lake Te Anau's northern end to Sandfly Point on the western bank of Milford Sound. To walk the pure wilderness is to immerse yourself in the sights, sounds, smells, and feel of nature left to herself —it is utterly impossible to emerge without a greater sense of the earth's rhythms. It's a walk closely regulated by park authorities, both for the safety of hikers and for the preservation of this wilderness area.

You set out from Te Anau Downs, 17 miles north of Te Anau township, where a launch takes you to the head of the lake for a fare of NZ$16.50 ($11.07) for adults (children pay half fare). You'll sleep in well-equipped lodge/huts with bunk beds, cooking facilities, and toilets, but you must carry your own food and cooking utensils. Overnight huts are manned by custodians, should you need any assistance along the way, and there's a NZ$4 ($2.68) fee per person per night at each hut. At Sandfly Point, another launch ferries you across Milford Sound for fares of NZ$6 ($4.03) for adults, NZ$4.50 ($3.02) for children. Upon arrival, you may elect to spend the night at Milford or to return to Te Anau, but prebooking is a must, whichever you choose.

You must be over 10 years of age, an experienced tramper, and apply to **Fiordland National Park Headquarters**, P.O. Box 29, Te Anau (tel. 7521). Bookings are accepted beginning in July for the tramping season, which runs from mid-November to early April. No more than 24 people are booked to start the walk on any given day, and applications begin coming in early for specific days.

There are two ways to walk the Milford Track: as a member of an organized group or as one of the ranger-organized "Independent Walkers." THC Milford and THC Te Anau offer an excellent package plan, which includes guides, cooked meals at the overnight huts, and accommodations at each end of the trek. As an independent, you take care of all these details yourself, with the able assistance of park rangers.

ACCOMMODATIONS: Between Christmas and the end of February, accommodations are tightly booked in Te Anau (most are booked by the week by holidaying Kiwi families), and you should book ahead as far as possible or plan to stay outside the township itself (possibly out Milford Road, at Milford Sound, or at Lake Manapouri, 12 miles to the south). Other times, there are usually ample accommodations available. If you do arrive roomless, go by the Mount Cook Lines office (tel. 494) on the grounds of THC. Mount Cook runs a local booking service at no charge.

A Hostel

Te Anau's **YHA Hostel** is a real standout, one of the most attractive in the country. It adjoins a sheep meadow in a very central location, and has 39 beds in six pine-paneled rooms with central heating. There's a nicely equipped kitchen, a lounge (with a pot-bellied stove), dining room, and laundry, and in summer, overflow accommodation is available. Rates for Seniors are NZ$6 ($4.03); for Juniors, NZ$3 ($2.01).

Cabins

If you want to do some tramping in the Fiordland National Park on a lesser scale than the Milford Track, park rangers will supply a map of trails and overnight hut locations. The **park huts** are basic shelters that provide a place to bunk down and cook simple fare. For those where fuel (cut wood) is provided, the overnight fee is NZ$4 ($2.68) per person; where you gather your own firewood, you pay NZ$2 ($1.34).

Te Anau Motor Park, on the Manapouri Highway (mailing address: P.O. Box 81; tel. 74-57), sits on 25 wooded acres across the road from the lake. Clint and Jill Tauri, the knowledgeable and friendly owners, are very helpful to guests in planning sightseeing activities. There are a variety of accommodations here: cabins sleeping two; small A-frame chalets (with front decks); family cabins, which have one large bedsitting room that sleeps four, private bath, stove and kitchen supplies, and blankets; a bunkroom with innerspring mattresses; caravan sites; and tent sites. There are three kitchen and shower blocks with laundries, indoor dining area, tennis court, game room, TV lounge, and food shop. Everything is kept in tip-top condition, and rates are budget oriented. Cabins and A-frames are NZ$12.50 ($8.39) double; family cabins are NZ$17 ($11.41) double, NZ$5 ($3.36) per extra adult, NZ$3.50 ($2.33) for children; NZ$5 ($3.36) per person in the bunkhouse; and NZ$3 ($2.01) for tent and caravan sites, NZ$1 (67¢) extra for power points.

About a half mile outside the town of Manapouri (12 miles south of Te Anau), there are excellent facilities at **Manapouri Holiday Camp and Motel** (mailing address: Te Anau Road, Manapouri; tel. 624). Its location is directly across from the lake, one of the most beautiful in New Zealand, and is run by American (from San Francisco) Joelle Nicholson and her son Aaron, whose woodworking skills account for such touches as scalloped beams and knotty-pine wainscotting. There are two- to eight-berth cabins, self-contained motel flats with color TV and lake views, a fully equipped on-site caravan (except for toilet), and campsites. All units have electric heaters and attractive, homey interiors. There's a kitchen with dining tables, fridge, freezer, and cooking unit; a game room with pool table and Ping-Pong; a spa pool, sauna, children's play area with trampoline, and a food shop. Rates for cabins are NZ$6 ($4.03) for adults, NZ$4 ($2.68) for children; motel units are NZ$29 ($19.46) single, NZ$8 ($5.37) per extra adult or child; the on-site caravan is NZ$17 ($11.41) double; camping and caravan sites are NZ$2.50 ($1.68) for adults, NZ$1.75 ($1.17) for children. Highest recommendation.

Incidentally, the Manapouri Motor Inn, just down the road from the camp, serves excellent bistro meals at budget prices.

Bed and Breakfast

Matai Lodge, 42 Mokonui St. (tel. 73-60), has five bed-and-breakfast units in a long block with toilet and showers at one end. The rooms (one with H&C) are all very pleasant and have electric heater, electric blankets, and comforters. The lounge, with beamed ceiling and lots of old brass ware, has a pot-bellied stove, comfortable chairs, color TV, and tea and coffee facilities. In the dining room, where your continental breakfast is served, you can also have a home-cooked evening meal at a reasonable cost. There's a hot spa pool on the premises. The hosts, Mike and Rosina Shakespeare (yes, they are descendants of you know who) will store baggage for trampers who are walking the Milford Track or Holyford Valley. Bed-and-breakfast rates are NZ$20 ($13.42) single, NZ$30 ($20.13) double, and off-season rates are also available on request.

If Lake Manapouri is your choice (or Te Anau is full), you couldn't do better than the **Grandview Guesthouse,** 12 miles from Te Anau just off the highway (mailing address: c/o Post office, Manapouri; tel. 642). It's one of the truly classic guest houses, approached by way of a lovely garden path. Mrs. Murrell and her son (the house has been in the family since 1889) run the 16-bedroom guest house with traditional hospitality. Rooms are beautifully done up, and no. 4 is especially nice, boasting an exquisite carved-wood fireplace with cloisonné bowls on the mantel, walls hung with a set of eight matched gold-framed prints, antique chairs, and a Persian carpet. Each of the other bedrooms is perfectly kept, with wicker chairs, starched curtains, electric blankets, and charming antique furnishings. Ample bathrooms are at the ends of hallways. A huge antlered red deer head is mounted over the guest book. The lounge displays a wonderful collection of paintings by artists who have stayed here to capture the irresistible scenery of Fiordland. John Moore, whose winter scene hangs over the tea table, "used to paint outside, dash in to get warm, then dash out again." The lounge also has an open fireplace, piano, a good selection of books, and cozy furnishings—no TV to intrude on the peaceful setting. The gracious dining room has gray walls lined with framed photographs of the area; tables are covered in white linen and adorned with vases of fresh flowers. Outside, a short walk through a beech forest brings you to the lake. This is a true country retreat, and a perfect base for seeing this part of New Zealand. Bed-and-breakfast rates are NZ$24 ($16.11) per person, NZ$36 ($24.16) with dinner (which comes with fresh vegetables from the garden).

Motel Flats

Some of Te Anau's nicest motel units are at the **Redwood Motel**, 26 McKerrow St. (tel. 77-46), presided over by the friendly hosts Shirley and Allan Bradley. Its location is quite central, on a quiet residential street. There are six nicely furnished, sparkling-clean, and beautifully equipped units. All have central heating, color TV, and phone, and four even have their own washing machines (guest laundry on the premises for others). Parking is in individual car ports. There's also a three-bedroom house on the grounds with full kitchen, bath and shower, and private garden, which is ideal for families. A children's playground is also on the premises. If you arrive in Te Anau by public transport, the Bradleys will pick you up by courtesy car. Rates are NZ$28 ($18.79) single, NZ$35 ($23.49) to NZ$40 ($26.85) double. A continental breakfast is available at a small charge. Surcharge for one-night stay.

The **Abel Tasman Motel**, Te Anau Terrace (tel. 75-48), is right across the road from the lake, with another entrance on Quintin Drive. Dick and Noelene Evans' seven one-bedroom and one two-bedroom units are immaculate and equipped with color TV, radio, electric blankets, and heater. The two-bedroom unit has a double and a twin bedroom, with two single beds in the lounge—it sleeps six persons comfortably. On the premises are a laundry, five-hole putting green, car wash, and children's play area with sandbox. Except for kitchens (you do the dishwashing), units are serviced daily. Rates are NZ$42 ($28.19) double.

Those using the Best Western Holiday Pass discount will find the **Black Diamond Motel**, 15 Quintin Dr. (tel. 74-59), convenient as well as comfortable. It's just a short walk from the lakefront, Fiordland Travel, and almost anything else in Te Anau. The nicely decorated units all have full kitchens and lounges, and they come in one- and two-bedroom sizes. Each has a heater, and one of those marvelous fairy-down comforters is on every bed. There's a playground for the kiddies, a laundry and a car wash for the grownups. For a small extra charge you can be served a continental breakfast. Rates are NZ$40 ($26.82) single, NZ$42 ($28.19) double.

MEALS: In the new **Waterfront Merchants Complex**, 92 Te Anau Terrace (diagonally across from Fiordland Travel), you'll find **Pop-In Catering** (tel.

78-07), a window-lined restaurant serving light meals at very moderate prices in a setting that overlooks the lake. Plans are to build on a glass-walled conservatory, which will afford 180° views, and I can't think of a nicer place to eat. Everything is home-cooked right on the premises. Sandwiches, meat pies, salad plates, and some hot meals are offered, and when the new addition is completed, the menu may well be extended. At any rate, my best advice is to check this one out first. Hours are 8 a.m. to 5 p.m. off-season, 7 a.m. to 8 p.m. during summer months.

Bailey's, next door to the Luxmore Motel on Mildord Road, is a small, cozy self-service restaurant, which also features home-cooking. It's a pleasant place in which you're likely to find locals and regular visitors. The menu covers everything from sandwiches, hot pies, and cakes, all for less than NZ$1 (67¢), to hot meals of chicken, steak, veal, ham, and seafood for prices of NZ$5 ($3.36) to NZ$7.50 ($5.03). Licensed to sell wine with meals.

The setting is rustic, the food inexpensive at THC Te Anau's **Grubsteak Bar** (tel. 74-11). The atmosphere is much like that of a frontier saloon, with a pot-bellied stove and bare wooden tables. Grills of steak, lamb, chicken, etc., come with coleslaw and french fries, and are priced under NZ$6 ($4.03); children 12 and under pay half. It's fully licensed, and hours Monday through Thursday are 5 to 9 p.m., open Friday and Saturday until 10 p.m.

The THC Te Anau can pack a very good **picnic lunch** for your Milford Sound day trip or tramping if you notify them the night before at a price of NZ$7.50 ($5.03).

THINGS TO SEE AND DO: Lake cruises are the main attraction in Te Anau, and **Fiordland Travel Ltd.** (tel. 74-16) can give you their latest brochure with current times, rates, and special concessions on launch trips. The most popular is that to **Te Ana-au Caves,** which runs year round. The tour includes an underground boat ride into the glowworm grotto in the "living" cave, so called because it is still being formed. A crystal river cascades down the cave tiers at the rate of 55,000 gallons per minute, creating frothy white falls. On the second level of the waterbed you'll see the glowworm grotto. In my opinion, the day trip is preferable to the evening, since the scenic ten-mile lake cruise begs to be enjoyed in daylight.

The primary reason for coming to Te Anau is to go on to **Milford Sound,** and right here I am going to stick my neck out and recommend that even if you're driving you park the car in Te Anau and book a coach and launch tour either through Fiordland or the THC. My reasons are twofold: first, while the road to Milford is remarkably good for such terrain, after you pass Te Anau Downs you'll need to keep your eyes straight ahead, thus missing a good bit of some of the most splendid scenery to be found this side of heaven; and second, coach drivers provide a wealth of information on the scenery through which you're passing, which adds immeasurably to the pleasure of the 2½-hour drive. Fiordland's half-day trip includes coach and cruise fares; if you book through THC, they'll arrange NZZRS coach booking.

There's a sightseeing splurge, which I heartily urge if time and money permit—Fiordland's day-long **Triple Trip** bus and launch excursion, which takes you to Doubtful Sound, Wilmott Pass, Deep Cove, and the West Arm Power Station. Doubtful Sound is ten times larger than Milford, and some say it's more spectacular, although just how one can judge between two superlatives is beyond me! Its still waters mirror Commander Peak, which rises 4000 feet in vertical splendor. The power station, with its seven great turbines, is impressive, as is the trip to the top of Wilmott Pass. From mid-August to mid-May, departures from Fiordland Travel are at 10 a.m.; check with the booking office at other seasons. Adult fares are NZ$55 ($36.91); children pay half price. The Triple Trip can, of course, be broken down and each done separately.

There's also a very good-value five-trip ticket, which includes the Milford Sound cruise, Te Ana-au Caves, cruise on the lake, coach excursion across Wilmott Pass to Deep Cove, and the Doubtful Sound cruise. At NZ$75 ($50.34), it's a NZ$12.80 ($8.59) savings over the separate fares of NZ$87.80 ($58.93).

Other activities include Fiordland helicopter flights, scenic floatplane excursions, raft trips on the Waiau River, jet-boat rides, and fishing with any one of the experienced guides available. Check with Fiordland Travel Ltd. for these or other activities, and with Park Headquarters for nature walks and tramping tracks. Then, head for glorious Milford Sound.

THE MILFORD ROAD: Highway 94 from Te Anau to Milford Sound leads north along the lake, with islands and wooded far shores on your left. The drive is, of necessity, a slow one as you wend your way through steep climbs between walls of solid rock and down through leafy glades. Keep an eye out for the chippy little flightless keas, which sometimes perch along the roadside to satisfy their insatiable curiosity about visitors to their domain. **Homer Tunnel,** about 63 miles along, is a major engineering marvel: a three-quarter-mile passageway first proposed in 1889 by William Homer, begun in 1935, and finally opened in 1940. It was, however, the summer of 1954 before a connecting road was completed and the first private automobile drove through. If timetables are posted for one-way traffic, be sure to observe the traffic flow going in your direction—there's two-way traffic much of the year, one-way during periods of heavy travel

Some four miles past the tunnel, you'll see **"The Chasm"** signposted on a bridge (the sign is small, so keep a sharp eye out). By all means take the time to stop and walk the short trail back into the forest, where a railed platform lets you view a natural sculpture of smooth and craggy rocks along the riverbed of the **Cleddau River.** As the river rushes through, a sort of natural tiered fountain is formed by its waters pouring through rock apertures. Marvelous! Absolutely unique! Well worth the time and the short walk.

Accommodations en Route

The only accommodations between Te Anau and Milford Sound are at **Te Anau Downs Motor Lodge** (mailing address: P.O. Box 19, Te Anau; tel. 77-53), an excellent Best Western property. There are B&B rooms with private facilities at NZ$22 ($14.77), and NZ$33 ($22.15) including dinner. One-bedroom motel flats are neat, modern units with cooking and eating utensils, fridge, electric rangette, and color TV. Rates for these units are NZ$38 ($25.50) double, plus NZ$8 ($5.37) per extra person. There's a laundry available to all guests. Also, proprietor Dave Moss runs a licensed restaurant with a local reputation for serving the largest and best roast dinner in the area at reasonable prices. As usual, Best Western Holiday Pass discounts apply.

3. Milford Sound

No matter what time of year you arrive or what the weather is like, your memories of Milford Sound are bound to be very special. Its 14 nautical miles leading to the Tasman Sea are lined with mountain peaks, which rise sharply to heights of six and seven thousand feet. Forsters fur seals sport on rocky shelves, dolphins play in waters, which reach depths up to 2000 feet, and its entrance is so concealed when viewed from the sea that Captain Cook missed it entirely when he was charting these waters some 200 years ago.

It rains a lot in Milford—more than in any other one place in New Zealand, in fact. I personally don't mind the rain, for the sound (which is actually a fiord carved out by glacial action) shows yet another side of its nature under dripping skies—the trip out to the Tasman in the rain is as special in its own way as one when the sun is shining. Ah, but on a fine day, when the sky is blue, the water varying shades of green and blue and dark brown, the bush, which flourishes even on sheer rock walls, a deep, shiny green—that day is to be treasured forever.

In summer months, coaches pour in at the rate of 30 or more each day for launch cruises. That tide slows in other months, but the launches go out year round, rain or shine. As is the custom at New Zealand's isolated beauty spots, the THC hotel is the center of things, and in the case of THC Milford, that continues a tradition that began in 1891, when Elizabeth Sutherland (wife of the sound's first settler) built a 12-room boarding house to accommodate seamen who called into the sound.

ACCOMMODATIONS: Milford Lodge, the only accommodations other than THC Milford, is a simple, dormitory-type lodging in gorgeous surroundings just one short, beautiful mile from the sound. It's owned and run by the THC, and open only from November 7 to April 6. Basic rooms, most holding three beds, provide beds, blankets, sheets, and towels—nothing more in the way of furnishings. Five rooms have H&C; five others have showers; and the toilet and shower block is immaculate. There's a big lounge and a cheerful dining room, which serves low-cost meals. If you're thinking of walking the Milford Track, this is where many hikers spend the first night back—perhaps to prolong a too-rare close communion with nature in the wooded site. Rates are NZ$13 ($8.72) per person.

On my reseach trip for this edition, the accommodation situation at Milford was in a state of flux. While the THC is out of reach for budgeteers, a tentative decision was made in the summer of 1983 to convert at least a part of the gracious luxury hotel into hostel-type dormitories. As this book is written, there is still no definite timetable for that to happen. It's a good idea, however, to check with the **THC Milford** (tel. Milford Sound 6) to see if that change has come about. If you fall under Milford's spell and decide to stay at the THC, expect to pay rates from NZ$65 ($43.62) and up, except from the first of May until the end of September when they fall to NZ$41 ($27.52) and NZ$52 ($34.90).

MEALS: You can eat very inexpensively at the **cafeteria** just below the THC hotel in a building that also holds the Public Bar. Or you can bring a picnic lunch with you from Te Anau. Or enjoy the smörgåsbord (NZ$7.50, or $5.03 U.S.) or snack (NZ$3.50, or $2.35 U.S.) lunch on the launch cruise.

You can choose from all those things, or you can treat yourself to a very special splurge and lunch in the **THC Milford,** next to a window looking out on the Sound and Mitre Peak (time is allowed between coach arrival and launch departure). The smörgåsbord lunch, which features the freshest of seafoods, along with soup, dessert, coffee, and cheese, costs NZ$11 ($7.38). Add another bit for a glass of wine and dine happily in anticipation of the launch cruise ahead.

THINGS TO SEE AND DO: Cruise Milford Sound. It must be seen from the deck of one of the launches, with the skipper filling you in on every peak, cove, creature, and plant you pass (the narrative, filled with anecdotes, is so entertaining you won't want to miss a word!), to be fully appreciated. Both the THC and Fiordland Travel Ltd. run excursions. There's a one-hour trip for NZ$11 ($7.38), and a two-hour cruise for NZ$13.50 ($9.06), which takes you out into the Tasman where you see the shoreline close and understand how it is that it escaped Captain Cook's keen eye. Even in warm weather, a jacket or sweater will likely feel good out on the water, and if it should be raining, you'll be glad of a raincoat. There are smörgåsbord and snack lunches available (see "Meals," above).

If you can stay over long enough, there are some marvelous **walks** from Milford Sound. Some climb into the peaks, others meander along the shore or up close to waterfalls. Ask at Park Headquarters in Te Anau or at the reception desk of THC Milford. It's worth the effort to know this timeless place from the land as well as the water.

READER'S TOURING COMMENT: "I found the place so beautiful that I felt compelled to stay—$41 at the THC!!! But worth it" (Ian McPherson, Oxford, U.K.) [*Author's Note:* This reader's comment is listed to validate my own admittedly "rave" comments on Milford Sound!!]

4. Te Anau to Invercargill or Dunedin

If time is short, you may want to head straight for Dunedin from Te Anau. If not, don't miss another very special place, **Stewart Island,** New Zealand's "third island," and almost as far south as you can go in this world before reaching Antarctica.

The drive to Dunedin takes about 5½ hours over good roads. Take Highway 94 across Gorge Hill into Lumsden, across the **Waimea Plains** to the milling center of **Gore,** through farmlands to **Clinton,** and across rolling downs to **Balclutha.** From there, it's Highway 1 north along the coast past **Mosgiel** (named after Scottish poet Robbie Burn's farm) to **Lookout Point,** where you'll get your first look at Dunedin. Along the way, you may want to stop in **Mossburn,** where **Wapiti Handcrafts Ltd.** (mailing address: P.O. Box 6; tel. 87), on the main street, makes and sells deerskin fashions. They are handsome creations and slightly lower in price here than in shops around the country. They also manufacture a range of smaller items for souvenirs and gifts. As you approach Balclutha, look for **Peggydale** (mailing address: P.O. Box 7; tel. 82-345), an ideal stopping point for tea, scones, sandwiches, or salad plates in the lovely Tea Kiosk. Peggydale handles a wide range of handcrafts—leather goods and sheepskin products (some made in their leathercraft shop), pottery, weaving, hand-knits, etc.—even paintings by local artists. They'll send you a mail-order catalog on request.

If Invercargill is your destination, you'll take Highway 94 only as far as Lumsden, then turn south on Highway 6 to ride through rolling farm and sheep country all the way down to Invercargill.

Chapter IX

SOUTHLAND

1. Invercargill
2. Stewart Island
3. The Coast Road to Dunedin

INVERCARGILL IS NEW ZEALAND'S southernmost city, the "capital" of Southland, a region you entered when you turned south at Lumsden and which extends as far northwest as Lake Manapouri, as far east as Balclutha. It is the country's coolest and rainiest region, yet the even spread of its rainfall is the very foundation of its economy, the raising of grass and grass seed, which in turn supports large numbers of sheep stations.

Its coastline saw settlements of Maoris (in limited numbers) and whalers, with frequent visits from sealers. From its waters have come those succulent Bluff oysters and crayfish (rock lobsters) you've devoured in your New Zealand travels. In fact they account for about 90% of the value of fish landed in this area.

1. Invercargill

The first thing you'll notice about Invercargill is its flatness—a bump is likely to take on the dimensions of a "hill" in these parts! Actually, that flatness is due to the fact that a large part of the city was once boggy swampland. In its reclamation, town fathers have turned what might have made for a dull city into a distinct advantage by planning wide, level thoroughfares and great city parks. Invercargill is a *spacious* city. Many of its broad, pleasant streets bear the names of Scottish rivers, revealing the home country of many of its early settlers.

Among its many attractions, perhaps primary is its proximity to Stewart Island, the legendary anchor of Maui's canoe (which became, of course, the South Island, with the North Island seen as the huge fish he caught). Day trips to Stewart Island are possible any day by air and several times a week by the ferry, which runs from nearby Bluff.

ORIENTATION: Invercargill's streets are laid out in neat grid patterns. Main thoroughfares are **Tay Street** (an extension of Highway 1) and **Dee Street** (an extension of Highway 6). Many of the principal shops and office buildings are centered around the intersection of these two streets. **Queens Park** is a beautiful green oasis (81 hectares) right in the center of town and the site of many activities. The **Southland Progress League, Inc.**, 40 Don St. (mailing address: P.O. Box 311; tel. 84-538), serves as a local tourist office and can furnish a list of local accommodations (although they are *not* a booking agency), as well as supply sightseeing details. The **railway station** and **NZZRS depot** are on Leven Street and the post office is on Dee Street. There is good rail, bus, and air service to and from Invercargill. Drivers will find **AA Headquarters** in Gala Streets.

ACCOMMODATIONS: You should have no trouble finding a place to lay your weary head in Invercargill. There are good budget accommodations in ample quantity.

A Hostel

The **YHA Hostel** is at 122 North Rd., Waikiwi (tel. 59-344). This is an extension of Dee Street, before it becomes Highway 6. There are 48 beds in the five rooms, showers, and a kitchen. There's a barbecue and picnic area available for use during the day, and the resident manager can arrange reduced fares to Stewart Island on a standby basis. He can also advise about hostel-type accommodations on the island (there are tentative plans for a YHA hostel, but no timetable as yet). Seniors pay NZ$4 ($2.68); Juniors, NZ$2 ($1.34).

Bed and Breakfast

The interesting old **Gerrards Railway Hotel,** on the corner of Esk and Leven Streets (tel. 83-406), is just across from the railway station. Built in 1896 of rosy-pink brick with white trim, its facade has recently had a face cleaning and rooms have been redone. These are not fancy accommodations, but comfortable, clean, and very centrally located. Rooms with or without private facilities are available, and showers and toilets are conveniently located for those which share. Bed-and-breakfast rates for rooms without facilities are NZ$20.50 ($13.76) single, NZ$28.50 ($19.13) double; with private facilities, NZ$26.50 ($17.79) to NZ$29.50 ($19.80) for one or two people. Children under 9 stay free; under-15s pay NZ$6 ($4.03).

Cabins

The **Southland A&P Association Caravan Park,** at the Showgrounds on Victoria Avenue (tel. 88-787), has two cabins that sleep up to four, and three that sleep up to six. On the premises is a kitchen, showers and toilets, a laundry, store, car wash, and play area. There are facilities for the handicapped, plus 50 campsites and 60 caravan sites. Rates for cabins are NZ$12 ($8.05) for two; caravan sites, NZ$4.50 ($3.02) per adult (children half); tent sites, NZ$4 ($2.68) per adult.

Motel Flats

Mitchells Motel, 85 Alice St. (tel. 45-04), is a pretty brick-and-wood complex right on the edge of Queens Park on a quiet residential street. Its ten units are more like individual homes than flats, some with one bedroom, others with two. Each is nicely decorated and furnished, and has a separate living room, telephone, color TV, radio, full kitchen, and private bath. Most have at-door parking. There's also a spa pool and playground. Pam and Peter are the attractive, friendly owner-operators of this Best Western motel, and they and their three young sons take a great interest in guests' welfare—they know Invercargill well and are eager to help you see it all. A cooked or continental breakfast is available at a small charge. Rates are NZ$30 ($20.13) single and NZ$36 ($24.16) double. Holiday Pass discounts apply.

The **Don Lodge Motor Hotel,** 77 Don St. (tel. 86-125), has 23 nice self-contained units, all with parking at the door. Each unit has a telephone, color TV, fridge, tea and coffee facilities, and private shower. Cooked or continental breakfasts are available. There's also a good, moderate-price restaurant on the premises (see "Meals," below). Rates are NZ$28 ($18.79) single, NZ$32 ($21.48) double.

The attractive blue-and-white, one-story **Tayesta Motel,** 343 Tay St. (tel. 76-074), has nine one- and two-bedroom units, with large picture windows in the lounge, fully equipped kitchen, central heating, telephone, color TV, and radio. There's a laundry, play area with swings and sandpit, and at-door parking. Lola Staite is the friendly hostess at this Best Western. Continental or cooked breakfasts are available at small charge. Rates are NZ$32 ($21.48) single, NZ$36 ($24.16) double, and Holidy Pass discounts apply.

MEALS: Invercargill has numerous coffeeshops offering good value. The coffee lounge in the **D.I.C. Department Store** has good morning and afternoon teas as well as light lunches, all inexpensive.

For quiches, salads, cakes (especially the carrot cake), and other light lunches, try **Joy's Gourmet Kitchen,** 122 Dee St. (tel. 83-985). It's open from noon to 2:30 p.m. Monday through Friday, and your lunch will run under NZ$6 ($4.03).

The beautiful and elegant **Grand Hotel,** 76 Dee St. (tel. 88-059), is a joy to go into, even if you don't eat. The lovely formal dining room is not for budgeteers (unless you decide after seeing it that this is your splurge), but you can enjoy elegance at a moderate price if you go along for their bistro meals in the **Prince of Wales Bar.** Seafood dishes are famous here, and you'll also find a nice selection of roasts, lamb, beef, etc. Lunch will run from NZ$6 ($4.03) to NZ$7.50 ($5.03), dinner slightly higher. Serving hours are 11:30 a.m. to 2 p.m. and 4 to 6:30 p.m. Monday through Friday. If you decide on the elegant dinner, hours are 6:15 to 8:15 p.m. Fully licensed. *Special note:* If oysters are on the menu in any form, let that be your order—the chef, who has been here 18 years, is noted for his oyster dishes, of which there are no fewer than ten!

The **Carvery,** at the Kelvin Hotel, corner of Kelvin and Esk Streets (tel. 82-829), is especially good value, much patronized by locals. Huge roasts are carved to your order, and the NZ$7 ($4.70) lunch includes three courses. At night, expect to pay NZ$9 ($6.04). Bistro lunches are served every day except Sunday in the **Nibble & Noggin Bar** from noon to 2 p.m. Fully licensed.

The **Hungry Knight Restaurant,** in the Don Lodge Motor Hotel, 77 Don St. (tel. 86-125), serves all three meals, all at moderate prices, and service is continuous from 7 a.m. until 10 p.m. seven days a week. The menu is comprehensive, with a nice selection of seafood, steak, chicken, etc. Lunch will run about NZ$6 ($4.03); dinner, anywhere from NZ$7 ($4.70) to NZ$9 ($6.04).

A Smörgåsbord Treat

Friday night in Invercargill means the seafood smörgåsbord and carvery at the **Ascot Park Hotel**—to residents as well as visitors, so booking ahead is a very good idea (in fact, I heard about this feast way up in the North Island when I mentioned coming to Invercargill). The Ascot Park, on the corner of Racecourse Road and Tay Street (tel. 76-195), is a luxury hotel of the first order, and the smörgåsbord is spread in an enormous room with different levels for tables. The spread is just about as enormous as the room, with every kind of seafood currently available, endless fresh salads, great roasts for non-seafood lovers, and luscious desserts. You'll see parties of locals chatting away with visitors, and there's a party atmosphere all through the place. The price is NZ$13.50 ($9.06), for which you get *full* value, indeed. Highly recommended.

THINGS TO SEE AND DO: Allow at least a full hour to visit the **Southland Centennial Museum and Art Gallery** on Gala Street by the main entrance to Queens Park. The collections inside include such fascinating items as stone tools, relics recovered from a 1795 shipwreck, artifacts from sealer and whaler days, a colorful figurehead from an English barque, which went down near Bluff in 1881, and a multitude of other exhibits, which will bring alive much of the history and natural resources of this area. In addition, there's a a tuatarium, the only place in the country you can view the little monsters in a simulated natural setting. In front of the museum, examine the section of fossilized forest, which dates from the Jurassic era of some 160 million years ago. Hours are 10 a.m. to 4:30 p.m. Monday through Friday; 1 to 5 p.m. on Saturday, and 2 to 5 p.m. on Sunday and public holidays.

Queens Park, right in the heart of the city, is just one (the largest) of Invercargill's parklands (a total of 1200 hectares) and might well keep you occupied for the better part of a day. Within its 81 hectares there's a rhododendron walk, iris garden, sunken rose garden, grove of native and exotic trees, wildlife sanctuary with wallabies, deer, and an aviary, duckpond, a winter garden, an 18-hole golf course, tennis courts, and—perhaps most of all, a cool, green retreat for the senses. A very special thing to look for is the beguiling children's fountain encircled by large bronze animal statues. Over the years this beautiful botanical reserve has seen duty as grazing land, a racecourse, and a sporting ground. The entrance is from Queen's Drive at Gala Street. There's a delightful Tea Kiosk for light refreshments.

Drive out to **Bluff,** Invercargill's port some 27 kilometers to the south. This is home port for the Stewart Island ferry, and site of the mammoth Tiwai Aluminium Smelter (the only one in the country) whose annual production is 150,000 tons. If you'd like to tour the complex (a fascinating experience), contact **Tiwai Smelter Tours,** NZ Aluminium Smelters Ltd., (mailing address: Private Bag, Invercargill; tel. 85-999). You must be at least 12 years of age and wear long trousers or slacks, heavy footwear, and clothing that covers your arms. There's no charge, but usually tours are limited to two a week, so it pays to book in advance.

There are two great **walks in Bluff** (ask the Southland Progress League office in Invercargill for the *Foveaux Walk, Bluff* pamphlet). The "Glory Walk" (named for a sailing vessel, *England's Glory,* which was wrecked at Bluff) is 1½ kilometers long and passes through native bush and trees, which form a shady canopy overhead. Ferns and mosses add to the lush greenery. The Sterling Point–Ocean Beach Walk begins where Highway 1 ends at Foveaux Strait. It's almost seven kilometers long, following the coastline around Bluff Hill, with marvelous views of beaches, offshore islands, and surf breaking against coastal rocks. Parking facilities are provided at both ends of the walk, and you are asked to follow the signposts and to leave no litter in your footprints.

INVERCARGILL TO STEWART ISLAND: The highlight of any Invercargill visit is a trip out to Stewart Island, about 30 kilometers across Foveaux

Strait. You can go by the venerable 627-ton **ferry** vessel *Wairua,* which sails from Bluff carrying up to 287 passengers (visitors and returning islanders), fresh milk, and almost every other commodity the island uses. It's a glorious two-hour voyage across waters, which are comparatively shallow, but which can be exceedingly turbulent. The *Wairua* usually sails on Monday, Wednesday, and Friday, with additional sailings during summer and holiday periods. It leaves Bluff at 8 a.m. (you must be aboard by 7:45 a.m.), arrives at Oban at 10 a.m., and does not depart until either 1:45 or 3 p.m., leaving you time for a saunter around the charming Stewart Island port and the interesting minibus tour of the island's 20 kilometers of paved road. Fares for the day excursion are NZ$21.50 ($14.43) for adults and NZ$11 ($7.38) for children. Booking is absolutely essential; book through the Marine Division, Ministry of Transport, P.O. Box 18, Bluff (tel. 8119).

Southern Air also flies between Invercargill and Stewart Island, and during the 15-minute flight, the nine-seater Britten-Norman Islander gives you breathtaking views of the coastline, changing colors of the waters below, which mark the passage of an oceanic stream flowing through the strait, bush-clad islands, and Stewart Island itself, where you land on a packed-clay runway and are minibused into Oban. Southern's schedules also allow for a day visit, but both days of the week and flying hours vary considerably, so best check when you're there. These flights are extremely popular and you should either book ahead by telephone or through travel agents or airline offices (Mount Cook Lines and Air New Zealand can both make bookings) before you arrive in Invercargill. Adult fare is NZ$34 ($22.82) each way; children pay NZ$19 ($12.75). From time to time they offer a luncheon excursion, which includes the flight, minibus tour of the island, and lunch for NZ$74 ($49.66). Southern Air's Invercargill telephone is 89-120.

2. Stewart Island

Seen on the map, Stewart Island is not much more than a speck. But seen from the deck of the *Wairua* or from the air, its magnitude will surprise you. There are actually 1600 kilometers of coastline enclosing 1680 square kilometers of thick bush, most of it left in its natural state, bird sanctuary, and rugged mountains. Only a tiny stretch of that long coastline has been settled, and it's the little fishing town of Oban that will be your landfall. There are about 20 kilometers of paved road on the island, which are easily covered by the minibus tour, and many of the houses you see are the holiday "batch" or "crib" of Kiwis from the South Island who view Stewart Island as the perfect spot to escape the pressures of civilization.

The pace here is quite unhurried—few cars, friendly islanders more attuned to the tides and the running of cod and crayfish than to commerce, and a setting that is a botanist's dream. The Maoris called the island Rakiura, "heavenly glow," a name you'll find especially fitting if you are lucky enough to see the southern lights brighten its skies or to be here for one of its spectacular sunsets.

While its beauty and serenity can be glimpsed in the few hours of a day trip, I heartily recommend at least one overnight to explore its beaches, bush, and people so as to savor this very special place to the fullest. Incidentally, should you hear yourself or other summer visitors referred to as "loopies" by the islanders, not to worry—it'll be said with affection.

The town of **Oban** centers on Halfmoon Bay and holds a general store, post office, travel office, craft shop, hotel, forestry office, small museum, and the pier at which the ferry docks.

ACCOMMODATIONS: There is no booking agency as such on Stewart Island, but pretty Beryl Wilcox and her husband Lloyd, who operate **Stewart Island Travel** (mailing address: P.O. Box 26, Stewart Island; tel. 69 or 105), can send you a complete list of accommodations and prices, and will do all they can to help you book. Accommodations are extremely limited, and in summer they're booked months in advance, so if your plans include a visit here, write or call just as soon as you have firm dates for your visit. It is sometimes possible to rent one of the holiday homes or apartments not currently in use, and Beryl is the one to contact. Where a P.O. Box is not listed below, the address is simply Stewart Island.

Hostel

There is no YHA hostel on Stewart Island.

Very basic "tramper accommodations" can be arranged through **Ann Pulen** (tel. 19). Rates are NZ$4 ($2.68) per person per night.

Cabins

Horseshoe Haven (P.O. Box 25; tel. 156K) is run by Bettie and Colin Garrie at Horseshoe Bay. They have A-frame chalets, simply but comfortably furnished, at NZ$21 ($14.09) double, NZ$5 (3.36) per extra adult. They also have a dormitory block, with rates of NZ$6.50 ($4.36) per adult, NZ$3 ($2.01) per child. Tent sites are NZ$3 ($2.01) per adult, NZ$1.50 ($1.01) per child. Horseshoe Haven is about 2½ miles from Oban and on a good swimming beach.

Motel Flats

Ferndale Caravans (P.O. Box 117; tel. 58) is on Halfmoon Bay, and has fully furnished luxury caravans with awnings, which rent for NZ$24 ($16.11) double, NZ$7 ($4.70) per extra adult, NZ$4 ($2.68) per child. Contact Leslie and Alan Gray.

Elaine Hamilton has five self-contained motel units at **Rakiura Motels** (P.O. Box 96; tel. 27K), about one mile from Oban. Units sleep up to six, are heated, and have kitchens and private baths. Rates are NZ$30 ($20.13) double, NZ$9 ($6.04) per extra adult, NZ$5 ($3.36) per child under 12.

A Licensed Hotel

Stewart Island's only hotel is the **South Sea Hotel** (P.O. Box 91; tel. 6), run by Bruce and Carol Ford. The two-story hotel sits right in the curve of Halfmoon Bay, across the street from the water. Its public bar, bar lounge (whose windows overlook the bay), and licensed restaurant are the center of much island activity, and even if you lodge elsewhere, you're likely to find yourself in and out of the South Sea many times during your stay. Rooms all share the bath and toilet facilities down the hall, and there are exactly six singles, nine twins, and three doubles. This is the kind of charming, old-fashioned inn that seems exactly right for an island—the guest lounge, for example, has an open fire glowing on cool days, and the staff takes a personal interest in all guests (and in casual visitors, for that matter). Rates are NZ$19.50 ($13.09) per person, with children under 10 at half that. Breakfast is extra, at NZ$5 ($3.36). Surcharge for one-night stay.

MEALS: The **Travel Inn Tearoom,** adjoining Stewart Island Travel (just opposite the deer park in the center of town), serves sandwiches, meat pies, salad rolls, cakes, etc., from 9 a.m. to 3 p.m., all priced under NZ$1 (67¢). Eat in the tea room, or take away.

One of the best seafood meals I've had in New Zealand was in the large, pleasant dining room at the **South Sea Hotel.** My fish was truly fresh and fried to perfection, the salad bar was more extensive than I would have expected on an island where so much must be imported, the dessert was luscious, and the service included a friendly chat about how best to spend my time on Stewart Island. Other main courses included beef, lamb, and chicken, but seafood is their specialty, and in a setting like this it seems the logical choice. Lunch hours are noon to 2 p.m., and the set price is NZ$7.50 ($5.03). Dinner is served each night from 6 to 8 p.m. and costs NZ$14.50 ($9.73)

The South Sea Hotel can pack a **picnic lunch** if notified in ample time, and there's a general store where you can pick up picnic makings for a day in the bush.

THINGS TO SEE AND DO: The only thing not to miss is the hour-long **minibus tour** given by Beryl Wilcox at Stewart Island Travel (tel. 69 or 105). Beryl will not only cover every one of those 20 kilometers of paved road, she'll give you a comprehensive history of Stewart Island—the whalers who settled here, the sealers who called in (it was, in fact, the mate of a sealer who gave his name to the island), the sawmill and mineral industries, which came and went, development of the fishing industry, etc.—and will point out traces they left behind scattered around your route. She also knows the flora of the island (you'll learn, for instance, that there are nine varieties of orchids on the island) and its animal population (no wild pigs or goats). You'll see many of the 18 good swimming beaches and hear details of the paua diving, which has proved so profitable for islanders (much of the colorful shell that went into those souvenirs you've seen around New Zealand came from Stewart Island). From Observation Point right to the road's end at Thule Bay, Beryl gives you an insider's view of her home. And questions or comments are very much in order—it's an informal, happy hour of exchange: a perfect way to begin a stay of several days, an absolute essential if the day trip is all you will have. The fare is NZ$6 ($4.03)

The **Rakiura Museum** in Oban is open only on ferry days between 10 a.m. and 1:30 p.m. Its collection is a bit small, but nonetheless interesting, with such relics as an 1816 globe, which shows Stewart Island as a peninsula (Captain Cook's mistake, which wasn't corrected for many years), and other bits and pieces of the island's history.

Visit the small **deer park** just across from Stewart Island Travel. Small red deer are right at home in the enclosure and seem delighted to have visitors.

Just next to the deer park is the **Forest Service Office,** which has an interesting display of island wildlife in a small exhibition room. More important, the rangers there can supply details on many beautiful **walks** around Oban and farther afield. If you're interested in spending a few days on the island tramping, I suggest you write ahead for their informative booklets on just what you'll need to bring and what you may expect. There are recently upgraded tramping huts conveniently spaced along the tracks (ranging in size from 6 to 30 bunks), but they are heavily used and must be booked with the rangers (no charge). A two-night stay is the maximum at any one hut.

Popular short walks around Oban are those to Golden Bay, Lonneckers, Lee Bay, Thule, Observation Point, and the lighthouse at Acker's Point. Ringarina Beach is a mecca for shell hounds (I have New Zealand friends who serve entrees in paua shells they've picked up on the beach here!), but your finds will depend on whether the tides are right during your visit. *Important:* If you're here on a day trip, check locally to be sure you can make it back from any walk you plan in time for the ferry or air return.

You can engage local boats for fishing or visiting nearby uninhabited islands at prices that are surprisingly low. A half-day trip to Ulva Island is only NZ$10 ($6.71) for adults, NZ$5 ($3.36), for children; a full day in Paterson Inlet, NZ$25 (16.78) for adults, half that for children; a twilight cruise in Paterson Inlet (7 to 10 p.m.) is NZ$10 ($6.71) per person; half-day's fishing, NZ$15 ($10.06) per person. Contact Phillip Smith (tel. 44), master of the *Seastar,* or check with Stewart Island Travel.

3. The Coast Road to Dunedin

You can drive from Invercargill to Dunedin in a little over three hours by way of Highway 1, through Gore, through farmlands and mile after mile of grazing sheep. It's a pleasant drive, and if time is a factor, one you'll enjoy. *However,* if you have a day to spend on the road, let me urge you to take Highway 92 and allow a full day to loiter along the way, rejoining Highway 1 at Balclutha. If you make this drive, pick up the useful folder *Southeast Otago Scenic Reserves* from the Southland Progress League office in Invercargill, which will detail the reserves through which you will pass.

The **Invercargill–Balclutha Coast Road,** as it is known, takes you through a region of truly unique character. Although you'll not be driving at any great altitude anywhere along this route, there are great folds in the land covered with such a diversity of native forests that from Chasland on you'll be in one national forest reserve after the other. Short detours will take you to the coast and golden sand beaches, prominent headlands, and fine bays.

Highway 92, let me hasten to add, is not paved its entire length—however, even paved portions are in good driving condition, albeit at a slower speed than the faster Highway 1. Picnic spots abound, so you can take along a packed lunch from Invercargill, or plan to stop in the country pub in Owaka's only hotel for lunch (stop for refreshments even if you lunch elsewhere—it's an experience you wouldn't want to miss). One very special detour you might consider follows.

Just beyond Fortrose, follow the Fortrose–Otara road to the right, and when you pass the Otara School, look for the turnoff to **Waipapa Point.** The point is the entrace to **Foveaux Strait,** a treacherous waterway that has scuttled many a sailing vessel and that is now marked by a light, which was first used in 1884. Follow the Otara–Haldane road to Porpoise Bay, then turn right and drive a little over one kilometer to the **Curio Bay Fossil Forest,** which is signposted. This sea-washed rock terrace dates back 160 *million* years and is the original floor of a Jurassic subtropical forest of kauri trees, conifers, and other trees, which were growing at a time when grasses had not even evolved. At low tide, you can make out low stumps and fallen logs that have been petrified after being buried in volcanic ash, then raised when the sea level changed. You can then retrace your way around Porpoise Bay and follow the signs to Waikawa and continue north to rejoin Highway 92 on to Chaslands.

There are a few simple rules you must follow when stopping in the scenic reserves. If you picnic, you may light fires *only* in the fireplaces provided in picnic areas, and be sure to extinguish them thoroughly (only dead wood is permitted as fuel); dogs and cats may only be brought into the reserves with permission from the Reserves Board; it is an offense to pick or damage any of the trees, shrubs or plants in the reserves; and (need I add?) you are expected to leave your picnic area clean and tidy.

If you'd like further details about this lovely part of a lovely country, write the Secretary, **South East Otago Reserves Board,** P.O. Box 896, Dunedin (tel. 70-650).

Chapter X

DUNEDIN AND MOUNT COOK

**1. Dunedin and Surroundings
2. Mount Cook
3. Mount Cook to Christchurch**

YOU WON'T FIND PIPERS in the streets of Dunedin—and the citizens of "New Edinburgh on the Antipodes" are quick to tell you they're *Kiwis,* not Scots. Still, one look at the sturdy stone Victorian architectural face of the city with its crown of upreaching spires will tell you that the 344 settlers who arrived at this beautiful Upper Harbour in March of 1848 could only have come from Scotland. And when you learn that Dunedin is the old Gaelic name for Edinburgh, that the city produces New Zealand's only domestic whisky, has the only kilt store in the country, and that there are no fewer than nine listings in the city directory under the heading of "Pipe Band," there's no mistaking its Scottish nature!

A reader once wrote that "very few people are lukewarm about their feelings when it comes to bagpipes—either they are very enthusiastic or they're *anti-* bagpipes." I think she's right, and you might as well know up front that I am one of those enthusiasts who will drop everything at the skirl of a bagpipe and travel miles to listen to its curious music. Which fact may account in large part for the place Dunedin holds in my affections. That affection, however, is mightily reinforced by the city's serendipitous character—lighthearted chatter in pubs hiding behind somber facades, instant friendliness, which belies that much-touted "dour" Scottish nature, and spirit of fun unexpectedly discovered in almost any Dunedin gathering, the *twinkle* in Dunedin's eye.

The city's foundations were planned on the solid bedrock of a "Free Church," but its fortunes changed drastically with the goldfield discoveries in Otago, which brought thousands pouring in to bring, along with the gold speculators, the bustle of industry and commerce. From 1861 to 1865 its population erupted from 2000 to over 10,000, and it has since that time never lost its position of prominence among New Zealand's cities. Amazingly, it has held onto its priorities of education (the first New Zealand university was founded here), conservation of its natural beauties (witness the green Town Belt, which encircles the city), and humanitarian concerns (the Plunket Society for good infant care originated here).

Dunedin, then, is likely to be one of your most fondly remembered New Zealand cities—and you really shouldn't go away without exploring the long Otago Peninsula that curves around one side of that beautiful harbor.

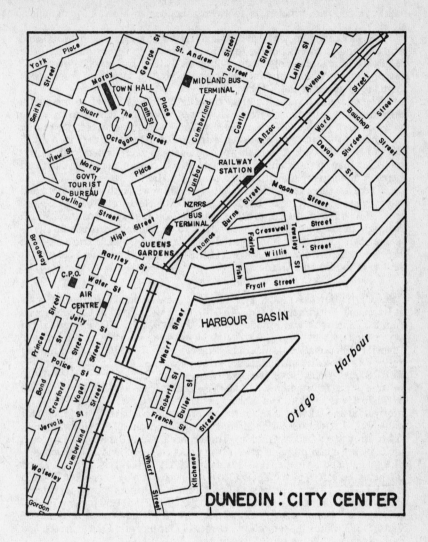

DUNEDIN : CITY CENTER

1. Dunedin and Surroundings

ORIENTATION: Most cities have a public square, but Dunedin has its eight-sided **Octagon,** a green, leafy park right at the hub of the city center. Around its edges you'll find **St. Paul's Anglican Cathedral** and the **Town Hall.** Within its confines, there's the beautiful illuminated musical fountain, which puts on a colorful show every night between 9 and 10 p.m., a statue of Scotland's beloved poet Robert Burns (whose nephew was Dunedin's first pastor), shady pathways, and park benches for footweary shoppers or brown-bagging lunchers.

The city center, at the head of **Otago Harbour,** is encircled by a 500-acre strip of land left, by edict of the founding fathers, in its natural state, never to be developed regardless of the city's growth. Thus it is that when driving to any of Dunedin's suburbs, you pass through verdant forestland from which there are glimpses of the harbor.

The Octagon divides the main street into **Princes Street** to the south, **George Street** to the north. Most city buses leave from the Octagon at the intersection of High and Princes Streets. There's frequent bus service during the week, a little spotty on weekends. Fares are zoned and range from NZ$.35 (23¢) to NZ$.70 (47¢). A smooth-working **one-way street system** makes driving easier than in most cities; all central streets have metered parking; and there's a municipal parking building near City Hall

There are three very good lookout points from which to view the city and its environs: **Mount Cargill Lookout** (eight kilometers from the city center, turn left at the end of George Street, then left on Pine Hill Road to its end, then right onto Cowan Street, which climbs to the summit); **Centennial Lookout,** or Signal Hill (turn into Signal Hill Road from Opoho Road and drive three kilometers to the end of Signal Hill Road); and **Bracken's Lookout** (at the top of the Botanic Gardens).

USEFUL INFORMATION: You'll find the **New Zealand Government Tourist Bureau** at 131 Princes St. (tel. 740-344), two blocks from the Octagon (open from 8:30 a.m. to 5 p.m. Monday through Friday). They offer a multitude of services and information.... Also helpful with visitor information is the **Otago Council Public Relations Office,** 119 Princes St. (tel. 774-176).... The **railway station** (a sightseeing attraction, see below) is at the foot of Stuart Street, the NZRRS **bus terminal** several blocks away on Cumberland Street (tel. 772-640 for train or bus information).... **Air New Zealand** has its ticket office in John Wickliffe House next to the Chief Post Office (CPO) (tel. 75-749 for flight information and booking).... Fares on airport coaches are NZ$5 ($3.36) for adults, NZ$2.50 ($1.68) for children, and they drop you off at **Airport House,** 114 Rattray St. at Queens Gardens. The airport is a full 20 miles from the city, which makes a taxi prohibitive... **Taxi ranks** may be found at the Octagon, all terminals and near the CPO. Flagfall is NZ$1.20 (81¢), NZ$.75 (50¢) per kilometer thereafter, plus NZ$.45 (30¢) if you call a cab by phone (tel. 774-455 or 771-771).... The **Chief Post Office (CPO)** is at Princes and Water Streets, open Monday through Thursday 8 a.m. to 5:30 p.m., until 8:30 p.m. on Friday. ... Central 24-hour gas (petrol) stations are: Kaikorai Service Station, 433 Stuart St.; Downtown Motors Ltd., corner of Gardner and Police Streets; and Everedi Service Station on Princes Street.

ACCOMMODATIONS: Dunedin has many fine accommodations in almost all price ranges. It also has, however, a large student population (with lots of visitors!) and a great deal of through traffic en route to the Southern Alps and Southland. All of which adds up to *book in advance.* This especially holds true during summer months.

Hostels

A grand old early-1900s mansion houses Dunedin's YHA hostel, **Stafford Gables,** 71 Stafford St. (tel. 741-919), with lovely flower beds leading up to its entrance. Centrally located close to the CPO, it is also near food stores and a large supermarket. There are 60 beds in 19 rooms with high ceilings, carpeting, and attractive wallpaper. One of the two comfortable lounges also serves as a game room, and there are kitchens, a dining room, and a laundry and drying room. Rates for Seniors are NZ$5 ($3.36); for Juniors, NZ$2.50 ($1.68).

Out on scenic Otago Peninsula there are hostel-type accommodations in historic **Larnach Castle** (mailing address: Larnach Castle, Otago Peninsula, Dunedin; tel. Dunedin 761-302). The four-berth rooms, plus showers and toilets, are upstairs in what was the hayloft of the 112-year-old stables. A kitchen is in the old groom's room downstairs, and the tables and chairs are from an old priory in Dunedin. An open fire and coal range (with radiators running from it) furnish the heating. Otherwise, the stables have been restored to their original state. Rates when you furnish linens are NZ$18 ($12.08) for two; when linen and quilts are furnished, NZ$20 ($13.42) single, NZ$25 ($16.78) double.

Cabins

The **Aaron Lodge Motor Camp,** 162 Kaikorai Valley Rd., near Brockville Road (tel. 64-725), is a whole complex of cabins, cabin blocks, and motel flats on a main artery with a grassy hill out back. Seven motel flats are in front (see "Motel Flats," below), and there are 15 family rooms in two large red-and-gray cement cabin blocks. Four- or five-berthed, all are spacious, and have carpets, large wardrobes, a table and chairs, and electric heater. Beds can be curtained off for privacy. There's a modern kitchen, shower, laundry with dryer, and TV room. Across a grassy lawn and up the hill are eight two-berth cabins with built-in beds, a shelf, and a chest of drawers. No separate shower for the cabins, but there is a small kitchen and laundry with a washing machine. There's a children's playground on the premises, and a dairy adjacent. Rates for all cabins are NZ$5 ($3.36) per adult, NZ$2.50 ($1.68) per child, with a minimum of NZ$15 ($10.06) on the larger cabins, NZ$7 ($4.70) on the smaller ones. Tent and caravan sites are also available. The Aaron Lodge is owned and managed by Mr. and Mrs. George and may be reached via the Bradford or Brockville buses from the Octagon.

The Y

The centrally located **YWCA,** Kinnaird House, Moray Place (tel. 776-781), is a modern brick, four-story, elevator building with a garden courtyard. The 120 beds are in centrally heated rooms, which include singles, doubles, and four-berth bunk rooms. Furnishings are basic, but a nice size and neatly fitted with tables and chairs, chests of drawers, and good cupboards. Floors are linoleum, and bedspreads are bright and cheerful. There's a pleasant, airy dining room, a comfortable sitting room, a color TV room, and a laundry with a drying room. The Y takes casual guests for unlimited stays, has no age limits, and is open to men and women, couples and families. Rates for bed and breakfast are NZ$15 ($10.06) per person the first night, NZ$14 ($9.40) thereafter. Lunch costs NZ$3.50 ($2.35); dinner, NZ$5 ($3.36). There are special rates for families. Book well ahead, and send a deposit of NZ$10 ($6.71).

Bed and Breakfast

The gabled brick **Sahara Guest House,** 619 George St. (tel. 776-662), sports elaborate iron grillwork, is just a five-minute walk from the Octagon and is on major bus routes. Built as a hospital back at the turn of the century, it now holds 12 nice-size rooms with H&C, with one to three twin beds, all immaculate and cheerful. Room 12 is especially bright, with a stained-glass window. Behind the main house is a block of one-bedroom motel units, which sleep up to four, with full kitchens, central heat, color TV, radio, and telephone. There are tea and coffee facilities in the TV lounge, and over the fireplace is a gallery of photos of sports teams who have been guests here. Also, central heat, a laundry, off-street parking, and a swimming pool. The dining room is spacious and inviting. Bed-and-breakfast rates are NZ$16 ($10.74) for adults, NZ$8 ($5.37) for children under 12, and there's a surcharge for a one-night stay. Motel-unit rates are NZ$30 ($20.13) for one or two people, also with a surcharge.

Motel Flats

The seven motel flats at the **Aaron Lodge Motor Camp** (see "Cabins," above, for complete description), 176 Kaikorai Valley Rd. (tel. 64-725), are all one-bedroom units and have central heating, color TV, radio, and electric blankets. All are nicely carpeted and well maintained. Rates are NZ$28 ($18.79) for one or two persons.

There are one- and two-bedroom units at the centrally located **Argyle Court Motel,** on the corner of George and Duke Streets (tel. 779-803). Each has a kitchenette with fridge and stove, TV, and telephone. The seven units are nicely decorated, and the Argyle is handy to a shopping center. Rates start at NZ$28 ($18.79) for one or two persons. A continental breakfast may be ordered at a small extra charge.

The **Alcala Motel,** at the corner of George and St. David Streets (tel. 779-073), is an attractive Spanish-style complex just a ten-minute walk from the Octagon. Each unit has a full kitchen, telephone, color TV with video, radio, and thermo-mattresses. There's a laundry, spa pool, sauna, and off-street parking. A continental breakfast is available at small fee. A licensed restaurant and shops, hairdresser, and service station are close by. Rates start at NZ$28 ($18.79) single, NZ$34 ($22.82) double.

There are 20 units at the **Dunedin Motel,** 624 George St. (tel. 777-692), nine with two bedrooms, the rest with one. All are nicely decorated, and although located on a main street just a five-minute walk from the city center, units run back from the street, creating a quiet and peaceful atmosphere. All have telephone, radio, color TV, electric heater, and electric underblankets. Rates are NZ$26 ($17.45) single, NZ$34 ($22.82) double. Take the Normanby Gardens or Opoho bus.

The **Best Western Tourist Court,** 838–842 George St. (tel. 774-270), has ten spacious units in a two-story building running back from the busy main street. Each can sleep up to six, and has a full kitchen, color TV, radio, telephone, central heat, and electric blanket. There's a guest laundry, and a continental or cooked breakfast may be ordered for a small fee. Units are exceptionally well appointed, and each has an iron and ironing board. It's on a main bus line, but within easy walking distance of the Octagon. Rates are NZ$32 ($21.48) single, NZ$39 ($26.17) double. Best Western Holiday Pass discounts apply.

There are three **Farry's Motels** in Dunedin, all in the heart of the city; 193 High St., 575 George St., and 112 Stafford St. (tel 779-333 for all). Units are nicely furnished, with wide picture windows in lounge, and each has central heating, fully equipped kitchen, color TV, radio, and telephone. All are very well kept, and two-bedroom units sleep up to seven. There's a laundry, children's play area, and off-street parking. Continental breakfast is available at an extra charge at the George Street address. Rates at all are NZ$28 ($18.79) single, NZ$34 ($22.82) double for one-bedroom units, NZ$36 ($24.16) double for two-bedroom suites.

Adjacent to beautiful St. Kilda Beach and a good children's playground, the **Beach Lodge Motel,** 38 Victoria Rd., St. Kilda, Dunedin (tel. 55-043), is run by Dave and Wendy Kennedy, who go out of their way to make this a "home away from home." The 18 units in this Best Western member range in size from bedsitters to three-bedrooms (which sleep up to nine). All are of a nice size and contain a kitchen (continental breakfast may be ordered, and an office shop sells frozen motel meals), TV, radio, telephone, and thermo-mattress or electric blanket. There's a spa pool, guest laundry with dryer, a car wash, and off-street parking. For a peaceful retreat after strenuous sightseeing or a quick swim to start the day off, you couldn't have a better location than the Beach Lodge—the safe beach (with a lifesaving club station) is a 300-yard walk across a golf course and sand dunes, and there's a view of hills in the distance. The drive into the city is direct and takes about five minutes. Rates are NZ$33 ($22.15) single, NZ$37 ($24.83) double. Best Western discounts apply.

Its central location and superior accommodations make the **Abbey Motor Lodge,** 900 Cumberland St. (tel. 775-380), good value-for-money. Run by Pat and Margaret O'Connor, the Abbey offers two classes of accommodations: motel flats and serviced hotel rooms. While the luxury hotel rooms are beyond most budgeteers' reach except as a Big Splurge, the beautifully furnished and equipped motel units are a bargain for a couple or larger party. Decorated under Margaret's careful supervision to be, in her words, "restful to the eye," they border on the luxurious, with leather sofa and chairs set off by warm shades of brown and burnt orange, and beamed ceilings. Each has a kitchen, TV, radio, and balcony, and three have waterbeds. On the premises are a sauna, spa pools, indoor heated swimming pool, laundry, an excellent licensed restaurant (see "Meals," below), and lounge bar. Rates are NZ$39 ($26.17) single and NZ$45 ($30.20) double, and since this is a Best Western member, Holiday Pass discounts apply.

In a newer, three-story building, the Abbey has truly luxury serviced hotel rooms decorated with the same care and good taste, each with fridge and tea and coffee facilities, and one "executive suite" is downright elegant, with antique furnishings and its own spa bath. Rates (just in case you're tempted) for these start at NZ$55 ($36.91) single, NZ$65 ($43.62) double. Those discounts apply here too. (Even if you don't book here, drop in to the lounge bar—very popular with locals—and have a look at the interesting prints of early Dunedin hung in the lobby and lounge.)

A Licensed Hotel

The three-story triangular **Leviathan Hotel,** 65–69 Lower High St. (tel. 773-160), is a Dunedin landmark dating back to the 1890s. It's on a corner directly across from the Early Settlers Museum and one block from the railway station and bus depot. The old building is in excellent condition and offers a high standard of central, budget accommodation plus 12 fully equipped suites, which are much favored by visiting M.P.s. Rooms are attractively decorated and furnished with built-in wardrobe, chest of drawers, and overbed lights. All have color TV and electric heater. Seventeen singles and two twins have H&C only; the rest come with private facilities. Two family units sleep five. There's a game room with a pool table, two TV lounges, and a writing room with chairs grouped around a brick fireplace. The elegant dining room serves meals in the moderate range. There's an elevator, hall telephones for guests, and a garage in the building with free parking. Rates for rooms with H&C are NZ$20 ($13.42) single; with private facilities, NZ$30 ($20.13) single, NZ$39 ($26.17) double. Children under 12 pay half. Surcharge. Suites accommodating up to five, with full kitchen, bath and shower, TV, radio, etc., are NZ$41 ($27.52) double, NZ$4 ($2.68) per extra adult, NZ$2 ($1.34) per extra child.

MEALS: There's a **Cobb & Co.** in the Law Courts, 53–65 Stuart St. (tel. 778-036), where good food is served at moderate prices—the average main course costs NZ$5 ($3.36). Fully licensed, with hours of 7:30 a.m. to 10 p.m., seven days a week.

Dunedin residents have long treasured **Stewart's Coffee House,** 12 Lower Octagon (tel. 776-687), for its fresh-roasted coffee (you'll love the smell!), its cozy basement location—also very central—and sandwiches, which far surpass those in most such places, both in quality and selection. For example, the plain old egg sandwich becomes a curried egg sandwich at Stewart's. There's soup and a nice array of cakes and other sweets. You can, of course, get tea, but it's the coffee that's a standout, and you can buy it by the pound to enhance meals back in your motel kitchen. Open from 9 a.m. to 5 p.m. Monday through Thursday, until 8:30 p.m. on Friday.

Special Note: One of the nicest things to do in Dunedin when feet are weary and a light snack has enormous appeal is to go in to the **Methodist Friendship Center** (in the Methodist Mission Building, just off the Octagon), where you'll find volunteers behind the counter in a large, rather plain but cheerful room. Their motto is "talk and tea from ten to three," and they're right in our price range—two cookies and tea or coffee cost NZ$.30 (20¢), and they can serve as dessert if you'd like to bring in your own lunch, as many people do. You'll be treating yourself to a refreshing, inexpensive break, and contributing to a worthy cause at the same time.

The **Hotel Southern Cross,** 118 High St. (tel. 770-752), holds two dining facilities, one in the budget range, the other very pricey but very elegant. The **Hogshead Bar and Restaurant** (entrance on Princes Street) is informal, with the look of a London pub. From noon to 2 p.m. and 5 to 8:30 p.m. (opens at 6 p.m. on Sunday) the self-service counter dishes up a roast (pork, chicken, beef, or lamb on alternate days) and two vegetables or three salads for NZ$6 ($4.03), and specials of curries, stews, etc., for well under that. On the hotel's top floor, the posh **Copperfield Room** offers a stunning panoramic view of Dunedin plus à la carte lunches with main courses of such delicacies as co-quilles St. Jacques mornay, crayfish Newburg, and duckling (as well as the usual roasts) for around NZ$8 ($5.37) and dinners, which run about NZ$18 ($12.08). Also at the Southern Cross, you can join the "after five" business crowd in the **Capella Bar,** a fun place well off the tourist path. Both the Hogshead and the Copperfield Room are fully licensed.

For old-fashioned elegance at moderate prices, it's the **Savoy Restaurant,** at Princes Street and Moray Place (tel. 778-977). It dates from 1912, was gutted by fire, then faithfully restored to its exact original condition. There are three large rooms, seating 400 in all, and the rooms are something to behold! Tudor Hall is oak paneled, with leaded-glass windows depicting colorful coats-of-arms, brass chandeliers hanging from the ornate plaster ceiling, and red linen tablecloths with an overcloth of Scottish lace. Both the smaller, mahogany-paneled Tudor Lounge and the Warwick Room have much the same decor. Owner Stewart Clark prides himself on "lunches and dinners individually served in elegant surroundings," and the Savoy has gained quite a reputation for its light lunches at prices in the NZ$4 ($2.68) to NZ$6 ($4.03) range (curried rice, filet of sole, Spanish omelet, etc.). An à la carte menu lists such selections as wienerschnitzel, ham steak Hawaiian, and sweet-and-sour chicken, which are priced from NZ$6 ($4.03) to NZ$8 ($5.37). Fully licensed and open from noon to 8:30 p.m. Tuesday to Friday, 5:30 to 9 p.m. on Saturday.

Chef and owner Brian Stewart run two very good eateries in the **Robbie Burns Hotel,** 370 George St. **Zapatas,** downstairs in the Robbie Burns Pub, features a good array of Mexican dishes, plus roast beef, seafood, etc. There are frequent menu changes, depending on what fresh meats are available locally. Lunch only is served, from noon to 2 p.m. Monday through Friday, at prices of NZ$3 ($2.01) to NZ$5 ($3.36). This place is extremely popular with locals, and your best bet to avoid the crowds is to get there exactly at noon or close to 2 p.m. On Thursday, Friday, and Saturday only, Brian opens **Foxy's Café,** upstairs at the same address (tel. 778-100), in four rooms, which look as they might have 125 years ago when the hotel was built. The charming room, which holds the dark, carved bar, also has a handsome fireplace, and fittings throughout are reminiscent of days long gone. Starters include tacos and enchiladas, as well as mussels Provençal; grills feature steaks in a variety of sizes and styles; and other main courses include a seafood basket, chili con carne, tandoori chicken, Italian pasta, and Mexican pancake. All grills are served with potato and side salad. Prices are in the NZ$6 ($4.03) to NZ$11 ($7.38) range on the à la carte menu. Hours are 5 to 10 p.m., and it's a good idea to book.

You may find yourself going back to **Carnarvon Station** for its lively bars as much as for its moderately priced meals in what can only be called about the most special ambience in Dunedin! The fully licensed restaurant is a tribute to the early days of New Zealand rail travel by the owners, Wilson Neill Wines and Spirits (they're the ones who distill New Zealand's only domestic liquor). The imaginative dining areas (seven in all) have such names as the Ticket Office, Parcels Office, Signal Box, and Southern Platform. There are two ornate old railroad dining cars, as well as the Station Carvery. The Northern Platform Refreshment Counter and the Waiting Room (complete with fireplace—there are not fewer than 12 fireplaces throughout) are both bars (with a wine list of over 300 wines), and light snacks are served in the Waiting Room, as well as fine coffees and liqueurs. Many of the fittings are from a suburban Dunedin station and date back more than 100 years. Carnarvon Station is an interesting place, a fun place, a place of fascination for railway buffs, and a warm, relaxing place that's guaranteed to generate an immediate affectionate response just for the tender, loving care with which it has been created. Besides all that, the food is very good. Budgeteers will appreciate the inexpensive lunch served from noon to 2 p.m. Monday through Saturday (it's self-service), when starters like gigantic shrimp cocktail and marinated mussels, and main-course selections of salads, fish, chicken, etc. (served with side salad or french fries), go for NZ$1.75 ($1.17) to NZ$3.95 ($2.65). The à la carte menu at night features a nice selection at NZ$7 ($4.70) to NZ$9 ($6.04), served from 6 to 10 p.m.—and you must book ahead. From 6 to 9 p.m. there's a choice of three roast meats with vegetable and potato in the self-service Carvery for NZ$6 ($4.03); half price for children—and it isn't necessary to make reservations. Sunday-night family suppers are served from 5 to 8:30 p.m., also with a children's menu (no need to book ahead).

During my Dunedin stay to research this edition, Wilson Neill Wines and Spirits were getting things underway to open another restaurant, similar to Carnarvon Station but with an African theme (same moderate price range, I am assured). As yet unnamed, it will be in the **Bowling Green Hotel,** 71 Frederick St. (tel. 741-949), and I'm sure it will be worth stopping by if done with the same style, flair, and good food as Carnarvon Station. If you get there, drop me a note reporting on the new place.

My highest recommendation goes to the **Abbey Motor Lodge Restaurant,** 900 Cumberland St. (tel. 775-380). You'd want to save this for a special semi-splurge, since prices are a little higher than moderate (although not in the stratospheric range), but an evening at the Abbey is a real treat and well worth pinching some pennies in other areas. It's a lovely wood-paneled room with beamed ceilings, spacious seating, beautiful china and crystal table settings, and a Viennese chef. A cozy (and very popular) lounge bar adjoins, and is fun to visit before or after dinner. As for the food—it's superb. From the ribeye steak Madagascar (flamed with cognac and served in a green peppercorn sauce) to the noisettes of lamb à la niçoise to the venison steak Saint Hubertus, dinners are prepared and served to perfection. And what the chef does with fresh seafood can only be called fantastic—try the filet of sole stuffed with a shrimp and scallop mousse and poached in white wine. There's a dessert trolley which is an artistic as well as culinary triumph, liqueur coffees, and after-dinner cheese. Dinner prices are à la carte, with main courses ranging from NZ$8.50 ($5.70) to NZ$14.50 ($9.73). At lunch, light meals and salads (omelets, triple-decker sandwiches, etc.), grills, and fish are in the NZ$5.50 ($3.69) to NZ$7 ($4.70) range. For lunch or dinner, try not to miss this one. Fully licensed, with hours of noon to 2 p.m. and 6 to 10 p.m. every day.

THINGS TO SEE AND DO: First of all, if you find yourself in the vicinity of Water and Princes Streets, diagonally across from the CPO, you'll be standing on what was the waterfront back when the first settlers arrived in Dunedin and what had been a Maori landing spot for many years. Look for the **bronze plaque** that reads: "On this spot the pioneer settlers landed from a boat off the John Wickliffe on the 23rd day of March, 1848, to found the city and province." It's a good jumping off point for your exploration of the city as it is today.

Now, for all my fellow **bagpipe** lovers, let me suggest that your first order of business be to arrange to hear the lovely instruments while you're in this little bit of transported Scotland. You may be in town for a scheduled event when they're featured (inquire at the GTB), but if not, just take yourself to the **Otago Council Public Relations Office,** 119 Princes St. (or tel. 774-176), and ask for Marie—she'll do her best to get you to a pipe-band rehearsal, if nothing else (which could turn out to be more fun than a formal performance!). Now, on to regular sightseeing activities.

There are marvelous **scenic drives** around the city and out the peninsula, so stop by the GTB and request their brochures: Dunedin's *Golden Arrow Scenic Drive* and *The Otago Peninsula*. Both provide maps and clear directions, and the first is keyed to golden arrows along the route, which give you a good one-hour view of the city and its immediate environs. Most of the area's other major attractions are out on the 18-mile-long Otago Peninsula, a splendid drive with quiet harbor scenes on one side, the restless ocean on the other. If you aren't driving, Newtons Coachlines run excellent bus tours covering both routes, with stops for such attractions as Larnach Castle. Check with the GTB for departure times (that's the departure point for the tours as well). For the peninsula tour, adults pay NZ$10 ($6.71); children, NZ$5 ($3.36).

In the City

The **Otago Early Settlers' Association Museum and Portrait Gallery** (tel. 775-052) is a fascinating look back into the daily lives of Dunedin's first

European citizens. It's on Lower High Street, just down from the railway station. Look for the sole surviving kerosene streetlamp, one of many used on the city's major streets in 1865. Inside, there's a reconstructed blacksmith's shop, three period room reconstructions, *Josephine,* a Class E steam engine, which pulled the first Dunedin–Christchurch express, a Penny Farthing Cycle you can actually ride (although you won't go anywhere since it's held by a frame and mounted on rollers—still fun, though), and all sorts of other relics of life in these parts many years ago. In the Portrait Gallery, faded sepia photographs of early settlers peer down with stern visage at visitors—one has to wonder what they think of their progeny who wander through. Hours are 9 a.m. to 4:30 p.m. during the week, 10:30 a.m. to 4:30 p.m. on Saturday, and from October through March, 1:30 to 4:30 p.m. on Sunday. Adults pay NZ$1 (67¢); children NZ$.20 (13¢). There's a family ticket for NZ$2 ($1.34).

Olveston, (tel. 773-320), on Cobden Street off Queens Drive, is a "must see" of any Dunedin visit (the Golden Arrow Drive will take you right past it). It's one of the country's stately homes, fully furnished, open to the public—and it's magnificent. The double brick house is Jacobean in style, faced with Oamaru stone and Moeraki gravel, surrounded by an acre of tree-shaded grounds. A much-traveled and very prosperous businessman, a Mr. Theomin, built the 35-room home in 1904–1906, and it's as much a work of art as those works he gathered to house within its walls. The house was bequeathed to Dunedin in 1966, and there are now two caretaker families who live on the premises keeping everything in perfect condition. There are just under 300 oil portraits in Olveston, including those of some 37 New Zealand artists. The dining room's Regency table and Chippendale chairs are still set as they were for the first Plunket Society dinner, which was held here in 1907; in the butler's pantry you'll see Beleek and Wedgwood china, Delft pottery, and Waterford crystal. At every turn there is evidence of the comfort and convenience, as well as visual beauty, built into this home. Guided tours are conducted at 9:30 and 10:45 a.m., and 1:30, 2:45, and 4 p.m., and although reservations are not required, they are given preference. Admission for adults is NZ$2 ($1.34); for children, NZ$1 (67¢).

Don't miss a visit to the **Dunedin Public Art Gallery,** in Logan Park at the end of Anzac Avenue. It holds a huge painting by Frances Hodgkins, Dunedin born and considered to be the finest painter ever produced by New Zealand. In addition, there's a fine collection, which includes Rembrandt, Landini, Lorrain, and Monet, that was given to the gallery by Esmond de Beer, whose family has a long connection with Dunedin. Open 10 a.m. to 4:40 p.m. Monday through Friday, 2 to 5 p.m. on weekends and holidays.

The Otago Peninsula

There is an excellent Newtons Coachlines tour visiting Penguin Place, Glenfalloch, and the Albatross Colony (all described below) departing the GTB at 1:45 p.m. on Monday, Wednesday, and Saturday from January to April. Fares are NZ$14 ($9.40) for adults, half that for children (the Albatross Colony is optional, and an additional NZ$4, or $2.68 U.S.).

To explore the peninsula's 40 square miles, head out Portobello Road, which runs along the harbor. **Glenfalloch Gardens** (tel. 761-006) is a good morning or afternoon tea stop. At the 24-acre estate, allow time to wander through native bush, under English oaks, and among primroses. Glenfalloch is noted for its magnificent roses, azaleas, and rare rhododendrons. Light lunches as well as teas are available in the gardens outside the chalet, with strolling peacocks occasionally fanning their glorious plumage. The gardens are open daily from 10 a.m. to 4:30 p.m., and adults pay NZ$1 (67¢); children are admitted free.

Your next stop is **Larnach Castle** (tel. 761-302), about two miles north of the gardens and a bit inland (signposted). It's a neo-Gothic Victorian mansion right out of one of those old English movies, except much more grand than anything you've ever seen on film. William Larnach came from Australia in the late 1860s to found the first Bank of Otago. He began building the grandiose home (which he called "The Camp") in 1871 for his French heiress wife. It took 200 workmen three years to build the shell and a host of European master craftsmen another 12 years to complete the interior. Total cost: £125,000. Larnach's concept was to incorporate the very best from every period of architecture, with the result that the hanging Georgian staircase lives happily with Italian marble fireplaces, English tiles, and colonial-style verandas. One of the most magnificent examples of master craftmanship is the exquisite dining room ceiling, which took the master carver some 14 years to complete.

William Larnach died by suicide, after rising to the post of M.P. but suffering a series of personal misfortunes—committed in his typically dramatic fashion in a committee room in the Parliament Buildings in Wellington. After his death, the farm around the castle was sold off and the Crown used the castle as a mental hospital. Later it served as a cabaret, then a tourist resort. It is now the private home of Mr. and Mrs. Barry Barker, who found it in a thoroughly dilapidated condition in 1967 and have spent the intervening years lovingly restoring it to its original glory. Pick up a printed guide at the reception and wander as you choose, climbing the spiral staircase to battlements, which look out onto panoramic views, strolling through gardens and outbuildings. The stables now house hostel-type accommodations (see "Accommodations," above), but you're free to walk around its ground floor. Hours are 9 a.m. to 5 p.m. in winter, until dusk other seasons. Admissions (which fund restoration work) are NZ$3 ($2.01) for adults, NZ$1 (67¢) for children.

Other places you'll want to visit on the peninsula include a Maori church at Otakou; an excellent aquarium at the Portobello Marine Laboratory operated by the University of Otago near Quarantine Point, and the **Albatross Colony** at Taiaroa Head.

The magnificent royal albatross, perhaps with an instinctive distrust of the habitations of mankind, chooses remote, uninhabited islands as nesting grounds. With the single known exception, that is, of this mainland colony. The first egg was found here in 1920, and a sanctuary was promptly established. Today the colony consists of about a dozen pairs each year. You can make arrangements to view the birds (at a respectful distance) through the GTB, with a NZ$4 ($2.68) donation required to help with the sanctuary's maintenance.

Near the albatross colony is **Penguin Place,** where the dignified yellow-eyed penguin can be viewed sharing a coastline habitat with a frolicking southern fur seal colony. Admissions are NZ$2 ($1.34) for adults, NZ$.50 (33¢) for children. Book through the GTB.

SHOPPING: Dunedin offers excellent shopping. A few tips: Some of the cheapest **liquor** on sale in New Zealand can be purchased at the bottle shop at the Robbie Burns Hotel, 370 George St. The markup is also slight on New Zealand wines. Open Monday to Thursday 11 a.m. to 10 p.m., on Friday and Saturday until 11 p.m. The **Rehabilitation League** shop, for good-quality souvenirs, is centrally located at 115 George St. The **City Bookshop,** 21 Moray Pl., buys and sells secondhand volumes, specializing in New Zealand books.

Shops stay open to 9 p.m. on Thursday instead of Friday nights in South Dunedin and Port Chalmers.

AFTER DARK: The **Regent Theatre,** on the Lower Octagon (tel. 778-597), often has international artists such as Kris Kristofferson, Glen Campbell, Johnny Cash, and Rita Coolidge in performance. Check local newspapers or call the theater for current appearances. Tickets are in the neighborhood of NZ$13 ($8.72).

There are concerts—symphony, string quartets, piano soloists, etc.—from time to time in **Town Hall** (tel. 740-005), at Moray Place in the northwest Octagon.

The **Fortune Theatre,** on the corner of Stuart Street and Moray Place (tel. 778-323), presents theatrical performances in a century-old leithstone building, which was once the Trinity Methodist Church. Prices run from NZ$4 ($2.68) to NZ$8 ($5.37).

The **Tam O'Shanter** lounge bar in the Robbie Burns Hotel, 370 George St., is a favorite gathering spot for the younger set, where you'll find university students and the 9-to-5-ers making merry almost any night of the week. The **Plough Bar,** at the same address, has a quieter ambience, and the emphasis is on good conversation, which, while lively, is almost never loud. Take your pick, but don't miss dropping in at the Robbie Burns if you're a pub person.

At **Carnarvon Station,** in the Prince of Wales Hotel at 474 Princes St., there's live music in the courtyard every Friday and Saturday night.

DUNEDIN TO MOUNT COOK: The five-hour, 206-mile drive is on good roads, leaving Dunedin on Highway 1 and driving north through hills and along the coastline. Some 57 miles from Dunedin, you might want to stop at the **Mill House,** in Waianakrua (tel. Herbert 515), a handsome three-story stone building, which was once a flour mill, but is now a handsome restaurant and motel complex. The colonial-style dining room is beamed and attractively furnished, and lunches (from noon to 2 p.m.) are reasonably priced. There's a wine license, and it's open every day except Tuesday.

At **Pukeuri,** turn inland onto Highway 83, where the road rises slowly to reach Highway 8 at **Omarama,** where you begin to see the Southern Alps glistening in the distance. At Lake Pukaki township, you turn sharply left and take Highway 80 along the lake and Tasman River to the glacial beauty of Mount Cook.

2. Mount Cook

Tiny Mount Cook Village is known the world over for its splendid alpine beauty and its remoteness. It sits within the 173,000 acres of **Mount Cook National Park,** some 2510 feet above sea level and surrounded by 140 peaks over 7000 feet high, 22 over 10,000 feet, and the most famous of all the Southern Alps, Mount Cook, which soars 12,349 feet into the sky. A full third of the park is permanent snow and ice, and the famed **Tasman Glacier** is the longest known outside of arctic regions—18 miles long and 2 miles wide. More difficult to get onto than either Fox or Franz Josef, it is still accessible for guided strolls or for one exhilarating downhill swoop on skis.

The park's most noted plant is the mountain buttercup known as the Mount Cook lily, a pure-white blossom with thickly clustered petals and as many as 30 blooms to a stalk. There are, however, more than 300 species of native plants growing within park boundaries. Many have been marked by park rangers so you may identify them as you walk. Bird sounds fill the air, most notably that of the mischievous kea, that curious little native parrot, which has clearly earned the nickname "Clown of the Snowline." Most animal life has been introduced—Himalayan thar, chamois, and red deer. Hunting permits are issued by park rangers.

ORIENTATION: A T-intersection at the end of the highway marks the entrance to **Mount Cook Village.** Turn left and you pass the THC's Glencoe Lodge, a modern, moderately priced motor hotel, then the lower priced Mount Cook Motels, the youth hostel, post office, grocery shop, Alpine Guides Mountain Shop, and finally the **National Park Visitor Centre** (open daily 8 a.m. to 5 p.m.). Rangers can give you the latest information on weather and road conditions, and it's a strict requirement that trampers into the wild must check in with them. They can also fill you in on high-altitude huts, picnic grounds, and recommended walks in the area. During summer months and school holidays, they conduct guided walks and present excellent slide shows. Turn right at the intersection and you pass Mount Cook Chalets before reaching the elegant, peak-roofed, internationally famous Hermitage.

And that is Mount Cook Village—a singularly underdeveloped pocket for mankind in this glorious alpine terrain.

ACCOMMODATIONS: Most accommodations—at any price level—are owned by the THC, and the pickings are poor in the budget range. One alternative, if you're driving, however, is to book in at nearby locations: Fairlie, Tekapo, Ohau, Omarama, Otematata, and Kurow are all under a two-hour drive and all have motels aplenty, with well-equipped motor camps at Fairlie, Tekapo, Omarama, Otematata, and Kurow. Needless to say, with such a scarcity of rooms, advance booking is an absolute necessity!

A Hostel

There are 25 bunks in five rooms at this pretty alpine-style **YHA Hostel.** Cooking facilities are good, and there is a large common room, which is often used to accommodate half a dozen extra mattresses on the floor. Best of all, the large peaked window wall frames a fair share of that gorgeous snow-capped mountain scene. Booking is essential during summer months. Contact: Hostel Warden, P.O. Box 26, Mount Cook (tel. 820). Rates are NZ$3 ($2.01) for Seniors, NZ$1.50 ($1.01) for Juniors.

Camping

Camping and caravaning are permitted free in the park (*not* in the bush), but only at designated sites, which have water and toilets. If you use these facilities, remember that the lighting of fires is prohibited within park boundaries. Check with the Visitors Information Centre for locations and conditions. Hikers and mountaineers have the use of 12 huts in the park, all of which have stoves, cooking and eating utensils, fuel, blankets, and radios with emergency lines. Only two of these are within reach of the casual tramper—the others are at high altitudes and you would need to be an experienced, expert climber to reach them. Fees for overnight use of the huts are NZ$4 ($2.68) per person, and arrangements and payment must be made at the Visitors Information Centre.

Chalets

The THC-owned **Mount Cook Chalets** (tel. 809) are A-frame prefab structures, but are attractive, comfortable, and convenient, with fold-out couches and several bright chairs in the felt-floored living area. There's a hotplate, electric fry pan, and small fridge, bathroom facilities, and electric heaters. Two curtained-off sections hold two small bunks in each, and linen is provided. It's an efficient use of space, which manages to be pleasing to the eye as well. The complex includes parking space and a laundry with washers, dryers, and irons. Rates are NZ$35 ($23.49) double, NZ$7 ($4.70) per extra adult, and no charge for children under 12.

Motel Flats

Bookings for **Mount Cook Motel** (tel. 809) are handled through the Hermitage. Ceiling-high windows capture all that mountain beauty outside, and each of the 32 units can sleep up to six people. All units have full kitchens, table, chairs, and electric heater, and are nicely decorated in shades of brown and orange. No radio or TV, but there are laundry facilities and at-door parking. Rates are NZ$44 ($29.53) double, NZ$7 ($4.70) per extra adult, and no charge for children under 12. Even though you book through the Hermitage, you check in at Glencoe Lodge.

A Licensed Hotel

There are four budget rooms at the elegant (and expensive!) **THC Hermitage.** All are singles, and none has a view. They're rather basic, but all are papered and brightly decorated, have telephones, and are centrally heated. And you have the use of all those posh hotel facilities, just as if you were paying the regular tariff of NZ$72 ($48.32) to NZ$81 ($54.36) double. Instead, you'll be putting out only NZ$20 ($13.42).

MEALS: At Glencoe Lodge, the **MacDonald Room** serves a table d'hôte six-course dinner for NZ$18 ($12.08). They'll pack a picnic lunch of chicken, sandwiches, hard-boiled egg, cheese, and fruit for NZ$7.50 ($5.03).

The **Alpine Room** at the Hermitage serves a sumptuous smörgåsbord lunch (salads, cold meats, desserts), beautifully presented, for NZ$11 ($7.38)—breakfast costs a whopping NZ$9 ($6.04)!

Both these restaurants serve very good—and very splurgy—à la carte dinners featuring seafood and game.

Off the reception foyer of the Hermitage, you can get light meals, pies, cakes, sandwiches, tea, and coffee in the coffeeshop.

Budgeteers, however, will gravitate to the **food shop** in the Hermitage, which stocks ample supplies of dairy and canned goods, produce, frozen meats, and hot pies, and is open daily from 9 a.m. to 6 p.m.

THINGS TO SEE AND DO: No need to tell you what to see—it's all around you! And if you missed the **skiplane scenic flights** at Fox and Franz Josef, you'll have another chance here. The planes lift off some 2000 feet above sea level to begin an hour-long flight, which includes glimpses of Fox and Franz Josef and a five-minute snow walk; the less expensive 40-minute flight surveys the Tasman Glacier only. Fares are NZ$78 ($52.35) and NZ$55 ($36.91) respectively for adults, NZ$59 ($39.60) and NZ$41 ($27.52) respectively for children.

Skiers will undoubtedly head for the Tasman, but you should know that skiing is neither inexpensive nor for those whose expertise leaves *anything* to be desired! Skiing on the glacier involves two runs of about seven miles each, with skiplanes returning you to the top after the first run and flying you out at the end of the day. Before you embark on the great adventure, you'll have to convince the Alpine Guides that you're reasonably good on skis. The 1983 price for this glorious day to add to your ski tales was NZ$140 ($93.96)!! Another possible additional expense (several, in fact) lies in the fact that you may have to wait for the weather to break, which could be a few days, and that means additional lodging, eating, and drinking expense.

All those high-priced activities (and in my opinion, they're worth every penny if you have the pennies!) do *not* mean there are no budget activities at Mount Cook. First of all, the sheer grandeur of the place costs nothing and is there for all. Park rangers will furnish a map of **easy walks,** which take anywhere from half an hour to half a day—no charge, and you'll commune with Mother Nature all the way. Individual booklets are available to explain about the flora you'll be seeing. Also, there's a coach trip up the Tasman Valley to **Husky Flat,** with time to putter around the edge of the Tasman Glacier. It's an hour-and-a-half trip, with departures at 9 a.m., 11 a.m., and 2 p.m. Fares are NZ$13.50 ($9.06) for adults, half that for children.

Alpine Guides, opposite park headquarters, rents ski and climbing equipment, and can furnish guides to take you mountain climbing. There's a four-day hike, which leaves you at Fox Glacier via a transalpine crossing. These are *not,* however, budget activities.

READER'S SKIING TIP: "Book ahead for the glacier—as soon as you get to NZ, go to a travel agent, or write to Alpine Guides, Mt. Cook Ski Region, Mt. Cook, and arrange through them. Reserve all the days you plan to be at Mount Cook even though you will only ski on the Tasman one day. Also, the guides do not actually test you before going on the glacier. It is not really difficult skiing, but it is not for the beginner, either. If you are apprehensive about your ability, be able to describe your technique to the guide. They are expert at getting you down the mountain under all sorts of tricky conditions. Relax and enjoy it; you'll never recover from the scenery" (Candy Carter, Truckee, Calif.).

AFTER DARK: The liveliest spot after dark is the **Tavern** at the Hermitage, as campers and hostelers come crowding in after a day on the slopes in all that mountain air. Open only to THC residents (which includes motels and chalets), the **Snowline Bar** is more elegant and features more mountain views. The house bar at the Glencoe is the **Chamois Bar and Lounge.** That's Mount Cook Village's entire nightlife—maybe you should bring along some cards or a good book?

3. Mount Cook to Christchurch

This is about a five-hour drive of some 233 miles. Follow Highways 80 and 8 to **Fairville,** about 93 miles. At **Lake Tekapo,** take a minute to visit the chapel, whose altar is made from a large block of Oamaru stone and features a carved shepherd. The chapel was built of rock, wood, and stone from the area, and is dedicated to early settlers. Highway 79 takes you through **Geraldine** back to Highway 1, through the Canterbury plains filled with grazing sheep. And across the level terrain, you'll see the spires of Canterbury's capital, Christchurch, long before you arrive.

READER'S TOURING TIP: "We stopped in **Fairlie,** gateway to the MacKenzie High Country, around noon, hoping to find a good restaurant, preferably of the health-food orientation, for a light lunch. And we did. The **Sunflower Centre,** 31 Main St., is owned by Val Parker, who is assisted by her sisters Tui and Bette. Val travels throughout the country lecturing on whole-food cooking. We were cordially welcomed into their bright, clean, and attractively decorated restaurant where luncheon and teas are featured. We enjoyed a delicious quiche and salad of home-grown vegetables and greens. A varied menu of sandwiches of whole-grain breads, fruits, salads, good hearty soups, and freshly baked quiche is offered. The adjoining section of the restaurant displays local pottery, weaving, woodcrafts, and whole-food cookbooks" (Betty Henrikson, Edgartown, Mass.).

Chapter XI

CHRISTCHURCH

1. The City and Its Surroundings

CHRISTCHURCH IS AS ENGLISH as Dunedin is Scottish—in fact it's more so. Gothic buildings built of solid stone are everywhere, modern glass-and-concrete buildings scattered among them like afterthoughts. London's red buses are emulated here. English trees, brought out by settlers as a bit of home, flourish along the banks of the Avon River. A primary preoccupation of its citizenry is with private gardens of the English variety. And cricket, that most English of all sports, is played by all little Christchurch boys. One of its most prized appellations is that of the "Most English City Outside England."

It is also a prosperous city—New Zealand's second largest—staunchly conservative, with much to be proud of. An equitable climate (2120 hours of sunshine annually), an airport considered to be the finest in the country, civic centers and sports arenas that outshine all those in other New Zealand cities—all are factors in Christchurch's 20th-century image.

For the visitor, Christchurch offers sophisticated restaurants and entertainment, as well as excellent accommodations and a variety of sightseeing attractions.

1. The City and Its Surroundings

ORIENTATION: **Cathedral Square** is the center of things, the point from which to get your bearings. Above it rise the spires of the Gothic Anglican Christchurch Cathedral from whose tower you can look out over the flat, neatly laid-out city. The Avon River runs lazily through the heart of the city, spanned by no fewer than 37 bridges as it wends its 15-mile course from Ilam (to the west of Christchurch) to the sea. The graceful willows that line its banks are said to have come from Napoleon's graveside on St. Helena.

Colombo Street bisects Cathedral Square north to south and is the city's main thoroughfare. Local buses leave from the square, with zoned fares ranging from NZ$.30 (20¢) to NZ$.60 (40¢). During certain off-peak hours, fares are reduced by one-half (check with the Information Centre or local newspapers), and a ten-ride concession ticket is available. Driving can be difficult until you master the city's complex **one-way street system,** and since all on-street parking is metered, one of the following centrally located municipal parking buildings is your best bet: Oxford Terrace near Worcester, Manchester Street near Gloucester, and Lichfield Street near Durham. Check locally for the locations of others.

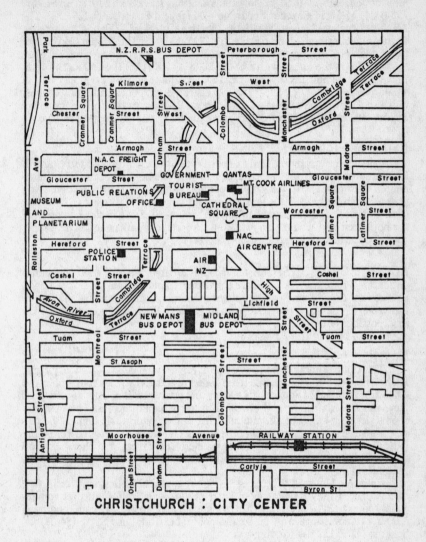

CHRISTCHURCH : CITY CENTER

USEFUL INFORMATION: Look for the **New Zealand Government Tourist Bureau** in the Government Life Building on Cathedral Square (tel. 794-900), open 8:30 a.m. to 5 p.m. Monday through Thursday, until 8 p.m. on Friday. . . . The **Canterbury Information Centre** is at 75 Worcester St. (tel. 799-629), with hours of 8:30 a.m. to 5 p.m. weekdays. The *Christchurch and Canterbury Official Guide* is published bimonthly by the Canterbury Promotion Council, distributed free of charge through hotels and the Information Centre, and gives up-to-date information on goings on in the city and surrounding area. . . . The **railway station** is on Moorhouse Avenue, south the city center. The NZRRS **bus depot** is on Victoria Street, north of Cathedral Square. For bus or train information, call 799-020. . . . **Newmans Coaches** leave from 110 Tuam St. (tel. 795-641); **Midland Coaches** depart 40-42 Lichfield St. (tel. 799-120). . . . The **Air New Zealand** ticket office is in the Bank of New Zealand Building on Cathedral Square at Colombo Street (tel. 797-000). . . . The **Mount Cook Lines** ticket office is at 91 Worcester St. (tel. 488-909). . . . Airport coaches leave from the west side of the square with a NZ$1.20 (81¢) fare. Call 794-260 for information. . . . You'll find **taxi ranks** at Cathedral Square and all terminals. To call a cab, phone 799-799 or 795-795. . . . There's a large, centrally located **post office** in Cathedral Square. . . . Two central 24-hour gas (petrol) stations are **Dallington**, at 712 Gloucester St., and **Blue Star**, at 515 Moorhouse Ave.

Christchurch Airport

Christchurch International Airport is the busiest in the country, and is located seven miles from Cathedral Square, out Memorial Avenue. The **Information Service Centre** will book accommodations and transportation at no charge. There's a cafeteria, snackbar, and fully licensed (expensive) restaurant; car-rental desks; three major banks with money-changing desks; hairdressers for both men and women; showers; and a large duty-free shop. The airport coach to Cathedral Square costs NZ$1.20 (81¢).

ACCOMMODATIONS: Christchurch has an abundance of good accommodations in all price ranges. Most are convenient to public transportation, a boon to those not driving who will be able to consider motels because of the ease of transport. Those using the Best Western Holiday Pass will find no fewer than nine possibilities.

Hostels

The **Cora Wilding Youth Hostel**, 9 Evelyn Couzins Ave., Avebury Park, Richmond (tel. 899-199), is on a tree-shaded residential street about a mile and a half from Cathedral Square. It's a lovely old white mansion with stained-glass panels in the front door and crowned by turrets and cupolas. There are six rooms sleeping 40, all bright and cheerful, and a comfortable lounge. To one side is a large parking area, and in the rear, a children's playground across the park. The laundry has coin-operated washers and dryers, and there's a shop selling food and provisions. Rates for Seniors are NZ$5 ($3.36); for Juniors, NZ$2.50 ($1.68).

Rolleston House, 5 Worcester St., on the corner of Rolleston Avenue, (tel. 66-564), is centrally located, about a five-minute walk from Cathedral Square. Eight rooms hold 47 beds, and there's a kitchen, laundry and drying room, and a dining room/lounge with piano and pool table. Rates are NZ$6 ($4.03) for Seniors; NZ$3 ($2.01) for Juniors.

The **Latimer Hostel**, 268 Madras St. (tel. 798-429), was once a YWCA but is now a privately run hostel and B&B with a young, enthusiastic management. The free courtesy van tries to meet every plane, bus, or train arrival (if you don't see it, telephone them). This is a large red-brick building with white trim, and rooms are nicely done up. There's a guest lounge with TV, kitchen, tea facilities, laundry with a drying room, dryer, ironing board, and sewing machine. In winter electric heaters are put into rooms. Accommodations are of the dormitory (sleeping bag) and single- and double-room variety, and all rates include bed and breakfast. For sleeping bag accommodations, the rate is NZ$6.50 ($4.36) per night; single rooms are NZ$12.50 ($8.39); doubles are NZ$20 ($13.42); and there are weekly rates of NZ$42 ($28.19) single and

NZ$69 ($46.31) double. Manager John Ryder will give a 10% discount on the first night's accommodation with the presentation of this book.

Cabins

Russley Park Motor Camp, 372 Yardhurst Rd. on State Highway 73 (tel. 427-021), is only two miles from the airport, close to Riccarton Racecourse, and about six miles west of Cathedral Square. Ten chalets in a green, grassy setting are all individual dark-timber structures with slanted roofs and natural light-wood interiors. All have foam mattresses, floor mats, jugs, toasters, cooker, dishes and cutlery, cooking utensils, and electric heaters. Small chalets sleep three in two single beds and one upper bunk. The large ones will sleep five in two singles, one double, and one upper bunk, and have dividing curtains for privacy, as well as a small front porch. Also available are three deluxe chalets (same as the large, but with H&C and fridge). Tourist chalets sleep five, with two separate rooms plus kitchen, lounge, shower, toilet, two-ring rangette, electric fry pan, and blankets (linen is for hire). Amenities include a modern shower/toilet block (bath for ladies), kitchen, TV lounge and pool room, spa pool, children's play area, laundry with automatic washing machines and dryer. There's a food shop close by. Caravan and campsites are also available. Rates for cabins are NZ$12 ($8.05) double, NZ$3.50 ($2.35) for additional adults, NZ$2 ($1.34) for children. Camp and caravan sites are NZ$6 ($4.03). Sheets and blankets can be hired. Take the Riccarton no. 8 bus.

The Y

The **YMCA,** 12 Hereford St. (tel. 60-689), is a centrally located, recently renovated complex of three buildings—one contains the pool, sauna, gym, etc., and two hostel buildings house 65 young men (limited accommodations for young women) in single rooms. All have a desk, chest of drawers, closet, and electric heater. Tea facilities are provided, and there are two tidy TV lounges, pool tables, and a dart board, as well as a washing machine. Age limits are 16 to 35, but the friendly managers, Bruce and Isabel Morris, are flexible on that issue. YMCA facilities are available to all guests at reduced rates. Breakfast during the week is a full, cooked affair; it's continental on weekends. Rates are NZ$15 ($10.06) per person, and dinner costs NZ$5 ($3.36). Full board (breakfast and dinner) is NZ$60 ($40.27) weekly. Send a NZ$10 ($6.71) deposit to the YMCA, P.O. Box 2004, Christchurch, to book in advance.

Bed and Breakfast

Wolseley Lodge, 107 Papanui Road, near Bealey Avenue (tel. 556-202), is within walking distance of the city center, a lovely old green-and-white home set in a flower-filled, tree-shaded lawn. There are 13 rooms in this stately, elegant house, all with H&C and nicely furnished. All have electric blankets and reading lamps. The lounge has overstuffed chairs and TV, and the dining room overlooks the garden. There's a guest kitchen for making tea, and a laundry with washer, dryer, and ironing board. A large parking lot is in the rear. Susan and Owen Roberts are the charming hosts. Rates for B&B are NZ$18.50 ($12.42) per person (reduced rates for children). The optional three-course dinner is NZ$12 ($8.05)

Don Evans, the charming—and caring—host at **Windsor Private Hotel,** 52 Armagh St., off Cranmer Square (tel. 61-503), has built a devoted following, primarily beacause of his personal interest in all his guests. The carefully renovated, rambling old brick home has 37 rooms (some with H&C), all nicely decorated. Hallways are heated for the trip to conveniently placed bathrooms. The TV lounge holds lots of chairs and stacks of magazines, and there are tea facilities as well as a laundry. Breakfast often includes omelets or some other special item. Parking off the street is available. Bed-and-breakfast rates are NZ$19 ($12.75) per person, with slight reductions for parties of three or four. Children pay half.

The **Hereford Private Hotel,** 36 Hereford St., opposite the Arts Centre (tel. 799-536), is just one block away from the city center. There's no H&C in the clean, comfortable, high-ceilinged rooms, but toilets and baths are ample and conveniently located. The large, window-lined TV lounge is light and airy, and there's a second, smaller telly room, as well. Guests have full use of the kitchen facilities, and separate tea facilities are provided. A single room (with breakfast) costs NZ$10 ($6.71); doubles, NZ$17.50 ($11.75). Call them from terminals for free transport to the hotel.

John and Mary Mills run the homey **Aarangi Guest House,** 15 Riccarton Rd. (tel. 438-504), a two-story white house with a car park at the rear. Rooms have H&C, electric blanket, and electric heat. There's a TV lounge furnished in a comfortable, family style, and the dining room is small, but cozy. Close by is a laundromat and a large, American-style shopping mall. The airport coach stops just outside the door. Rates for bed and breakfast are NZ$15 ($10.06) per person, and you can have the evening meal for NZ$6 ($4.03).

Finally, two charming Kiwi housewives who are neighbors offer bed and breakfast in their private homes on a quiet, residential street just a block off a major bus line. Guests are welcomed into the family at both, with a good deal of personal attention (lots of help on what to see and do). **Mrs. Kaye Stokes,** 29 Clissold St. (tel. 556-951), has a recently renovated home with flower-filled front sun porch, lots of rimu paneling and antique furnishings, and two nice double rooms. No H&C, and the bathroom is at the foot of the stairs. **Mrs. Roberta Conway,** 11 Clissold St. (tel. 554-806), has one double room. The charge for this kind of one-on-one Kiwi family hospitality is NZ$15 ($10.06) per person, including breakfast.

Motel Flats

Units at the **Alexandra Court Motel,** 960 Colombo St. (tel. 61-855), are spacious and nicely decorated, have outside patios, and all bathrooms come with both bathtub *and* shower (important to me, since a long soak can work wonders at the end of a long day of travel). There's an electric fireplace (complete with mantel) in each unit, which makes for a homey atmosphere, and equipment includes an iron and ironing board in addition to such standards as color TV, radio, and phone. The guest laundry also holds a dryer. One-bedroom units can sleep up to four; those with two bedrooms will sleep six. All have complete kitchens. There's at-your-own-door parking, with covered car ports, at all except four units (with covered parking space for those across the courtyard). Judith and Lester Walker, the friendly owners, are extremely helpful in such matters as delivery of rental cars, same-day dry cleaning, and sightseeing information. The no. 4 city bus stops out front, and there's a Cobb & Co. restaurant close by, as well as a swimming pool and golf course. This is a Best Western, so Holiday Pass discounts apply to the rates of NZ$34 ($22.82) single, NZ$38 ($25.50) double. During holidays, minimum rates apply, and there's a surcharge.

Just six blocks from Cathedral Square, the **City Court Motel,** 850 Colombo St., on the corner of Salisbury Street (tel. 69-099), welcomes families with children. There's a one-bedroom unit and five with two bedrooms (two large enough to sleep eight). A bonus here is the washing machine in every unit. The immaculate and spacious units all have large kitchens, color TV, electric heater and blanket, and bathtub. The lawn holds a picnic table and a children's play area, and there's a seven-day food store just across the street. Babysitters can be arranged. Rates are NZ$26 ($17.45) single, NZ$28 ($18.79) double.

The **Holiday Lodge,** 862 Colombo St. (tel. 66-584), has 15 spacious and immaculate two-bedroom units, housed in two blocks on either side of a parking lot. Those in a yellow stucco building are all duplexes with bedrooms and a glassed-in sun porch upstairs. All units have color TV, telephone, radio, electric blanket, electric heater, and bath with tub and shower. There's daily maid service, a laundry, and a children's play area. Rates for singles are NZ$26 ($17.45); for doubles, NZ$28 ($18.79). Surcharge.

Within easy walking distance of Cathedral Square, the **Belmont Luxury Motel,** 168 Bealey Ave. (tel. 794-037), consists of one U-shaped block of units arranged around a flower-bordered lawn and a town-house-style two-story structure, all set back from the street for quietness. Interior decoration in these units is of the highest standard—one of the most tastefully done-up motels I've seen in New Zealand—and each unit has full carpeting, kitchen, innerspring mattresses, electric blanket, telephone, radio, color TV, and individual electric heating. There are bedsitters and one- and two-bedroom units, and family units accommodate up to five comfortably. There's a laundry on the premises, and a seven-day food store just down the street, but the motel can supply a pre-packed meal ready for heating, as well as a continental breakfast (both at extra charges, of course). Rates are NZ$40 ($26.85) for one or two persons. This is a Best Western, so Holiday Pass discounts apply to all rates. Surcharge.

Another attractive Best Western is the **Diplomat Motel,** 127 Papanui Rd. (tel. 556-009), with 16 units set in grounds, which are lavishly planted and landscaped. There are bedsitters and two-bedroom combinations, all of ample size and nicely decorated, with full kitchen, color TV, radio, and telephone. All have beamed ceilings, writing desks, and private patios. A heated swimming pool (including one for toddlers) and a luxurious spa in a Swedish-type setting are on the grounds. Rates are NZ$36 ($24.16) single, NZ$40 ($26.85) double. Surcharge. BW discounts apply.

MEALS: There are two **Cobb & Co.** restaurants in Christchurch. These are the family-style restaurants with colonial decor, which serve excellent meals at moderate prices (main courses average NZ$5.50, or $3.69 U.S.). They're fully licensed and serve from 7:30 a.m. until 10 p.m. You'll find them at the Caledonian Hotel, 101 Caledonian Rd. (tel. 66-034), and the Bush Inn, on the corner of Waimairi and Riccarton Roads (tel. 487-175).

The **Shades Tavern** is right in the center of things, upstairs at the Shades Shopping Precinct, Cashel Street, City Mall (tel. 50-859), and has something for everyone in one of the most pleasant settings in town. Lots of light woods, diamond-paned windows, capiz-shell lampshades, an open fire in the lower (mezzanine) level, wide windows with a view on the top level, and the Boatshed Bar and pretty garden room on the main level. Even more pleasant than the setting is the staff, a collection of Kiwis who seem genuinely interested in all their customers, from the youngest to the oldest. In fact, children are catered to here with really caring service. That's not to say this place lacks sophistication, for it doesn't. In short (after being longwinded!), this turned out to be one of my favorite stopping places in Christchurch, even if just for a cup of coffee, when you're given the same top-flight service as if ordering the most expensive meal. The menu is an extensive one, with such offerings as spaghetti bolognese, deep-fried chicken, roast chicken with mushroom sauce, wienerschnitzel, ribeye steak (in three varieties), a crockpot, salads (including a vegetarian salad), and a long list of sweets. And hot, fresh-baked bread is on the menu. Prices run from NZ$1.50 ($1.01) to NZ$10 ($6.71), with most main courses in the NZ$5.50 ($3.69) to NZ$7 ($4.70) range. There's a children's menu at about NZ$2 ($1.34), and half meals are available on request. Fully licensed. Hours are 11 a.m. to 8 p.m. Sunday through Wednesday, until 10 p.m. on Thursday, Friday, and Saturday. Highly recommended.

The elegant dining room at the **Town Hall,** on Kilmore Street between Colombo and Victoria Streets, serves a beautiful and bounteous smörgåsbord from noon to 2 p.m. Monday through Friday. Floor-to-ceiling windows look out on the sphere-shaped fountains, and the groaning board is set with an inviting display of salads, meats, hot dishes, fruit, sweets, and cheeses. The price is NZ$9 ($6.04), and there's a low-cost family menu from 5:30 to 7:45 p.m. starting at NZ$6.50 ($4.36). From 8 to 10:30 p.m., Monday through Saturday, it's a full à la carte menu from NZ$8 ($5.37), and there's a late-supper serving from 10:30 to 11:30 p.m. Monday through Saturday from NZ$6 ($4.03). Licensed.

The **Gardens Restaurant** (tel. 65-076), in the Botanic Gardens, is in an octagonal red-brick building with wrap-around windows looking out to the gardens—a delightful place to eat. The garden-like interior has green rugs with white garden-type furniture and fringed Victorian lampshades hanging from the domed white wood ceiling. You can park under the trees at the Armagh Street entrance and walk over the rustic bridge to reach the restaurant. Lovely morning and afternoon teas are served, and a NZ$5 ($3.36) smörgåsbord lunch is set up under a yellow awning. After lunch, take a ride on the Toast Rack, an electric tram with upright seats (from whence the name), for a half-hour tour of the gardens. Tours leave the restaurant daily at regular intervals, September to May, weather permitting. The restaurant is a popular one, so it's a good idea to phone ahead to reserve. Lunch is served every day from noon to 2 p.m.

Meals at the **Coachman Inn Restaurant,** 144 Gloucester St. (tel. 793-476), are excellent value. This is an attractive room with rustic interior, lots of natural brick, heavy dark-stained timber beams, and lighting by old-fashioned lanterns. The Coachman specializes in steaks, and has won the New Zealand Restaurant Association Award of Excellence. Prices for peppered porterhouse, T-bone, garlic sirloin, lamb chops, and pork chops range from NZ$4.70 ($3.15) to NZ$6.50 ($4.36). Tender, juicy steak sandwiches are on the menu at NZ$3.95 ($2.65), and there's a nice variety of entrees and desserts. It's fully licensed, and there's an adjoining bar for a pre- or after-dinner drink. Hours are 7:30 a.m. to 11 p.m., seven days a week.

The **Coffee Pot Restaurant,** 16 New Regent St. (tel. 790-087), is run by a charming couple, Vince and Yolande Grant, and ranks high among Christchurch's budget eateries. Main courses of roast (pork, beef, or lamb), fried chicken, ham, and fish are accompaneid by four vegetables, plus mashed or roast potatoes, and range in price from NZ$5 ($3.36) to NZ$6 ($4.03). Half portions are available on request. Lovely desserts like hot apple pie and custard, ice-cream sundaes, pavlovas, trifle and cream from NZ$1.75 ($1.17) to NZ$3 ($2.01). Lunch is served from noon to 2 p.m. Tuesday through Friday; dinner, from 5 to 9 p.m. Tuesday through Sunday. Closed Monday. BYO.

I'll have to confess right here that there must be a little Greek in my soul, and perhaps that colored my enjoyment of **Mykonos Taverna,** 112a Lichfield St. (tel. 797-452). However, it certainly didn't affect my judgment of the food—there's Greek food, and then there's Greek food, and I fancy I know the best when it comes my way. The home-style cooking here is as good as any I've ever had, from the classic moussaka to souvlakiarni (barbecued kebab with lamb, onions, capsicums, and tomatoes) to the flaky, sweet baklava for dessert. Marika, mother of Paul Chisnall, one of the owner-partners here, is responsible for the delectable meals, many from recipes handed down in her own family. The restaurant is aptly named, for once you climb the stairs in the converted warehouse and enter Mykonos, you're in an authentic taverna setting, with plain white walls, simple wooden tables and chairs, photographs and wall hangings from Greece, and candles and fresh flowers on the tables. And if you come along on Wednesday, Friday, or Saturday, there's a three-piece Greek band (bouzouki and all) whose lively music draws patrons, waiters and waitresses, and kitchen staff out onto the floor for dancing. This popular place is pretty crowded on Friday and Saturday night, yet you're never hurried—it's a place to relax, stuff yourself on overgenerous portions, and loiter a while. Prices are in the NZ$8 ($5.37) to NZ$9 ($6.04) range for main courses, and there's a cover charge of NZ$2 ($1.34) on music nights, a minimum charge of NZ$10 ($6.71) on Friday and Saturday. Bring your own wine to wash down all that good food. Hours are 6 to 11 p.m. Tuesday through Saturday, and you'd best reserve ahead.

A Big Splurge

You'll be dining in magnificent Gothic splendor at **Grimsby's,** Cranmer Courts, on the corner of Kilmore and Montreal Streets (tel. 799-040). The marvelous old stone building was opened in 1876 as Christchurch Normal School, which operated until 1954, when it became the Post Primary Department of Christchurch Teacher's College until 1970. After that it lay vacant and was severely vandalized until developers took it in hand in 1980 to create co-op apartments in one wing and this elegant restaurant on the ground floor. You enter through heavy wooden doors into a medieval hall, thence into a high-ceilinged dining room beautiflly furnished, with tables resplendent in crisp white linen, exquisite china, crystal, and silverware. Classical music plays softly in the background. Service is as elegant as the surroundings, and the food is worth every effort involved in managing a splurge meal. The cuisine is English and French, and lunch offerings might be sole amandine, lamb noisettes, or entrecôte Café de Paris, while the dinner menu features beef steak and oyster pudding, beef Wellington, roast venison, scallops Parisienne, and rack of Canterbury lamb. Lunch prices run from NZ$7.50 ($5.03) to NZ$9.50 ($6.38) for main courses on the à la carte menu, with omelets at NZ$5.50 ($3.69). At dinner, the price range is NZ$9.50 ($6.38) to NZ$16 ($10.74) for main courses. Lunch hours are 11:30 to 2 p.m. Monday through Friday; dinner, 6 to 10:30 p.m. Monday through Saturday. BYO. Highly recommended—you'll have had a Big Splurge of true elegance after a meal at Grimbsby's!

READER'S MEAL SELECTION: "The **Darfield Tavern,** in Darfield, a small town 45 kilometers east of Christchurch on Highway 73 going to Arthur's Pass National Park, serves lunch from noon to 2:30 p.m. and includes a choice of ham steak, chicken, or sausages. Platters contain coleslaw and a generous serving of delicious chips (fries). The tavern is clean and well lighted, and during lunch hour is filled with locals in for a pint of brew, all of whom are interested in talking to Americans" (Kenneth Ogren, Oakland, Calif.).

THINGS TO SEE AND DO: Your first stop should be at the **Information Centre,** 75 Worcester St. (opposite Noah's Hotel), to look over their exhaustive supply of informative brochures on Christchurch and all of Canterbury. Look for the *Riverside Scenic Walk* brochure, and especially if you're driving, pick up a copy of their inexpensive guide to *Canterbury Picnic Spots.*

In Cathedral Square, climb the 133 steps in the 120-foot **Christchurch Cathedral** tower for a splendid panoramic view of the city and its environs. Adults pay NZ$.30 (20¢); schoolchildren, NZ$.20 (13¢). The cathedral is open from 9 a.m. to 4 p.m. weekdays and Saturday, 12:30 to 4:30 p.m. on Sunday.

There are many good **coach tours** for seeing the city and its surroundings, the best and least expensive being those given by the **Transport Board's Red Buses,** which leave Victoria Square daily at 2 p.m. One tour takes you through the garden suburbs and past impressive city buildings for fares of NZ$5.15 ($3.46) for adults, NZ$2.65 ($1.78) for children. Then there's one which takes the spectacular Summit Road to Lyttelton Harbour, with panoramas of snow capped Alps, plains, and sea, includes a launch trip on the harbor, and makes a stop at the baronial Sign of the Takahe for tea on the way back. Adult fare is NZ$6.70 ($4.50); children pay NZ$3.35 ($2.25). Highly recommended.

You can also make these tours with the help of Information Centre brochures, which give explicit directions. There are also excellent **walks,** both inside the city limits and beyond, with pamphlets available from the center to direct you.

You'll really catch the flavor of Merrie Olde England if you paddle a canoe down the lovely **Avon River,** which is landscaped its entire length. Canoes are for rent at NZ$1.50 ($1.01) per hour from **Antigua Boatsheds,** Cambridge Terrace (tel. 65-885), as they have been from this same company for over a century. Open daily 10 a.m. to 4 p.m.

Christchurch's flat terrain invites **cycling,** and bike lanes are marked off in several parts of the city, including parks. Parking lots even include bike racks. Join the bikers by renting from **Rent-a-Bike,** 82 Worcester St. (tel. 64-409), at NZ$1 (67¢) an hour, NZ$4 ($2.68) per day.

Among the interesting places to visit in the city are: **Canterbury Museum,** on Rolleston Avenue (tel. 68-379), which has an excellent permanent Antarctica exhibit, along with New Zealand birds, Oriental art, Maori culture, and a recreation of a 19th-century Christchurch street. Hours are 10 a.m. to 4:30 p.m. Monday through Saturday, 2 to 4:30 p.m. on Sunday. Admission is free, although they are grateful for donations. The museum is at the entrance to the 75-acre **Botanic Gardens,** where show houses display tropical plants, ferns, mosses, and a comprehensive collection of cacti and succulents. It's impressive in the spring, when there are hosts of daffodils. Hours are 7 a.m. to sundown for the gardens, 10 a.m. to 4 p.m. for the show houses. Within the gardens, you'll find the **McDougall Art Gallery,** which holds an impressive collection of Australasian and European art, with constantly changing exhibits. Hours are 10 a.m. to 4:30 p.m. Monday through Friday, 1 to 5:30 p.m. on Saturday and Sunday. In the same area, there's the **Arts Centre,** on Worcester Street off Rolleston Avenue (tel. 60-989). They offer live professional theater nightly, a craft workshop, gallery, two restaurants, and from time to time working craftspeople who will demonstrate their work.

The 100-acre, 15,000-square-foot **Ferrymead Historic Park,** 269 Bridle Path Rd., Heathcote (tel. 841-708), holds a fascinating collection of vintage cars, railway and fire engines, etc., in an old-style township. Take Ferry Road south and make the first right turn after Heathcote Bridge. If you're not driving, the no. 3 bus from Cathedral Square will get you there. It's open daily from 10 a.m. to 4 p.m., and admission is NZ$2.50 ($1.68) for adults, NZ$1.50 ($1.01) for children (under 5, free).

Christchurch **gardens** are known throughout the country, and there is fierce competition every year between neighborhoods. To view some of these glorious gardening achievements, visit **Royds Street,** opposite Boys' High, which has won the competition for many years running. In the business community, it's the exquisite garden at **Sanitarium Health Food Company,** 54 Harewood Rd. off Papanui, which comes out on top time and time again. However, just about any street you stroll will display garden patches of exceptional beauty, and if you express your delight in seeing them, the nearest gardener will have you deep in conversation in no time flat!

Christchurch is the American supply base and communication center for **Operation Deep Freeze,** a scientific study program in Antarctica, some 2000 miles to the south. As a result, there's a steady flow of air force and navy personnel through the city. It is sometimes possible to tour the base, and if you're interested, contact the Public Relations Officer, Operation Deep Freeze, Christchurch Airport (tel. 583-079).

The **Willowbank Wildlife Reserve,** 60 Hussey Rd. (tel. 596-226), is a delightful natural park and zoo in a Maori village, only 15 minutes' drive from the city center. Take Papanui Road to Main North Road, turn left into John's Road, then left at Gardiners Road. It's open daily from 10 a.m. to 6 p.m., and adults pay NZ$2 ($1.34); children, NZ$1 (67¢).

If you're driving, take a day and visit the picturesque village of **Akaroa,** 52 miles east at the tip of the Banks Peninsula. It was settled by the French in 1840 and its street names reflect its roots. A beautiful drive to a delightful village.

SHOPPING: The **Rehabilitation Servicemen's Shop,** 146 Gloucester St., has a limited, but very good, selection of souvenirs. You'll find the **Duty-Free Shop** at the corner of Gloucester and Colombo Streets, one block from Cathedral Square, with a huge selection of items (much larger than at either international airport). Shops in the nearby suburb of **New Brighton,** five miles east of Cathedral Square, are open for Saturday shopping until 9 p.m.

AFTER DARK: For current after-dark happenings, check the *Tourist Times, Christchurch and Canterbury Visitors' Guide* (which has the largest theater listings), or *What's On in Christchurch.* You'll find several pubs in the city (which are constantly changing) listed that have music and dancing.

In the **Arts Centre,** there is a Jazz Cellar with music and dancing from 9:30 pm. on Saturday. You bring your own wine, and there's a small cover charge.

Mykonos Taverna (see "Meals") is an after-dark event on Friday and Saturday night if you're a lover of Greek music and dancing. And the **Coachman Inn cocktail lounge,** at 144 Gloucester St., has live entertainment Wednesday through Sunday from 6 p.m. to 1:30 a.m.

Chapter XII

THE ABC's OF NEW ZEALAND

LISTED BELOW ARE SOME of those everyday practical details which can produce a first rate boondoggle if you don't have them at hand when traveling in a foreign country.

ACCIDENT COMPENSATION: As a visitor to New Zealand, you are automatically covered, from the time you arrive until you leave, by the same no-fault accident compensation plan as Kiwis. And it doesn't cost you one red cent! Benefits include compensation for reasonable expenses directly resulting from the accident, such as medical and hospital expenses, as well as lump-sum payments for permanent incapacity. No matter if the accident was your fault or not, you'll be covered 24 hours a day. Benefits are determined by the Accident Compensation Commission, and the State Insurance Office handles claims. Their head office is in Wellington, and you should contact them immediately if you should—God forbid!—have an accident.

AMERICAN EMBASSY: The Embassy of the United States of America is at 29 Fitzherbert Terrace (Thorndon), Wellington (tel. 722-068). Hours are 8:15 a.m. to 5 p.m.

AMERICAN EXPRESS: There are American Express offices at 95 Queen St., Auckland (tel. 798-243), and 226 High St., Christchurch (tel. 66-772). They will accept mail for clients (you're a client if you have an American Express credit card or their travelers checks), forward mail for a small fee, issue and change travelers checks, and replace lost or stolen travelers checks and American Express credit cards.

BANKING HOURS: Banks in international airports are open for all incoming and outgoing flights; others are open 10 a.m. to 4 p.m. Monday through Friday.

CIGARETTES: You can bring in 200 cigarettes per person, as allowed by Customs regulations. Most brands for sale in New Zealand are English or European, although more and more American brands are appearing on the market.

ELECTRICAL APPLIANCES: New Zealand's voltage is 230 volts, and plugs are the three-pin flat type. If your hair dryer or other small appliances are different, you'll need a converter/adapter. Most motels and better hotels have built-in wall converters for 110-volt, two-prong razors, but if you're going to be staying in hostels, cabins, or guest houses, better bring a converter/adapter.

EMERGENCIES: Dial 111 anyplace in New Zealand for police, ambulance, or to report a fire.

FILM: Film is expensive in New Zealand, so bring as much as you can with you. You're not limited by Customs regulations, just by baggage space. Most brands are available in larger cities.

HAIRDRESSING: Prices are reasonable to cheap, and neither barbers nor hairdressers will be looking for a tip.

HOLIDAYS: Kiwis love a long holiday weekend, so most holidays are juggled to fall on a Friday or Monday—sometimes including both days. They will be a big factor in the availability of accommodations, since everybody and his brother packs up and goes to another part of the country at the drop of a long weekend. Banks and most shops close for national holidays. National holidays are listed below:

January: New Year's Day
February: New Zealand Day, February 6 (the date the Treaty of Waitangi was signed)
April: Good Friday, Easter, Easter Monday (and in some counties, the following Tuesday); ANZAC Day, April 25 (the date on which New Zealand and Australian troops landed in Gallipoli in 1915)
June: Queen's Birthday (first Monday)
October: Labour Day (last Monday)
December: Christmas Day and Boxing Day (December 26)

Individual regions celebrate their date of founding with Anniversary Days, which are usually rearranged, if necessary, to fall on a Monday.

During school holidays (Christmas through the beginning of February), the entire population of New Zealand seems to be on the move. Families usually holiday together (annual office leaves fall within this period, as a rule), and many book as much as a year in advance in popular resort areas. There are two-week school holidays in May and in August when the same thing happens, although to a lesser degree.

KIWI: Has two meanings: if not spelled with an initial capital, it means that round-bottomed, long-beaked, nonflying bird, which has become New Zealand's symbol; when there's a capital "K," it means a native New Zealander, and it's used with the utmost affection.

LANGUAGE: English is spoken by all New Zealanders, Maori and Pakeha. You'll hear Maori spoken on some TV and radio programs and in some Maori settlements, but it's seldom used in conversation in the presence of overseas visitors.

LAUNDRY: No matter if you'll be staying in hostels or motels, there will usually be a well-equipped laundry on the premises for your use. Cities have commercial laundromats, but most visitors have little need for them.

MAIL DELIVERY: New Zealand post offices will receive mail for you and hold it for a month. Just have it addressed to you c/o Chief Post Office of the city or town you'll be visiting. American Express will receive and forward mail for its clients.

MEDICAL ATTENTION: Not free like accident compensation, but so inexpensive by comparison to costs elsewhere that it would almost pay to get sick while in New Zealand! Medical facilities are excellent and health care of a very high standard. Pharmacies observe regular local shop hours, but each locality usually will have an Urgent Pharmacy, which remains open until about 11 p.m. every day except Sunday, when there will be two periods during the day it's open. You'll find them listed in local telephone directories. There's a minimal extra charge for prescriptions filled during nonshop hours. Should you need a doctor, either consult the Government Tourist Bureau or prevail on your motel or guest house host to direct you to one.

METRIC MEASURES: New Zealand uses the metric system of weights and measures, and listed below are some of the conversions you may want to know:

> *1 kilometer* = ⅝ mile (1 mile = 1 3/5 kilometers). A simple way to figure miles is to divide kilometers by 8, then multiply by 5
> *50 m.p.h.* = 80 k.p.h.
> *1 meter* = 39 + inches (about 3 ¼ feet, or a little over a yard)
> *1 kilogram* = 2.2 pounds (1 pound = 0.45 kilograms)
> *1 gram* = 0.035 ounces (1 ounce = 28 grams)
> *1 U.S. gallon* = 3.8 liters

OFFICE HOURS: Usually 9 a.m. to 5 p.m., Monday through Friday.

PAKEHA: The Maori word for "fair-skinned people," which has come to mean all New Zealanders of European descent. There's nothing derogatory in its use.

POSTAGE: Rates run as follows:

	To Australia	To USA	To UK/Europe
Airmail (10 grams)	NZ$.40 (27¢)	NZ$.58 (39¢)	NZ$.70 (47¢)
Aerogrammes	NZ$.35 (23¢)	NZ$.40 (27¢)	NZ$.45 (30¢)
Surface (20 grams)	NZ$.30 (20¢)	NZ$.35 (23¢)	NZ$.35 (23¢)
Postcards	NZ$.40 (27¢)	NZ$.58 (39¢)	NZ$.70 (47¢)

PUB HOURS: 11 a.m. to 10 p.m.; closed Sundays. The drinking age is 20 in pubs, 18 in licensed restaurants.

RADIO AND TV: The BCNZ (Broadcasting Council of New Zealand) is the major broadcaster in New Zealand, operating TV Channel 1 and TV Channel 2, both color since 1974, and Radio New Zealand. The majority of TV productions come from Britain and America, and you'll be surprised and pleased to know that commercials are never shown on Sunday! Television transmission hours are 11:30 a.m. to 11 p.m. Sunday through Thursday, and 10 a.m. to 12:30 a.m. on Friday and Saturday.

RESTROOMS: There are "public conveniences" strategically located and well signposted in all cities and many small towns. You'll find public restrooms at most service stations. Local *Plunket Rooms* are a real boon to mothers traveling with small children, for they come with a "Mother's Room" where you can change diapers and do any necessary tidying up. The Plunket Society is a state-subsidized organization, which provides free baby care to all New Zealand families, and their volunteers are on duty in the Plunket Rooms—no charge, but they'll welcome a donation.

SHOP HOURS: Usually 9 a.m. (sometimes 8 a.m.) to 5:30 p.m. Monday through Thursday, until 9 p.m. on either Thursday or Friday. Most shops close on Sunday, although an increasing number are staying open in larger cities, and it's becoming more usual for Saturday to be a half day in large cities. Bottle shops connected to hotels sell alcoholic beverages during pub hours, 11 a.m. to 10 p.m., but never on Sunday.

STUDENT DISCOUNTS: Not many. Expect to pay full price most places.

TAXES: The only tax you'll have to pay in New Zealand is the departure charge of NZ$3 ($2.01)—never a sales or hotel tax.

TAXIS: Taxi ranks are located at all terminals and in major shopping streets, and you may not hail one on the street within a quarter mile of a rank. They're on call 24 hours a day, and telephone numbers are in local directories, but there's an additional NZ$.40 (27¢) charge if you ring for one. Rates vary from place to place, but all city taxis are metered (in smaller localities, there's often a local driver who will quote a flat fee). Drivers don't expect a tip just to transport you, but if they handle a lot of luggage or perform any other special service, it's very much in order.

TELEGRAMS: All telegrams are sent through the post office, either by telephone or in person. The cheapest rate is "Letter Rate," which takes about 24 hours for delivery; rates for telegrams sent after regular post office hours can be as much as double.

TIME: New Zealand is located just west of the International Date Line, and its standard time is 11 hours and 30 minutes ahead of Greenwich Mean Time. A 30-minute daylight saving is permanently observed, which puts New Zealand exactly 12 hours ahead of GMT. Thus at noon in New Zealand, standard time in Sydney is 10 a.m.; London, midnight of the previous day; San Francisco, 4 p.m. the previous day; New York, 7 p.m. the previous day; Singapore, 7:30 a.m.; and Tokyo, 9 a.m. same day.

TIPPING: Kiwis don't do it. And they don't expect visitors to do it. Their theory is that all workers in their country are paid a living wage and they can jolly well live on it. Restrain that uncontrollable urge if you can—then give in to it when someone has rendered a very special service (carried a ton of luggage, come to your rescue in a puzzling situation, etc.). It's not easy for Yanks who are accustomed to tipping at every turn, but once you get the hang of the system, what a relief! And what a saving! And the nicest thing about the whole situation is that you'll get the same friendly service whether you tip or not—I once actually had a taxi driver (who had juggled my bags a few times in the course of one journey) turn down a tip!

WEATHER FORECAST: There's a "Traveller's Rundown" every morning on the radio, which gives a roundup of weather in all tourist areas. Weather reports are also given at the end of the 6:30 p.m. TV newscast. To unscramble those Centigrade temperatures and convert them to Fahrenheit, multiply the Centigrade reading by 9, divide by 5, and add 32 degrees.

NOW, SAVE MONEY ON ALL YOUR TRAVELS!
Join Arthur Frommer's $25-A-Day Travel Club

Saving money while traveling is never a simple matter, which is why, over 21 years ago, the **$25-A-Day Travel Club** was formed. Actually, the idea came from readers of the Arthur Frommer Publications who felt that such an organization could bring financial benefits, continuing travel information, and a sense of community to economy-minded travelers all over the world.

In keeping with the money-saving concept, the membership fee is low—$14 (U.S. residents) or $16 (Canadian, Mexican, and foreign residents)—and is immediately exceeded by the value of your benefits which include:

(1) An annual subscription to an 8-page quarterly tabloid newspaper *The Wonderful World of Budget Travel* which keeps you up-to-date on fastbreaking developments in low-cost travel in all parts of the world—bringing you the kind of information you'd have to pay over $25 a year to obtain elsewhere. This consumer-conscious publication also provides special services to readers:

Travelers' Directory—a list of members all over the world who are willing to provide hospitality to other members as they pass through their home cities.

Share-a-Trip—requests from members for travel companions who can share costs and help avoid the burdensome single supplement.

Readers Ask . . . Readers Reply—travel questions from members to which other members reply with authentic firsthand information.

(2) The latest edition of any TWO of the books listed on the following page (except for *The Adventure Book,* which is available at only $7.50 to members).

(3) A copy of *Arthur Frommer's Guide to New York*.

(4) Your personal membership card which entitles you to purchase through the Club all Arthur Frommer Publications for a third to a half off their regular retail prices during the term of your membership.

So why not join this hardy band of international budgeteers NOW and participate in its exchange of information and hospitality? Simply send $14 (U.S. residents) or $16 U.S. (Canadian, Mexican, and other foreign residents) along with your name and address to: $25-A-Day Travel Club, Inc., 1230 Avenue of the Americas, New York, NY 10020. Remember to specify which *two* of the books in section (2) above you wish to receive in your initial package of members' benefits. Or tear out this page, check off any two books on the opposite side and send it to us with your membership fee.

FROMMER/PASMANTIER PUBLISHERS   Date_____
1230 AVE. OF THE AMERICAS, NEW YORK, NY 10020

Friends, please send me the books checked below:

$-A-DAY GUIDES
(In-depth guides to low-cost tourist accommodations and facilities.)

☐ Europe on $25 a Day	$10.95
☐ Australia on $25 a Day	$9.95
☐ England and Scotland on $25 a Day	$9.95
☐ Greece on $25 a Day	$9.95
☐ Hawaii on $35 a Day	$9.95
☐ Ireland on $25 a Day	$7.95
☐ Israel on $30 & $35 a Day	$9.95
☐ Mexico on $20 a Day	$8.95
☐ New Zealand on $20 & $25 a Day	$9.95
☐ New York on $35 a Day	$8.95
☐ Scandinavia on $25 a Day	$7.95
☐ South America on $25 a Day	$8.95
☐ Spain and Morocco (plus the Canary Is.) on $25 a Day	$8.95
☐ Washington, D.C. on $35 a Day	$8.95

DOLLARWISE GUIDES
(Guides to tourist accommodations and facilities from budget to deluxe, with emphasis on the medium-priced.)

☐ Egypt	$9.95	☐ Canada	$10.95
☐ England & Scotland	$7.95	☐ Caribbean (incl. Bermuda & the	
☐ France	$8.95	Bahamas)	$10.95
☐ Germany	$9.95	☐ California & Las Vegas	$7.95
☐ Italy	$7.95	☐ Florida	$9.95
☐ Portugal (incl. Madeira & the Azores)	$9.95	☐ New England	$9.95
☐ Switzerland	$9.95	☐ Southeast & New Orleans	$9.95

THE ARTHUR FROMMER GUIDES
(Pocket-size guides to tourist accommodations and facilities in all price ranges.)

☐ Amsterdam/Holland	$3.95	☐ Montreal/Quebec City	$3.95
☐ Athens	$3.95	☐ New Orleans	$3.95
☐ Boston	$3.95	☐ New York	$3.95
☐ Hawaii	$3.95	☐ Orlando/Disney World/EPCOT	$3.95
☐ Dublin/Ireland	$3.95	☐ Paris	$3.95
☐ Las Vegas	$3.95	☐ Philadelphia/Atlantic City	$3.95
☐ Lisbon/Madrid/Costa del Sol	$3.95	☐ Rome	$3.95
☐ London	$3.95	☐ San Francisco	$3.95
☐ Los Angeles	$3.95	☐ Washington, D.C.	$3.95
☐ Mexico City/Acapulco	$3.95		

SPECIAL EDITIONS

☐ How to Beat the High Cost of Travel	$4.95	☐ Memorable Weekends	$10.95
☐ New York Urban Athlete (NYC sports		(NY, Conn, Mass, RI, Vt, NJ, Pa)	
guide for jocks & novices)	$9.95	☐ The Adventure Book: 237 Adventure	
☐ Where to Stay USA (Accommodations		Trips World-wide (8½ × 11 with 115	
from $3 to $25 a night)	$8.95	color photos)	$14.95
☐ Fast 'n' Easy Phrase Book		☐ Museums in New York (Incl. historic	
(Fr/Sp/Ger/Ital. in one vol.)	$6.95	houses, gardens, & zoos)	$8.95
		☐ Travel Guide for the Disabled	$10.95

In U.S. include $1 post. & hdlg. for 1st book; 25¢ any add'l. book. Outside U.S. $2 and 50¢ respectively.

Enclosed is my check or money order for $_____

NAME_____

ADDRESS_____

CITY_____ STATE_____ ZIP_____